D0072291

THE BARBARY COAST

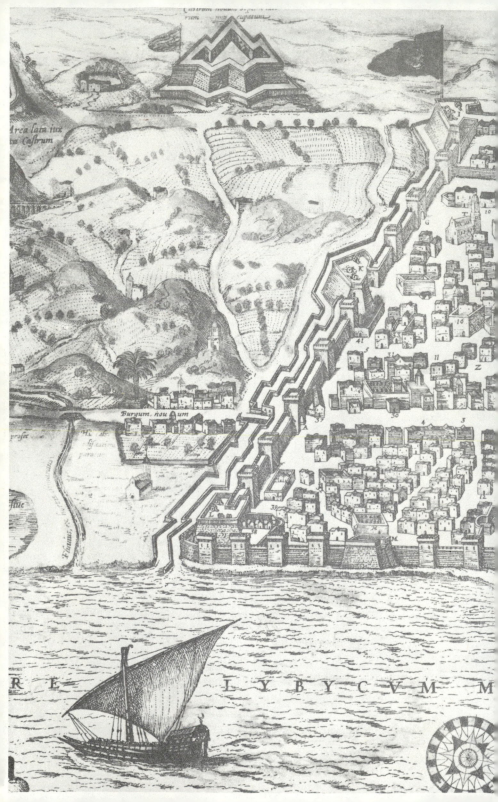

Castrum novum ergo a latere nunc expugatum.

Area lata iuxta Castrum

Burgum nouum

Hic aedificationes parant.

prospe...

...fiue

Flumen...

RE LYBYCVM M

JOHN B. WOLF

THE BARBARY
COAST *Algiers Under the Turks*

1500 to 1830

W · W · NORTON & COMPANY · NEW YORK · LONDON

OTHER BOOKS BY JOHN B. WOLF

Diplomatic History of the Bagdad Railroad, 1936, 1973
France: 1815 to the Present, 1940
History of Civilization (with Hutton Webster) 2 vols. 1943
The Emergence of the Great Powers: 1685–1715, 1952
The Emergence of European Civilization, 1962
Louis XIV, 1967
Toward a European Balance of Power, 1970
Early Modern Europe, 1972
Louis XIV: A Profile, 1972

The text of this book was set in Linotype Fairfield with Garamond display by Fuller Typesetting of Lancaster. Printing and binding were done by Murray Printing Company. Book design by Marjorie J. Flock.

FIRST EDITION

Library of Congress Cataloging in Publication Data
Wolf, John Baptist, 1907–
   The Barbary Coast.
   Bibliography: pp. 339–351
   Includes index.
   1. Algeria—History—1500–1830.   I. Title.
DT291.W64 1979   965′.02   79-11044

ISBN 0-393-01205-0

1 2 3 4 5 6 7 8 9 0

For my Theta

Contents

❖ ILLUSTRATIONS FOLLOW PAGES 115 AND 243

Preface

WHEN LOUIS XIV ceased to be a problem and became a book, I looked around for a new topic that might be interesting and instructive. I was committed to friends to write two rather long essays that, we hoped, might appeal to undergraduates, but I also wished to undertake a more substantial project that would carry over into the first years of retirement. It should not be so extensive that there would be a serious question about the probability of its completion, and yet it should be a project formidable enough to justify working on it.

How did the Turkish community of Algiers come into focus? Everyone who has attempted to explain human behavior knows that it is most difficult to say why a person does "this" rather than "that." My decision may unconsciously have been in part the result of the fact that my first research paper, written some fifty years ago as an undergraduate at the University of Colorado, dealt with an aspect of Franco-Ottoman relations in the sixteenth century. The project earned me a table in the stacks and gave me my first understanding of some of the problems involved in the use of diplomatic correspondence to explain characteristic processes in an historical development. I well remember that in my paper Kheir-ed-din Barbarossa appeared as a fabulous character, half myth, half historical reality, who wandered on the edges of my investigation. Obviously there are other, perhaps more important, reasons for my choice, but since this is not a psychiatric examination, they will have to remain behind the curtain. Perhaps it is enough to say that I did not want to do anything further with Louis XIV for the immediate future.

A quick glance at the secondary materials available on the topic of the North African corsair communities convinced me that the field was uncrowded and even suggested that a book in English might be welcome. In my innocence I also concluded that the project would provide a relatively simple and very interesting area of study for my

last years of teaching and the early ones of retirement. It has proven
to be interesting; simple it was not.

The Guggenheim Foundation graciously granted me a second fel-
lowship that allowed me to travel in the Mediterranean basin and explore libraries and archives for materials. Several years later the Social Science Research Council gave me a grant that enabled me to
microfilm extensively both archival materials and rare books. During
these years the Newberry Library provided me with a study and the
unlimited use of its superb collection. The University of Illinois
Chicago Circle granted me a sabbatical that permitted my return to
Europe for a full year's study and travel. I used part of that period
to explore the Spanish coastlines exposed to corsair attack where one
can still see the defensive measures taken both by the king and the
peasants. And finally the Folger Shakespeare Library invited me to
give a seminar that made possible four months' research in Washing-
ton in the Library of Congress and the Folger. In addition to the
Folger and Newberry Libraries I also owe a debt of thanks to the
Public Record Office, the British Museum, the Archives Nationales,
the Archives des Affaires Étrangères, the Archivo de la Corona de
Aragon, the Bibliothèque Nationale, and the Library of the University
of Amsterdam for permitting extensive microfilming of their materials. I shall place these microfilms in the Newberry Library when
this book is finally in print. In addition to the above I must indicate
my indebtedness to the Libraries of the University of Chicago, the
University of Illinois, and the University of Minnesota (Bell Library). Every student of history knows how important these institutions are for our métier.

Library and archival work provides a student with much pleasure and occasional excitement, but sooner or later he must ask himself: "What are you going to do with all this information?" The
question is not always a welcome one. It forces one to identify the
significant processes that seem to be emerging from the research,
and to ask the further question: "Will this information produce a
useful, perhaps important, book? Indeed, is it a book at all?" There
is no way to avoid the fact that my research into the processes at
work in the Maghrib between the sixteenth and the nineteenth centuries was introducing me into a wide variety of problems: government of a disorderly society, high politics of Europe and the
activity of the corsair communities, commercial expansion and the
interests of Christian merchants, slavery and redemption, tribal customs, ethnology, government in nomadic and semi-nomadic societies,

naval architecture and warfare, weapons and military organization, and a host of lesser things. Indeed, my research was in the act of becoming a series of Roman candles or skyrockets shooting off in every direction, but largely unfocused either by a central theme or any consideration of significance. To borrow Winston Churchill's expression, the study that had begun as a delightful toy or even a charming mistress was in the process of becoming a monster that would grow and grow unless I could discover some way to contain it.

Obviously were I to follow all the facets that were opening before me I would need several stout volumes to present my findings. But what editor would consider so extensive a work on the Maghrib, and, moreover, who, outside of a small handful of scholars, would be willing to read it? Clearly such a work would be out of the question; a series of monographs would better serve the few scholars interested in the subject. And yet this did not mean that a general book would not be useful. In fact, there was no book available in English dealing with the Turkish-corsair community of Algiers.

With the decision to limit the focus, it was apparent that the Turkish-corsair community of Algiers must be at the center of the stage. It would be impossible to include the histories of Tunis and Tripoli, since their divergent economic and political structures would only serve to enlarge the book beyond reasonable size without contributing much that would be either significant or novel. My study of the characteristic developments in the evolution of Algiers during these three centuries easily led to the assumption that there were two important themes that could be usefully explored. The first is the historical evolution of the political society that was founded in the "heroic era" of the Moslem corsairs and finally ended with the French invasion of 1830. To my knowledge the Algerian experience is the only example of a government by a foreign army of occupation that lasted three hundred years. Its history is both interesting and enlightening. The second theme is the adaptation by the European Christian powers to the problems presented by the existence of a corsair community committed to a "holy war" against Christendom. It was complicated by the fact that the Algerian regency was technically a part of the Ottoman empire and yet it became independent of the sultan and ignored his firmans. It was difficult for the European princes to understand that the Algerian corsair community could and did make war on whatever power it might be pleased to pillage without consulting the sultan or even in face of the sultan's wishes. It seemed often to be simple piracy rather than

xii	*Preface*

corsair privateering in the mode usual in Europe. I have tried to focus around these two themes.

I have discussed my findings with friends more knowledgeable than I, and I wish to thank particularly Professors Paul Bamford and Andrew Hess for listening to me and making suggestions; they of course are in no way responsible for the results. I fear that I have bored other friends whose interests are far from the Maghrib with my discussions; I should ask their pardon rather than blame them for my mistakes. I also want to thank my wife, Theta, for her generous aid in the development of this book; without her the book might never have been finished. Finally I also owe a debt to Mr. James Mairs, Vice President and Senior Editor of W. W. Norton & Company, for his patience and support, as well as for his part in the final preparations of this manuscript for the printer.

John B. Wolf

Jupiter Inlet Colony, Florida
November 7, 1978

THE BARBARY COAST

I *The Conquest of Algiers by the Turks*

IN 1830 A FRENCH expeditionary force landed at Algiers and quickly overthrew the Turkish regime that had controlled this section of the Maghrib[1] for more than three hundred years. The origins of the Turkish government are shrouded in myth and fiction, relieved by a scattering of facts, but this central section of the Maghrib had already a long history when the Turks first arrived. Phoenician, Roman, Visigoth, Byzantine, and Arab invaders, conquerors, and rulers as well as massive movements of nomadic tribesmen who lived on the edges of the Sahara, all had contributed to the gene pools of the population as well as to the history that stretched out into the past. In Roman times the population was divided between "folk in dwellings of hair" and "folk in dwellings of clay"— the nomadic tent compounds and the more settled towns and villages. This division was still valid when the Turks arrived in the Maghrib in the sixteenth century, and again when the French captured the city of Algiers in the nineteenth. This was a land of high plateaus, mountains, deserts, and a relatively small area suitable for agriculture. Its coast was largely inhospitable; the harbors were few and the anchorages only partly suitable for commercial activity. There were port towns with a past dating at least to Carthaginian and Roman times, but for most of them their prosperity had never been spectacular. Much of the land of the central Maghrib was inhabited by nomadic herdsmen, some Arabs and others Berbers, who occasionally exchanged their hides, wool, and animals for the products of agriculture and of the workshops of villagers and townsmen.

The Arabian conquest of the Maghrib that began in the seventh century left two important items of culture in the area: the Mo-

1. Maghrib: an Arabian word for North Africa from Tripoli to Morocco, now in common use; also known as the Barbary Coast.

hammedan religion and the Arabic language. One distinguished historian insists that the conversion of the peoples of North Africa to Islam was indeed a revolution that dwarfs the French and Russian revolutions of our day, but, unfortunately there are no documents and few artifacts to tell us how it occurred. What did happen, however, was the multiplication of Mohammedan cults from the most puritanical fanaticism to more tolerant patterns, a fact pregnant with the history of the land. On the other hand, since the Koran was written in Arabic and since a considerable number of Arab nomadic tribesmen migrated to the Maghrib, the language and the culture of the Arabians was, and has continued to be, important.

But the Arabs were never able to establish a political system to encompass the entire area. Their conquests from Egypt to Spain were too widespread geographically for easy controls in the era in which transportation was limited to horses or sails. There were several dramatic "reorganizations" of the land between Tripoli and Morocco in the centuries before the Christian Middle Ages, usually led by men from the desert areas where religious fanaticism and an urge for plunder gave reason for conquering the more effete, luxury-loving people of the towns. This was the story of the towns from the time that urban centers first developed; the tribesmen from the mountains descended upon them and looted their wealth.

In the thirteenth century the Maghrib from the area we today call Tunis to Morocco came to be divided among three Berber kingdoms that managed to dominate both the towns and the tribesmen in their area. The Hafsid dynasty that was established in the eastern area (approximately the territory called Tunis today) continued to rule into the sixteenth century. In the west the confederation of tribes under shepherd kings known as the Beni Marin emerged as victors over the Almohad rulers in the middle thirteenth century, and proceeded to create, or to encourage, the development of a high civilization in the territory we know today as Morocco, a civilization that reached a peak toward the end of the fourteenth century. In between these two Berber kingdoms another Berber tribe, under a shepherd king Abd-al-Wadid, established the Ziyanid dynasty at Tlemcen, an important commercial center for the exchange of African and Mediterranean goods, and extending eastward to Constantine and the frontiers of the Hafsid kingdom. However, the Ziyanids were in a precarious position from the very beginning, for their lands were coveted by the stronger neighbors to the east and to the west. The Marinids invaded and captured Tlemcen, while the

Hafsids captured Constantine in the eastern part of the kingdom. As a result no strong power emerged in the central Maghrib. By the opening of the fifteenth century, there was no real central authority. There were tribes with patterns of movement from pasture to pasture, some of them settling long enough to raise a crop of wheat before continuing their movement. There were petty cities, some of them still with commercial contacts with the rest of the Mediterranean; these were in effect independent city states, ruled by their religious or patrician leaders.

Thus the Maghrib at the end of the fifteenth century presented a picture of political and military decadence and economic decline. The Hafsid dynasty was still in power in the east, but weakened and largely unable to control the powerful Arab tribes, or to govern the towns over which it pretended suzerainty. To the west there were still Moroccan states with some political and military power, the one centered at Fez being the most important, but in Morocco, too, decadence rather than political vigor best describes the government of the land. The central Maghrib, the territory we know as Algeria today, was without any government that could even pretend to speak for the entire land; it was a political swamp of petty independent towns and villages, nomadic or semi-nomadic Berber and Arab tribesmen, of which the tribes in the Kabylie were perhaps the strongest. It was this central Maghrib that was to become the regency governed by the corsair community of the Ottoman Turks with the town of Algiers as its capital, but this did not occur without conflict that involved the two powers emerging in the fifteenth century at either end of the Mediterranean basin: the Spanish kingdoms and the Ottoman empire.

Let us look first to the emergence of the Spanish empire in the west. The marriage of Ferdinand and Isabella brought two of the three kingdoms[2] on the Iberian peninsula under a more or less common direction, even if it did not really unite the kingdoms of Castile and Aragon into a single Spanish state. Ferdinand's Aragon continued to center its attention on the Mediterranean islands and Italy and to be governed by diplomats and merchant-oriented politicians, while Castile, a kingdom dominated by soldier noblemen, had a more predatory political outlook. No sooner had Granada, the last Moorish kingdom on the peninsula, been conquered, than men of Castile

2. The third kingdom was Portugal. For a time it was a question whether Isabella of Castile would marry into the House of Aragon or that of Portugal. The final decision was fateful for all three kingdoms.

looked across the Straits for new fields of military activity. Isabella sent a spy to reconnoiter the land on the other side of the water. His report: "The entire country is in a state that it seems that God has wished to give it to their Majesties." The policies of the Catholic kings in the conquered kingdom of Granada further reinforced the need for Spanish action in North Africa. Their first reaction to their Moorish subjects was toleration; a bishop who respected Islamic culture and a law that allowed the practice of Mohammedan religion gave the Spanish Moors, known as Moriscos, almost ten years of relative freedom to continue to live as they had in the past, but at the turn of the sixteenth century this tolerant policy changed and the Catholic kings managed to provoke a revolt among their Morisco subjects. The resultant repression sent thousands of them, as émigrés, to the Maghrib and farther east to the Levant, where they became advocates of a holy war, a jihad, against the kingdoms of Spain. Some of them took to the sea, attacked the coasts of their erstwhile homelands, and pillaged Spanish fishermen and small traders who came in their paths. The Catholic kings were soon deluged with petitions for aid against these raiders who sacked villages, churches, and monasteries and enslaved the poor people who fell into their hands.

Had Isabella lived, the complaints and petitions might have resulted in the Castilian conquest of the Maghrib. When she died (1504) she left a codicil to her will urging her successor to extend Castilian control of North Africa from the Straits to Tripoli, but the death of her son-in-law, Philip (1506), the madness of her daughter Johanna, and the subsequent contest between Ferdinand and the regency government of Castile, prevented immediate action. The union of the two Spanish crowns was further endangered because Ferdinand might produce an heir to Aragon who would have no place in Castile, but the Castilian regency refused to allow Ferdinand to make any move that might disinherit his grandsons by Isabella, Charles and Ferdinand von Hapsburg, in Castile. This dynastic problem was not the only thing preventing a Castilian invasion of North Africa. In 1492 a Castilian expedition under Christopher Columbus had discovered a New World that, by the early sixteenth century, was attracting Castilian noblemen and soldiers seeking wealth and power across the Atlantic, and thereby draining into the New World adventurers who might have invaded Africa.

For his part Ferdinand and the important people of Aragon were more interested in Italy and the contest that was developing there between the European states than in any adventure for conquest. He and his Aragonese advisors were more tolerant of Moriscos and Islam than the Castilians, and oriented more toward diplomatic than toward military solutions. They did recognize, however, that something had to be done to curb the "piracy" of the Morisco raiders that was ravaging Spanish commerce and coasts, but they were unwilling to invest the wealth and manpower needed to conquer the land. The policy they adopted can best be described as "containment" rather than conquest; Ferdinand attempted to check the piracy by controlling the ports from which the pirates could operate.

The actual course of Spanish occupation of port towns on the North African coast had begun in the last years of the fifteenth century when the Duc de Medina Sidona occupied Melilla, but it was almost a decade later before a Spanish force took Mers-el-Kébir (1505) to establish a proper harbor for their ships. In the next six years under the impulse of Archbishop Jiménez de Cisneros and others, Pedro Navarro managed to conquer Oran, Bougie, Valez, and Tripoli (1508–11). The violence of the Spanish attacks and the brutal treatment of the conquered populations sent a tremor of terror along the entire coast, and those towns as yet unvisited by the Spanish armada quickly asked Ferdinand to accept their submission to his rule as vassals. This suited Aragonese policy, for Italy was much more important at that moment than North Africa, and Ferdinand was quite content to establish presidios or fortifications in the principal harbors along the coast. Bougie, Algiers, Valez, Oran, Mers-el-Kébir, and Melilla were either occupied by Spanish troops or forced to accept a Spanish fortress in their harbors with guns that could command all the traffic. With the exception of Oran, Mers-el-Kébir, and Tripoli, the actual government of the towns was left in the hands of the natives. Obviously this policy was motivated by the need to curb the activity of corsairs operating against Spanish possessions rather than by any religious considerations. It proved to be inadequate for, as we shall see, following Ferdinand's death one presidio after another was wrested from Spanish hands until only Oran and Mers-el-Kébir remained.

The basic difficulties of this policy of containment may have been inevitably rooted in the religious fanaticism of the Berber and Arab peoples of North Africa, a fanaticism that was fanned by tyrannical Spanish treatment of the Moorish inhabitants of Spain. The latter—the Moriscos—who were forced to accept baptism or migrate, who were imprisoned and burned for their Moslem faith and customs, spread far and wide the tales of Spanish (that is, Christian) intolerance, tyranny, brutality, cruelty—to make the name "Spanish" a hated thing. The Spanish garrisons in the presidios suffered from this fact. Situated on islands in the harbors, they were isolated from the mainland of Africa so much that their bread and meat, even their water, often had to come to them by sea. In the sixteenth century, when transportation and communication were hazardous, this dependence upon outside help was disastrous. Nonetheless, these presidios were strong. They had cannons that could sweep the harbors and bombard the towns, and the garrisons were armed with the arquebus. Since the natives had no such firearms, they were not even prepared to repulse the occasional *razzias* (raids) that the Spanish troops undertook against them. Only when the Spanish soldiers were overloaded with loot and strung out in their line of march could the Berber or Arabian horsemen armed with lances and swords hope to defeat them.

Almost at the same time that the Spanish began to establish their presidios in the harbors of North Africa a handful of adventurers from the Levant arrived in the central Mediterranean to begin a story that is almost as fabulous and unbelievable as those of Cortez or Pizarro in the New World. Their leader, Aroudj, and his brothers may have been the sons of an ex-janissary and the daughter of a Greek Orthodox priest. Myth tells us that the boys were brought up to be pious Mohammedans, their sisters to be Christians, but the only solid facts that we have about Aroudj are that, before he arrived in the west, he had once been a galley slave, captured by the Knights of St. John at Rhodes, and that after his ransom or escape, an Egyptian emir outfitted him and his brothers as corsairs to raid Christian merchants. His first benefactor was not the Ottoman sultan, but rather an Egyptian prince whose domains were soon to be overrun by that sultan and his armies. About the turn of the sixteenth century, Aroudj, accompanied by his brothers Isaac and Kheir-ed-din, arrived at Tunis to begin their career in the western Mediterranean. They were corsairs, warriors in the jihad, against Christendom; Aroudj was also fighting a war of revenge against the men who put him to the oars in the galleys of the Knights of St. John. The Hafsid ruler of Tunis welcomed the adventurers and agreed to allow them to use his harbors in return for a share of the loot taken from Christian ships. By 1510 tales of the exploits of these corsairs had spread widely in both East and West. The capture of two large and richly laden papal galleys was only one of the many extraordinary attacks that gave Aroudj the reputation of a brave, bold, daring man. The number of his own ships grew with those commanded by other Levantine reis[3] who had worked their way westward to place themselves under Aroudj's leadership; his corsair flotilla numbered over a dozen vessels. They could station themselves in a line, each within sight of his neighbor, which would allow them to attack and capture any ship that might try to cross through their net. Had the now famous Aroudj Reis been willing to spend the rest of his life as a corsair admiral, his fame and fortune would have been assured. But Aroudj developed other ideas; he saw in the amorphous political structure of the central Maghrib possibilities for the creation of a political sovereignty for himself and his brothers that would yield power, prestige, and salvation in heaven. His efforts to achieve it cost him his arm at Bougie and his life in the effort to extend his power to Tenez and Tlemcen.

In the first years after the establishment of the Spanish presidios, however, it was not these Levantine corsairs who distressed Ferdinand's government. While the Levantines did have firearms, their ships were brigantines and small galleons armed at best with small cannons that could have no impact on the walls of Spanish fortresses. What bothered the Spanish were the Morisco raiders who came ashore in small vessels powered by six to eight oars on a side, vessels that could be easily hidden in the estuaries of the Spanish rivers while the raiders, aided by Moriscos who had not yet migrated, moved to capture slaves, burn churches, and pillage monastaries. These "pirates" were hard to discover, harder to control. The Levantine corsairs, no match for the heavily armed Spanish galleys that patrolled the Mediterranean, found enough ships belonging to the petty Italian states—Genoa, Sicily, Naples, Tuscany, and the Papal States—to makes prizes and enslave the crews. The first serious conflict between the Levantines and the Spanish came when the town of Bougie invited the former to help them drive the Spanish from the presidio that controlled their commerce. The corsairs' cannons were ineffective, and Aroudj and his men were quite unprepared for the ferocity of the Spanish artillery and arquebus fire that was poured out at them. Aroudj's arm was broken off by a cannon ball, and his men retreated in much disorder. Several years later, after Ferdinand's death (1515), when the Algerians begged him to help them against the Spanish presidio in their harbor, Aroudj

---

3. The reis was captain or commander of a corsair vessel. We shall use the term in this sense throughout this volume. The singular and plural have the same form.

again found that his artillery was too weak to accomplish the task. Thus, though the Levantine corsairs were operating in the mid-Mediterranean basin, as long as Ferdinand lived they were still inferior in power to the Spanish.

The Levantines, however, as Mohammedans themselves, were in tune with the native populations and therefore more flexible than the Spanish in their movements to establish themselves in North Africa. Their first solid base was the little town of Djidjelli, a small port town some 180 miles east of Algiers, where by chance they appeared with a prize loaded with Sicilian wheat at a moment when ·the town was threatened by famine. The grateful natives invited Aroudj to become their "king." A few years later Ferdinand's death provided a new opportunity for the Levantine corsairs. The *baldi* (native Moors of Algiers) and the Arab sheik whom they had invited to rule their town, believed that the king's death absolved them from their oath of allegiance. They invited Aroudj to bring his Levantines to Algiers to help them drive the Spanish from the presidio in their harbor. Aroudj first visited Cherchell (Caesarea in Roman times), a town on the coast about 150 miles west of Algiers inhabited almost exclusively by refugees from Spain, where one of his late lieutenants had set himself up as "king." Aroudj wanted no rival; he landed at Cherchell, parlayed with the "faithless" lieutenant, seized and beheaded him. The Levantines at Cherchell were then joined with Aroudj's men and, except for a small garrison left at Cherchell, proceeded to Algiers.

Once at Algiers Aroudj failed to dislodge the Spaniards, but he did manage to strangle the sheik who governed the town and to force its inhabitants to accept him as their "king." Shortly afterward when he learned that leading members of the baldi were quietly negotiating with the Spanish for assistance in expelling the Levantines, Aroudj rounded up the plotters in a mosque and summarily executed the richest and most influential of their number. This did not make the Levantines more loved in Algiers, but it did discourage other attempts to shake their rule.

Curiously enough this brutal seizure of power did not prevent other towns from appealing to the Levantine corsairs for assistance. In the west the town of Tenez and the old capital Tlemcen were both plagued with problems of succession to the city thrones. In each case this led one faction to seek outside support from the new ruler of Algiers. Aroudj left his brother Kheir-ed-din, soon to be called Barbarossa, in charge of the town of Algiers, while he and his brother Isaac, with a little army of Levantines, marched westward. At first the little army was so successful in securing allegiances from natives that it seemed that the entire Maghrib between Algiers and Tlemcen would soon be subservient to the rule of the Levantine adventurers. But at this moment the son of the murdered sheik of Algiers appealed to the Spanish governor of Oran, explaining that unless the Levantines were checked the entire Maghrib would fall under their government. The governor petitioned for aid from the new king of the Spains, Carlos I, soon to be called Charles V, emperor of the Holy Roman Empire, ruler of the Burgundian Netherlands, as well as most of Italy and Spain. The young king sent an expeditionary force that proved to be much too strong for the Levantines. Both Aroudj and his brother Isaac were killed along with most of their men. Only a remnant returned to Algiers to tell of the disaster.

The defeat of the Levantine corsair army and news that the Spanish were preparing another expedition to drive Kheir-ed-din and his men from Algiers were the deciding events that were to give form to the government of the corsair community and the corsair state that was to become the regency of Algiers. A Turkish chronicler, probably inspired by Kheir-ed-din himself, tells us that news of his brothers' deaths distressed and sorrowed Kheir-ed-din. The pious corsair reis then called the principal baldi of the city and told them that he planned to return to the Levant, but that he would leave their town under the protection of his Levantines and Andalusian Moors. Protests arose from all sides! Our chronicler tells us that the baldi begged Kheir-ed-din not to leave them. He then made the condition that if he should stay, he wished to invite the sultan of the Ottoman empire to give him protection. There was much discussion, and finally the Algerian notables persuaded him to send his trusted deputy, Hadj Hassan, to the sultan to secure the needed aid while Kheir-ed-din himself would remain in Algiers to defend the town. Our chronicler does not tell us whether or not the sultan, Selim Khan, the Grim, asked pointed questions about the Levantines' earlier relations with Egypt, but he does assure us that the sultan accepted Kheir-ed-din's offer to place his conquests under the mantle of the Ottoman empire as a western sanjac (province) in return for military aid. Kheir-ed-din became a Turkish pasha, and henceforth money coined at Algiers would bear the image of the sultan.

It probably was not as simple as the chronicler of the *El-Zorat-*

el-Nayerat tells it, even though Christian chroniclers give us about the same story. Nonetheless it is a fact that sultan Selim I accepted Algiers as a new Ottoman frontier province, and sent two thousand janissaries and four thousand other Levantines enlisted into the Algerian militia as well as some cannons and munitions of war.

This was the decisive step in the development of the Turkish regency of Algiers that was to last until 1830. The introduction of Turkish janissaries provided the military muscle needed not only to defend Algiers against the Spanish but also eventually to extend the Turkish conquest to the entire central Maghrib. Furthermore, by introducing the divan of the janissaries as the governing institution for the soldiers, it brought an institution that in the future was to be central to the government of the regency.

Had the Spanish response been more prompt after the death of Aroudj, it might have saved the Spanish kingdoms much wealth and many lives, but the viceroy of Sicily, Moncada, did not understand this fact. He was slow in preparing an expedition to capture Algiers; he did not get under way until after Kheir-ed-din had added Bône, a port town near the Tunisian frontier, to his government, and had reinforced the fortifications of Algiers. When he did land an army of Spanish and Italian soldiers, Moncada and his council of war decided to wait for their assault on the town until after native allies from Tlemcen could join them. The Spanish army sat before Algiers for a week. Then a violent storm arose, dashing twenty-six of the forty Spanish ships on the rocks and ruining much of the inadequately sheltered supplies. In the confusion that followed, janissary troops from the city, supported by Berber tribesmen anxious for booty, attacked the disorganized Spanish forces and completed the disaster. The price of slaves in Algiers dropped to a new low as hundreds of Spanish and Italian soldiers were put on sale. The Turkish account tells us that over three thousand soldiers and thirty-six officers were captured on the beaches, and that many more were killed.

Reinforcements from the Ottoman sultan and victory over the Spanish army emboldened the corsairs to enlarge their spheres of activity. Heretofore they had operated largely in the central Mediterranean; now they raided the coasts of Catalonia, Valencia, and the islands of the western Mediterranean. The depredations were so vicious that a special Cortes of the kingdom of Aragon held in Barcelona in the winter of 1519-20 voted a subsidy of ten thousand ducats a year to be paid by the principality of Catalonia and the kingdoms of Valencia, Majorca, and Sardinia. When we remember that the Spanish kings had so much trouble securing funds from the kingdom of Aragon (which included the aforementioned principalities), the true importance of this grant is seen. The grant was to be used to build a naval force to meet the Moslem corsairs and to construct the fortifications and watch towers that still bear witness to the fact that the Spanish kingdoms were under siege from the sea.

The Spanish naval patrol was directed against the principal bases available to the corsairs. The port of Algiers was still under the control of Spanish guns in the presidio on the island in the harbor. Kheir-ed-din's ships operated from the smaller harbors along the coast, and, more importantly, from the island of Jerba, where Aroudj had taken the corsair navy after the Genoese attack on La Goulette, the most important Tunisian port, convinced the sultan of Tunis to deny them shelter in his ports. The Spanish landed a force of some thirteen thousand men at Jerba, some of them armed with the *escopetus*, a new firearm more effective than the arquebus. The Berber sheik who had gladly given haven to the corsairs for a percentage of their "loot," was soon ready to swear allegiance to the king of Spain and promise to deny his harbors to the corsairs, but it was only a few years until his allegiance and his promises were forgotten. Perhaps had the young Carlos I (Charles V) of Spain not been so busy with many other things, he might have stifled the threat that Kheir-ed-din's corsair-janissary community at Algiers posited for Spain and Christendom.

We will better understand why the kingdoms of the Spains did not take more aggressive action against the embryo corsair community in these yearly years if we recall some of the problems confronting the young King Charles.[4] For one thing the Spains were far from ready to accept his government. There was a rebellion in Valencia in 1519, one in Castile in 1520, a communeros revolt in 1520–21: Charles's Spanish subjects had no wish to be assimilated into a single kingdom with a single law. Indeed, this had to wait until the eighteenth century to be accomplished only partially; Charles's Spanish subjects did not have a common recognized will or goal. And yet Spain was only one of his problems. Charles was elected Holy Roman Emperor in 1519, just in time to become in-

---

4. Charles von Hapsburg (1500–1558) was heir to his parents' lands in the Netherlands, the Burgundian inheritance, and his grandfather's Austrian lands on the Danube; he also was heir to the thrones of Spain, and he was elected to the imperial throne of the Holy Roman Empire. In Spain he was Charles I, in Germany Charles V.

volved in the Lutheran Reformation. He also inherited the problems of the Burgundian realm that included conflict with France over succession. Thus the problems of Burgundy joined with those of Italy to force Charles into wars with Francis I of France, the Hapsburg-Valois wars that filled a half century. These wars drained both his and his French opponent's treasuries. Nor did the problems end there: Charles was contemporary not only of two vigorous and vain West European kings, Francis I of France and Henry VIII of England, but also of Suleiman, the Magnificent, sultan of the Ottoman empire, and he was forced to come to the aid of his brother Ferdinand, who ruled in Germany as "king of the Romans" when the Turks besieged Vienna in 1529.

While Charles was deeply involved in the politics of Europe, Kheir-ed-din tried to establish a Moslem power in the Maghrib. He was a statesman as well as a good politician, a man of personal charm when it was needed, and a grim representative of his era as a brutal ruler when it suited his purposes. Kheir-ed-din Barbarossa recognized that his brother's policy of acquiring sovereign power over towns in the hinterland was sound, indeed absolutely essential, for the successful development of the Turkish-corsair-janissary state; he also was a pious Moslem leader who envisaged the eventual reconquest of Spain as an important goal for Islam. When Charles's intolerant religious laws of Castile were extended to Aragon, Kheir-ed-din became involved in helping Moriscos escape from Spain; the experience apparently convinced him that the reconquest of that kingdom could never be accomplished until all of the Maghrib was under a single Moslem power that could generate armies to return to Spanish soil. Aroudj was clearly the founder of the corsair community, but it was Kheir-ed-din Barbarossa who was the skillful politician, military organizer, and commander who created the Algerian Turkish regency. He gave it its characteristic form and legitimized its existence by connections with the Ottoman empire (see Chapter IV, below).

However, it was no easy problem to bring the anarchic territory of the Maghrib under a single rule; indeed, it probably could not be done. When Kheir-ed-din began his rule, the Spanish presidios controlled traffic in the port towns of Algiers, Oran, Tenez, Valez, Bône, and Bougie as well as several others of minor importance. The ancient capital cities of Tlemcen and Constantine in the east and west of the central Maghrib were accustomed to managing their own affairs and wanted no interference from outside. In the mountains and plateaus the Berber and Arab tribes, under their sheiks and emirs, had no interest in paying tribute or recognizing the overlordship of outsiders. Kheir-ed-din's problems may not have been as politically significant as those confronting Charles V, but they were every bit as difficult in light of the resources available to him. He had one important advantage: the Spanish Christians provided a common enemy, hated because of their religion and the violence of their naval officers; the port towns could expel them only with the aid of the Turks. This was Kheir-ed-din's first political lever.

But if being a co-religionist was a plus, there were minuses. At either extreme of the territory in the central Maghrib, Kheir-ed-din encountered military forces better prepared to fight his Turkish janissaries than the Arab and Berber peoples. In the west the Spanish held Oran and Mers-el-Kébir, where they had cannons, fortifications, and men armed with the arquebus. They were much stronger than any force that Kheir-ed-din could hope to bring against them, a real barrier to any westward expansion of his government. South of Oran was the sultan of Fez, whose endemic war against the Spanish did not make him more willing to see a strong government arise in the central Maghrib that would expand to Tlemcen and perhaps beyond. He also was armed with modern weapons, the arquebus and small cannons, and he had soldiers with discipline unknown to the Berbers and Arabs in Kheir-ed-din's area. Moroccan power had been greatly strengthened by the migration of the Moriscos from Spain. The sultan had welcomed them, and they brought handicraft skills, including the gunsmith's art, as well as willing recruits to the sultan's armies. Unless these Moroccan soldiers could be joined to the Turkish janissaries in a free alliance, the reconquest of Spain would be an absurd dream; however, the Moroccans were unlikely to give up their independence simply to aid aggrandizing Turkish power. On the other extreme of the central Maghrib, Kheir-ed-din encountered another military force also more sophisticated than the Arab and Berber tribesmen. The sultans of Tunis, the last of the Hafsid dynasty, ruled a land where the production of wheat, olive oil, wool, hides, fruit, and many other commodities made a considerable exchange of goods on the international market possible, and thus also provided larger tax revenues than were possible in the central Maghrib. The sultan of Tunis also had mercenaries, many of them Christians, who understood the use of firearms before the Turks appeared. These Hafsid rulers were hated by most of their subjects, but they knew how to make allies of the powerful Arab families and thus to rule the land. Kheir-ed-din and his successors were to find that Tunis was a barrier to expansion eastward; indeed, the sultans of Tunis coveted Constantine and the Kabylie hills to the west of their domains as much as the Turkish regency rulers wished to expand eastward to Le Kef and Kairouan.

In the decade 1520–30 the Turkish-corsair regime experienced both victories and defeats in its efforts to build a state in the central Maghrib. One setback could have been fatal to the regime had the Spanish been able to take advantage of the corsairs' embarrassment. After an easy victory over the leader of a Kabylie confederation of the Koukou tribesmen led by their most important sheik, Ben-el-Kadi, and the occupation of the towns of Constantine and Bône in the eastern part of the territory, Kheir-ed-din was confronted by the intervention of the sultan of Tunis. This alliance between the Koukou tribesmen and the Tunisians was to be a constant problem for the rulers of Algiers in the following centuries. Ben-el-Kadi, joined with the Tunisians, not only defeated the little janissary army but also drove it back on Algiers and forced the Turks to abandon that port city. Kheir-ed-din retired to Cherchell with his fleet, and appealed to the Ottoman sultan, Suleiman the Magnificent, for aid. The Ottoman sultan, however, could not help much, for his armies were deeply engaged in the conquest of the Island of Rhodes, and he was preparing for the invasion of the Danube basin that would bring his soldiers to the walls of Vienna. Fortunately for Kheir-ed-din the Koukou tribesmen and their leader, Ben-el-Kadi, were quite unprepared to take over the government that the Turkish corsairs had begun to erect; rather than attempting to supplant the Turks, they systematically looted Algiers. Both the baldi and the Morisco émigrés were convinced that the Turkish regime was the lesser of two evils.

For his part Kheir-ed-din sent his corsairs out to loot the Christian shipping and thereby to secure money needed to reorganize his forces; he also made an alliance with a Berber tribe, the Kalâa, hostile to the Koukous. In his next encounter Ben-el-Kadi was defeated and the Turkish corsair community reestablished a secure hold on the Mitidja,[5] the territory immediately surrounding the city of Algiers. The Koukous wanted peace; they sent Ben-el-Kadi's head

5. This was a narrow band of territory from Tenez to the west of Algiers, to Dellys to the east; it was known as the Mitidja, or Dar-es-Sultan, and was governed from Algiers throughout the era of Turkish domination. The rest of the land came to be divided among three beyliks. (See map.)

to Algiers as a token of submission. In the future, however, the Koukous were often allied with the rulers of Tunis against the Turkish-corsair rulers in Algiers, but for the moment Kheir-ed-din had established a Turkish overlordship in the eastern part of his domains.

In the west the Turkish-corsair expansion was facilitated when the port town of Mostaganem accepted Kheir-ed-din's protection against the Spanish. This provided the corsairs with a secure harbor not far from Oran to which they could bring artillery and war supplies for the conquest of the western lands bordering Oran and the sultanate of Fez. The corsairs also helped the Moors of the city of Valez to expel the Spanish garrison, and thereby secured access to another port on the Moroccan coast, to the west of Oran. The fact that Mostaganem allowed transport by sea made it possible for Kheir-ed-din's forces to capture Tlemcen, the ancient capital of the central Maghrib. It was an easy conquest, for one faction in the city called in the Turkish-corsair soldiers to support their candidate for the throne of the city. Unlike the Spanish, whose policy was to establish a native ruler and require him to give an oath of allegiance to the Spanish king and then retire leaving the town under "friendly" government, the Turkish policy was to establish a janissary garrison in any town that came under Turkish control, and thereby assure the loyalty of the community. The Spanish at Oran were unhappy about this; they tried several times to send forces to expel the Turks, but when, in 1543, they did succeed in taking the town they were unable to hold it with their own soldiers whose religion was despised by the townsmen, and the Turks soon returned.

Kheir-ed-din's most troubling problem of these early years was in Algiers itself. The Spanish garrison in the presidio on a little island in the harbor of the city made impossible the use of the harbor by his ships. Their little flotilla was unable to brave the cannons in the Spanish fort, so the corsairs anchored elsewhere or were pulled up on the beaches beyond Algiers. Kheir-ed-din began a new siege of the little fortress in 1529. The Spanish garrison fought bravely, but it lacked food, water, and war materials. The supply ships from Spain arrived a few days after the governor of the fortress surrendered; they could see Spanish slaves demolishing the fortifications and using the rock to begin the construction of a mole, or breakwater, that would join the island with the mainland and provide a reasonably safe shelter for ships against a Mediterranean storm. The Turkish chronicler tells us that when the king of Spain heard of the fall of the presidio of Algiers "that cursed of Allah (King

Charles) shewed his fingers in rage" and called a council of state. All members were silent except one named Doria, who came forward with the proposal to attack Barbarossa (the Christian name for Kheir-ed-din). The king of Spain then made peace with France and Doria sailed with a mighty fleet to attack Cherchell where Barbarossa made his biscuits.

Our Turkish author was correct in that Andrea Doria[6] did attack Cherchell in 1530. He landed troops who freed several hundred Christian slaves; then they began to loot the little town. It proved to be a bad enterprise, for Cherchell was largely inhabited by émigré Moriscos, who knew how to fight and were happy to kill Spaniards or Italians. While his soldiers were involved with the Moriscos, Doria learned that Kheir-ed-din's corsair fleet was on the way to relieve the town. Since it was a force larger than his, Doria sailed away, leaving his soldiers there, stranded as slaves.

The capture of the Spanish presidio in the harbor of Algiers and Doria's abrupt retreat before the oncoming corsair fleet not only emboldened the Turkish-corsair regime but also enhanced Kheir-ed-din's prestige with the sultan at Istanbul. Henceforth the corsair admiral was an important factor in the politics and naval strategy of the central Mediterranean.

6. Andrea Doria (1466–1560), a Genoese condottiere admiral, owned a fleet of war galleys that were available to rulers with money and influence. He was first in the employ of Francis I of France, then he joined Charles V, and during the rest of his career he was the most important "Spanish" admiral in the Mediterranean. Some critics claimed that he fled from any engagement that might damage his own ships; others insinuated that he and Kheir-ed-din, who also owned the warships that he commanded, did not hurt each other, just as "wolves never kill each other from common interest." The Doria family continued to serve the Spanish kings as condottiere sailors throughout the sixteenth century.

II *Kheir-ed-din Versus*
Charles V

THE CAPTURE of the presidio in the harbor of Algiers (1529)
came at the end of a decade that had seen the princes of
Europe entangled in wars from the plains of Hungary to
the Pyrenees. The Valois king of France, Francis I, had been a
prisoner of war in Madrid, the king of Hungary was killed in a
battle with the Turks, the city of Rome was sacked by the soldiers
of the Catholic king of Spain, and the North German princes had
formed an alliance of the "Lutheran party" to oppose the will of their
emperor. Only when the Turkish armies arrived before Vienna in
1529 did the Germans unite to drive the Ottoman forces out of
Austria. That same year the so-called ladies' peace made at Cam-
brai temporarily ended the Hapsburg-Valois war, but did not prevent Francis I from sending an emissary to both the Sultan Suleiman and Kheir-ed-din proposing a joint Franco-Turkish action
against Andrea Doria's condottiere fleet in revenge for Doria's de-
serting the French service for the Spanish. This was the age that
Machiavelli described in *The Prince,* an age of unscrupulous, pragmatic political leaders determined to secure advantage for themselves.

Francis's request may have interested the sultan and his advisers,
for Doria, on Charles's orders, had conducted a raid into the Gulf of
Corinth only a year before. But Suleiman's advisers had other things
to consider. The failure at Vienna in 1529 had been caused by the
troops of Charles V as well as by those of his brother Ferdinand,
the King of the Romans, who actually ruled in Germany. Could it
be that the road to Central Europe through the Danube was
blocked by the power of the Spanish Hapsburg Imperial complex?
Then there was the clamor of the Morisco émigrés in Suleiman's
court, who urged the Turkish sovereign to right the wrongs being
done to Moslems in Spain. In all this, the pasha of Algiers, Kheir-

ed-din, appeared as a key figure. He and his corsairs had been landing on the Spanish coasts to carry off booty, slaves, and Moriscos who wished to escape Spanish tyranny. These refugees were hailing him as the Moslem hero who might some day lead a victorious army into Spain itself. Suleiman decided to call Kheir-ed-din to Istanbul to discuss the building of an Ottoman fleet and the possible intrusion of Ottoman power into the western Mediterranean.

This was a serious question for the Ottoman sultan. The Turkish host had always been a "land animal"; its victories were accomplished by foot soldiers and horsemen; the sea was an unfamiliar environment. Jean Chesneau, writing about 1540, explained that "the Turks, with the exception of a few corsairs, know little or nothing about the sea. Even today when they wish to outfit a naval armament, they go into the mountains of Greece or Anatolia to take shepherds, whom they call *gouionari* and put them in the galleys . . . thus the Turks have never done well at sea . . . but Barbarossa has changed this somewhat." Chesneau's estimate was partially wrong. Andrew Hess, the distinguished U.S. historian interested in the Ottoman empire, has pointed out that Ottoman naval units had operated in the Aegean against the Venetians and in the Red Sea against the Portuguese as early as the second decade of the sixteenth century. Nonetheless, it is true that the Ottoman naval power grew strong after Kheir-ed-din and his corsair captains joined the sultan's naval establishment. The Ottomans lacked neither the skill nor the shipyards to build a navy. In the fifty years following 1530 they were to astonish the world by the speed with which they built excellent war galleys, made them ready for the sea, and proved themselves capable of fighting in that unfamiliar element.

When Sultan Suleiman called Kheir-ed-din to Istanbul in 1532, the question was: should there be a war in the Mediterranean between the Ottoman and the Spanish empires? Could this war break the power of the Hapsburg ruler in Spain so that he would never again help to block Ottoman drives up the Danube river? Could an Islamic force reconquer Spain and right the wrong that was being done to the Moriscos? Our Turkish chronicler, the sixteenth-century Spanish historians, and Fernandez Cesáreo Duro, the most important modern Spanish historian of the Spanish navy—all believed that Suleiman accepted Kheir-ed-din's proposal for such a war, and gave him freedom to build a navy in the shipyards at the Golden Horn.

If such a war was to be waged, the first priority for the Ottoman power had to be the securing of Tunis as a base for further operations. Tunis is situated at the narrow waist of the Mediterranean sea. To the north, Sicily, Naples, and Malta, Christian-held harbors, provided naval bases for the Spanish galleys, where food, water, wood, and other supplies were readily available. The recent establishment of the Knights of St. John at Malta and Tripoli underlined the fact that this was the important part of the Mediterranean sea if there should be a war between the Ottoman Turkish and the Spanish Hapsburg powers. Algiers was farther westward; without Tunis it was not a suitable base for such a war. A friendly Tunis could supply the springboard for further Ottoman operation westward; if Tunis were hostile these operations would be impossible.

The Hafsid ruler of Tunis was hostile to the Turkish-corsair community of Algiers and its pasha, Kheir-ed-din; he was also vulnerable to attack. The Spanish historian-geographer Marmols, probably knew Tunis better than any of the Christian writers of this era. He tells us that Mulei Mohammed, who ruled Tunis for twenty-eight years, had many sons, but they were all so debauched that he did not know which one should succeed him. He finally fixed on Mulei Hassan, the youngest, born of an Arabian princess whose relatives, he hoped, would support the young man. When Mulei Hassan came to the throne, he systematically killed or blinded not only his brothers and sisters but also his nephews and sister-in-laws. Only one young Hafsid prince, named Arrachid, escaped the slaughter and reached the camp of a friendly Arab sheik, Addula. Without artillery the Arabs could do nothing against Mulei Hassan, so Arrachid appealed to Kheir-ed-din. The corsair pasha saw this as an opportunity; he took Arrachid with him to Istanbul, where the sultan listened to his story and agreed to order Kheir-ed-din to attack Tunis. Suleiman gave Kheir-ed-din a fleet, extended his title to that of beylerbey of North Africa, and gave him instructions to ravage Calabria and Sicily, and then to move on to the capture of Tunis. When the fleet left the Golden Horn, the Hafsid prince Arrachid remained in Istanbul in a safe prison. Kheir-ed-din did not want a vassal sultan; he wished to rule directly.

Kheir-ed-din's army was composed of some eighteen hundred janissaries, sixty-five hundred Albanians, Anatolians, and Greeks, and six hundred renegades. After sailing past southern Italy with a number of landings for loot, slaves, water, and wood, the Ottoman armada landed its forces near La Goulette, the harbor for Tunis, on August 16, 1534. It met practically no opposition. Mulei Hassan fled from the city to the safety of his Arabian relatives, and Kheir-ed-din marched into the city of Tunis, welcomed by Arrachid's friends and relatives and the general population. Most of Arrachid's friends had been in prison; they thought that their freedom meant that the Hafsid prince would return with the Turkish army; when they learned that the Turks intended to govern Tunis on their own account, they attempted a revolt, which was quickly crushed by Turkish arquebus fire. The Tunisian notables then agreed to accept the Ottoman Sultan as their lord, and Kheir-ed-din as beylerbey; it was relatively easy after the conquest of the city of Tunis to extend Ottoman control to the other towns and cities of the eastern Maghrib that were normally under Tunisian suzerainty. Very quickly Kheir-ed-din was, nominally at least, in control of the coastal towns from La Goulette northward and around to the port of Bône, which was under the jurisdiction of Algiers. In the meantime Mulei Hassan, on the advice of a German renegade, sent an appeal to Charles V for help against the corsair-Turkish invaders.

It required little understanding of the political situation in the central Mediterranean to know that the king of Spain could not long remain indifferent to this Turkish conquest of Tunis. Even before Mulei Hassan's request for aid was placed before him, Andrea Doria urged that the Spanish king must move to drive the corsairs and Turks out of that land. The time was propitious: France and the Hapsburg empire were at peace; Charles's sister had become queen of France. A mighty expedition was quickly brought into being. Charles himself tells of the "galleys, galleons, carracks, fusts, ships, brigantines, and other vessels" that he assembled to transport his army of Spanish, German, Italian, and Portuguese troops. "We left," he wrote, "[asking] for the aid and guidance of our creator . . . and with divine assistance and favor, to do that which seems most effective and for the best against Barbarossa." The artists who created the great series of tapestries still to be seen at Seville have left us pictorial evidence of the magnificence and power of this military expedition. These sixteenth-century war machines were ponderous, slow-moving affairs, but, if the weather did not interfere, they could place great power at the disposal of the commander.

It was a powerful expedition that left Spain in June 1535: over four hundred sails, ninety royal galleys, twenty-four thousand troops and fifteen thousand horses. Kheir-ed-din could not match such a force: Suleiman was campaigning on the Persian frontier and his viziers in Istanbul did not have the means to supply the beylerbey of North Africa with soldiers to confront the Christian army. Thus when the Spanish landed near Carthage, only a few Arabs were there to witness the debarkation, and only minor night attacks harassed the landing. The emperor moved toward Tunis, cutting down olive trees and burning the villages; he stopped at La Goulette long enough for a stiff fight to capture that fortress and gain control of the lake that it defended. It would seem from the accounts of eyewitnesses of this struggle that the sun and thirst were enemies as serious as the Turks. The fall of La Goulette left part of the corsair navy in Charles's hands,[1] but Kheir-ed-din had had the foresight to leave some of his naval force at safe harbors north of Tunis. When the Christians moved on the city, the corsair-Turkish soldiers beat a hasty retreat across the country to their ships, leaving Tunis to Charles's soldiers, who proceeded to sack the city and murder many of its inhabitants.

Marmol, an eyewitness, gives us a description of the sack of Tunis that makes one's blood run cold. Leading dignitaries of the city went to Charles when Kheir-ed-din left, and begged him to spare them in return for money and supplies, but Charles had promised the soldiers the right to sack the town. While they were talking, the soldiers "without waiting for orders broke in the gates and began to sack the city with all the license and cruelty that one is accustomed to see in such encounters." In spite of the emperor's orders, many were killed, some in trying to save their goods from the soldiers, some soldiers by their fellows, to steal loot that they had found; some of the Christian slaves who had been liberated also looted, and a number of them were killed by men coveting the loot. "On the streets one saw piles of men, women and children . . . The king of Tunis [Mulei Hassan] assured us," writes Marmol, "that more than seventy thousand were killed and forty thousand men, women, and children were made prisoners." The sack lasted three days, during which the soldiers "dug in the earth and blew up houses" in their efforts to uncover hidden treasure. Marmol tells us that at the end of the siege the soldiers emerged from the city loaded with goods and things, and leading slaves.

While the sack was in progress, Mulei Hassan, in the entourage of the emperor, did nothing to protect his people; perhaps there was nothing that he could do, but Tunisians remembered this as long as he lived. Charles confirmed the fact that his puppet king of

1. Charles wrote that the fortress fought bravely, but finally fell and left "us a number of galleys, brigantines, galiotes, and fusts with a great quantity of artillery. . ." (Correspondenz II, p. 193).

Tunis was not loved by his people. He wrote, "none of Mulei Hassan's subjects made any demonstration for him" and the city was "pillaged and sacked . . . with the consent of the king of Tunis who saw that its inhabitants did not support him." The emperor-king went on to tell his sister that he had freed "eighteen to twenty thousand Christian slaves [who had not been killed by the corsairs as was expected], some of them my subjects, others of diverse Christian nations . . . including seventy-one Frenchmen." The emperor's letters fairly beam with his satisfaction at the results of the expedition.

Considering the low opinion that he had of Mulei Hassan, and his knowledge that it was shared by the people of Tunis, it is surprising that Charles reinstalled him as vassal king. He must have known that this solution could not possibly last. The Spanish policy in 1535 was obviously the same that Ferdinand had inaugurated in the first decade of the century. Charles rebuilt the fortification of La Goulette, which guarded the harbor and provided a base for operations on the narrow waters of the Mediterranean as well as southward toward Jerba and Tripoli. This presidio was then garrisoned with Spanish soldiers and equipped to supply the Spanish fleet. Charles also sent Doria with the armada to capture Bône and the port town of Africa (Mahdiya); he then made an effort to bring the other towns of the Tunisian territory under the control of his new vassal, Mulei Hassan. It undoubtedly would have been too expensive to attempt to garrison and govern all of the Tunisian territory, but it was unwise to trust his conquest to so weak and unstable a character as Mulei Hassan.

The conquest, however, greatly strengthened the Spanish king's position in the Mediterranean. La Goulette, on the southern rim of the Strait of Sicily, more or less completed his control of the entry into the western Mediterranean sea. Six years earlier Charles had given the Knights of St. John the island of Malta and the North African port of Tripoli. With these vassals of his kingdom of Sicily established in these two points and with his bases in Sicily and Naples, Charles could effectively shut off an invasion from the east.

Only Algiers remained as a thorn in the Spanish position, a fact that Kheir-ed-din immediately and dramatically demonstrated. While the Spanish empire was celebrating its king's victory at Tunis, he led his corsairs to the islands of Majorca and Minorca very soon after he had escaped from Tunis. At Maon the invaders came into the harbor just as the inhabitants were joyously celebrating the victory at Tunis over the "pirates" who had so long plagued the island. One account tells us that the corsairs carried off eight thousand people into slavery. This is probably an exaggeration, but the raid did force the Spanish king to realize that Algiers had to be his next target.

In January 1536, Charles wrote to his viceroys in Catalonia and the other territories of the kingdom of Aragon to announce the assembly of a Cortes to provide money, men, and materials for a descent on Algiers. A victory there would crown the system of defense and assure his Spanish and Italian possessions security against the corsairs. The emperor-king was sure that victory would be his because Sultan Suleiman was deeply engaged in conflict with the ruler of Persia, who, incidentally, had Spanish military advisers to teach his armies the use of "modern" weapons. Unfortunately, however, for the people who inhabited the coasts of the territories of the kingdom of Aragon, the king's project was soon jettisoned. Charles did not know that Le Forêt, the French ambassador to the Sublime Porte,[2] was making a treaty of commerce and friendship with the sultan that was the basis for the famous capitulations by which French merchants and French consuls enjoyed special privileges in the Ottoman empire, as well as for the entente between Francis I and Suleiman that, a few years later, would introduce the Turkish naval establishment into the port of Toulon. Francis I was anxious to take a stronger position vis-à-vis Hapsburg Europe, and the Spanish Hapsburg king had to react to French ambitions rather than to the question of Algiers.

The occasion for a new war between Charles V and Francis I was the death of Duke Maximilian Sforza of Milan, which allowed Francis I to reaffirm his rights to that territory. Charles, after a violent denunciation of the French king, sent an army into Provence, while his admiral, Doria, cruised on the coast (1536). The invasion did not go well: before the summer was over, twenty thousand of the fifty thousand Spanish troops had died of starvation or epidemic disease. Francis, too, was unable to act effectively, so the campaign simply proved that these two could not reach a definite conclusion by battle. Charles's suggestion that they meet in single combat was no solution.

While Charles was thus engaged in war with his French rival, Suleiman managed to free himself from Persian pressure, and was thus able to turn his attention to the west. He may have accepted Kheir-ed-din's proposals for war against Spain, but his immediate objective was control of the Ionian Sea, the Straits of Otranto, and

2. The court of the Ottoman sultan.

perhaps southern Italy. This area had the same importance to the Ottoman empire that the Straits of Sicily had for the Spanish. It was of utmost importance to secure it before moving westward, especially after Charles V's conquest of Tunis. The narrow seas could be secured by bribery or force. Indeed, Suleiman's agents did manage to corrupt the governor of Otranto, but the proposed treason was discovered before the Turkish navy was ready to act. The Turkish armament that put to sea in 1537 under Lufti Pasha with Kheir-ed-din Barbarossa as his lieutenant, included some four hundred ships of all kinds; it carried three thousand cannons, twenty-five thousand soldiers of which five thousand were armed with the arquebus, and the rest with bows, arrows, and spears. As this armada moved toward Italy a tremor of fear ran up the peninsula as far as Rome, where the Bishop of Maçôn wrote that "Our Holy Father and all his court are in great fear of the Turks, so much so that they think they will have to abandon the city. . . . The Pope is sending agents to the King of France and to the Emperor Charles to exhort them to make peace." The news that the Turks had two hundred ships each carrying one hundred horses convinced the Italians that an invasion was imminent.

The Turkish force landed at several points, both north and south of Otranto, but its chief mission in 1537 was to seize control of the islands in the Ionian Sea and the Straits of Otranto. Lufti Pasha failed to take Corfu early in the season, but Barbarossa returned before the summer was over and captured the Venetian fortifications on that island. The Spanish governor of Calabria sent a cavalry force to Brindisi, but he could not prevent the Turks from ravaging the coast and stopping all commerce. Since the main target of the summer's campaign was the Venetian holdings in the Ionian Sea and thus control of the outlet of the Adriatic, Venice was more threatened than Spanish Italy. Thus in spite of the fact that there was a strong party in Venice anxious to make peace, by February 1538 Pope Paul III succeeded in bringing Venice and Spain into an alliance with the papacy against the Turks: the Ottoman armada had created a Holy League.

The next year Kheir-ed-din was in command of the Ottoman navy in the Ionian Sea; his lieutenants Dragut and Salah were both corsair reis, captains with reputations for valor, and Salah later held the office of beylerbey of North Africa. The Algerian Turkish historian tells us that his fleet consisted of one hundred twenty-two "light galleys"; a Christian writer gave him eighty-five galleys, thirty galiots, and a small fleet of supply ships. Against this force the Holy League mustered fifty-five galleys from Venice, twenty-seven from Rome and the Knights of St. John (Malta), and forty-nine from Spain. Charles's admiral, Andrea Doria, was in command of this entire fleet, but Duro tells us that the other two admirals did not always obey his orders, a fact that contributed to the failure of the League navy. The two fleets made contact with each other in September near Prevesa. After a more or less uncertain action two Christian and three Turkish ships were sunk, and five Christian ships captured. The next day, Doria withdrew the Christian fleet rather than risk further fighting; his action credited the Turks with victory. Skeptics in the West, like the contemporary French historian Brantôme, remembered that Doria's own ships were involved and explained that Barbarossa and Doria, both corsair admirals, were like wolves "who do not eat each other," or crows "who do not peck out each other's eyes." The Turkish historian was more pleased: "Such wonderful battles," he wrote, "as those fought between forenoon and sunset of that day were never seen before!"

Doria's forces were not really damaged at Prevesa; after the engagement he moved northward to the Dalmatian coast where he captured a Turkish fort, Castelnuova. In place of the three hundred fifty men who had guarded it for the Turks, he installed thirty-five hundred Spanish troops and strengthened the walls of the fortification. The Venetians regarded this as a Spanish intrusion of their domains, a danger to their control of the sea routes to the east; as a result, a few months later a Venetian agent was in Istanbul attempting to come to an agreement with the Turks. Venice preferred Turkish to Spanish influence in these waters.

The Spanish, however, did not hold Castelnuova long. The very next year Kheir-ed-din brought an army and a mighty fleet and recaptured the fortification. Of the thirty-five hundred Spanish soldiers, only eight hundred escaped death or enslavement. The summer of 1539 saw the Turkish armada capture the remaining Christian outposts in the Ionian and Aegean seas. Kheir-ed-din sent slaves and booty to Istanbul, where parades advertised the Ottoman victories. The expulsion of the Spanish from Castelnouva did not alter the Venetian desire for peace; in October 1540 they signed a treaty with the sultan that confirmed the remaining Venetian holdings and rights to trade in the Levant.

In the same time that Venice came to an agreement with the Ottoman empire, a curious episode in the west well illustrates the political climate of the mid-sixteenth century. Charles was aware that his rival and enemy, Francis I, was in close contact with Suleiman. For his part, Charles had long been in contact with the Persian shah, whose armies could distract the Ottoman sultan from European adventures. Now Spanish diplomacy sought to detach Kheir-ed-din from his allegiance to the sultan, much as it had previously detached Andrea Doria's Genoese fleet from France. The contacts with Barbarossa found him willing to talk, but his terms seemed too high. In return for joining Spain against France and the Sultan he wanted the entire North African coast from Tripoli to Morocco! This seemed to be too much for Charles, but the discussions continued until the Spanish finally learned that Barbarossa was keeping the sultan and the king of France up to date on the negotiations. There was nothing in Kheir-ed-din's career to suggest that his attachment to Islam was a sham or that his allegiance to the sultan was insincere; even so, in the sixteenth century, an age described by Machiavelli, it was quite in character for the king of Spain to attempt to buy the admiral pasha of his most dangerous enemy. The ploy did not happen to be as successful as it had been in the case of Andrea Doria.

The failure of these negotiations seems to have been one of the immediate factors in Charles's decision to make a descent on Algiers in order once and for all to destroy the pirate nest. Before undertaking that adventure, however, his agents made secret contact through the governor of Oran with Hassan Agha, a Sardinian renegade, who was Kheir-ed-din's calif (viceroy) in Algiers. As a result of these negotiations they believed that he would surrender the city as soon as the Spanish landed in force and set up siege lines. Like the negotiations with Barbarossa, the imagined agreement with Hassan Agha proved to be without foundation. The Spanish were more hatred by the men who had been saving Moriscos from Spanish tyranny than they knew.

While Spanish agents were dealing with Kheir-ed-din, and later with Hassan Agha, in hopes of assuring either an alliance with Algiers or an easy conquest of the city, Emperor Charles was also preparing to free himself and his armies by agreement with Francis I. A truce in 1537 was followed by the treaty of Nice, ending hostilities between the Hapsburg and Valois rulers; the next year at Aigues-Mortes a sensational meeting of the two rulers seemed to consolidate their friendship so completely that Charles actually traveled across France and visited Paris en route. The peace still remained unbroken in 1541, so that Charles could plan the massive military project against Algiers with some confidence that the king of France would not interfere. Indeed, Francis, informed of the project through the Holy Father, gave assurances of neutrality.

The projected invasion of Algiers was planned and organized with great care, but Charles remained in Germany until late in the season so that the actual departure of the armada with its cargo and troop ships was delayed until 18 October. It was a formidable force. The Turkish chronicler set the number at ninety thousand men; the Spanish, a little more conservative, tell us that the force included twenty-four thousand German, Italian, and Spanish troops, twelve thousand marines, over two thousand horses, plus the cannons and siege equipment deemed necessary for the task. The fleet included sixty-five galleys and well over four hundred transport vessels of all kinds and sizes. When this armada anchored before Algiers, the bay was blackened with ships. The Turkish chronicler gives us the feeling of awe that such a military display could inspire. He tells us that the guardian of the port said that "this fleet covered the entire surface of the sea, but I was unable to count all the vessels for they were so numerous that they did not permit the count that I started." This same chronicler insists that Hassan Agha encouraged his people by saying: "The Christian fleet is enormous . . . but do not forget the aid that Allah gives his Moslems against the foes of religion." He added: "Paradise is in the shade of the sabers . . . happy are those to whom Allah offers the chance of the martyr." The Algerians needed this encouragement; against this massive force they had some fifteen hundred janissaries, six thousand armed Andalusian Moriscos, and an undetermined number of Levantine "marines." Hassan also attempted to rouse the baldi of Algiers in defense of their city, but from all accounts these men were hardly of much use as soldiers.

The landing encountered minimal interference from Berber horsemen tribesmen, who harassed the left flank of the landing party. However, Charles did not order an immediate assault. He first sent an arrogant demand that the city must surrender to him, the king of kings, ruler of rulers. The answer was a firm and equally bombastic refusal. Nonetheless, there seems to have been much discussion in Algiers of the possible alternatives to a siege, but a persistent story informs us that a "holy man," a marabout named Kara Josef, announced that Allah had informed him that He would save the city if it would only resist the intruders. Hassan Agha and his soldiers, who knew something about sieges and war, must have wondered whether it might not be best to come to an agreement with the emperor. Nonetheless, the decision was to resist.

On the 24th of October the Christian army was ready to begin its operations, but about 9 p.m. a violent storm broke out. The ships anchored off the coast were soon in trouble. Our Turkish chronicler tells us that "the tempest that Allah loosened against them threw ashore many of their ships from which Moslem captives [galley slaves] escaped . . . the Arabs of Algiers fell on the crews of these ships and massacred them." Many of the Christian ships did break their cables and, with the supplies and war materials, were dashed on the rocks. Indeed, the entire coast was strewn with debris. Doria managed to cut loose most of his galleys and put them to sea, but the greater part of the fleet was wrecked. The troops, unprepared for such a storm, were soaked with rain, their powder and the fire for their arquebuses were wetted, and their morale shattered. At this point the troops in Algiers made a sortie that only the valor of the Maltese Knights of St. John prevented from becoming a rout. Moslem spears and arrows were better suited to the weather than the Spanish arquebuses, but the soldiers under the Knights of St. John were better disciplined than those pouring out of the city gates. One of the famous men in the emperor's entourage was Cortez, the conqueror of Mexico; he urged that Charles should try to stand off, wait for the storm to pass, and then make another effort to take the city. But Charles listened to Doria, Martin d'Alcaudette (the governor of Oran), and others on his staff, who pointed out that he did not have food, or powder, or men with morale. The twenty to thirty thousand men without food would soon become a rabble rather than an army. Retreat appeared to be inevitable.

Charles led the debris of his army around Cape Matifou where the war galleys and as many of the ships as could be saved were finally anchored, and managed to put the men to sea without further damage. Brantôme, a contemporary French historian, regretted that the soldiers had eaten their beautiful horses, but he, along with many others who either saw or heard about the disaster, wondered "why God did not favor so saintly and just a Christian enterprise." Was it "because He wanted to make men believe that nothing is sure until the fact is accomplished"? This was a question that was echoed in one account after another. The most eloquent of these, a pamphlet written by Nicholas Villaganon, a knight of St. John, was entitled *Carlo V Imperatoris Expeditio in Africam ad Algieram.* The subtitle translated into English ran "A lamentable and piteous treatise very necessary for everie Christian Manne to reade wherein is Contayned not only the high enterprise and valeantness of the Emperor Charles V and his army . . . but also the myserable chaunces of wynde and weather, with dyverse other adversities able to move even strong hearts to feayle the same and pray to God for his ayde and seccourse. . . ." This pamphlet was translated into nearly every European language; it is surprising that it did not shake men of their belief that God was on their side.

The Turks, naturally, were more satisfied with the results of the battle and the storm. Our chronicler tells us that "when the infidels saw the losses that had been inflicted on them by the Moslem sword and what the cold and the torrential rains had added . . . their sadness redoubled and their fears overburdened them for they recognized the extreme danger of the situation to which they were subjected." This was perhaps even an understatement. Our author goes on to say that the "shores of North Africa from Delleys to the east of Algiers to Cherchell were littered with the bodies of men and horses," that the Algerians had captured over two hundred cannons and that, upon hearing the news, Suleiman sent Hassan Agha a magnificent robe, an autographed letter, and the title of pasha. Our chronicler ends his story with the much-quoted boast: "Since that day Algiers seems like a young bride who contemplates her beauty and her jewels . . ."

It was a glorious day for Islam, a day celebrated in the following two centuries as Algiers' greatest victory. Even the Jews celebrated the defeat of the Christian enemy; they were on the bottom of the social ladder in Algiers, but they preferred Turkish scorn to Spanish tyranny.

There is an unauthenticated story that may well have been true: Kara Josef made such a pest of himself as the "savior of Algiers" that the newly elevated pasha and the divan of the janissaries *invented* another marabout who, rather than Josef, had assured the city that it was the will of Allah to resist. As for Josef, he was quietly strangled. Someone has said of such stories: "If it was not true, it probably should have been."

Emperor Charles V's defeat at Algiers was the opening of the long, often amorphous, struggle between the Hapsburg Mediterranean empire ruled by Charles V and then by his son Philip II, and the Ottoman Empire in the eastern end of that sea. Algiers was not the central point in this conflict, but the Algerian corsairs who had studied the art of naval warfare under Kheir-ed-din played very important roles in it. Kheir-ed-din, as the Sultan's admiral, ruled the Ottoman naval establishment until his death in 1546, and, after him and his son, two of his most trusted lieutenants rose to the role of beylerbeys of North Africa and admiral pashas of the Ottoman navy. As for Algiers, it continued to be called "the theater of the wars," the western base of the Ottoman empire. It was the Moslem counterpart of the island fortress of the Knights of St. John at Malta, where the knights were establishing a community of warrior rulers to govern the island and to supply a base for the corsair activity of the crusading order.

III *The War Between the Ottoman and the Spanish Empires*

I N THE HALF-CENTURY following Charles's disaster at Algiers, soldiers and sailors fighting under the flag of the Spanish Hapsburg kings, or of states vassal to them, intermittently fought with men subject to, or vassals of, the Turkish sultans. It was a curious war, interrupted by truce, by simple inaction, by failure of both parties to find the funds needed to continue. Its course was altered or impeded on the one side by the Spanish problems in the Netherlands, France, England, and Germany; on the other, by Suleiman's conflicts with his sons, with the rulers of Persia, and Ottoman incursions into central Europe. But at no time did the Spanish seriously consider another descent on Algiers. The emperor's failure to wipe out the pirates' nest was the third attempt in a generation to land at Algiers that ended in failure. Many superstitious persons feared that God himself was the author of the defeat, while others realized that the effort had been unwise in that it attempted a landing so late in the season. Nonetheless, after that debacle in 1541 the Spanish did not soon again attempt to conquer at Algiers. There were a number of interesting proposals by the Duke of Alba, the Italians Lanfreducci and Bossio, and others for an assault on the city, but none persuaded the Spanish kings that they were practical until the later years of the eighteenth century when another landing ended in disaster.

KHEIR-ED-DIN IN THE WESTERN MEDITERRANEAN

Interestingly enough the next exchange between Charles's states and the Moslem power resulted in a Turkish invasion of the western Mediterranean. By 1542 Suleiman was at war with the Hapsburgs in

Austria and Charles was again at'war with Francis I over Milan. As if to complicate the situation further, Henry VIII of England found himself at war with the Scots and France. These diverse political embroglios resulted in a treaty between Francis I and Suleiman by which the French agreed to provide a base at Toulon for the Turkish fleet as well as a subsidy to assist its operations so far from the Golden Horn. When Kheir-ed-din, admiral pasha of the Ottoman navy, appeared in the western Mediterranean with a huge armada that terrorized Spanish Italy and threatened Spain itself, it was no longer a question of a Spanish landing at Algiers, but rather of a Turkish landing on Spanish soil.

Kheir-ed-din's invasion of the western Mediterranean coincided with increased corsair activity from Algiers. As beylerbey of North Africa and admiral pasha of the sultan's navy, he directed the holy war against the infidel to maximize the amount of loot and number of slaves taken. The Ottoman navy made landings all along the Italian coast, sometimes in cooperation with the small Franch naval establishment, sometimes on its own. One of these incursions resulted in the capture of the governor of the chateau of Reggio, Don Diego Gaëtano, and his beautiful, talented daughter. The young woman attracted Kheir-ed-din's attention, and he finally persuaded her to become his wife. Further up the coast, the Ottoman and French forces cooperated in the siege and capture of Nice. In that operation, the Ottoman artillerymen clearly proved their superiority, and Ottoman discipline was much better than the French. But the thing that bothered Kheir-ed-din most seems to have been that the French ran out of powder and had to beg supplies from the Turks; Kheir-ed-din became wary about a people whose supply of munitions was exhausted before they ran out of wine!

This Turkish invasion of the western Mediterranean momentarily turned the naval balance of power against the Spanish empire, but the total effect of the Franco-Ottoman cooperation on the balance of power was relatively small. Indeed, on the contrary, the experience of the Ottoman naval forces at the Toulon base during the winter of 1543–44 left scars on both the host and the guests that made future cooperation less likely. From all accounts the Turks did behave properly; their discipline did not break down. Nonetheless the French who had been forced to leave their homes and city to make way for the Turks resented the experience. Even more distressing for the future of the Franco-Ottoman alliance was the inability of the French treasury to meet the costs of supporting the Turks for the entire winter. Kheir-ed-din became convinced that Francis I had failed to keep his word and as a result conceived a deep dislike for both the French king and his people, a dislike that he passed on to his son Hassan. On the other hand Francis decided that the costs of maintaining a Turkish navy were simply too great; it would be better to make peace with Charles V.

Charles V also wanted peace with France. He had problems in Germany, where the Lutheran heresy had become a fixture and where the North German princes were defying his authority. The two rulers made peace at Crespy in 1544. Suleiman, also bothered by internal problems and a possible new war on his eastern frontier, was equally willing to reach an agreement to end the war in the Mediterranean. The result was a truce between the Spanish and Ottoman empires.

THE DRAGUT INTERLUDE

The truce between the sultan and the king of the Spains had an immediate effect on the regency community at Algiers. Hassan Pasha, beylerbey of North Africa after his father's death, was as loyal a subject of the Sultan as Kheir-ed-din had been. The truce with Spain had to mean a cessation of the corsair raids. He therefore directed his attention to the problem of bringing the hinterland between the coastal cities and the Sahara under the control of the government at Algiers; his successes and failures were to be important for the future of the regency. However, the corsair community, as distinct from the janissary corps and the Morisco militia at Hassan's disposal, could find no such outlet for its activities. As long as the beylerbey of North Africa paid attention to the firmans from Istanbul, the reis would be unemployed. These men, however, had given their lives to the jihad and plunder; they were both pious Moslems bent on revenging their fellows against the Christian Spanish empire and "privateers," sea captains who were turning war into a business that could yield huge profits for themselves and the owners of their ships. One of Kheir-ed-din's most trusted companions and perhaps his best friend, Dragut, became the leader of these men.

Like so many of the Moslem heroes of this first epoch, Dragut's origins are clouded by myth. Marmol tells us that he was born on the Island of Rhodes before the Knights of St. John were expelled. Brantôme says he was born in Anatolia; others simply assert that he was a Greek, which is probably true. No matter, at an early age he came to the attention of Kheir-ed-din and quickly rose to a position of power and influence in the inner circle of the Turkish-corsair community. At Prevesa, Dragut commanded one wing of the fleet, but a year later he had the misfortune to be captured by Doria's nephew and found himself on the oar bench of a Christian galley. A number of distinguished people of this era had this experience, including a grand master of the Knights of St. John, Aroudj, and others who pulled oars beside poor wretches who were never to be ransomed. When Kheir-ed-din was at Toulon with the Turkish fleet, he made an agreement with Andrea Doria by which Dragut was freed. It was an expensive bargain: the Genoese house of Lomellini obtained the concession to establish a coral fishing port and factory on the island of Tabarque off the coast near Bône, and Doria got 3,000 gold ducats. Before long, Doria regretted his bargain, for Dragut refused to recognize the truce between the sultan and the Spanish king and soon became the leader of the corsairs who continued their depredations on Spanish commerce and the Spanish and Italian coasts.

Dragut's most spectacular exploit was the capture of a Maltese galley carrying the treasure of the Knights of St. John, some twenty thousand gold ducats in all. But he had to have a port for his operations; Algiers was denied him, and with the Spanish in control of La Goulette, Tunis was also out of bounds. Like Aroudj before him, he established a base on the island of Jerba, where a native sheik happily provided him with supplies and a harbor in return for a share in the loot taken by his corsairs. The Spanish protested at Istanbul, but when the sultan ordered Dragut to come to his court to answer questions, the corsair chief refused. His head was safer when he was in the central Mediterranean than it would be at the sultan's palace.

As his little flotilla grew and prospered, Dragut felt the need for a better harbor. He managed to secure two small towns on the coast opposite Jerba, but neither of them was satisfactory. There was a small port city that would suit his needs, Mahdiya (also known as Africa); it was a walled town with a reasonably safe harbor, but its leading citizens wanted nothing to do with the corsairs. Dragut managed to corrupt a man who helped him introduce Levantine marines from the corsair ships into the town; the next morning the fait accompli could not be reversed. It was a trick quite reminiscent of Aroudj's adventures forty years earlier. The walls of Mahdiya were weak, but when they were invested by determined men, Mahdiya became a formidable position.

From Mahdiya, the corsairs spread out in the central Mediterranean with results disastrous to the Spanish. The Spanish government protested to the sultan: either Dragut was a pirate or he and the Sublime Porte (the government of the Ottoman empire) were breaking the truce. Dragut was probably a pirate with ambitions to wage a jihad in his own or in the sultan's name. We must recognize, however, that Dragut was not the only one to rupture the truce. Christian corsairs operating from Malta, Sicily, and Minorca also "broke the truce" by attacking Moslem commerce in the eastern Mediterranean and capturing pilgrims sailing from North Africa to the Levant on their pious mission in the holy places of Mecca and Medina. Had Dragut been content to operate out of Jerba, he might have been ignored, but Mahdiya was too close to La Goulette and Sicily; it was dangerously near the center of the Spanish Tunisian vassal state of Tunis. In 1550, the governor of La Goulette called on Doria and the Spanish fleet to rid him of this unwelcome neighbor.

The Genoese squadrons, strengthened by troops from Sicily, descended on Mahdiya in force. Dragut, warned of the attack, had the wisdom to withdraw his corsair fleet before the Spanish arrived (September 1550), but he left five hundred Turkish Levantines to defend the town. Although these men held out bravely, they finally did have to surrender. Then it was the same story that was told so often in this era: The people who really paid the bill for Spanish wrath and soldiers' greed were the townspeople. They had not wanted Dragut or his corsairs in the first place; when their city was captured from the Turkish Levantines, it was the townspeople who were pillaged, raped, murdered, and enslaved. Pedro Navarro had established the pattern of Spanish violence earlier in the century; his successors in 1551 saw no reason to depart from it. The fate of Mahdiya was left to Charles V and his Spanish council. They decided that the city would be too expensive to garrison and fortify, so the alternative was to destroy it. Its walls, houses, and mosques were systematically blown up, and its people expelled or enslaved.

The Spanish excused their assault on Mahdiya on the grounds that they were acting as allies of the sultan of Tunis, helping him to rid his lands of unwelcome pirates who had taken over one of his harbors. In Istanbul, men saw the adventure differently. The Ottoman government was in serious difficulty because of a conflict that had developed between Suleiman and his heir; the latter found support and refuge in Persia. But even with this unhappy involvement, the sultan was not ready to see the Spanish make their grip firmer on the central Mediterranean. If they added Mahdiya and perhaps Jerba to the holdings of the Knights of Malta at Tripoli and Malta and their ports in Sicily and Naples, the central Mediterranean would be closed to the Turks. But it was not simply the fear of Spanish control in that sea that inspired Suleiman to forgive Dragut. The new king of France, Henri II, was urging the re-establishment of the Franco-Ottoman entente and common action against the Hapsburgs. Henri II was interested in upsetting the Hapsburgs in Germany; a diversion in the Mediterranean would be useful to support his German policy.

In any case the Turkish response to the capture of Mahdiya was quick. A powerful Ottoman naval force appeared off the Italian coasts in August 1551. After several landings it passed by Malta and sailed on to Tripoli to besiege that port occupied by the Knights of St. John from which Christian corsairs had operated against Turkish commerce. Doria's response was weak; in July he had lost eight galleys in a storm. Tripoli was doomed. A French ambassador on the way to his post at Istanbul stopped by Tripoli, where he observed the progress of the siege at close hand. When it became evident that the Knights must surrender, the ambassador persuaded the Turkish admiral, Sinān Pasha, to allow the knights at Tripoli to be evacuated in the French ship in return for immediate surrender. The Turks were reluctant to make any agreement with "dogs"; thirty years earlier the Knights of St. John had promised Suleiman in solemn treaty not to engage again in corsair activity against the Ottoman commerce in return for the right to evacuate their fortress at Rhodes with the honors of war. The knights did not keep this article, but they rightfully pointed out that Suleiman really gave them this right to leave with honor because he could not take their fortification without further great losses. Finally Sinān Pasha agreed as much to save his own men as to favor the French ambassador. The knights of Tripoli were allowed to leave freely; the soldiers who made up their army were enslaved. When the French ship delivered the refugees from Tripoli to Malta, the French ambassador was coldly received by the grand master, who believed that the French had aided the Turks with both information and war supplies.

The capture of Tripoli was a significant victory for the Ottoman empire, for it provided a port that connected the Mediterranean with the caravan routes into the Sahara and black Africa beyond, as well as a haven for ships from the west carrying pilgrims on the route to Mecca and Medina. Dragut, again in favor at Istanbul, became pasha of Tripoli with a squadron of some forty war galleys at his disposal.

He strengthened the fortifications and developed the harbor into a major base for the Turkish fleet.

The Spanish capture of Mahdiya in 1550 and the Turkish response at Tripoli in 1551 were signals for the reopening of the Hapsburg-Ottoman war in the Mediterranean. The entente between Henri II of France and Suleiman soon linked this conflict to the one that was in progress in Northern Europe, where the French king had come to the support of the North German princes in their war with Emperor Charles. Transportation and communication were slow in the sixteenth century, but European problems had a way of becoming pervasive and intertwined anyway.

THE EXTENSION OF THE ALGERIAN REGENCY

Henri II was not as astute a politician as his father had been, but he did understand that the cooperation of the beylerbey of North Africa was important for the success of his war in the Mediterranean. The beylerbey was Hassan ben Kheir-ed-din, and he had learned from his father to distrust the French. Furthermore, he was convinced that the consolidation of Turkish control over the territory of the central Maghrib between the sea and the Sahara was the most important task of the moment. The French recognized his reluctance to join wholeheartedly in the war effort, and so the French ambassador at Istanbul persuaded the sultan to replace him as beylerbey. His recall came just when he was about to establish a firm hold on Tlemcen in face of opposition from Fez. Hassan Corso, a janissary agha (commander) who was popular with the corps and was as well an astute soldier, completed the conquest after Hassan was recalled, and established five hundred janissaries in Tlemcen to assure Turkish control over that important city on the western frontier. When the new beylerbey, Salah Reis, arrived, he fully supported the policy of extending the authority of the Turkish regency into the hinterland of the city of Algiers; he also more readily supported the progress of the Franco-Turkish war against Spain.

Salah Reis, an Egyptian, was one of Kheir-ed-din's most trusted lieutenants. From commander of a simple corsair vessel, he rose to admiral pasha of the sultan's navy when Kheir-ed-din died. He came to Algiers just when the emirs of the Tuggurt and Ouaregla, Arab tribesmen on the borders of the Sahara, refused to pay tribute to the Turkish regency. If this rebellion were to be successful, it would soon be repeated by other tribes within the territory, for the payment of any tribute was unpopular, indeed hated; the nomadic and seminomadic peoples believed themselves to be free. This particular revolt against the Turks was inspired by the tutor of a young sheik; he persuaded the tribesmen to believe that Allah would load favors on anyone who killed a Turk! Salah Reis had to forget the Mediterranean war for the moment and mount an expedition into the Sahara. The tribesmen were no match for the janissaries; their spears and swords were of little avail against men armed with the arquebus and a few small cannons. Salah Reis overwhelmed them, forced them to make peace, and beheaded the tutor, who, presumably, was responsible for the rebellion. According to the Turkish chronicler, Salah Reis returned to Algiers with fifteen camels loaded with gold and other booty in the form of cloth, jewels, hides, and livestock as well as with five thousand negro slaves.

Salah Reis was next confronted with a rebellion by the Koukou Kabylie tribesmen, which was backed by Spanish gold. This rebellion was suppressed as vigorously as the one in the south, but it prevented any action against Spain. In the fall of 1553 Salah Reis's corsairs assisted the sultan of Fez in recapturing the port of Valez from the Spanish, but he could not make any serious effort on the part of Algiers until 1555, when he finally was able to make an assault and take Bougie, which was, except for Oran, the most important Spanish holding on the entire coast. The Spanish were slow to supply their garrison, with the result that the governor of Bougie was unable to defend himself when he was besieged from both land and sea. The unfortunate man finally agreed to surrender if he and his officers were allowed to return to Spain. When he arrived home, the Spanish government immediately tried him for cowardice and misgovernment and beheaded him.

Once in control of Bougie, Salah Reis recognized that Oran and Mers-el-Kébir should be the next targets for the Algerian regency. Accordingly he made plans for an assault by both land and sea similar to the siege that had succeeded so well at Bougie. But, as the pious father Diego de Haëdo put it, "Thanks to the grace of God," before the siege could really get under way, Salah Reis died of the plague. When the news of his death reached Istanbul, the Sublime Porte decided to call off the projected siege of Oran and ordered the Turkish galleys to return to the Golden Horn. Algiers was far away, and there were some in the sultan's entourage who believed that the beylerbeys of that distant sanjac might be using the war to consolidate a semi-independent state in the Maghrib. With the prestigious figure of Salah Reis out of the picture, it might be very unwise to allow the janissary agha, Hassan Corso, to be the man who captured Oran. In a very real way, they were right, for, as we shall see, the janissaries were furious when the Turkish galleys departed, leaving them without the resources to capture the Spanish fortifications. It was this action that sparked the first rebellion of the janissary corps of Algiers, an event of great importance for the future of the regency.

While the Algerian beylerbeys were using the war to strengthen their hold on the central Maghrib, the conflict in Italy, the Netherlands, and Hungary was exhausting the limited resources of the contestants. Sixteenth-century warfare had become an expensive enterprise, too expensive for the slender resources available to the rulers. Armies were composed of mercenaries who had to be paid; cannons, powder and shot, and other supplies that were now so necessary for conducting war on land and sea were expensive. Neither the tax revenues nor the loans from the bankers were enough to pay the ever increasing costs of war. By 1557–58, princes in France, Spain, and even the Ottoman empire were either bankrupt or very near to it. Both Henri II of France and Philip II of the Spains realized that peace was essential and that no military decision could dictate it. There were other political problems urging peace: the religious issue in both France and the Spanish Netherlands; the death of Mary Tudor in England, which broke the bond between Spain and that kingdom; and a number of minor difficulties facing both kings, all joined to lead to the treaty of Château Cambrésis in 1559. This treaty ended the Hapsburg-Valois wars that had filled the first half of the sixteenth century.

While Philip II negotiated peace with the king of France, he also considered the possibility of peace with the Ottoman empire. His advisers assured him that Suleiman needed peace as much as he did, and, indeed, Suleiman was in the act of negotiating a peace with Philip's uncle, Emperor Ferdinand, who had succeeded Charles on the imperial throne in Germany. Suleiman was not as pliable as the Christian kings had hoped he would be. He did make peace with Ferdinand on condition that the German emperor pay all the subsidies that had been due to the Ottoman empire since the last treaty, but when Philip's agents tried to be included in the treaty, Suleiman insisted upon separate negotiations between the Ottoman and Spanish empires. Philip considered several alternatives. It seemed that bribes for the grand vizier might be the best route. He offered ten thousand écus a year; the money could be placed in the vizier's name either in Venice or Istanbul, providing that the peace was honorably kept. Then for reasons that are obscure, Philip suddenly decided that a truce with the sultan would be beneath his dignity; he returned to his plans for keeping the Turks out of the western Mediterranean basin.

FROM JERBA TO LEPANTO

The task ahead was clear. Spanish control of Malta, Sicily, Naples, and La Goulette at Tunis provided strong bases for patrolling the narrow seas between the eastern and western ends of the Mediterranean. If the Spanish navy could regain control of Tripoli and capture Jerba, it should be easy to contain any Turkish thrust westward, even if the Turks continued to hold Algiers. Algiers was not a good harbor for a large fleet of warships. Tripoli, however, had been captured by the Turks, and Dragut was in the act of making that harbor into a second Algiers, a corsair's nest and a base for the Ottoman fleet.

It was an article of faith in Sicily that the Turkish navy would not risk an adventure beyond Levantine waters except in the summertime, when the weather would be dependable. With this reasoning, the Spanish decided upon an assault on Tripoli at the very end of the summer season of 1559. They were optimistic about the results: The fortifications were still weak, the tribesmen in the hinterland of Tripoli were willing to help since they had come to hate the Turks. However, like Charles's assault on Algiers in 1541, this attack on Tripoli required the cooperation of Spanish naval and military officers of the Spanish Mediterranean empire, who were scattered from Barcelona to Genoa, from Sicily to Oran. It was difficult to bring them all together in a common enterprise in this era when communications were slow, even ponderous. There had to be food for men and horses, powder and shot for the guns, naval supplies to keep the ships at sea, and all had to be brought into port at the same time that the German, Italian, and Spanish soldiers who were needed for the enterprise were ready to embark on the transports. Small wonder that there were delays. Bad weather set in about the time the armada was ready to move; the ships had to put in at Malta to avoid a serious storm, and it was only in the winter of 1560 that the ships could leave the island harbors. In the meantime, sickness had taken a serious toll; ten percent of the men could not leave Malta with the fleet. Then, rather than move directly against Tripoli, where Dragut was arming himself to meet them, the Spanish decided upon a landing at Jerba to capture the "pirates' nest" there. The corsairs had left the island before the Spanish arrived and had dispatched a vessel to Istanbul to beg for help.

Madina Celi, the Spanish commander, took time to establish a puppet government for Jerba and to build a small fortification for a garrison that would remain and assure the Spanish control over the island; he was sure that the Turks would not intervene so early in the season. He was wrong. Piali Pasha, with a strong Turkish flotilla, arrived off Jerba unexpectedly. The Spanish intelligence was faulty, and Spanish preparations to fight were even less effective. Part of the fleet was up on the shore, immobilized; the rest of it was not prepared to fight. Of forty-eight galleys and galiots twenty-eight were either captured or destroyed; the rest escaped after being badly damaged. Turkish marines landed at Jerba, captured the bulk of the Spanish supplies, and then besieged the newly constructed fortification. The garrison held out bravely, hoping for relief, but finally in July, when supplies of food and water gave out, it surrendered. This was a terrible blow to Spanish prestige, and not only to its prestige but also to its safety, for the victory emboldened the corsairs in the western Mediterranean and encouraged the Moriscos to believe that at last they might count on aid from the east in their conflict with the Spanish oppressors. Ten years later, the most serious Morisco rebellion of the century was to follow from this belief.

Philip's naval problems in the Mediterranean did not end with the defeat at Jerba. Dragut surprised and sank several of his galleys off the southern coast of Sicily, and a storm destroyed twenty-five of them, killing nearly the entire complements of men and sailors. It was 1564 before the Spanish navy could again make a serious show of force in the central Mediterranean. The Turks, however, were not able to take advantage of this weakness. The Ottoman system was so ponderous that it could function only when the sultan was with his armies; this meant that when Suleiman was involved in the east with the Persians and his rebellious son, his forces in the west were immobilized. The naval arm remained strong, but it did not leave Levantine waters until the sultan returned to Istanbul.

While the war galleys of both empires were inactive, the corsairs, both Moslem and Christian, swarmed the seas in search of prey. The western seas were covered by corsairs operating from Algiers, Bougie, Tripoli, and some of the smaller harbors like Cherchell and Bône. On the eastern seas, corsairs operating from Minorca, Sicily, Malta,

and other Italian ports sought prizes in the Levant. The governments of Genoa and Venice did not encourage this activity, and yet
their officials governing Genoese and Venetian islands like Crete,
Cyprus, Chios, and others looked aside when Christian corsairs came
to their harbors for wood, water, and food; they often even allowed
them to sell part of the cargoes of their prizes. These Christian corsairs were as much of a thorn in the Ottoman empire as the Moslem
counterparts were for the Spanish. On one occasion, five Maltese corsairs captured a galleon belonging to Kiz-ler Agha carrying several
important ladies from the sultan's seraglio and the chief of the sultan's black eunuchs. Other Christian corsairs captured important people intent on visits, official business, or pilgrimages to Mecca. The
most dangerous and daring of these corsairs were knights from the
two orders of crusader monks: the Tuscan order of St. Stephen,
and above all, the Knights of St. John, who operated from Malta.

The order of St. Stephen, recently (1562) founded and patronized
by the dukes of Tuscany and operating from Tuscan harbors, were
relatively unimportant; they were few in number and largely
acted as an arm of the dukes' service. On the other hand, the Knights
of St. John regularly operated six to ten first-class war galleys, and
their grand master commissioned swarms of privateer corsairs to raid
from Malta.

The religious crusading order of the Knights of St. John dated
back to the era of the Crusades. It was originally founded to provide
hospital service for the crusaders in the Holy Lands. In time, its members became warrior knights, and by the fifteenth century they had
developed into an order of crusading sailors with a powerful fortress
base on the Island of Rhodes and "chapters" established in France,
Provence, Spain, England, Italy, and Germany. Some of these chapters were very wealthy, for it had been a pious practice for good
Christian noblemen to leave a part of an estate to these warrior
monks, with the result that the Knights of St. John owned and operated vast holdings of agricultural land and maintained chateaus all
over the countryside in Roman Catholic Europe.

The Knights of St. John were recruited from the sons of noblemen. No one without four grandfathers who were noblemen could
become a knight. There were a few exceptions, but the order was
largely made up from the second or third sons of noble families who
were destined for the church but also wished a military career. These
men were perhaps culturally a cut above the joldacs, or privates, who
made up the janissary corps, and surely better prepared to carry arms

than ox-drivers, camel herders, and plowboys from Anatolia. None-theless, distinct comparisons can be made: Both knight and joldac were expected to be bachelors; both were bound in the discipline of the corps to which they belonged. When a young man joined the Knights of St. John, he was sent to sea in one of the order's warships on a "caravan" against the foe. After a fixed term at sea, he could be sent back to Europe to manage estates or carry on other business of the order. When, or if, the order's island fortification was in danger, the knights could be recalled to help defend it. We should remember in passing that with all its property to manage, the order was very rich and thus was often viewed with covetous eyes by Europe's princes. When Henry VIII reformed the English church, the con-fiscation of the property of the Knights of St. John was one of his first acts.

At Malta, as at Rhodes in the preceding century, the knights lived in houses belonging to the "languages" of the order: the French were the most important numerically, but English, Provençal, Spanish, German, and Italian houses also provided places for those adventurers who combined their religious activity with war. Some of them lived exemplary lives; some were riotous philanderers, though no one questioned their valor or bravery. In 1465 they stood off a powerful Turkish assault when the sultan attacked their stronghold at Rhodes; in 1521 they surrendered only when it was obvious that Suleiman's armies would eventually storm their walls. The knights were organized politically as an aristocratic republic of soldier monks. They elected their grand master and gave him powers similar to those exercised by the pashas, aghas, and deys of Algiers. Since the order was smaller in numbers than the janissary corps and since so many of the knights lived in Europe in the commanderies of the order, the dangerous cliques, common to Algiers, did not develop as readily nor was there the rebellion and violence later to be common to the Maghrib regency.

As we have noted, early in his reign, Suleiman had succeeded in driving the Knights of St. John from Rhodes after a prolonged and costly siege. He allowed them to leave "with the honors of war" only because his forces were not really able to win a knock-out vic-tory. The Turks understood that one of the conditions of the peace had been an agreement by the knights not to continue their war against Ottoman commerce. However, once Charles had installed them on the island of Malta (1529) and in the harbor city of Tripoli, the "galleys of the religion," as they were called, again attacked Turkish shipping and landed on Turkish soil to take slaves. In Turkish eyes, Malta was as much a nest of vipers as Algiers was in the opinion of the Spanish. Just as Charles decided several times that he must capture the pirate stronghold of Algiers, Suleiman and his advisers realized that they must take the strongholds of the Knights of St. John. The capture of Tripoli in the early 1550s was simply the first step toward liquidating the Christian positions so dangerous to the Ottoman empire. Tripoli, Malta, Tunis with La Goulette: these were the next natural targets for the Turkish fleet and soldiers.

The decision to attack Malta was made in 1564; the next May a formidable Ottoman force arrived before the island and landed troops and supplies for the siege. So impressive a military force could not be assembled in the sixteenth century without advertising the fact of its existence. The Christian West knew that an attack was to come, but would it be Malta, La Goulette and Tunis, Crete, or even Cyprus? No one could know which would be the target. The grand master of the Knights of St. John, Jean de la Valette Parisot,[1] was sure that his island would be attacked, and he did everything he could to prepare for the storm. He recalled as many of his knights as he could from their European posts, hired additional levies of soldiers in Italy, strengthened his fortifications, and laid in supplies for a siege. He was not able, however, to persuade any of the European princes to send him aid. The Spanish, concerned for La Goulette and Sicily, did not wish to leave themselves open for an easy attack, and the princes of northern Europe were concerned with their own problems largely related to the religious schism. The grand master and his knights with some nine thousand soldiers in their service prepared to fight alone; they were to show the world that they were worthy heirs to the tradition that grandmaster de l'Isle Adam and his men had established forty years earlier in the defense of their island fortress of Rhodes.

The Ottoman invading force landed some forty thousand men with great quantities of siege equipment, but their command was divided between Piali Pasha, the admiral, and Mustapha Pasha commanding the land forces. When Dragut arrived from Tripoli with his

1. This remarkable man, son of a French noble house, joined the Knights of St. John, was captured by the Turks, and served as galley slave on the vessel of Reis Abdarahaman Castagli. After his ransom he, by a turn of fate, captured his former Turkish master and put him to the oars. His story, as commander of the knights under siege, is one of a man with an iron will, a cold calculating intelligence, and complete faith in his God. With good reason the knights renamed their capital city "Valette."

contingent, he also carried a commission from the sultan that gave him command. The knights were under the single and devoted orders of Grand Master de la Valette, who skillfully managed the defense. It would be folly to try to tell the story of a siege that lasted five months: both attackers and defenders showed great heroism; both were subjected to frustrations, fears, and terrible losses. The story of the siege was told in Europe in many popularly distributed maps and pamphlets that still testify to the interest that was generated by the heroic defense.[2]

Even though the defenses were in ruins and the defenders weakened by losses to a point where continued resistance seemed nearly impossible, the knights and their soldiers fought on, hoping for relief. Numerous messengers were smuggled out of the city with urgent demands for help, but the viceroy of Sicily still feared that the Turkish armada would be turned against his island if he denuded its fortifications. However, he did finally round up and dispatch a small relief force. On September 1, the Turks launched a massive offensive; the battle that had gone on for months had somehow to be ended. Again they were repulsed and again with new losses that dispirited and demoralized the Turkish soldiers. "Was it the will of Allah that Malta should not be taken?" Events seemed to prove that this was the case. Then, the second week in September, the small Christian task force landed on the coast opposite the scene of the battle and cautiously moved toward the Turkish siege lines. The Turkish commander did not wait to find out whether this was a massive support for the defenders, or simply, as was the actual case, a token enterprise to help maintain Christian morale. He lost his nerve and ordered a withdrawal that managed to embark his army, but he abandoned much of its equipment and supplies before the reinforcements from Sicily could do more than harass his rear guards. It was a disastrous defeat for the Ottoman military forces, and a victory for the Knights of St. John, that made the expression "The Great Siege" synonymous with the siege of Malta. It had been a victory of 600–700 knights and 8,000–9,000 soldiers over a besieging force that must have numbered between thirty thousand and forty thousand men. Small wonder that Grand Master de la Valette was hailed as hero by the entire Christian world, Protestant and Catholic alike. On the other side, the Turks could count the death of Dragut as one of

2. The Newberry Library has a superb collection of these maps that purport to show the progress of the siege. Ernle Bradford's *The Great Siege* (New York, 1961) is the best popular account in English.

the tragedies of the contest. Dragut was wounded in action and failed to recover; he had proven himself to be their best captain; his death was as much a serious blow as that of the thousands of the Turkish soldiers killed besieging the ramparts of the two Maltese fortifications. After the departure of the Turks, the knights thanked God and began to reconstruct their walls. Everyone feared that the Turkish host would return the next year and easily accomplish the task that had failed in 1565. The fortifications were in ruins, the supplies of food and war material practically exhausted, and the defenders weakened by losses that they could not retrieve. The Ottoman empire, however, was essentially a "land animal"; its successes at sea under Kheir-ed-din and his successors had not convinced Suleiman that the sea was a suitable field for his own military action. He decided to retrieve the Turkish reputation lost at Malta by an assault on central Europe via the Danube. The death of Emperor Ferdinand (1564) served as a pretext for demanding payment of arrears in tribute money. The new Emperor Maximilian added a further pretext for war by interfering in Transylvanian politics. Thus in 1566 a mighty Turkish force left the Golden Horn for Belgrade and Buda Pest (Ofen) but it never pushed on for a contest with the German empire, for Suleiman died en route, and the attack simply disintegrated. His heir, Selim II (later surnamed "the sot") succeeded in establishing himself as sultan, but he did not join the Turkish forces on the Danube, and, without the sultan as the leader, the army was unable to act. Historians often mark the beginning of the decline of the Ottoman empire with the date of Suleiman's death. It is probably correct, but for some time after 1566, capable viziers, trained in the heroic era of the Ottoman state, continued to direct the course of empire, so that the Christian West could hardly have been expected to know that this formidable foe was in decline.

Indeed, during the years immediately following the death of Suleiman, the grand vizier, Mehemet Sokolli, a statesman in the mold of Suleiman's best viziers, governed the Ottoman empire. Famine in 1567–68 curtailed his activity and probably contributed to his making peace with Maximilian, but it did not prevent him from beginning the construction of a fortress opposite the island of Cyprus that could be used to reduce that Venetian possession. In 1569, he was obliged to fight petty wars on the southern shores of the Black Sea, on the Persian frontier, and against Arabs on the shores of the Red Sea, but these "brush-fire" wars did not dissuade him from his real objective: Cyprus. In 1569, there was an explosion in the arsenal at

Venice, possibly the work of an Ottoman agent, and the shipyards near Istanbul worked at full speed. Sokolli's preparations for an attack on some part of the Christian holdings in the Levant sent chills in the hearts of statesmen in Venice. They soon understood that Cyprus was to be the next victim of Turkish aggression.

Christian diplomacy turned on the possibility of an alliance that would unite Spain and Venice, but, in the years following the siege of Malta, Philip II's Spain had other problems more pressing than those of the Mediterranean. The Spanish king tried at first to be associated with Maximilian's peace with the Ottoman empire, but Sokolli insisted that a Spanish ambassador must be sent to negotiate for the king of Spain. There followed numerous "under-the-counter" suggestions for negotiation that failed to bring any agreement. The war with the Ottoman empire had quieted down; Spain's Mediterranean fleet had recovered enough to guarantee Spanish control over the routes between Spain and Italy and to place a serious check on the activities of the Moslem corsairs in the western and central Mediterranean. Peace with the Turks might be desirable, but it was not necessary. Furthermore, it might cost the king the subsidies granted him by the pope to fight the infidel. However, the most serious problem for the king of Spain in these years was centered in the Netherlands, where Calvinist fanatics had desecrated the churches and refused to obey the regent. Spanish policy vacillated for months over the proper response. Finally the party advocating drastic military action in the north won out, and the Duke of Alba was sent to the Netherlands with the flower of the Spanish and Italian troops from the king's Mediterranean territories. It was not long before Philip's desk was covered with dispatches telling of "brisk" fighting in the Netherlands and the attacks of English and Dutch corsairs in the Channel and on the sea lanes of the Atlantic. Thus, by the time the Ottoman naval power began to grow again and plans were being made for the descent on Cyprus, Philip was deeply engaged in the Netherlands.

Nonetheless, after 1569, the tension in the Mediterranean world began to mount, for the West was warned that Selim II would probably attempt to emulate his ancestors by a striking military victory to provide spoils to decorate mosques and a pageant spectacle of a victory march in Istanbul. The fortifications opposite Cyprus suggested that Venice would pay the bill for an "easy" victory. But when the shipyards on the Golden Horn came to life with feverish activity to enlarge an already powerful Ottoman fleet, the Spanish could not exclude the possibility that La Goulette, Malta, Sicily, or even Spain itself might be the target for this armada. This latter possibility was underlined by the fact that on Christmas day in 1568 a Morisco fanatic aroused his fellow countrymen to rebellion in Granada. Was he an agent for the sultan? The rebellion got underway slowly at first, but then supplies and some volunteers arrived from North Africa and the Morisco rebels were able to come out of the mountains and attack towns and villages on the plains. When they learned that Ottoman agents proposed that the French king should again turn over to them the port of Toulon, this Morisco rebellion seemed dangerous indeed. None of the North African ports were big enough or protected enough to allow a large Ottoman naval force to use North African bases, but Toulon would be adequate for such a force.

It turned out, however, that the Turkish naval power was to be used for the conquest of Cyprus in case the Venetians should be unwilling to surrender their holdings there without a fight. And yet the Moriscos—encouraged by volunteers from North Africa and a flow of supplies collected by popular subscription in Algiers that even went beyond the wishes of Euldj Ali, the beylerbey—became a dangerous enemy before the end of 1569. With his best troops committed under the Duke of Alba in the Netherlands, Philip II was much embarrassed by this rebellion.

While the corsair community at Algiers expressed sympathy for their co-religionists in Spain and sent them a few men and considerable munitions of war, Euldj Ali and the divan realized that without the Ottoman fleet and a large Ottoman land force, Spain could not be reconquered. However, the rebellion in Spain was useful to the beylerbey of North Africa, for it immobilized the Spanish naval forces as well as much of the Spanish army that remained in the Mediterranean basin. It gave Euldj Ali an excellent opportunity to try again to extend Algerian control over the entire North African Coast; Kheir-ed-din's effort to make Tunis a part of his regency had resulted in Charles V's expedition and capture of Tunis. The Spanish fortification of La Goulette, as well as the native puppet government that Charles had established as his vassal, were both still in existence in 1569. The prince that Charles had imposed upon the Tunisians had been deposed (and blinded) by his son years before, but the son made peace with the Spanish and misruled Tunis about as badly as his father had. In 1569, there were many important people in Tunis who wished to be rid of their ruler, and several of them had approached Euldj Ali for Algerian assistance in driving out the tyrant. By paralyzing the Spanish armies, the Morisco rebellion provided an excellent opportunity to consolidate Algerian power in North Africa. A conquest of Tunis would make up for the fact that, in the west, Oran and the sultanate of Fez had proved to be too strong for the Algerian janissary army's westward expansion.

The Morisco rebellion also may have entered into the calculations of the Sublime Porte regarding Cyprus. In 1570 the harassment of Venetian ships and merchants signaled the warning that it would be dangerous to resist Ottoman pressure. In mid-March a Turkish spokesman appeared in Venice to demand the return of Cyprus to the sultan as legitimate overlord of that island. The Venetian senate refused by an overwhelming vote, and Venice prepared for war. But Venice had not been seriously at war for over thirty years; her ships, her men, her fortifications were poorly prepared for the oncoming struggle; without allies, Venice would be doomed to defeat.

At this point a vigorous personality made a striking difference in the course of events. It would be folly to attribute the formation of the new Holy League solely to Pope Pius V, and yet this impressive old man of humble origins and great faith became the center of what he saw as a new crusade. His own words provide a clue to the intensity of his feelings:

Oh century burdened with evils, the Turks . . . will destroy Christendom bit by bit. Consider their humble origins, born with the Sythians in the Caucasus of India, living in brigandage with no notice by the world. . . . Little by little their force grew, they had the audacity to invade Christian lands, they occupied Cilicie, subjected the Armenians, fought the Thraces of Asia and Ciliciens of Cappadocia . . . moved as a torrent to the frontiers of the Euphrates and Tigris, overran the peoples of Mont Taurus and and Mont Amanus. Where will Turkish cupidity end? We see Ottoman arms carried to the Tanais, the Volga, the Borystheme, the Sea of Hyreanie; after having devoured almost all of Asia, they took Constantinople, seized Greece, overthrew the throne in Cairo; Egypt, and Syria fell into their hands. Suleiman reduced part of Hungary, he took Rhodes, besieged Malta, occupied the isle of Chio by fraud, took Szigeth from the Hungarians, Selim today, after having violated the laws of nations, violated his own faith. Avid to extend his tyranny, he assails the kingdom of Cyprus!

But the Holy Father was more than a firebrand urging action; he was also a diplomat and he proved himself capable of persuading Philip II that Spanish interests demanded a serious naval war against the Ottoman empire. The negotiations for the treaty were difficult, tortuous, prolonged. The first session took place in Rome on July 2, 1570; the treaty was finally complete and the signatures were exchanged on May 25, 1571. The delay was in part because the Venetians had to see whether or not they could reach a satisfactory agreement with the Turks before they would be willing to commit themselves to a program of action that would undoubtedly have bad effects on their Levantine commerce. There was a strong "peace party" in the Venetian senate that wanted no interruption of Venetian business activity. Only after they were convinced that no agreement could be made that would save Cyprus and their commerce, did the Venetian senate decide for the Holy Alliance and war. The high tide of that alliance came with the battle of Lepanto.

Much has been written about this battle. For some it appears the turning point in the history of the Mediterranean—the decisive act that broke the power of the Turkish navy. And yet the fact that three years after Lepanto, a Turkish armada transported an army and took Tunis and La Goulette from the Spanish, would seem to throw some doubts on this interpretation. No matter what conclusions might be reached about its decisive character in the history of the Mediterranean basin or of Europe as a whole, the Christian victory at Lepanto was a serious blow to Ottoman prestige and the occasion for Te Deums of thanks in the cathedrals of Italy and Spain, as well as of northern Europe. The commander of the Christian navy, Don Juan of Austria, proved himself to be a worthy son of Charles V and the hero of a generation of young noblemen who aspired to fame and fortune. While his half-brother, King Philip II of Spain, and His Holiness, Pope Pius V, as well as many others who helped to prepare and command the Christian armada, must share the glory of the victory, tradition was right to make Don Juan *the* hero of Lepanto.

The fleet of the Holy League was slow to assemble because it came from so many different political authorities, but assemble it did, and ponderously it moved toward the Ionian Sea, where it had a rendezvous with destiny. The Ottoman fleet, too, suffered from the problems of logistics, but the fact that it was under a single command made it easier to control. The encounter of the two fleets has been described many times, both in the sixteenth century and since; most impressive are the accounts in the Spanish collection of documents drawn from manuscripts presented to the king; they are both vivid and immediate, even though for the most part each of the writers actually witnessed only a small segment of the battle. The men of both armadas invoked divine assistance and were assured by their religious leaders that death in this conflict would guarantee entrance into paradise. When the ships came together, it was either victory or death, and each man on the League's armada must also have remembered Don Juan's announcement that, as victors in this fight, they would be hailed as saviors of their religion and civilization, while defeat would result in their ignominy and disgrace. The Turkish officers, if we are to believe the accounts of prisoners taken in the battle, were a bit overconfident. The Turkish navy had met and defeated the Christians at a number of engagements since the battle of Prevesa over thirty years earlier, and they fully expected to repeat the performance. This overconfidence may account for the fact that many of the Ottoman ships fouled each other by contact before they reached the Christian line.

The two fleets came together slowly, majestically. Don Juan had placed the six mighty Venetian galleasses in the front of the large semicircle that made up his line. These huge ships, each mounting sixty cannons capable of smashing into the sides of a galley, were the dreadnoughts of the era. They had to be towed into position, but, once the battle started, their fire was disastrous for the Turks. The Turkish fleet also was marshaled in a huge semicircle on the interior side of the Bay of Lepanto so that the two ends of the line were dangerously near the shore. The two fleets came together slowly, majestically—deliberately driven by short oar strokes. They began to exchange shots when the ships were within range of the cannon fire; then they came together, grappling ship to ship, with men swarming over the sides. Every personal account that we have left to us fairly breathes with the drama of sixteenth-century naval warfare. The Turkish armada had some two hundred-plus galleys and sixty-six galiots and fusts, manned by twenty-five thousand soldiers and an unknown number of sailors, galley slaves, and free oarsmen. The League naval force contained six big galleasses and three hundred-odd galleys manned by twenty-five thousand or more Spanish, Italian, and German soldiers, as well as the usual complement of slaves, free oarsmen, and sailors who maneuvered the ships. From the list of dead and wounded presented to the king of Spain after the battle, it is clear that both armadas were commanded by some of the most distinguished men of their nations; important noblemen and high officers from the civil and military administrations of all the states involved in the conflict were among the casualties. A surprisingly large number of Turkish pashas as well as Spanish grandees were killed.

There have been many analyses of the victory. Obviously the galleasses were an important factor, but so much of the battle was fought by men, almost or really in hand-to-hand combat, that Don Juan's insistence on putting his Spanish, German, and Italian troops on the papal and Venetian, as well as on his king's Spanish and Italian galleys, gave the Christians a slight advantage when the ships grappled. The added fact that the majority of the Christian soldiers and marines had some personal armor, while the Turks had practically none, was also a Christian advantage—as was the fact that most of the Christian troops were armed with firearms, while the Turks, with few exceptions, had only bows and arrows, pikes and scimitars. There can be no doubt about the fact that men from both sides fought bravely; Louis XIV might have said that he did not know whether a man was brave or not when he was fighting a boat, since the brave and the cowardly both could be sunk, but accounts of Lepanto abound with the personal valor of the combatants.

The many accounts of the fighting presented to Philip II testify to the rudeness of the battle. The Christians tried to hold off the Turks with cannon fire, but sixteenth-century sea fighting could never be settled by artillery; the decisive act often came in hand-to-hand combat. Don Juan's *Real* and the flagship of the Turkish navy came together in something more than a symbolic duel between the two admirals: the fight did not end until the Turkish commander's head was stuck on a pike as a token of victory, and the great standard of the Ottoman navy—the banner that came from Mecca—was in the hands of the Christian admiral. Don Juan sent it to the Escorial as evidence of his triumph. On the wing of the Turkish armada, the beylerbey of North Africa, Euldj Ali, commanded the Algerian flotilla. He alone of the Ottoman commanders survived the battle to enjoy the fruits of a personal victory in the face of the general defeat. He not only attacked and captured the flagship of the Knights of St. John and brought their great flag to Istanbul as evidence of the corsair's valor, but also managed to evade the Genoese galleys commanded by Doria and brought his wing of the fleet out of the conflict and back to Istanbul relatively unharmed. One has only to follow any of the accounts of Lepanto to know that it would be folly to give a completely rational explanation of the battle. Once the ships were engaged, Tolstoi's explanation of war in an era when hand-to-hand combat was possible, is perhaps the most satisfactory way to explain the result.

After the battle, the two navies left the scene without further action. There were those who believed that Don Juan should have followed his victory with an assault on the heart of the Ottoman empire, but such criticism was founded in ignorance. The Christian navy was badly battered by the fight. The Venetian squadrons withdrew to the north to lick their wounds and replenish their supplies; the Italian and Spanish vessels, many of them almost ready to sink, had trouble working their way back to the ports of Naples and Sicily. Any talk of an attack on Istanbul completely ignored the fact that Lepanto had been a brutal engagement, and sixteenth-century navies were fragile affairs that could not be pushed too far without great hazard. It was not only the Ottoman navy that needed rest and repair.

The next year (1572), there were hopes in Europe that a Greek rebellion in the Morea would provide opportunity for military invasion of the Ottoman empire. The insurrection never occurred, but there was another naval sweep into Turkish waters by a Christian armada. This naval force did reach the Greek islands, but the opponent it encountered was Euldj Ali, whose talents as an administrator and skill as a commander made him a worthy successor of Kheir-ed-din. Euldj Ali recreated a Turkish navy in the winter of 1571–72; the new galleys were modeled after those of the Algerian corsairs—they were lighter with a shallower draft than the Christian or the older Ottoman galleys and thus much more maneuverable. He armed them with heavier cannons and provided his soldiers with firearms; thus, the new Turkish ships were faster and better armed than those lost at Lepanto. However, Euldj Ali could not match the number or the firepower of the Christian fleet, so he refused to be drawn into a pitched battle. At least twice, he withdrew behind a curtain of smoke created by his guns, leaving the Christians without a target, and then reappeared to harass and threaten their rear. The naval action of 1572 came to nothing.

The year 1572 was, however, one of crisis. Pius V died, and his successor could not really take his place as the soul of the Holy Alliance, especially since the Venetians were already negotiating with the Turks for an end to hostilities. At the same time, the Saint Bartholomew's Day Massacre of the Protestants in France abruptly changed the course of Franco-Spanish relations by ending the plan for French intervention in the civil war in the Netherlands.

The following year (1573) found the Venetians at peace with the Ottoman empire and Don Juan in possession of Tunis. His assault on Tunis in 1573 was a repetition of his father's invasion. However, Don Juan's victory proved to be ephemeral. The Spanish had been in doubt whether to attack Tunis or Algiers; they were even more confused about the disposition of their conquest after Tunis had surrendered without much of a fight. There was talk of making Don Juan king of Tunis, but that seems to have been only an idea rather than a program. Before the question could be settled, the Turks made it an academic one. In July 1574 Euldj Ali and Sinān Pasha appeared at Tunis with some two hundred and thirty galleys, and forty thousand men. By September they had conquered Tunis and La Goulette. This expedition was decisive evidence that although the battle of Lepanto may have singed the beard of the Turkish sultan, it had not crippled his empire.

Euldj Ali's victory at Tunis and La Goulette was costly in both men and money for both the Ottoman and the Spanish empires. Fernand Braudel insists that as a result these two "political monsters," the Spanish and the Ottoman empires, withdrew from the conflict in an informal peace several years before they actually made a truce that, in effect, ended their confrontation. He also believes that the inaction resultant from this withdrawal was responsible for the decay of the Turkish navy. After 1580, however, the whole Turkish empire began a decline that sapped the armed forces and the vigor of Turkish policy. North Africa continued to be technically a province subject to the Ottoman sultan, but the Sublime Porte's power and desire to control the activities of the corsair-Turkish communities followed the pattern of decay in the empire. After Euldj Ali's death, no beylerbey for North Africa was appointed, and the pashas who were sent there as governors on three-year assignments ceased to be political-military figures. They went to North Africa to recoup the money that they had to pay for their offices. Thus the informal truce that finally brought peace between the empires at the two ends of the Mediterranean had important consequences for the development of the Turkish-corsair community of Algiers. As we shall see, the triennial pashas, unable or unwilling to assert the authority of the Grand Seigneur, allowed the real power in the regency to slip out of their hands. Furthermore, while the corsair community did not share in the relaxation of warfare between the Ottoman and Spanish empires, the rapid decay of Spanish commerce that began at the end of the sixteenth century forced the corsairs to look beyond Spanish and Italian ships and coasts for booty, with the result that the holy war of the sixteenth century took on a piratical tinge in the century that followed.

IV The Regency Government: Sixteenth-Century Rule of the Beylerbeys

IT IS NO EASY THING to reconstruct the processes that created the government of the regency of Algiers. Since the principal actors did not leave us usable records, we must be content with memoirs, geographical accounts, and contemporary histories that often frustrate rather than inform. Without the two books of Fr. Diego de Haëdo, it would be nearly impossible to reconstruct any good picture of the development of the institutions that were at the base of the structure of the regency. For Tunis and Tripoli, for which no such account exists, the problem is nearly insurmountable. There are, it appears, records in the archives at Istanbul, but for the sixteenth century, they seem to be limited to some tax and tribute accounts that provide only minimal understanding of the Turkish-corsair community that became the regency of Algiers. Thus we are left with Marmol and other geographers, Turkish writers like the author of *Ghazewat* and the *Maritime History of the Turks,* and the numerous Christian historians who have left us accounts of the Spanish kings and their soldiers who played a part in the Mediterranean world (Sandavol, Mariana, Marmol, and others). All of this means that we often need to use historical imagination and inference to piece together the story that must be told if we are to understand the corsair-Turkish communities on the northern coast of Africa.

Again we must start with Aroudj and his brothers, whose careers resembled and paralleled those of the famous conquistadors who invaded the Americas at the same time that our Levantine adventurers sailed westward toward Tunis and Algiers. Unlike the Spanish adventurers, however, these Levantines did not leave their homeland to create a new Turkish province or to make themselves rulers over a conquered people. They were corsairs, armed with a commission from an Egyptian prince, who saw themselves as warriors in a jihad, a holy war against the enemies of their god, a war that could give them a crown in heaven as well as wealth in this world. As we have seen at first they were satisfied to accept the sultan of Tunis as a sort of overlord or protector who allowed them to use his ports in return for a share of their booty. When their depredations led to an attack on La Goulette by a Genoese fleet, the ruler of Tunis urged them to move their activities to the island of Jerba, where they had some sort of an arrangement with native sheiks, who helped them supply their fleet in return for money or captured goods. Success allowed the brothers to increase their fleet and also attracted other corsair captains to leave the Levant and join them in the central Mediterranean. After a decade as corsairs, Aroudj and his brothers found themselves owners of a flotilla. In the next dozen or so years, Aroudj lost an arm trying to drive the Spanish from Bougie; saved Djidjelli from starvation and became its "king"; captured Cherchell from one of his wayward captains, whom he quickly beheaded; and managed to murder the sheik who ruled Algiers and placed himself on the throne. His cannons were still too small to batter the walls of the Spanish presidio in the harbor of Algiers, but he did have enough power to try to extend his little empire westward toward Oran. We know little about the structure of his government for this haphazard "empire," but after he was killed in conflict with the Spanish, his brother Kheir-ed-din attached this embryo state to the Ottoman empire and gave form to its political structure.

The political situation in the towns of the Maghrib had played into Aroudj's hands. The towns were governed by local "sultans" with many relatives and therefore many chances for contest for the "thrones." Invitations for intervention were welcomed by the corsair chief. These little towns also were threatened or partly controlled by the Spanish governors at Oran and Bougie. Thus it was easy to excite the fanatical Berber people against the enemies of their god when the corsairs were willing to come to their aid. After Aroudj was killed, his little Levantine band was in great danger, for it was clear that the Spanish would attack Algiers and that the corsair government, unpopular with both the baldi of the city and the Kabylie tribesmen in the hinterland, could be assaulted from all sides. Furthermore, the Hafsid sultan of Tunis claimed to be suzerain over most of the land and people to the east of Algiers and threatened to join the Kabylie to drive the Levantines from the land.

The corsair community, even with the aid of Andalusian Moriscos, was in great danger. With Aroudj and his army removed from the scene, Kheir-ed-din had to find new support or face destruction.

As we have seen, he placed his little "empire" under the protection of the Ottoman sultan. His Turkish chronicler tells that he explained his decision to the "important people" of Algiers (a nice question might be: "Who were these 'important people'?") in a great speech: "I see only one choice to make. This city should be under the protection of Allah, and after him, of my sovereign lord and master, the powerful and fearful emperor of the Ottomans to whom everywhere victory directs his feet." Of course the oration was an invention. The Ottoman sultan was not yet Kheir-ed-din's "sovereign lord and master"; Aroudj and his brothers started their westward venture under the protection of and with a commission from an Egyptian emir. Time had proven that they had chosen the wrong ruler, for Selim had conquered all Syria and Egypt since they had left the Levant. However, the corsair leader was a politician-statesman with great skill and understanding; he knew that the Ottoman sultan would be pleased to add the Maghrib, or part of it, to his domains, especially if it cost him very little. As we have already seen Kheir-ed-din did not go to the Levant in person; he sent his trusted lieutenant, Hadj Hassan, to find the sultan in Syria and to offer to place Algiers under his government in return for military aid against the Spanish. This would provide the Turkish empire with a western sanjac to push its influence deep in the western Mediterranean basin.

Fresh from the conquest of Egypt, Selim I (surnamed both the "grim" or the "dread") apparently agreed with Kheir-ed-din that a province in the West would be advantageous, particularly since it would not cost much in either blood or treasure. We do not know how much the Turkish sultan understood about the political situation in the western Mediterranean, but it is likely that Andalusian Moriscos had reached his court with their laments about Spanish tyranny long before Kheir-ed-din's emissary arrived. In any case, the sultan sent two thousand janissaries and allowed the Algerians to recruit another four thousand soldiers in Anatolia; he also gave Kheir-ed-din cannons, arms, and war supplies, and the titles of pasha and governor of the western province. This comprised the military and political muscle that permitted Kheir-ed-din to defeat the Spanish invaders in 1519. Had it not taken so long for the viceroy of Sicily to get his expedition under way, the corsair community of Algiers might have been destroyed before it came into bloom, but as we have noted earlier, the janissary army and a severe storm saved Algiers and flooded the slave market with thousands of Spanish soldiers who could not return to their boats.

The arrival of the janissaries with the title of pasha for Kheir-ed-din proved to be the decisive fact for the future history of Algiers. The first two thousand men of the famous janissary corps were probably the sons of Balkan Christians taken from their homes by the "boy tax" that recruited manpower for the sultan's military and political machines, but the four thousand recruits were undoubtedly Anatolians whose chances in their own land were slender and who were therefore willing to listen to the Algerian recruiting agents. Since the Algerian janissary militia continued to expand by drawing recruits from Anatolia and elsewhere in the Ottoman empire, the Algerian corps ceased to be the elite body of slaves of the sultan, converts to Mohammedanism, and became a mercenary corps drawn from the Mohammedan populations of the Levant. Later in the century when the janissaries were allowed to join the corsair ships and the "Levantines" who had heretofore fought those ships were enrolled in the janissary corps, a large number of renegade Christians who "had turned Turk" were also admitted as members of the militia. No matter whether they were Levantine Turks or Christians turned "Turk," the corps resisted all efforts of the natives of Algiers of North Africa to join it. From the first to the last, the Algerian janissaries insisted that their company should be a foreign "army of occupation" —conquerors rather than an indigenous force.

Our pictures of the Algerian militia came from Christian slaves, mission priests, European consuls, and merchants; the men of the corps have contributed little or nothing to our documentation. As a result, it is undoubtedly true that our picture may be biased, and yet the bulk of the testimony fits together and has an overall aura of authenticity. Critics have asserted that the militia were recruited from the criminals, beggars, and ne'er-do-wells of the sanjacs of Anatolia, Syria, and the Balkans; all this may be true, but they were also recruited from young peasants who could find no place for themselves in the villages. Like Europe of the sixteenth through the eighteenth centuries, the east produced a surplus of males for whom there was no good place in the economy. Of a hundred births, about fifty reached the age of twenty, more or less evenly divided between boys and girls, but in the next ten years the mortality among the young women was much higher than that of the men. The result was that in Western Europe, men with land and animals or other wealth could marry several times, replacing wives who died; in Moslem countries where polygamy was possible, this condition became more serious for young men without land or wealth or status. They were squeezed out by the forces of demography. Obviously such men heard the drums and the recruiting speeches of the Algerian recruiting officers who assured them of status and importance and position; when they joined the corps, they became the "powerful and illustrious lords of Algiers" for whom the rest of the population must stand aside. It seems not to have been difficult to find men who would willingly join this janissary militia.

Obviously most of the recruits came from the bottom layers of society. There are stories of generosity, kindliness, even some culture among them, but most of the janissaries seem to have been illiterate, ignorant, gross, ill-mannered, irrational, and religiously prejudiced. Some were brutal and given to violence. Like men of their age in Europe, they had grown up in a society where the gibbet or the axe ended many men's lives, where the law and manners were violent, unfair, and often brutal: How could too much more be expected of them?

In the last quarter of the sixteenth century, new opportunities were added to the Algerian janissary militia. The soldiers much resented the fact that they were not permitted to go to sea on the corsair ships and share in the booty. The reis customarily fought their ships with corsair "marines" recruited from the Levant port towns and renegade Christians. Since so many of the reis were themselves Christian renegades, this latter group made up a considerable number of their crew. In 1568 Mohammed Pasha, in an effort to reduce the hostility that had developed between the corsair "marines" and the janissary militia, decreed that the janissaries could go to sea with the corsiars and that the Levantine and renegade "marines" could join the militia. This did not alter the fact that the Algerian janissaries were all "foreigners" rather than Algerian baldi or Kabylie tribesmen, nor did it end the conflict between janissaries and reis, but it did introduce a considerable number of ex-Christians into the corps. There is no evidence, however, that the renegades raised or lowered its cultural levels, yet they did provide a few men who could not only speak, but also write, European languages.

The militia was a military corps, organized as an army. The new recruit became a joldac (*yoldash*), or private, when he arrived in Algeria. This made him a "powerful and illustrious lord of Algiers":

he could not be arrested by any but his own officers, nor tried in any but the court of the agha. If he was sentenced to death, he would not suffer the indignity of a public execution. On the streets of Algiers, all must step aside for him, and anyone who dared to strike or abuse a joldac was in hazard of his life. These were the men of the "army of occupation," and they could demand and receive respect from all the occupied. It is not quite clear how the first members of his corps were housed. By the time that Haëdo was in Algiers, they had at least three caserns (barracks) each housing some six hundred men, and in the years that followed, the pashes built other caserns for the corps.[1] Some of the men, however, seem to have provided themselves with housing where six to twenty men lived together; a few of them married and were housed privately in the city. Each man received a ration of bread every day, the same for a simple joldac as for the agha; their meals, prepared in common kitchens, were simple, and largely without meat of any kind. The uniform of the janissary was distinctive, although neither elegant nor costly. The "powerful and illustrious lords of Algiers" lived more like monks than like noblemen as Europe understood such things, but they did enjoy respect and fear from their fellow men as well as a measure of economic security. Only when famine struck the entire town were they threatened, and then, as in 1579, the corps defended itself against hunger by rioting and invading the storehouses of the city—even the pasha's and caids' homes.

The corps was organized democratically. In theory every joldac carried the baton of the agha with him when he became a janissary. They were supposed to rise through the ranks from joldac to *adabuch* (sergeant) to *boulouk-bachi* (captain) to agha (commander). There were several other grades or places on the way up that seem not to have been filled by seniority alone, and, indeed, the "democracy through seniority" was sometimes by-passed to exclude an unpopular candidate. In a later period, one man was passed over for the rank of agha because his Turkish was weak, another because his wife had had a questionable reputation before she married him. Upward movement was assured by the fact that a man held the rank

1. The dates indicate earliest mention in archival materials available: (1) Caserne Makaroun (Rue Makaroun). Earliest mention in archives, 1603—built about 1571-72 by Ali-el-Fartes. (2) Caserne Bab-Azzoun at Place Bab-Azzoun; built before c. 1599. (3) Caserne d'El-Kherratin (Rue Bab-Azzoun) c. 1599-1600. (4) Caserne d'Osta-Moussa 1674-75 (?). (5) Caserne d'Ed-Droudj, 1694-95? (6) Caserne Vieille, 1660-61; probably much older. R. A., III, pp. 130ff.

of agha for only a short time; in the sixteenth century, there seem to have been three or four aghas each year; later the office was limited to two moons. After passing through the agha rank, the janissary was "retired." He could become a *spahi* (cavalryman), or he might be given some political post. As we shall see, in the seventeenth century, the situation changed radically as the janissary corps expanded its role in the corsair community.

Ordinary affairs of the militia, questions of conflict within the corps, and criminal justice were governed by the divan of the janissaries in which each member of the corps, in theory at least, had an equal voice. In actual practice the leaders of the corps often presented their decisions for ratification; the "democracy" was too cumbersome and frequently resulted in vocal disorder. In the sixteenth century, questions of general interest to the regency as well as to the militia were settled by the beylerbey or his califate in conference with the corsair reis and perhaps the garrison agha. They reserved all critical decisions to themselves: they ruled absolutely in the name of the sultan, and yet, and of course, they also consulted with their officers and reis on important problems. Toward the end of the period of the beylerbeys, the divan of the janissaries showed signs of a tendency to encroach on the power of the pashas appointed from Istanbul; in the next century, when the divan was expanded to include the more important officers as well as members of the militia, it did actually supplant the triennial pashas as the seat of power in the Algerian regency.

Some of the janissaries married local women and sired children who became the coulougli of Algiers, whose status was between the janissaries and the baldi. Naturally they wanted to enjoy their fathers' positions and privileges, but the majority of the corps, unmarried and hostile to the baldi, were bent on excluding from their company anyone born in North Africa. As we shall see, in the early seventeenth century, this led to a coulougli rebellion, after which there were even stricter rules concerning their status.

So many unmarried men inevitably created moral problems. Our good Father Haëdo tells us that (except for the renegades among them) the janissaries did not blaspheme or play cards or drink. They did not fight among themselves, but they did lead morally disorderly and scandalous lives. Debauchery and sodomy were their sins; they were sexually promiscuous, visited women of ill-repute, and commonly seduced young Christian and Jewish boys. They were accused of seeking ways to capture or buy Christian slave boys for sexual pleasure. Our priest is obviously scandalized; his testimony is reiterated so many times by other observers of Algiers in the succeeding centuries that it probably was relatively accurate.

In the years that Algiers was governed by beylerbeys and their califates, the problem of paying the janissary corps did not become critical. The beylerbeys were wealthy corsairs who owned in their own names a squadron of galiots and brigantines that scoured the Mediterranean Sea and its Christian coastal lines for slaves and booty. Along with the revenues extracted from the Berber and Arabian peoples subject to them, these rulers had no difficulty finding the funds necessary to pay the rather meager salaries of the 9,000–12,000 janissaries under their command. It was later when the triennial pashas saw their office as a means of recouping the costs of purchasing their places and titles that payment of the soldiers' salaries became a problem that shook the government of Algiers. Most of these pashas had no personal ownership in the corsair fleets; they depended upon the share of the booty allotted them for their own personal fortunes rather than the public need. Thus in the period that followed, much of the salary for the militia came from tribute collected in the hinterland. The joldacs by "sweeps" through the country were responsible for collecting tribute from the tribesmen. These excursions were a bit more orderly and regular than the razzias made by the Spanish from Oran, and yet, like the razzias, they were really brutal raids to force unwilling nomadic and seminomadic tribesmen to pay into the government treasury. In some cases, the presence of a body of 600–800 janissaries, accompanied by spahi cavalry and Kabylie vassal horsemen, was enough to persuade the "victims" that they must pay up. Indeed, before the Berber and Arabian tribesmen learned to use firearms, it was simple for a small company of janissaries to dominate many times their number of these native people.

In addition to the janissary corps, the sixteenth-century rulers of Algiers had the crews that fought the corsair ships more or less at their disposal. Before Kheir-ed-din placed his corsair community under the protection of the Sublime Porte, the Levantine, Andalusian, and Moorish recruits who fought the ships were the very core of the corsair captain's power. By the mid-sixteenth century, when so many of the corsair reis were themselves renegades, the crews also had a large admixture of ex-Christians. These "marines," however, were neither organized into military companies nor paid a regular salary; they were, in fact, the creatures of the reis under whom they sailed, and their share of the prizes taken in the cruise was their sole recompense. This booty, however, was large enough to draw the envy of the joldacs and probably partly contributed to the hostility that existed between the two groups. We do not know how many men were involved, but the fact that in the mid-sixteenth century there were at least thirty-eight galiots, and twenty-five brigantines, as well as a large number of smaller vessels, operating out of Algiers would indicate that there were at least fifteen thousand men in the business of privateering in the name of Allah.

These Levantine and renegade marines were often at odds with the janissary corps. The most striking confrontation came when the militia refused to allow the sultan's nominee as pasha, Mohammed Kurdogli (Tekeleri), to land in Algiers as a replacement for the pasha whom the janissaries had proclaimed on their own. As we shall see later, the marines, supported by the soldiers and guards that Kurdogli Pasha had on his ships, slipped into Algiers at night, over-powered the janissary guards, and seized and executed the rebel leaders. On other occasions the hostility between the janissaries and the Levantine marines merely caused disorder in the streets or taverns. Some of this hostility was quieted in the latter sixteenth century when Mohammed Pasha ordered the reis to accept janissaries as soldiers on the corsair vessels on an equal basis with the marines, and at the same time provided that the Levantines and renegades could join the janissary militia and enjoy the privileges and rights of the corpsmen. H. D. de Grammont believed that the conflict between the two groups continued to be the important factor in the evolution of the regency, but his opinion is not really supported by the facts. The continuing problem with the janissary corps was the necessity of finding money to pay its members as the number in-creased—perhaps doubled or more—in the ensuing years. C.-A. Julien explains that the introduction of the Levantines and renegades was a factor in the decline of privateering (corsair warfare), but this suggestion also flies in the face of harsh facts, since the great days of the Algerian corsairs came in the first half of the seventeenth cen-tury when the number of renegades in relation to Turks and Levan-tines was the greatest ever.

The corsair reis were organized in a loose-knit corporation called the taiffe, and since the important beylerbeys and their califates were themselves corsair reis, and owners of raiding galiots and brigan-tines, the taiffe worked closely with the government of the commu-nity. The reis were popular with the people: they brought wealth and fame to Algiers; they assured the city of sustenance when famine struck elsewhere; their largess gave tone to the entire society. There are, however, no serious studies of the taiffe, and no archival records of its development have been found. It is clear that during the greater part of the sixteenth century, the taiffe was definitely under the control of the beylerbey or his califate, who governed Algiers in the name of the sultan. During this period the reis were kept under strict control, indeed, one of them was executed because he disobeyed the sultan's orders not to molest French shipping. In the following century the pashas were unable to exercise such authority.

In the sixteenth century there were other troops, or armed men, at the disposal of the pasha at Algiers, some of them on a regular basis, others recruited for a specific action. There were a few hundred horsemen, the spahis, who apparently were either overage janissaries or recruits from the Levant. Their numbers were small, and they played no important part in the military institutions of the regency. Kheir-ed-din had a body of armed Andalusians at his disposal. These refugees from Spain were also enrolled in the armies of the sultans of Fez. Unlike African Moors, they understood the use of firearms; indeed, many of the refugees were gunsmiths who established the manufacture of arms in Algiers and other African cities. Kheir-ed-din probably used them on his privateering fleet as well as for his military needs at Algiers. We also find native Berber or Arab cavalrymen either in the service of the beylerbey or as allies on many of the expeditions into the hinterland as well as on the occasions of the Spanish landings at Algiers. These men were obviously motivated by hopes of loot; it is not clear that the beylerbeys or their viceroys ever paid them any regular subsidy. In the years following the sixteenth century, pashas and their caids (military commanders) regularly used native horsemen as auxiliary troops both for their "sweeps" to collect tribute or punish rebels, and for their conflicts with the Spanish, the Tunisians, or the Moroccans. There were other more or less informal troop concentrations. For example, a whole company of Spanish soldiers, captured when the Spanish attempted to take Mostaganem, were persuaded to renounce their religion and to fight for the pasha in return for freedom from slavery. However, none of these expedients actually freed the pashas from their dependence upon the janissary corps.

It is very difficult to determine the actual relationship that existed between the sultan's government in Istanbul and the beylerbeys who ruled Algiers. There can be no doubt about their dependence upon the favors of the imperial government, but this does not explain the basis for the appointments to the high office of beylerbey of North Africa, nor to that of the califate pashas who represented the beylerbey in Algiers. Kheir-ed-din's appointment was an obvious one; he presented the sultan with the western sanjac of North Africa, and by 1533, he was beylerbey of North Africa, admiral pasha in the Turkish navy, and an obvious favorite of the sultan. His prestige was great enough to allow him to pass on his honor as pasha and beylerbey of North Africa to his son Hassan. Yet Hassan could be, and was, removed from office when the French ambassador urged it. Paradoxically, however, he returned two more times as beylerbey when the situation demanded a strong ruler. The other beylerbeys, Salah Reis and his son, Mohammed, were also natural appointments; Salah Reis was Kheir-ed-din's most trusted lieutenant, and he himself became an admiral pasha in the Ottoman navy. His prestige allowed him to pass on the office to his son. The last beylerbey, Euldj Ali, had been a lieutenant of Dragut and became a high admiral pasha in the Ottoman service after Lepanto. All these men were patent appointments, and yet we hear of bribery and presents to viziers as important to secure the influence of the right people to obtain even these appointments.

If the appointment of the beylerbeys seems to have been made for obvious reasons, the basis for that of califate pasha is a little more difficult to determine. Most of them were corsair captains, about half were renegades, the rest were Greeks, Arabs, Albanians, or Turks. The first califate, the eunuch Hassan, was a creature of Kheir-ed-din; he had been in his service since his youth. The second, Hassan-ben-Kheir-ed-din, also presents no problems. But in the years that followed there were califates like Mami Pasha, an Albanian janissary who had come to the sultan's service through the boy tax and had risen to power and influence in the imperial court at Istanbul; others like Hassan Venitiano, Arab Ahmed, or Rabadan Pasha, were creatures and lieutenants of the beylerbey Euldj Ali. It seems that it was usual for the sultan to appoint the nominee of the beylerbey, and yet we learn that great sums of money had to change hands to assure these appointments.

Some of the problems arose as a result of the efforts of the janissary militia to interfere in the process of appointment. The disorderly patterns that were to mark the behavior of the corps in the seventeenth century appeared first after Salah Reis died of the plague before Oran, and the sultan ordered the lifting of the siege. The militia elected his califate commander, Hassan Corso, to be the new pasha. From all accounts Hassan was a great favorite of the troops, a man with both ambition and personal charm, but the sultan refused to be told who would become pasha of Algiers. Hassan Corso, however, ordered the beys of the eastern and western provinces of Algiers to refuse to allow the sultan's nominee, Mohammed Kurdogli, to land in their harbors. At this juncture the taiffe of the reis intervened by making contact with Mohammed Kurdogli and introducing him into Algiers at night with the support of their Levantine corsairs and the Turkish marines on his ship. The militia was completely surprised and unable to resist. Hassan Corso tried to pretend that he was not to blame, but he could not avoid execution (by being thrown on the hooks on the walls of Algiers, a horrible death even by sixteenth-century standards). Unfortunately for Mohammed Kurdogli, Hassan Corso had many friends who escaped the new pasha's vengeance; one of them hunted him down and murdered him in a holy shrine where he had tried to escape. The murderer was immediately elected pasha by the militia, but he died before he could be removed, by the sultan's orders, and an old janissary agha took charge until a new pasha could be appointed from Istanbul.

A few years later the militia again attempted to control the office of pasha. Hassan-ben-Kheir-ed-din had returned to power and obviously had plans to alter the military situation of the city. The son of a Moorish lady and married to a Kabylie princess, he allowed the Kabylie tribesmen to enter Algiers and buy arms. In September 1561, there were six hundred of them in the city, armed to the teeth, and obviously in the favor of the beylerbey. At this point the janissary leaders became suspicious: The agha Bosnoc Hassan and the bey Cousa Mohamet, with the support of the janissary divan, went to the palace, stopped the sale of arms to the Kabylie, ordered all armed men to leave Algiers, arrested Hassan and his nephew, and put them in irons to send them to Constantinople with a delegation that was to explain to the sultan that Hassan was trying to establish himself as an independent ruler in North Africa. However, Hassan was able to convince the Sublime Porte of his innocence; the delegation was arrested and executed, and a new pasha went to Algiers to arrest the leaders of the rebellion. They were sent to Istanbul and beheaded. Hassan returned a little later as beylerbey, backed by twenty Turkish galleys that assured his acceptance by everyone in the city. There was no evidence from his last period as beylerbey to support the claim that Hassan planned to establish an independent state based upon the support of the native Berber tribesmen, but there is reason to believe that he revenged himself on the janissaries when he undertook a new siege of Oran. So many of them were killed in this attack on the Spanish position that the survivors were convinced that Hassan deliberately placed the corps in the front of the assaults to pay them off for the humiliations that they had caused him. This assault on Oran failed when Philip II managed to bring superior naval power to bear upon the attackers.

The janissary divan did not again rebel against the authority of the beylerbey, but later in the century, when one of Euldj Ali's califates became both tyrannical and rapacious, the militia did manage to present its complaints to the sultan's divan and to secure the dismissal of a hated pasha; indeed, according to Haëdo, Euldj Ali had to pay a considerable bribe to save his creature from a fate worse than dismissal. And yet soon afterwards we find this man as Euldj Ali's califate pasha at Tripoli. All that we can be sure of is the fact that at this period the janissary divan was able to get some redress from the Sublime Porte to remove an unwanted pasha, even though it was unable to take matters into its own hands. Late in the century, when the sultan no longer gave the office of beylerbey to corsair admirals who were also pashas in his naval establishment, but rather to time-serving politicians or court favorites, the powers of the divan in Algiers waxed while that of the pasha and the Sublime Porte declined. Thus toward the end of the sixteenth century, Algiers came to mirror the malady of decay that was overtaking the Ottoman empire itself.

An important difference between the Levantine Turkish conquest of North Africa started by Aroudj and his brothers and that of the Spanish intrusion during the reigns of Ferdinand and Isabella was the fact that the Spanish contented themselves with the creation of presidios or fortified positions in the important harbors, while the Turks attempted to hold the hinterland tribesmen as well as the interior towns under their control, or at least under their suzerainty. From all accounts the Turks were hated by both townsmen and tribesmen almost as much as were the Spanish, but there was an essential difference: the Turks were also Moslems, and when a conflict between Turk and Spanish reached crisis proportions, the native North Africans usually supported the Turks. It was not easy, however, for the governor of Algiers, even with Turkish help, to push his authority into either Morocco or Tunis; in each case, Moslem rulers resisted the intrusion.

The Tunisian frontier was the most difficult in the sixteenth century because the Hafsid rulers of Tunis, on the basis of past history, could claim suzerainty over most of the towns and tribesmen between Tunis and Algiers. Kheir-ed-din's first excursion with Turkish aid was the conquest of Tunis in 1534. The next year Charles's victory in Tunis followed the usual Spanish pattern by establishing a presidio at La Goulette that would control the harbor and provide a base for operations. He then reestablished the hated Hamida on his throne. A few years later Hamida's son deposed him, but he, too, had to accept Spanish overlordship because of the fortification at La Goulette. In the meantime the Algerian pashas took Bône and Bougie from the Spanish, and the Turkish navy took Tripoli from the Knights of St. John, but La Goulette remained a difficult obstacle to Turkish power. Dragut was unable to hold his position in Mahdiya (also called Africa) south of La Goulette largely because that fortification, in conjunction with Malta and Sicily, gave the Spanish a secure hold on the central Mediterranean. It was not until the 1570s that Euldj Ali captured Tunis on the invitation of officers and tribesmen unhappy with their Hafsid ruler. Don Juan, however, soon after recaptured the city largely because La Goulette was still in Spanish hands. Two years after the battle of Lepanto, Euldj Ali, again as an admiral of the Ottoman navy and beylerbey of North Africa, captured Tunis and also took La Goulette. Henceforth Tunis remained in Turkish hands, but the conquest did not solve the problems of the pasha at Algiers because when Euldj Ali died, the Sublime Porte appointed separate pashas for Algeria, Tunis, and Tripoli so that in the years that followed, these regencies experienced quite different political evolutions, which often resulted in armed conflicts among them.

The conquest of the Berber and Arabic sheikdoms and "kingdoms" in the central Maghrib was most important for the development of the Algerian regency. Kheir-ed-din's son Hassan seems to have been responsible for dividing these conquests into the three beyliks that became the pattern for governing the hinterland of the Turkish-corsair regency. In the east, the beylik of Constantine included the harbor towns to the east of Algiers as well as the two important Kabylie tribes in the hinterland, the Abès and the Koukou. The actual "frontier" between Algerian and Tunisian authorities was vague, adjusted from time to time by military action. The bey established at Constantine ran his government with the assistance of a janissary garrison and caids who acted in his name. The bey and his caids were responsible for delivering to Algiers the regular payments of tribute that they collected; they were usually able to get enough to assure their own wealth as well as the payment to the pasha and divan of the regency. As in other governments of these preindustrial societies, the way to riches was through the possession of political and military offices.

The loyalty of the subjugated tribes in the beyliks was often questionable; indeed, when Lanfreducci and Bossi proposed a Spanish descent upon Algiers, they assured the king that the Kabylie tribesmen hated the Turks enough to join in the attack. The assurance that these tribesmen could marshal three thousand arquebusmen plus numerous cavalry would also suggest that in the course of the century the military difference between the tribesmen and the janissaries had changed to the disadvantage of the latter. This undoubtedly was true, for the beys later were obliged to establish strong points or fortifications along the important routes in order to maintain their authority and collect the taxes. The tribes would and did revolt on many occasions; however, whether or not their dislike of the Turks was greater than their hatred of Christians is another question. In any case, the Spanish king did not try to buy their aid with a few pieces of cloth and the baubles that Lanfreducci suggested.

Just as the frontier between the Algerian regency and Tunis was an uncertain line drawn by military force, the western frontier was fixed by the conflicts between the Algerians and the Spanish at Oran and the Moroccan sultanate of Fez. In both cases the Algerian janissaries faced soldiers also armed with guns and cannons. The Spanish had European soldiers, while the sultan of Fez had Andalusian Moriscos, refugees from Spain, in his army. Thus the military problems in the west involved both the difficulties of logistics and the firepower of potential enemies. The necessary bases were the town of Mostaganem on the sea, where military supplies could easily be landed, and Tlemcen, a fortified place in the hinterland of both Oran and Fez. The frontier shifted back and forth depending upon the power of the principals and the varying allegiance or loyalty of the tribes and towns. The bey of this western territory at first made his residence at Mazouna, where he would be safe from a Spanish razzia and yet in position to come to the aid of Mostaganem or the Kalâa tribes or Tlemcen. Later as Spanish power declined, the beys were established at Maskara, from which they could menace Oran. Like the beys of the east, they entrusted their relations to the tribes under their supervision to caids who could command troops in the garrison towns and more or less supervise the security of the routes and the collection of tribute.

The poorest and most difficult to control was the beylik of Titteri to the south, on the frontiers of the Sahara desert. The tribesmen in this beylik were mostly nomadic and often unwilling to pay tribute. To rule them the bey established his court at Medea and fortified garrisons at six or seven points in the territory. He had at his disposal a relatively small (under seven hundred) contingent of janissaries, a detachment of mounted spahis, and a varying number of native horsemen who either owed service to the regency or were hired for a specific enterprise.

A fourth area of the regency was ruled directly by the pasha and his government at Algiers; it was called the Mitidja or Dar-es-Sultan and included the coastal towns from Delleys to the east to Cherchell and Tenez to the west, as well as a narrow strip of the hinterland behind the coast. The pasha stationed janissary garrisons and a caid in the towns to assure their loyalty to the regime. Since most of this territory was easily reached by sea, the Turkish authority was relatively secure. And yet the tribesmen in the hills behind the towns, like those in the other beyliks, were governed by their own chieftains and often could not be controlled by the pasha's government. In the next century the ruler of Algiers had to confess that he could not compel a tribal sheik to give up captives that he had taken as a result of a shipwreck; his authority was limited to the amount of military force that he could bring to bear upon a recalcitrant tribal leader.

The processes of government for this confusing structure of pasha, divans, beys, caids, towns, and tribal units were unbelievably complex. The laws that were administered were drawn first of all from the Koran, but there were two Moslem sects (Maliki and Hanafi) with separate cadis and muftis on one side to judge the Turks, and on the other, to judge the rest of the Moslem population. The Jews and Christians came under the jurisdiction of the pasha and the divan for cases involving Moslems. For civil disputes, commercial questions, and criminal behavior involving their own countrymen, the Jews had their own courts, and the Christians had the consular courts. The Moslem rulers recognized that Koranic law did not apply to nonbelievers.

To rule this complex of jurisdictions the pasha-beylerbey or his califate was assisted by a half-dozen or so officers: a high admiral, elected by the taiffe, an agha of the janissaries who reached his office by seniority, an agha of the auxiliary troops who was appointed by the pasha. Each pasha had a lieutenant to aid his work. There were also secretaries, interpreters, and emissaries to carry out orders and transmit commands, and a treasurer to look out for the finances. In each of the beyliks, there was a bey appointed by the pasha and assisted by caids who had both civil and military positions; these men were responsible for the government of the provinces. Each town had its traditional government usually headed by a sheik-el-blad or mayor and a town divan usually composed of the richer citizens and officials. In the more important towns there was also a janissary garrison to guard the town and assure its loyalty to the regime; thirty to one hundred janissaries under a caid could usually guarantee obedience. The "law" often stopped at the town walls, for the nomadic and seminomadic tribesmen lived under their own customs; they were governed by a sheik or emir, often by hereditary right. It was the government of a patriarch in the case of a small unit; the larger groups—confederated dow-ars or tent villages—were ruled by an emir, a sultan, or a "king." The Koran was the written source of law, but custom, often more ancient than the Koran, also regulated men's lives.

It is small wonder that a califate pasha or even an experienced beylerbey had trouble untangling the complexities of this society, but when, toward the end of the sixteenth century, the sultan decided that he would govern the western sanjacs with the appointment of pashas for Algiers, Tunis, and Tripoli on three-year terms, his triennial pashas could not be expected to grasp the problems of his government. Confronted with a situation that could not be understood, they contented themselves with acquiring as much wealth as possible to recoup the costs of their purchase of the office, and hoped for an early return to Istanbul, where civilized life was available.

V The Regency Government: The Seventeenth-Century Experiment

THE SEVENTEENTH-CENTURY EXPERIMENT

A MEMORANDUM presented to Napoleon on September 7, 1802 informed the first consul that "from the frontiers of Egypt to the Straits of Gibraltar North Africa is held by men unacquainted with the public law of Europe . . ." Such information would not have surprised any European who had had contact with the Barbary States in the preceding centuries. The rulers of these lands, and especially those of the Algerian regency, had long since earned for themselves an unsavory reputation. European consuls who did business with them regularly referred to "these savages," "these ruffians," "these barbarians," "these tyrants," and other expressions not more complimentary. One of the sultan's officers wrote of them: "These are not men—they are worse than devils. I have never seen their like . . ." Other observers spoke of the government of Algiers as a "republic of brigands" and its officers as "brutal and barbarous people." The dey confided to the English consul in 1732 that "the Algerians are a company of rogues, and I am their captain." It would be easy to extend this picture by quotations from letters, pamphlets, and books written by their contemporaries who observed them, but before we accept the idea that all the rulers in North Africa were formed in a single mold, we should remember that our informants were men frustrated by their experiences with a government that often appeared to be an anarchy, or men who had been slaves or travelers who brought to North Africa their Christian prejudices. Indeed, few of the Christian writers had any sympathy for the culture of the Islamic world, and unfortunately, Moslem writers who might have corrected our impressions did not find it necessary to do so. Thus we are left with the distinct impression that the political system in the Barbary regencies more often than not brought cruel men to the positions of power.[1]

Perhaps we should expect the rulers of the Algerian regency to have acquired this unpalatable reputation. They were drawn from the ranks of the janissary militia, the corsair reis and their crews, and the renegades who threw in their lots with the corsair community. As we have seen, Kheir-ed-din secured the right to recruit his soldiers in the lands of the Grand Seigneur, and down to the end of the eighteenth century the rulers of Algiers sent recruiting agents to the Levant to persuade young men to become "high and powerful" seigneurs as members of the janissary corps. They picked up ox drivers, cutpurses, black sheep of families, as well as good, honest country lads who had no future at home. There was little in the cultural community of Algiers to change these young men, so when luck, seniority, favoritism, political cleverness, or simply a coup d'état brought one of them to the rank of agha or dey-pasha or indeed to lesser offices in the state, their Levantine culture came with them. The renegades in the janissary corps were usually not many notches above the cultural level of the recruits from Anatolia, Syria, or Dalmatia; many of them, captured by the corsairs, were Italian or Spanish peasant boys who easily sloughed off their Christian religion for the faith of their patrons. Others, for various reasons, were refugees from their homelands, but very few brought with them much education or background that would soften the mores of the land of their adoption. Most of the renegades seem to have shared their fellow Moslems' dislike or even hatred for Christianity, but a few of them still maintained some contact with their families in Italy or elsewhere on the northern shores of the Mediterranean. One striking case was a Tunisian renegade who made his family rich by fostering business relationships between them in Italy and the Tunisian market.

The joldac who arrived at Algiers as a new recruit in the seventeenth century may have been a "high and powerful seigneur" who could and did demand respect from the baldi, Christians and Jews,

---

1. Fisher's effort to correct this impression results in a clumsy "whitewash" that becomes ridiculous in face of so much evidence. He rejects all critical comments as prejudice, seizes upon any fragment of praise, and tries to make it a general rule. The result is that his book is marred as badly as those of Algiers' more violent critics. (*The Barbary Legend* [Oxford, 1957].)

but could one call him a "pampered darling"? He had been given clothes of about the same quality issued to slaves, as well as a fusil, an *ajataghan* (a sword), and a pair of pistols, but he was expected to pay for the weapons out of his salary, or if he wished to buy others of better quality, he must return those issued to him. In Algiers he was given a daily ration of bread made from wheat and rye flour, and when he was with the "tents" on a sweep to collect tribute, he was fed rice, flat bread, soup, and pilau. Any additional food that he might wish came out of his own pocket. If he was unmarried, he had free lodging in a casern; if he married, he was expected to take care of his own household. What was his salary? It is difficult to translate it into modern terms since the things that he might wish to buy or pay for were obviously different from desirable consumers' goods today. The joldac started at fourteen mezounes every two moons; his salary increased along with his seniority until, as agha or perhaps even dey, it increased to a little over two hundred mezounes each two moons. It is impossible to translate the mezoune into modern-currency equivalents, but by all accounts this pay scale was low; even by Algerian standards the joldac apparently often found it insufficient. Although food was cheap in Algiers, his additional rations did cost something, and entertainment in the whorehouse, the tavern, and the street made important demands on his income. The joldac often found it necessary to join a cruise as a soldier for a share in the booty, or even to operate a tavern or work as an artisan to make ends meet.

There is no sure way to fix the number of men in the Algerian janissary corps before the middle of the eighteenth century. Folio registers of the corps in the National Library of Algiers give us a little information about the seventeenth century, and a complete account for the year 1745. For the earlier periods we have educated guesses by men who were in the city, and, where they agree, the numbers are probably nearly correct. Kheir-ed-din's first contingents from the Levant did not count more than six thousand men, but by the end of the sixteenth century that number had grown to approximately twenty-two thousand. We do not know the proportion of renegades, Levantine Turks, and coulougli, but the Levantine recruits were undoubtedly in the majority. By the end of the seventeenth century, we have some figures suggesting that the corps was reduced to about twelve thousand, but others, perhaps more trustworthy, place it between fourteen and eighteen thousand. Our first accurate figure based on payrolls of 1745 gives the figures of 9,322 active members and 2,575 emeriti (retired). Paradis agrees with this figure for the third quarter of the century (about twelve thousand men). In the early nineteenth century, when recruiting in the Levant was no longer possible, the numbers decreased rapidly. Dr. Underhill placed it at eight thousand, and when the French arrived in 1830, there were only about twenty-five hundred fit for any duty. By that time, the deys increasingly had to rely on recruits for the "auxiliary" forces drawn from the native Berber population.

By the opening years of the seventeenth century, the janissary militia was largely a democratic institution. Every joldac who arrived in Algiers as a new recruit could hope to become agha for two moons if he lived long enough to reach that office. The simple soldier (*bequelar*) moved to the rank of corporal (*odabachis*) in command of a company of six to ten men. The odabachis elected the *boulouchardis* (captains), who might command a company or have other duties. The *agabachis* were drawn from the boulouchardis; this rank was limited to twenty-four men, but since the agha for the two moons was drawn from the agabachis, the term of service for the agha had been shortened so that there were at least six appointments each year. Several writers insist that the movement from bequelar to agha was based solely on seniority, but this is not quite true, for we know of several occasions when an agabachi was passed over by his peers and another was elected agha; the reasons given were probably not the true ones for they sometimes seem spurious. However, it was almost true that the janissary recruit carried the rank of agha in his bundle of clothes when he arrived at Algiers. The problem was to be able to live long enough to become a retired agha (*mezoulaga*) and thus to become a spahi or a retired soldier, or, perhaps, even an adviser to the powers that governed the regency.

The terms of service for the joldac were complex, and there is space in this account only to suggest the form. By the early eighteenth century (when we have the best evidence), the joldac served one year of active duty either in garrison or with the "tents" collecting tribute and then had a year free if he could hire one of his comrades to take his place. The usual duty was not too onerous. In Algiers the bachelor soldiers lived in the caserns; they did no special drill or practice being available only for service of the agha or dey. In the beylik garrisons, 100–300 janissaries would be quartered in the several towns and a smaller number in the forts along the main roads. They would be expected to join the tribute-gathering "sweeps." If all went well, the "tents" had a relatively pleasant time: the joldac had only his fusil, sword, and pistols to look after, since slaves and Moors cared for his tent, baggage, and supplies. When the Arab or Berber tribesmen resisted payment, the soldier had to fight, but even then the fact that the janissaries usually had small portable cannons gave them great advantage over their foes. Every so often, depending upon the dey's hopes for booty, tribute, or new territory, the corps were called out to fight on the frontiers, either against Tunis, Fez, or Oran (Spain), or to repress a serious rebellion by the tribes. On such adventures they were accompanied by auxiliary Moorish cavalry. Several of these ended badly for the janissaries; the Koukou tribesmen eventually acquired firearms and learned to fight open battles as well as to ambush scattered companies. It was not uncommon for the soldiers to dethrone their dey after such misadventures. Thus, by the eighteenth century the deys were usually careful not to become too involved in conflict with these dangerous vassals.

The janissary militia was an infantry organization, but it was not disciplined on the model of the emerging European armies of the seventeenth century. The foot soldiers fought largely without any seriously organized method; the joldacs lined up more or less haphazardly and fired their fusils at will. With the help of a few small cannons, they were usually superior to the swarms of Moorish horsemen. In the eighteenth century, between ten and fifteen percent of the corps were mounted as spahis under their own agha, but they, too, were largely undisciplined. While the corsairs at sea learned to manage warships on the model of those being developed in Europe, the soldiers did not copy the military practices that we associate with Le Tellier, Louvois, Martenet, and finally Frederick the Great.

Even without the discipline that we have learned to expect from soldiers, the janissary militia was and remained the most important military force in the regency down to the second decade of the nineteenth century. It also played a significant role in the political evolution of the community. As we have seen already, in the era of the beylerbeys, the janissary corps several times attempted to impose its will on the regency—once by insisting upon the elevation of one of its popular officers to the office of pasha, and another time by demanding that the beylerbey (even if he was the son of the great Kheir-ed-din) must not arm the Moors as a rival military force. These early efforts to control the government failed because the sultan was strong and the corsair reis refused to support the soldiers, but in the seventeenth century, when less effective men filled the office of pasha and the sultan's power had crumbled even in the Levantine sanjacs of the empire, the Algerian janissary militia was able to extend its power enormously. The instrument of control was the divan, or general council; it was attended by the senior officers of the janissary corps, the pasha, and the mufti, cadi, the four *cayas* (secretaries), plus the former aghas. At the opening of the seventeenth century, the pasha and the agha for the "two moons" presided. As we shall see, the decline in the prestige of the pasha during the first half of the century gave the divan the opportunity to usurp power and finally to displace the pasha for all but his ceremonial role.

The rules covering the meetings of the divan were simple enough. No member was allowed to carry arms of any kind, and armed guards maintained order. No member was allowed to use his fists for any offensive action on pain of death, but he was allowed to express his feelings with his feet, either by stomping or by kicking. One French consul was nearly killed when he was "footed" in the divan. All speech was in Turkish; dragomen translated into Berber or Arabic and the European languages when necessary. The "word" was taken in order of seniority or importance, although the most usual practice seems to have been for the speaker to orchestrate a chorus of shouting by the assembly. These sessions were incredibly disorderly as a result of this procedure. Foreigners who attended were often convinced that they were dealing with wild, violent, irrational men; the evidence seems to point to the fact that the leaders used this procedure to emphasize their programs and to shout down any objections. To an Englishman, however, such procedures seemed irrational; for instance, Francis Knight, who, in the second quarter of the seventeenth century, spent several years in Algiers as a slave, was apparently able to witness meetings of the divan. His account of procedures is worth repeating:

They stand in ranks, passing the word by *chouse* or *pursuivant,* jetting each other with their arms or elbows, raising their voices as if in choler or as a pot boileth with the addition of fire . . . They have a wise prevention of a greater mischief, for [they] are commanded upon deepest pains not to drink wine or any strong liquor before coming . . . or to carry a knife thither . . . It is such a government like which there is nowhere else in the world . . . (Francis Knight, p. 403).

However, beyond the accounts of slaves, travelers, and consuls who had only limited access to the meetings of the divan, we know little about its inner workings. There is a strong suspicion that the wealthy corsair reis and the owners of the corsair ships had much influence on decisions, particularly those concerning war and peace. We also know that within the corps itself, there were cliques headed by strong men; these were often responsible for the murder of an agha or one of the ministers, and they probably had an important role in the decisions of the divan.

The actual requirements that the soldiers imposed upon their rulers were relatively simple. The first, and undoubtedly the most important, was that they must be paid promptly every two months. When they were not paid, they became dangerous. This was what happened to the pashas sent from Istanbul for a three-year term. These men often enough were interested only in making enough profit out of their stay in Algiers to provide for their future life in the more civilized Levant. They were careless with the soldiers' pay, and as a result the soldiers, by using the divan as an instrument of power, gradually usurped the authority with which the beylerbeys had endowed their califate pashas. They took from the pashas the control of the public treasury and gave it to their aghas under the supervision of the divan. As we shall see, this did not work either. The pashas were made into "honorary" officials, but the aghas became targets for the cliques in the corps, and murder was substituted for orderly process.

Aside from the requirement that they must be paid, the janissaries had two other requirements that they imposed upon their rulers. The first was that the corps must be the only important and well-armed military force in the regency. There could be auxiliary troops, but they were to be paid less and kept in a subordinate position. It was not until the last years of the regency in the nineteenth century that a ruler of Algiers managed to free himself from the tyranny of the soldiers by developing a military force outside of the janissary corps.

The second requirement was that the soldiers must be recruited from outside the population of the regency. Men from the Levantine Ottoman empire or renegades were welcome; others were excluded. This requirement kept the army of occupation unconnected with the people that it dominated. But, as we have already seen, there was a problem. Some of the janissaries managed to marry native women and to produce children. These were the coulougli, the sons of janissaries. Naturally these men aspired to their fathers' profession. The unmarried members, however, regarded these sons as dangerous; in a conflict with the native population, they might easily side with their mother's people rather than with the corps. Thus the soldiers first limited the numbers of coulougli who were permitted to enroll and then passed laws to prevent their rising to posts of power or responsibility in the militia. Concern over the problem of the coulougli and consequent efforts to control them finally led to a rebellion in the early 1630s. Although the coulougli leaders expected to find support from either the Kabylie and the Algerian baldi, it did not materialize. The battle raged in the streets of Algiers until a major fortress, in which the coulougli had barricaded themselves, exploded. This accident in the powder room killed several thousand people, destroyed a section of the town, and ended the coulouglis' hopes for equality. They were not allowed to enroll in the janissary militia until after the great pestilence of 1648–50 so decimated the corps that more manpower was needed; and even then they were never allowed to rise to power as officers. In the eighteenth century, however, we find that several of the coulougli did succeed to important offices: they were beys and cadis, but never aghas.[2]

The other institution, also inherited from the sixteenth century, was the taiffe of the reis. As long as the beylerbey and his viceroys were men of the sea, owners of corsair ships, commanders in their own right, the reis had a voice in the affairs of the regency, and their interests were given consideration. However, when the sultan appointed pashas for a three-year term, they were usually men of the court rather than the sea, and the reis, like the soldiers, had to look out for their own interests. The exact story of the development of this body is shrouded in the obscurity of time; it produced no memoirists of its functions and no letters of its members to explain its history; so we are left with the insights of outsiders and evidence of the obvious impact that it had upon the course of events. The crews of the galleys and galiots that Aroudj and his brothers brought from their island home were obviously Levantines, probably also islanders. They continued to command the corsair fleet until the capture of Italians and others produced the renegades who, like Euldj Ali, proved to be at least as effective as the Levantines. At the end of the century, they were joined by European "seadogs" who, perhaps more pirates than pious renegades, taught the Algerian reis

2. There are many accounts of the rebellion of the coulouglis. Grammont's *Relations entre la France et la régence d'Alger au XVII Siècle*. R.A. XXIII, 414ff is a good summary. The *Gazette de France*, 1633, Père Dan, *Histoire*, and Francis Knight's *Relation* provide eyewitness accounts.

to sail the tall ships powered by canvas. Aroudj and later Kheir-ed-din seem to have used the captains of their ships as a sort of divan of the corsairs. By the mid-sixteenth century it had become the taiffe of the reis, a corporate institution that must have resembled a medieval guild more than a modern "employer's union." The taiffe elected the admiral of the corsair fleet, usually the richest member of the group whose personally owned ships were a significant contribution to the corsair navy. By the seventeenth century many of the corsair vessels were owned and equipped by private individuals, shipbuilders who gave them to successful captains to command the actual cruise. Some were even owned by groups of "partners" or "stockholders" who were proper capitalist entrepreneurs. However, the reis who commanded the ship employed his own slaves or "hired" slaves belonging to others and recruited his own marines. When ready for a cruise, the reis hoisted his flag as a signal to "volunteers" who joined his crew with no fixed pay, but with the promise of a share of the booty. A popular reis easily found all the men he needed. The seagoing reis, rather than the "capitalist" owners of the ships, belonged to the taiffe.

Grammont, the most knowledgeable of the nineteenth-century historians to write about Algiers, insisted that the taiffe of the reis was in competition with the janissary-controlled divan. There undoubtedly were periods when the janissaries and the reis were at odds with each other, yet a careful reading of the evidence can also suggest that for the most part the reis were able to influence the soldiers whenever their interests were involved. Even the revolution that created the office of dey—clearly controlled by the reis—was engineered so that the janissaries went along with the program proposed by the sea captains.

The reis were personally interested in questions of war and peace. They wanted war that would yield rich prizes; they wanted peace when the great naval powers appeared in the Mediterranean to bombard and sink their ships in the harbor and to fight them at sea. By the eighteenth century when the ships were largely owned by members of the regency government, the latter were willing to give the smaller states peace if the tribute that came with it approximated the value of the prizes that were possible if the policy were war.

Even without the sort of testimony that the historian likes to have, we can readily understand that the wealthy corsair captains—the reis—who owned slaves, ships, town hotels, villas, and farms outside the city, as well as gold, silver, jewels, and other valuables, had influence in a city that depended upon their valor for much of its economic base. Furthermore, many of them seem to have been better educated and more humane than the janissary joldacs. There are many stories to support this; even as late as the early nineteenth century when Mrs. Elizabeth Broughton was in Algiers, the reis were more acceptable than the soldiers because their experience gave them a wider horizon. In almost any society, men with wealth and knowledge superior to their fellow subjects are likely to be able to influence the course of political events.

The relations between the regencies of North Africa and the Sublime Porte in Istanbul were a continuing problem throughout the sixteenth to the eighteenth centuries. Kheir-ed-din placed his corsair community under the Grand Seigneur, and as we have seen, his immediate successors to that high office were all corsair reis, owners of fleets of galleys and galiots that scourged the sea for booty and slaves and, at times, joined the fleet of the Grand Seigneur to do battle with the Spanish empire. There was no question about the sultan's authority; an offending reis or officer of the janissary militia could lose his head at the sultan's order. Kheir-ed-din, Hassan-ben-Kheir-ed-din, Salah Reis, and Euldj Ali all rose to command the entire Turkish fleet with the title captain pasha as well as that of beylerbey. These men were powers in the Ottoman empire as well as in the North African territories. But when Euldj Ali died in 1587, the sultan, perhaps because he feared that a powerful officer so far from Istanbul might become independent, decided to suppress the office of beylerbey and to create instead the three regencies of Algiers, Tunis, and Tripoli, each to be governed by a pasha. As representatives of the sultan's authority, the pashas enjoyed many perquisites: a share of the booty and slaves captured by the corsairs, the right to receive "presents" for favors, and control over the revenues generated in the subject communities governed by the three beys and the pasha in Algiers. Thus the office was a juicy plum for ambitious or greedy courtiers and politicians in the sultan's entourage.

The shortness of tenure (three years) made it almost impossible for a new pasha to understand the political complexities of the city of Algiers and the governments of the beyliks with vassal sheiks and "kings" before it was time for a new pasha to take his place. Furthermore, these triennial pashas were usually not sailors or soldiers; they were political favorites who had acquired their offices at considerable expense; bribery was the way of life in Istanbul after the great sultans of the sixteenth century were followed by weak men often under the control of the sultana and the harem. The new pasha was most anxious to fill his pockets with gold and to return to Istanbul. This greedy behavior aroused the envy and anger of both the janissaries and the reis. The latter may have had their "labor union," the taiffe, to coordinate their actions and to influence the behavior of the divan, but the divan was indeed the instrument of the janissary militia, the army of occupation of the regency. Thus the divan became the focal point of the movement that eventually deprived the pashas of all authority, leaving them solely with a ceremonial office.

The proccess was slow, but by the 1630s an incident described by Père Dan, the French priest who went to Algiers to liberate slaves and stayed to write its history, illustrates the erosion of the powers of both the pasha in Algiers and the sultan as overlord. The Algerian corsair had captured a Venetian ship and sold its crew and cargo. After Venice protested in Istanbul, the sultan sent a messenger ordering the restoration of both. The pasha had the order read to the divan and insisted that there was nothing to do but obey. The next speaker shouted that the sultan was misinformed, and the whole divan took up the chant: "The order is not just," "The sultan's misinformed." Nothing came of the sultan's demands. A half-century earlier the pasha would have beheaded the guilty reis and the recalcitrant soldiers and restored the Venetian ship, but as Père Dan remarked, "Although [the sultan] knew the nature of these barbarians . . . he is content simply to send a pasha to represent his person." The pasha was more fearful of the soldiers than of his distant overlord.

In the years that followed, the erosion of the pasha's authority proceeded apace. Orders from Istanbul were obeyed only when the divan agreed. In the middle 1630s Père Dan remarked: "The state has only the name of a kingdom since, in effect, they have made it into a republic." Francis Knight, as well as the English and French consuls who managed to survive in Algiers in the first half of the century, all echo this opinion. The process was speeded up by the disaster that overtook the Algerian fleet when the Venetians surprised it at Valona in the late 1630s. The reis decided that they would never again go to the sultan's aid without a subsidy in advance. The next time the Sublime Porte ordered them to join the Ottoman fleet, the taiffe refused. Istanbul's first response was to order the pasha to take Admiral Bitchnin's head. But he was the richest man in Algiers and admiral of the fleet, and so his head was safe! The Sultan's order was a colossal blunder that could have ended all the relations between Algiers and the Ottoman empire, for Bitchnin seems to have plotted to seize power and make Algiers independent. Only the untimely death of the corsair admiral (possibly by poison) ended the plot.

The next time the sultan needed the Algerians, he did send a subsidy in advance, but that subsidy turned out to be the cause of a further breach. Ibraham Pasha announced that if the corsairs did join the sultan's naval establishment, they naturally would not be able to capture prizes in the western Mediterranean, and thus he would be deprived of his percentage share of the booty. He therefore demanded that ten percent of the subsidy be given to him (1659). This produced a revolution that ended the powers of the pasha of Algiers. A boulouk-bachi, Khalil, rallied the divan to an insurrection to "re-establish the ancient ways." These "ancient ways" were alleged to be a constitution that placed all effective powers in the hands of the janissary agha and the divan. Of course, this was pure mythology, but like revolutionaries in mid-seventeenth-century England, France, Barcelona, Naples, and elsewhere, the Algerian divan insisted that it only wanted a return to ancient forms. No one in this era would admit to being a "revolutionary." The result, however, was revolutionary. A few years later d'Aranda could write, "The pasha . . . acknowledges a kind of subjection to the Grand Seigneur in words, but takes little account of his orders . . . The soldiers are more dreadful to him than the Grand Seigneur." They had become the rulers of Algiers, leaving the pasha as a ceremonial officer, paid a regular salary, but without power.

The new situation was tacitly recognized in Istanbul by the fact that the sultan no longer appointed a new pasha every three years. Thus the office ceased to be a rich prize, for the incumbent henceforth received a fixed salary with a settled issue of bread and meat. He no longer could claim a percentage of prize money for himself. It was no longer an office that appealed to the sultan's entourage of place-hunters.

Throughout the rest of the century, letters from Algiers to foreign rulers were signed by the pasha, agha, and (after 1672) the dey of Algiers. But the pasha's role was entirely passive in all the decisions of policy. Only once did a pasha try to re-establish the ancient prestige of the office. In 1671 when the Ali Agha and his friends were murdered and no one seemed to want to take Ali's place, the pasha seized the flag and urged the janissaries to rally around him as the traditional officer of the regency. As we shall see, the reis had other ideas, and quickly persuaded the soldiers to call on one of their number to accept power on his own terms. He became dey with life tenure; the pasha accepted this defeat without a murmur.

The office of pasha, however, was not terminated even though the actual incumbent had become powerless. Hayes, writing from Algiers, explained to Colbert in 1681 that the pasha no longer meddled in any affairs; he simply signed any expedition that was presented to him. At the end of the century, de la Croix *fils* gives us the real reason why the Algerians were willing to keep the pasha and pay him a salary. He explains: "It is necessary to draw troops from the Levant . . . They are obliged to have recourse to the Ottoman Sultan who only gives it in return for recognizing him and a pasha . . . but they limit the pay of the pasha and give him no voice in affairs of state." [3] In the 1680s Baba Hassan conceived the idea of uniting the office of pasha with that of dey, a project that became standardized later in the eighteenth century when the sultan accepted the fait accompli and united the two offices rather than face a confrontation. The link that the office of pasha provided for the Sublime Porte at Istanbul and the real rulers of Algiers continued to be important throughout the seventeenth and eighteenth centuries. The janissary corps had to be filled by recruits from the Levant, and the Algerian recruiting officers were able to draw men from Syria, Anatolia, and the Balkans every two to four years with the full consent of the sultan's government.

The revolution that Ibraham Pasha provoked by trying to skim off ten percent of the sultan's subsidy was plainly inspired by the reis as well as by leading janissaries. Khalil, a janissary officer, led the rebellion in the divan, but the pasha was really attempting to force the reis to give him part of the subsidy. However, since the revolt of 1559 resulted in the assumption of power by the aghas in cooperation with the divan, it is clear that the janissaries in the divan had prepared for the rebellion by the gradual assumption of power in the preceding decades and had used Ibraham's indiscretion to consolidate their position. Khalil was murdered soon after the rebellion, but for the next twelve years the regency of Algiers was ruled, or misruled, by the agha and the divan. Ibraham escaped

3. A.E.E. Algérie, XII, fols. 275–76.

with his life when he agreed to retire to a ceremonial role, and his successors fared no better. But the janissaries were not really prepared to rule; their leaders were not politically educated, and the "return to the ancient constitution" did not produce a regime flexible enough to allow an orderly exercise of authority. The agha coming to power found himself tied by the "democratic" organization of the janissary corps and the anarchy in the divan. From the first day he was in danger of assassination, for the cliques that developed had no other regularized route to express opposition. The years between 1559 and 1571 were marked by one assassination after another; no agha who assumed power died a natural death. The government of the regency was nearly pure anarchy.

In all fairness to the efforts of the aghas to establish an orderly rule, we should note that there were outside forces operating on the corsair community that also contributed to the disorder. The new regime appeared at the same time that the Peace of the Pyrenees (1659) brought an end to the long Hapsburg-Bourbon war, thereby releasing both French and Spanish naval forces for coastal defense and convoy duty in the Mediterranean. Shortly afterwards, Charles II (1661) was recalled to the throne in England, and his subsequent marriage to a Portuguese princess gave him the port of Tangiers as her dowry. This provided the English navy with a port of call near the Straits. With Cardinal Mazarin's death in 1661, Louis XIV assumed control over his state, and very soon Colbert became a powerful personality in the French government. As we shall see in a later chapter, these events quickly altered the balance of naval power in both the Mediterranean and the Atlantic, to the disadvantage of the Algerian reis. English, Dutch, and French squadrons not only bombarded Algerian ports but also captured and sank Algerian corsair cruisers. The reis, their interests neglected by the soldiers who had assumed power in 1659, had good reason to seize power in the regency to protect themselves.

There were also other forces at work. The mid-seventeenth century in Europe saw the continued development of the "revolutionary" governmental program started by Cardinal Richelieu in France, by Gasparde Guzman, duke of Olivares, in Spain, by Frederick William in Prussia-Brandenburg, the Kammeralist ministers in Austria, and by lesser princes and ministers elsewhere in Europe. The disorder inherent in the heritage of political pluralism that came from the European past could no longer be tolerated by the emerging civilization of Europe. The great nobles as well as the independent towns were being brought under the control of the larger political entity by royal power. Soldiers responsible to the ruler, rather than simply to their captain or some quasi-independent marshal or general, were in the process of imposing internal peace upon the disorderly elements of European society. By the third quarter of the seventeenth century, a Wallenstein, a Bernard von Sax-Weimar, or the *grands* in sixteenth- and early seventeenth-century France who could challenge the king, were as little possible as a city government like the one at La Rochelle that stood off Louis XIII's army for an entire year. This concentration of power has been called "absolutism" perhaps because Louis XIII spoke of his *pouvoir absolu*. It was not that kings gained the complete power that the word absolutism suggests but rather that rulers absorbed the political and military powers of the great nobles and the independent cities; of course, they never held the complete powers that have become common to rulers in the centuries that have followed the French revolution.

The revolution of 1659 in Algiers, however, was not characteristic of the processes at work in Europe. While European princes were establishing their right to govern the great nobles and the commercial cities of their kingdoms, in Algiers the complex structure of quasi-independent towns, tribal sheiks and kings, and divergent corporate interests within the regency melted into near anarchy. The 1660s witnessed rebellions and refusals to pay tribute, and the inability of the janissary corps' leaders to reach a political solution after the seizure of power blocked the possibility of an effective response by the agha and divan. Murder and civil disorder were poor substitutes for the "absolute" power that was developing in Europe. The corsair reis were seriously threatened by this anarchy. They were the richest men in the community; they owned villas in the suburban areas of Algiers and townhouses in the city; they had slaves as well as wealth in goods and money, and they were accustomed to command. The anarchy threatened their wealth as much as the foreign navies interfered with their métier as corsairs. The reis could find allies in the ranks of the rich baldi and Jews who managed the commerce of Algiers and owned many of the vessels of the corsair navy. They, too, had a stake in the establishment of order, but neither the baldi nor the Jews had any military or political base from which to operate on their own. Thus, when the soldiers reduced the political process to cliques and murder, the rich merchants and shipbuilders had no recourse except through a revolution led by the reis.

The crisis of 1671 that produced that revolution was as much the result of the situation in Europe as of the problems in Algiers. When the so-called War of the Devolution ended in 1668, the naval powers were in a position to use their ships to bring some safety to their Mediterranean commerce. Unfortunately for the agha's rule, the end of that war also coincided with a serious naval defeat suffered by the Algerian reis who were aiding the sultan in the Cretan war. In an effort to recoup some of their losses, the reis captured any ships they met—no matter that they might be protected by treaty. The response was immediate: both English and French naval squadrons appeared before Algiers and demanded reparations and an end to this piracy. The aghas agreed but the sailors continued their depredations. The next year (1669) Vivonne arrived with a French fleet and required the agha to hang three of the reis who had illegally taken French prizes. In 1670 English, Dutch, Swedish, Maltese, and French naval forces patrolled the Mediterranean, forcing the Algerians to remain in port. With no prizes, the reis and the wealthy shipowners became more and more impatient. But the final blow came when Admiral Spragg surprised about a third of the Algerian fleet in the harbor of Bougie, managed to break the boom, and burned most of the corsair ships. (See Chapter 12.)

When the news reached Algiers, a revolt broke out. Agha Ali was able to quell the first outbreak and to behead some of its ring leaders, but another wave of violence swept him and his friends out of power and to their deaths. For a short time the revolt hesitated; no one wanted the post vacated by Ali. He was only the last of a series of aghas whose rule ended in murder. The pasha, perhaps hopeful that he could fill the vacuum, seized a flag and called upon the janissaries to follow him and reestablish the ancient constitution of the regency that recognized the sultan's rule. But the taiffe had other ideas. Some one proposed that Hadj Mohammed, a very rich retired reis who was respected by all as a man of good faith and who could probably find the money to pay the janissaries' salaries, should be asked to assume power. The crowd marched to Hadj's residence. He either did not know, or at least pretended not to know, whether they were attacking his house or honoring him. When offered the position of power, he first refused, but then reconsidered on the condition that his authority should be absolute. The reis Hadj did not want the title of agha; he became "dey," a title that signified both "maternal uncle" and "valiant hero." The reis pretended that they were returning to the "ancient constitution" founded by Kheir-ed-din. They insisted that, when Kheir-ed-din and his brothers had left home to cruise in the western Mediterranean, their father had recommended that they obey Kheir, for "he is your dai."

Hadj Mohammed had no intention of falling into the traps that had brought down one agha after another in the preceding years. He insisted upon the right to set up a government with the power to defend itself against the cliques that mushroomed so easily in the ranks of the janissary corps. The sailors were now to rule Algiers. Fortunately for him, in the rest of that decade, the sea powers of Europe were embroiled in a costly war that started when Louis XIV attempted to make the United Netherlands pay for its unwillingness to see the French king as sovereign of the Catholic (Spanish) Netherlands. It was to be almost another decade before the sea powers could again turn their attention to Algiers.

Hadj Mohammed did not attempt to rule by himself. His son-in-law, Baba Hassan, became for all intents and purposes, the ruler of Algiers, and it was he who initiated the changes in the government of the regency that were to become characteristic of the regime of the deys. In place of government by the divan, the deys instituted a regime in which ministers—the "powers"—assisted in managing the affairs of state. A treasurer, aghas for the janissaries and for the auxiliary troops, the admiral, a minister for foreign affairs, and a staff of secretaries, messengers, and other aids came to rule. The divan merely approved their decisions. Hadj Mohammed and Baba Hassan governed Algiers for more than a decade without any serious contests of their power. Hadj Mohammed was an old man, Baba Hassan a clever, unscrupulous politician; they supported the policies of the reis and kept a close watch on the development of cliques in the janissary corps. However, the European situation finally turned against them. During the first years of their government the Dutch War occupied the full attention of the naval powers, but after the Peace of Numwegen (1679) the fleets of England, the Netherlands, and France were all available to chastise any interference with the commerce of those nations. As we shall see in a later chapter, first an English fleet and then the French, bombarded Algiers and attacked the corsair navy. The second French bombardment was particularly brutal, and Baba Hassan was ready to negotiate. He did free most of the French slaves in Algiers and would have gone further to accommodate Louis XIV, but the French admiral Duquesne, duped by promises, released his hostage Mezzo Morto in hope of securing better terms. Mezzo Morto, also a corsair reis, promptly managed to murder Baba Hassan while Hadj Mohammed escaped to Tunis. Mezzo Morto became dey and refused to negotiate with Duquesne. A year later he did reach an agreement with a French agent and then persuaded the sultan to unite the office of pasha with that of dey. He hoped to establish a stable regime, but such a hope proved impossible to fulfill. Mezzo Morto managed to alienate the soldiers by involving them in an unsuccessful war against Tunis. He had to flee for his life, and in 1689 the soldiers elected one of their number to the office of dey. The reis had held power for just two decades before the soldiers reasserted the primacy of the janissary corps in the government of Algiers.

At this point the Sublime Porte, prompted by the French ambassador, who hoped to use Algiers in France's war against England (1689), appointed another pasha from Istanbul. The divan refused to allow him to land. The order was "Return to the place from which you came . . . we have no need for a pasha . . . if you do not return, you will see what happens to you."[4] Once again over a quarter of a century later, the sultan's viziers sent another appointee from Istanbul to be pasha at Algiers. He too was threatened with death should he attempt to land. The revolution of 1671 had created a political situation in which the dey was able to usurp authority both from Istanbul and the Algerian divan. It was to be another quarter-century before this power was firmly in the dey's hands, but prospects for a return to past government by "anarchy" or "murder" were considerably lessened.

The soldier deys had no difficulty in making peace with European states as soon as Europe became embroiled in the two great wars that filled the years 1689–1714; their only problem was to keep their own government out of Europe's conflicts. However even if they did not have to worry about naval bombardments, the soldier deys did become involved in conflicts on their frontiers. As we shall see in a later chapter, they succeeded in capturing Oran, but wars with Tunis and Morocco were not equally successful, and ill-advised policies and failures on the battlefield placed the dey's life in danger. It was never possible for the governors of Algiers to rule out the possibility that murder would end their careers and their lives, but the soldier deys did reduce that eventuality to a point where it was not uncommon for a dey to die a natural death.

4. Ismail Pasha to Louis XIV, R.A. CLXIII, p. 70.

VI *Algiers: Situation, Population, Society*

WHEN EIGHTEENTH-CENTURY literary men took notice of the Barbary Coast, their accounts were romantic and quite unreal. As one French scholar points out, "This 'Century of Light' produced hundreds of books on religion, medicine, grammar, music, agriculture, economics, politics, meteorology, exotic ethnology, and geography, but North Africa was neither wild enough nor exotic enough to merit attention from the *philosophes*." In many of the lexicons, dictionaries, geographies, and encyclopedic works, the peoples of North Africa were characterized in uncritical discussions based on unreliable evidence. It was not that they had no evidence to go on but rather that the literary men preferred to see the North Africans either as the "scourge of Christendom" or in the guise of Molière's Turk in the *Bourgeois Gentilhomme*. Either role fails to account for the complexity of North African life.

There was, however, a considerable wealth of material from which they could have drawn a picture of Algiers and its people. In the three and a quarter centuries between the time that Aroudj led his little squadron to the central Mediterranean and the French landed at Algiers in 1830, a host of merchants, soldiers, sailors, ex-slaves, travelers, consular and diplomatic agents, and literary people visited Algiers for one reason or another and left accounts of their experiences. These persons came from all parts of western Europe and from many classes of European society: some, like Haëdo and Dan, were priests involved in the ransoming of slaves; others like Sanson Napollon, Denis Dusault, and Cole were men of affairs; Marmol and Duquesne were soldiers; Morgan and Shaw were literary men and travelers; de la Croix was a savant, and Mrs. Broughton, the literary wife of a consul; Dapper, a Dutch geographer; Panati and Hayes spied to seek out the weakness of the land; Francis Knight, Dr. Underhill, and de Rocqueville were slaves. This list is far from complete. The Newberry Library in Chicago has forty or more contemporary accounts by ex-slaves, travelers, and publicists; the Bibliothèque Nationale and the British Museum each have over a hundred titles, and Playfair's bibliography lists 293 books or pamphlets published before 1789, not all by people who actually visited Algiers, but all attempting to elucidate Algerian conditions. As might be expected, much of this material is worthless, but there is enough valid experience for a reasonably trustworthy account to be put together.

While the people who visited Algiers had varied backgrounds and experience, they shared a common prejudice, since all were Christians. Unfortunately, Mohammedan officials, soldiers, and merchants who either lived in, or visited, Algiers have left us few documents available to Western scholars, even to those who know Arabic or Turkish. Thus, the picture we get of the life and customs of the people of North Africa is undoubtedly distorted. If we remember this, however, it is not impossible to cull out of the books, pamphlets, and consular, diplomatic, and naval letters and memoranda enough material to give us a reasonably acceptable account. We must be careful, however, not to go to the lengths that Fisher did in discounting all unfriendly or hostile comments and giving credence to all friendly ones. Prejudices can cut several ways.

The only easy route to visit Algiers was by sea, and all travelers agree that the city presented a beautiful as well as a formidable sight from the roadstead outside the mole that Kheir-ed-din built to provide a safe anchorage for his fleet. The mole was a secure breakwater that extended from the island that had been the old Spanish presidio to the shore. By the middle seventeenth century it had become a fortification bristling with cannons as well as a wall to hold off high seas. Beyond the mole, the walls of the city were studded with guns, and there were free-standing fortifications to assist in the defense against an invader. We have a number of memoranda written by spies or soldiers analyzing the problems of capturing Algiers. D'Arvieux's memorandum for the prince of Portugal and an anonymous one written for Colbert give us careful descriptions of these fortifications in the third quarter of the seventeenth century.[1]

1. Memorandum for Colbert, 1664, A.A.E., Algiers 12, 148; Memorandum for prince of Portugal, d'Arvieux, R.A. V, 363–72.

Neither considered the city impregnable; indeed to the contrary, both were optimistic about the chances for a successful assault. The city walls had about one hundred cannons, most of which faced the sea. Neither writer knew that some of them dated back to the days of Charles V's assault; in fact, after Algiers was taken in 1830, Europeans discovered that many of the guns "defending" the town could not be fired without endangering the gunners. There were five gates in the walls, two facing the sea, and four detached forts, one a half-cannon shot from the town. Accounts in the 1660s and 1670s, as well as others written before and after these dates, agree that the city could be taken by twenty-five to thirty thousand men suitably armed with siege equipment. A "footnote" to this optimism should indicate that the half-dozen or so attempts to take Algiers between the days of Kheir-ed-din and the opening of the nineteenth century had all failed; and yet the French expedition of 1830 met little serious opposition.

The city was impressive as one approached it from the sea. In the foreground the mole and the harbor were framed by the city walls, and the houses marched up the side of the hill in the form of an amphitheater. Walls and houses were a gleaming white in the African sunlight. There was little smoke to pollute the air and blacken the walls, and the citizens used whitewash in the hope of controlling the plague. When one entered the narrow streets, however, it became obvious that Algiers promised more from a distance than it could deliver close at hand.

Inside the walls, much of the "white beauty" gave way to dirty streets, some not wide enough for two people to pass easily. In those that were wider, the pedestrian was in competition with camels, horses, donkeys, even the ubiquitous rats, and his nose was assaulted by the stench of manure, garbage, and dirt. To be sure this was not unusual for any city in the early modern era; it has been said that one could smell Paris five miles away if the wind were right, and visitors who knew Naples, Barcelona, Marseille, and other Mediterranean cities to the north often contrasted Algiers favorably with the Christian port towns. Today in the native quarters and suks of Tunis, Algiers, Rabat, and other North African cities we still find the narrow streets, some with high walls on both sides— walls to give privacy to the households of the wealthy whose court-yards with pools and flowers make gracious and private living possible. On other streets, the shops of tradesmen and artisans push into the passageways, sometimes almost blocking traffic while their owners urge the passers-by to buy their wares or to join in the convivial entertainment of the wine or coffee shops.

In these earlier centuries the artisans were usually native baldi, Moriscos, Tagarines (refugees from Spain), coulougli, or Jews. Many writers insist that the refugees from Spain greatly enriched Algiers by their skills, while others tell us that the Moriscos were not as well received in Algiers as they were in Tunis, where the economy was more suitable to their abilities and the government more willing to receive them.

The wineshops and coffee houses in Algiers were nearly all owned and managed by renegades or Christian slaves who paid their masters a part of the profits, and very often became well-to-do themselves. Indeed, there are numerous accounts of slaves who refused to be freed or ransomed because they might lose their profitable businesses. In the eighteenth century we hear of janissaries operating shops of one kind or another, some of whom were over age and retired from active service, and others who found it more profitable to manage a shop and hire a substitute for the expeditions of the corps than to act out their role as soldiers.

One institution of Algiers that was universally praised by all visitors was the public baths. Obviously these baths were direct descendants of those that served the Romans centuries before. The most sumptuous of them had steam rooms, hot and cold water, negro servants skilled as masseurs, coffee and sherbets served by female slaves. Women patrons had certain hours reserved for them. Christians, Jews, and slaves could also patronize the baths. Dr. Underhill, in the latter eighteenth century, tells us of the lighting, the cold and warm water, the dressing rooms, towels and "flesh brushes," bath assistants, coffee, sherbet, tobacco, and even the possibility of having opium. His account corresponds suitably with those of earlier visitors. Most of the Christian commentators credited the Moslem concern about cleanliness for so excellent an institution; this may be correct, but the baths probably also were connected with traditions from classical antiquity.

There were no hostelries for Christians in the sixteenth and early seventeenth centuries; the traveler had to find shelter in the Jewish quarter. But in course of the seventeenth century, the European consuls developed compounds or *fonducks* for storing merchandise, for consular business, religious services, and eventually places where a visitor could find lodging. By the eighteenth century, when there were five to seven consular offices in Algiers, these services were reasonably well organized.

The Spanish hospitals maintained by the redemptionist fathers of the Holy Trinity and the Order of the Redemption of Captives (Trinitarians) were founded to care for Christian slaves, apparently in an effort to maintain their faith in their religion. But the hospital was available to Christian merchant seamen and even to some of the Moslem population. It seems to have been a "model" institution for the period, but the reverend fathers were not always able administrators. In the first years of the seventeenth century, it was in serious trouble. The director of one hospital borrowed money from Christians, Turks, baldis, and Jews at usurious rates of interest. One cargo of wool sent from Spain did not provide enough money to satisfy his creditors, and the French consul was arbitrarily constrained to assume some of the responsibility. By the eighteenth century when there were six or so of these hospitals situated in the slave quarters, or the *bagños*,[2] the fathers were permitted to impose a small tax on all goods brought to Algiers, to help support the hospitals. These provided services for Christians that were quite unavailable to the Moslem residents of the city.

In a later chapter we shall discuss the slave quarters and the problems of the slaves in Algiers.

Père Dan placed the number of mosques at one hundred, most of them small, and including all the little shrines or chapels guarded by a marabout or two. The impressive mosques of Algiers were built after his time by several highly successful, and therefore wealthy, corsair reis. Tassy tells us in agreement with most observers, that in the early eighteenth century there were ten large mosques and some fifty smaller ones. These mosques were serviced by the many different schismatical or heretical sectarians as well as by the three dominant Moslem sects: Santors, Cabalists, and Sunnaquites. There were two rites and two different teachings: the Turks and renegades usually patronized the mosques belonging to the Hanafi rite, which was liberal in its teachings on personal morality, while the migrants from Spain and the baldi mostly attended services of the Maliki rite, a more strict interpretation of morals and customs. In the smaller shrines and mosques a wide variety of doctrine was

2. The bagños were compounds where the slaves were housed. Several of them were places of "close" security; others were open all day, but usually closed at night. These bagños provided places for the catholic Mass, wines shops, food vendors, a market for stolen goods as well as housing for slaves. Their courtyards were busy, dirty, colorful, exciting, sordid—the word used depended upon the feelings of the writer who used it. The picture of the bagño is probably a correct presentation for the bagños at the end of the life of the Algerian regency.

common. Unlike the Christians of this era who still waged war against one another in the name of orthodoxy, all these different groups tolerated each other. The wild-eyed marabouts who preached their own version of religion were as acceptable as the teachers of the Koran in the schools.

By the eighteenth century, there were three colleges where boys learned the Koran and some literary culture probably in the same manner that Moslem boys still do as they sit around a teacher reciting the holy books to learn them by heart. There also were a number of small schools for children where a boy could learn to read, write, and do elementary arithmetic.

However, education, either religious or secular, was at a very low level throughout the era. Undoubtedly, the majority of Algerians, baldi, Turks, or Tagarines would share the surprise of one of their fellow countrymen who was astonished to hear that Europeans of the latter seventeenth century were spending their time trying to learn about the stars, "useless mathematics," and natural philosophy. Shaw, writing about 1720, was a most astute observer, well equipped with languages of the Near and Middle East. He met with Algerians of many different social levels, and gives the following account:

Philosophy, mathematics, and the knowledge of physic and medicine, which, a few centuries ago they had almost to themselves, are at present little known or studied. The roving and unsettled life of the Arabs and the perpetual grievances which the Moors meet from the Turks, will not permit either of them to enjoy that liberty, quiet, and security which have at all times given birth and encouragement to learning. As for the Turks, they are generally of such turbulent and restless dispositions, or else engage themselves so deeply in trade and the improvement of their fortunes, that they have no time at all for it; being wonderfully astonished, they have often asked me how the Christians can take delight or spend time and money on such empty amusements as study and speculation. (*Travels, I,* p. 353.)

De la Croix *fils,* writing in the 1760s, underlines this impression: "The people of Barbary are ignorant, without taste for Science or Arts, avaricious, cruel, defiant, suspicious, and vindictive. They have but small ability for commerce, even though they do much business . . . They live by piracy." (*Géographie Moderne,* pp. 294–95.)

In the sixteenth century, the Algerians depended upon cisterns and rain for their water, but in the early seventeenth century a refugee from Spain found an abundant, good spring on the mountainside and managed to build the aqueducts needed to bring water into the city. As a result there were over one hundred "fountains" in Algiers; some of them in the prisons (bagños) for the slaves, some in the caserns of the janissaries, some on the streets where the inhabitants could fill their jugs.

The public buildings lacked architectural distinction. Neither the offices nor the arsenal at the port were more than functional, and the "palace" itself was a square building quite without flair. The divan met in a large courtyard with the pasha and the dey seated on a dais; it was not distinguished in any way. The French were so unimpressed by this "palace" that they tore it down a few years after the conquest of the city.

All writers tell us that the population of Algiers was composed of the baldi (native Moorish Algerians), the Turks (renegades and Levantines), the Tagarines and Andalusians (refugees from Spain), Jews, "wild" Moors (Berbers) and Arabs from the hinterland of the city, Christian, and a few negro slaves. In the centuries before the modern era no one took an accurate census so that estimates of the numbers of each group, as well as of the total population, were, at best, educated guesses and, at worst, haphazard conjectures. The best figures seem to be those based on the number of "households" in the city multiplied by the supposed number of people in each household. Any figures, however, were probably compiled by adding the number of people in one quarter of the city, or one village, to an estimate rounded out to thousands. The figures for the seventeenth century should be bracketed by much smaller ones for both the first of the sixteenth century and the last of the eighteenth century: just how much difference there was, however, is quite impossible to determine.

The figures given by Père Dan (c. 1630), d'Aranda (c. 1657), d'Arvieux (c. 1675), and Tassy and Morgan (c. 1730) seem to indicate that seventeenth-century Algiers maintained its population at a reasonably stable figure of one hundred to one hundred twenty-five thousand freemen and slaves. This was the century of the greatest prosperity for the corsairs; loot and slaves poured into Algiers more rapidly in the first half of the century, but throughout the whole period the reis were able to contribute to the well-being of the community. Food was cheap and plentiful, and there was a constant renewal of the population from both the Levant and the hinterlands around the city. We have no reliable figures for birth or death rates, but we should not assume that the figures that have been established by demographers for parts of France and England can be applied to Algiers. It is probably true that without the constant renewal of population from the Levant and from the nomadic and seminomadic tribes, Algiers would have seriously declined in population during this seventeenth century.

Is there any way to discover the ethnic makeup of the population in this period? This question cannot be answered with any degree of accuracy. One writer after another, several probably copying their predecessors' writings, tell us that the city had one hundred thousand freemen and twenty-five thousand slaves, but the breakdown of the population into classes and ethnic groups creates confusion. For example, we have the figure of twenty thousand to twenty-eight thousand households of freemen, natives of Algiers who were exempt from taxes by decree of Kheir-ed-din. Add to this figure the Jews, usually put at about ten thousand individuals, the Tagarines and Andalusian refugee families from Spain, usually put at seven thousand households, the coulougli families at six to ten thousand individuals, the janissaries and renegades another fifteen to twenty thousand men, and twenty-five thousand Christian slaves. Such a breakdown—counting only four people to a household— would yield a population of nearly two hundred thousand. None of our informants claim such a large figure, so the breakdown must be faulty.

Furthermore, it is highly likely that the figure of one hundred twenty-five thousand must also be questioned if we were to attempt to establish the population at the end of the seventeenth century after the series of terrible visitations of the plague. Populations in Europe during these years were controlled by endemic diseases: small pox, diphtheria, several fevers and respiratory ailments, and the like, and the accidents of childbirth. These were all present in Algiers, and in addition there were dramatic visitations of the plague that killed so many people that it is hard to understand how the city survived at all. For example, we are told that in 1647 and 1648 ten percent of the population died each year. Then came the "great plague" of 1654 in which one-third of the population died. Eight years later (1662) ten thousand of the twenty-five thousand slaves died; no figure was given for the remainder of the population. Three years later came another "great plague," but no fixed figures for the death rate. For the next five years the plague was endemic, and then in 1671 came another "bad" year. From earlier and later accounts, a "bad" year supposedly meant anywhere the deaths of between ten and twenty percent of the total population. In the 1680s the plague was joined by famine and French bombardments, but the latter were ineffective as a check on population. During the "bad" years of 1687–88 the death rate was said to run between two hundred and two hundred forty a day (a figure that must be inaccurate, for it could mean that about seventy-five thousand of the one hundred and twenty-five thousand population died in a year). It should be noted that the fact that famine joined the plague during the 1680s may help to account for the political disorders of that period.[3] What are we to believe? In the early years of the eighteenth century, Algiers still had a considerable number of inhabitants, perhaps less than a half century earlier, but certainly the city was not deserted. The plagues and famine had undoubtedly taken a toll, but migration and the capture of slaves helped to stabilize the population.

For some reason, plagues came less frequently in the eighteenth century, and yet we have some more or less objective evidence that would indicate that plagues, on one occasion, almost halved the janissary corps in the latter part of that century. It is a reasonable assumption that the plague was only in part responsible for the population decline that began about 1720. We know that the decay of the corsair naval power and with it fewer prizes and less prosperity must be considered, and, with fewer slaves, fewer janissaries, and probably fewer immigrants from the hinterland, the total population had to go down in numbers.

North Africa historically witnessed the introduction of many ethnic types: Phoenicians, Romans, Germanic barbarians, Arab and Persian invaders, all criss-crossed the land, leaving traces of their blood with whatever was the original population. It would be most difficult to know just what bloodstreams made up the baldi, the Kabylie, the Arabs: Shaw, on finding blue-eyed, blonde-haired "Moors" decided that they were descendants of the Visigoths, and who is there to say him false? In the sixteenth century, the Spanish armies, Spanish slaves, and Levantine Turks added other genes to the bloodstreams, and in the years that followed, slaves from all over Europe, from Russia to England, from Scandinavia to Sicily, further complicated the ethnic mix. The fact that only a few negroes were brought to Algiers probably accounts for the fact that the natives' skin color

3. The best evidence on the effect of plague is probably in the consular letters, but all reports about Algiers, including the *Gazette de France*, discuss the plagues.

today is lighter than those in Morocco where sixteenth-century rulers introduced corps of soldiers drawn from the southern side of the Sahara. In any event, the visitor to North Africa today is quickly struck by the fact that the facial features, head shapes, and other indications of ethnic origin that one sees on the streets and in railway cars suggests that the population is related to every race on earth.

In the city the Turks were the ruling class, members of the army of occupation. Every ox-driver from Anatolia or mountaineer from Albania became a "high and powerful seigneur" the minute he arrived in Algiers. These rough, untutored men, along with the renegades who also became part of the janissary militia, were the rulers of the city. They alone could rise to positions of power in the military and political structure of the society. They stood outside the regular system of justice and punishment applied to the rest of the population. Most of the descriptions of the "Turks" are unflattering; some of them, however, seem to realize that the lot of the "high and powerful seigneurs" was not as rosy as it first appears. Francis Knight, writing in the early seventeenth century tells us:

> The Turk is he who fights for all, both by land and by sea, and by his power as conqueror keeps all other sort of inhabitants as vassals, as possessing goods by imagination, and the other [Moors] as possessing the essentials, for the Moors and Tagarines are the owners of the lands and ships, and the only armorers of them . . . whom I compare to the main sea, and the Turks are but rivulets or small streams that emptie themselves into the great ocean, for besides their pay and the shares they get at sea they [the Turks] enjoy . . . but little, of which the most part, the taverns, whores, and worst vices surve to spring them. In the summer they are slaves to the toyles and hazards of fortune . . . they have no free exemptions until they become Bullabashes [officers of the militia] . . . Some Turks there are of them that are excessively rich, yet but few. [spelling by Knight]

While Knight recognized that the average joldac was almost a slave himself, unrewarded for his services and preyed upon by those who catered to his vices, d'Arvieux, perhaps affronted by their arrogance and ignorance, tells us that the militia was composed of "bandits, rebels, fugitives from debts or crimes, young incorrigibles whose parents want to be rid of them—in a word the excrements of the lands of the Grand Seigneur"—hardly a flattering portrait of the men who ruled the community.

These pictures can be multiplied many times; it would be incorrect not to add that there is also evidence that individual members of the militia could be generous, kind, considerate. The slaves who worked in the caserns were often enough treated as colleagues or younger brothers rather than as servants. But the same men might force a Christian or a Jew to step into the mud, or worse, when he met them on the street, and should either Christian or Jew strike a joldac, no matter whether the latter had just arrived at Algiers, the punishment was death. Most of the joldacs remained unmarried and lived communally in caserns that were not much more commodious than the living quarters of the Christian monks. Their food was prepared by slaves, who also kept their quarters clean. Those members of the militia who married were obliged to find their lodgings elsewhere, but they did receive the same daily ration of bread as their brothers in the caserns. Many writers have emphasized the immorality of these janissaries who lived communally. It is to be expected that any company made up of unmarried men living in a community segregated from women might practice some sexual aberrations. They were accused of keeping concubines, of visiting whorehouses, and above all of homosexual relations. Some writers however, were impressed with their behavior: Tassy, for example, says that "their only play is with women or chess; they never gamble for money." He believed that he was praising them. Haëdo and Dan both commented that they did not blaspheme, although one wonders whether the good fathers' Turkish was adequate to understand the talk of joldacs. Were they veritable devils or just door devils caught by their fate? This question is unanswerable at this distance in time, but we do know that most of them lived both dangerously and simply and died without much wealth. Only when they were lucky enough to share in a rich prize and survive the dangers of the corsair cruise did they have any considerable surplus of money to spend on the pleasures that brought condemnation from Christian writers.

In addition to the recruits brought from the lands of the sultan, there were two other sources for the janissary militia: the renegades, who could become full members of the janissary corps and share equally with the Anatolian, Syrian, and Dalmatian recruits, and the coulougli, who were not allowed to hold high office either in the corps or in the government of the regency.

As we have noted, the coulougli were the children of janissaries and Moorish women. The Moors welcomed these alliances because they could thereby obtain a "protector" in the militia, the men contracted them for the various reasons that men have always had: some for money, some for sex, some perhaps for companionship and a home. The coulougli, however, were a problem. They very naturally wished to enjoy the privileges of their fathers, but the native-born Turks and the renegades would not allow them full membership in their company. As we have seen, in the first half of the century, attempts to limit the role of the coulougli finally led to a rebellion in which several thousand coulougli, poorly supported by Kabylie and friends, tried to take over the regency. The mass of the baldi, however, remained neutral, and an explosion of a powder magazine in a fortification held by the rebels ended the uprising. Thereafter the coulougli were strictly limited in their service in the armed forces.

The renegades played a more important role in the organization of the militia and in the government of the regency. They were both a source of manpower and of skills lacking in the recruits from the east. A distinction must be made between two groups of renegades. On the one hand, were Christian children captured in raids and sold, often enough, to a patron (master) who brought them up in his own house much as his own children. These youngsters found it easy to renounce the religion of their father for that of their patron, who in many cases made them his heir. There were others, adults who became renegades when they despaired of being ransomed and hoped to better their lot by denying their Christian faith. Among these were found several priests whose knowledge of Latin and ability to write brought them to important places in the government. Others were slaves who renounced their faith and joined the janissary corps. Their patron had some rights over their income until the slave could purchase his freedom. The other type of renegade was represented in footloose Europeans who presented themselves in Algiers and renounced their religion for reasons of their own. Many of these men were hard-bitten characters who left their homelands for very good reasons of personal safety; however, many of them also brought skills to the regencies that were unavailable in the Levant. In the early seventeenth century they taught the Algerians to build and sail the tall ships that could venture into the Atlantic. These men, however, were not pious warriors fighting a jihad for Allah; they were often little more than pirates who sought their fortunes under the star-spangled green banner of Algiers rather than the Jolly Roger. From the first they caused trouble in the city because they would not renounce their boisterous, immoral behavior patterns. And, if Morgan is to be credited, even in the eighteenth century, they could be seen sitting on expensive carpets or mats, playing with dice and cards, strumming guitars, singing like Christians, but inebriating themselves "like swine." Many Turks called them "men without faith"—they were neither Christian, nor Jew, nor Mohammedan. On the other hand, these men also were useful. They knew the European languages, European ways, and European skills. The picture of the renegade as a drunken, gambling wretch, unwanted in his own lands, is probably true for some and quite libelous for others.

In any case, the lot of the renegades was not without hazard. If he tried to return to his Christian faith, he risked horrible death at the hands of the Moorish executioner. If he were captured by a European naval officer and identified as a renegade, he was often summarily hanged. He did not dare, even as captain of his ship, to put in at a Christian port for fear of apprehension and execution. The term "renegade" has taken on an opprobrious connotation in all Western languages, because Christians did not distinguish between the various levels of renegade behavior.

The Berber or Moorish population of Algiers was made up first of the native baldi, the inhabitants of Algiers who were there when the Turks arrived; then of the refugees from Spain; and finally of tribesmen, mostly Kabylies, and others who drifted in from the hinterland. Dapper tells us that there were twenty-five thousand Moorish families living in Algiers; if we assume at least four to a family, this figure is probably exaggerated; nevertheless, the "Moorish" families made up a majority of the population. The Turks regarded them with mild contempt; they were peaceful, unsoldierly, unable to defend their own interests. As the result of a story about a patrol made up of baldi who, managing to provoke a pack of dogs to bark, then precipitously fled, the Turks had a proverb: "When dogs bark, the baldi run." Actually the refugee Tagarines and Andalusians were made of sterner stuff, as Spanish raiders often learned when they struck coastal villages inhabited by these refugee families. While these refugees were a minority in Algiers, they were nonetheless often very rich men who made their money by selling slaves back to their Christian families in Europe and investing the money in new corsair ships to capture more slaves. The Moorish population, as one might expect, was made up of people of all social ranks. Some were rich merchants, owners of corsair ships or outfitters of those ships; some were artisans and petty merchants, some professional people, and some were very poor, carriers of burdens and workers in the fields, not much better off than the slaves. Our Christian commentators had little opportunity to meet the native populations socially, so we have only the most formal sort of information about them, much of it quite untrustworthy.

The refugee families from Spain attracted much attention from travelers and other writers. We are told that they took to the sea in small raiding corsair ships and attacked their erstwhile homelands with the skill and knowledge that comes from familiarity with the land. Others brought to North Africa skills of many sorts: silk and woolen cloth weaving, gun manufacture, leatherworking, metal trades. In Tunis some ex-Morisco communities actually reproduced the villages that they had left, even to the names of the streets, and continued to use the Spanish language in their homes. Other Tagarines achieved fame by their rigorous defense against Spanish landings. Unlike the usual native custom of departing for the hills the minute a raiding party appeared, the Tagarines fought back and repulsed the raiders with considerable losses to both sides.

The Kabylie and other Berber peoples who migrated into Algiers were always a minority. Dapper says that there were about six hundred "Kabylese" families in the city in the latter seventeenth century. They played a very minor part in the native economy and even less in the corsair activity. Morgan writes that "the Turks have . . . disdain for these mountaineers," but this undoubtedly was simply the attitude of the army of occupation toward all the subjects of the regency.

If any Algerian Jew wrote memoirs or a history of his people in that city, the account has not survived. As a result, the Jews of Algiers are known to us through the writings of Christians, the vast majority of whom were rather more, than less, anti-Jewish. The English consul, writing in 1675, tells us that there were about thirteen thousand Jews in Algiers. The majority were native Jews whose forefathers had been in Algiers for a long time; they were mostly artisans who lived in a ghetto, dressed inconspicuously in black, and were easily recognized as Jews. The rest were "Christian or European Jews" who came from Spain, Portugal, or Italy, dressed in "European fashion," and merged into the European community. These latter were in contact with their co-religionists in Florence, Marseille, Amsterdam, London, and elsewhere. They had a "bad" reputation with most of the Christian observers, probably because they were in economic competition with them. Our informers insist that they were cunning, tricky, treacherous, dishonest. The French were sure that they were in close association with Prince William of Orange, both before and after he mounted the English throne. Even if this were true, English and Dutch observers were not less hostile to them than were the French.

One basis for this hostility was the fact that the Jews profited from the corsair activity. Some of the money needed to outfit the corsair ships came from Jewish merchants; some of the merchandise brought into Algiers by the corsairs was sold to Jewish entrepreneurs who then re-exported it to Italy, France, and even as far as the islands in the Atlantic; and finally these Jewish merchants were deeply involved in the business of transferring ransom money from Europe to Algiers for the release of slaves. This latter was a curious business involving the duke of Tuscany, who provided "prisons" for the security of slaves until their ransom money was actually transferred.

Eighteenth-century Europeans had another complaint against these Jewish merchants: the government of Algiers came to depend upon several of them for its financial stability with the result that Jewish advisers enjoyed almost a sub-rosa cabinet status that was the envy of the European consuls and merchants.

There undoubtedly was some foundation for the hostility we find generated against the Algerian Jews. Dr. Underhill, whose medical skills provided him money to pay off his ransom, used the services of a Jewish banker who was indebted to him for medical attention. Unhappily, the man died before the contract was negotiated and his son refused to recognize the obligation. Shortly afterward, the son fell ill and called in Dr. Underhill to attend him. The negotiations for a ransom were renewed. However, the Jewish merchant, arranging for Dr. Underhill's passage from Algiers, surreptitiously sold him to a Tunisian patron! Fortunately for the doctor, the ship was captured by a Portuguese man of war, and he gained his freedom. Like many others, Dr. Underhill generalized his experience and blamed his misfortunes on "Jewish character."

Others who generalized about "Jewish character" were much concerned about their competition. LeMaire (10 April 1734) urged the Marseille chamber to prevent Jewish merchants from loading French goods at that city's docks; the traffic should belong to Frenchmen. A few years earlier (5 August 1718) Consul Baume urged the king to punish French Jews in retaliation for the "illegal" traffic of Algerian Jews. Still others simply agreed with the Turks, who regarded the Jews as "less than dogs." Anti-Jewish attitudes and behavior have deep roots in both Christian and Mohammedan cultures.

Nonetheless, the Jewish community was allowed to govern its own affairs and to maintain its own courts except in cases that also involved Moslems. A Jew, condemned to death by a Moslem court, was always burned at the stake. The Moslem community shared the Christians' anti-Jewish prejudices so much that if a Jew wished to renounce his religion and become a Mohammedan, he first was obliged to become a Christian, after which he could become a renegade.

Nearly all our informers speak of the women of Algiers. Some who had been slaves assure us that they knew intimately whereof they spoke; others seem to repeat trite or fictitious myths; most seem to be describing the "outside" onlooker's impressions. The Berber Moorish women were presumed to be beautiful, even though most observers saw only their eyes. A Frenchman tells us that they were voluptuous, ignorant, and at the disposal of their men. Male slaves tell us tales of seductions in the house, seductions very dangerous for the slave, who, if caught, would suffer a horrible death hanging from a hook on the wall of the city. "Respectable" Algerian women veiled themselves on the streets, and it is probably true that they, like their descendants in our own times, hennaed their hair and painted their eyes and cheeks. The poor dressed wretchedly, the rich sumptuously. Today a visitor to the back-country villages of Algiers, Tunis, or those high up the Nile probably sees about the same sort of society that seventeenth- and eighteenth-century Europeans saw in the North African regencies. Oil, the automobile, and electricity may soon change these ancient patterns.

With what seems to be a bit of envy, one writer tells us that the marriage bond could easily be broken if the husband or wife decided that it was no longer useful. A man could easily rid himself of a "bad" woman.[4] Others simply point out that there was no love between husband and wife—only sex and family. Tassy insists that it mattered not whether a wife had a religious affiliation, or what one she had: A man could marry any woman he wished to have. Tassy tells us that the women were corrupted by the climate, becoming lazy and voluptuous, that their conversation was about the pleasures of sex and the means to please men. Their children, he said, respected their fathers but despised their mothers. Tassy, a Frenchman, retold as truth the old myth that Aroudj killed the "king" of Algiers because he wanted his wife. Perhaps his other evidence about Moorish women is made of the same whole cloth. Curiously, while Tassy tells us of seduction by women, Knight tells us of their "greed and impudence" and that they had no scruples against murder. Another Frenchman notes that in Algiers a Turk could marry a Moorish girl only after agreeing to pay the sum her father demanded, a

4. B.N., Mss. Franc. N.A. 4294.

situation exactly the reverse of that in France. He concludes that women were more valuable in Algiers than in France.[5] All agree that the Turks had a special problem with women. There were no Turkish women in Algiers, and if a Turk married a baldi, there was the problem of a settlement and the children became coulougli, but male children by a concubine, became Moors. If a Turk married a converted Christian slave, their sons became "Turks," the daughters were Moors.

The slaves of Algiers made up another large segment of the population. Although a majority were either Spanish or Italian, there were also slaves from every part of Europe. The vast majority were men, but landing raids and occasional capture of female passengers by the corsairs did produce a few women. Since an entire chapter of this book will be devoted to the problems of slaves, it is enough to note here that their conditions varied greatly. Some worked the oars at sea, some labored in quarries, on farms, at heavy road or construction operations; on the other hand, some were pampered servants, domestics who became part of the family, domestics clothed in fine costumes, whose work was light—perhaps even interesting. Others operated wine shops, were artisans, even overseers and master craftsmen in the shipyards; there were at least twenty-five thousand of these Christian slaves in the mid-seventeenth century who came from every walk of life, from nobleman to peasant, from physician to watercarrier; it is not surprising that their lot in Algiers was as varied as their origins.

With all these different peoples, there were inevitable language problems. The janissary corps and the high officials used Turkish; it was the official language of the divan and of all communications of the government (with few exceptions, when a letter might be written in a European language). Those members of the corps who did not learn Turkish as children (renegades and Dalmatians) had to acquire a working knowledge of the language, but non-Turkish speakers who appeared before the divan for any reason could count upon interpreters. According to Shaw, Martin, Dan, and others, there were a number of Berber dialects as well as Arabic dialects spoken by the tribes in the hinterlands. All the Arabic in Algeria, in contrast to that spoken in Tunis, where the Arab communities were more cultured, sounded archaic to Europeans, who knew the Arabic spoken in the Levant. The Jews, apparently, used Hebrew among themselves,

5. B.N., Mss. Franc., N.A. 4294, fol. 118.

the lingua franca when talking to others. This lingua franca was nearly universal; it was a mixture of Spanish, Portuguese, Italian, and French, with Spanish as the predominant component. Since there were so many slaves who would have no difficulty with this language, and since most of the people of Algiers had to deal with slaves in one way or another, this lingua franca could almost be said to be the language of Algeria. Slaves from English, Germanic, Slavic, and Greek parts of Europe added to the babble but could not impose their languages on the city.

Nearly every observer from Haëdo to Paradis had praise for the judges (cadis) who decided civil cases. The Koranic law was their guide, but the cadis apparently also used common sense and a measure of elementary justice in their decisions. The law was quickly applied with reasonable fees and apparent justice. D'Arvieux says: "It is surprising that a people as brutal and barbarous keep order and justice in their brigandage . . . while they are unjust to everyone else, they keep a remarkable justice amongst themselves." These same writers will also tell us how brutal was the criminal justice. A hundred or more blows on the soles of a man's feet either brought death or the loss of the feet; burning alive, suspension from hooks on the walls of the city, beheading, and strangulations were common events. The janissary who committed a crime was judged by his own court, and if guilty, strangled or beheaded quietly in a private ceremony, but all others were executed as public spectacles. There is also some disagreement about the amount of crime in Algiers; d'Arvieux, whose testimony seems to agree with the best evidence from others, writes: "The Moors are natural thieves, and Christian slaves imitate them closely—perhaps even surpass them, for all slaves are are not locked up at night; many lodge with their patrons and can go out at will. They go in groups, break into the walls of shops and in a few hours empty them. . . . if caught they rarely suffer beating with a stick." We are told that, for a slave, thievery was not as great a crime as was an attempt to run away; some observers believed that some patrons shared the loot.

When the traveler left the city of Algiers for the hinterland, he soon found himself in a wild country inhabited by people living under primitive conditions. There were numerous Berber and Arabic tribes living under the rule of their own chieftains or kings. Some were semi-nomadic; they would settle in rough villages long enough to harvest a meager crop of grain and then follow their herds during the season unsuitable for agriculture. Some of these tribes lived in the mountains, where inaccessibility assured them a high degree of independence. Others, like the Kabylie, were more or less settled in widely separated villages called *daskarats* with houses made from mud or stone. Their agriculture provided them with some surpluses of grain, wax, hides, and fibers that could be sold to the French at the Bastion or to Arab traders in the small port cities, for money to buy guns, powder and other commodities that they could not produce themselves. There was much variation in these hill villages: some were very primitive; others, like one whose residents made its living by copying holy books for Moslem readers, were relatively advanced in their cultural development. In the hinterlands and on the borders of the Sahara, the Arab and Berber nomads wandered with their herds, living in tents made from hair cloth. Shaw tells that these peripatetic villages, called *dow-ars,* moved from place to place much in the manner of the Israelites of Jacob's, and later of Moses', time.

Père Dan was one of the first Europeans to recognize the difference between Arabs and Berbers (Moors). He called the former "perpetual vagabonds," living in tents and moving from place to place. They were hated by the Moors, who failed to exterminate them and whose customs, language, and features were strikingly different. Dan apparently did actually visit several Arab dow-ars and seems to have admired the Arabs' lack of ambition that allowed them to despise worldly goods. A hundred-odd years later, Shaw, whose linguistic armament and travel experience makes him a reasonably good source, tells us that the Arabs were a lazy lot: "he follows no regular trade or employment, his life is one continual round of idleness or diversion . . . he loiters at home, smokes his pipe, and reposes himself . . . he has no relish for domestic amusements and is rarely known to converse with his wife or to play with his children." Shaw insists that the Arab women were swarthy and homely, while the Berbers were light-skinned, and their women, beautiful—"at least until thirty years of age." Shaw decided that the Berbers (Kabylie tribes in this case) must be descended from the "ancient Africans"; their language was not Arabic, but rather another difficult tongue that must have come from a distant past. His account of his travels in North Africa, as well as in the Levant, provides an important interestingly written source for anyone seeking to understand those lands in the early eighteenth century.

What was the relationship between these people and the Turkish masters of Algiers? By the end of the sixteenth century, the regency government had established control over the port cities as well as the larger interior towns. The beys, supported by janissary garrisons, placed caids in the larger towns to assure their authority, but the countryside remained a problem. Lanfreducci, writing in the 1580s, explains: "The Turks have no sovereignty over the interior of Barbary except that some Arabian and Moorish chiefs are in accord and pay tribute as the price of peace . . . according to our information, they are profoundly dissatisfied . . . The Turk has put himself on their backs for big extortions . . ."[6] Two hundred years later Paradis informs us that the Kabylie had never really been under the Turks, and now even less so, since they now had firearms. The only way the Turks can seem to rule is by favoring one factor or clan against another.[7] In 1830, when Hocine Dey signed peace with the French, "he gave the victors only the city, the casaba, and forts. As a sovereign elected by foreign troops who imposed their choice on the Barbary coast, he did not have the power to dispose of the kingdom that was not an hereditary fief in his family . . ."[8] The Berber peoples in 1830 were sure that the military convention of July 5 had nothing to do with them.

This was the pattern throughout the history of the regency; the story is studded with revolts against Turkish rule, wars with the Kabylie or other tribes, sweeps of janissary troops to impose discipline. And, even so, in 1700 the French consul could write: "Is it possible that you do not know that the Moors (the Berber tribesmen were Moors to the French) from Bougie to Gigery [Djidjelli] recognize no domination, pay no taxes to Algiers, that the Turks do not dare set foot with their camps there, and when an Algerian ship wrecks [on that coast], they cut it to pieces and kill the crew?" D'Arvieux has a similar story: at Bougie there were one hundred and fifty janissaries, but the latter did not dare to leave the town in small numbers because the Moors would cut them off and give no quarter. Only on market days was there peace. The market held at the town gate was a place for truce—at least until noon, when it ended. Many of the consular accounts tell the same story: the pasha and later the dey could not really claim much authority over the tribesmen. Every year a contingent of janissaries made a "sweep" through the hinterland to collect "tribute"; it was almost always a disorderly action often accompanied by sharp violence. By the eighteenth century the

6. R.A. LXVI, p. 549.

7. R.A. XLI, 76–77.

8. L. Rinn, "Le royaume d'Alger sous le dernier dey," R.A. XLI, pp. 121–22.

Algerian regency had established "forts" or "blockhouses" along many of the more important routes, but even with this sort of military pressure, the Turkish authority was often, one might almost say usually, ignored unless it was supported by a strong contingent of troops.

The Turks did have a military advantage. In the sixteenth century the Moorish or Arab tribesmen did not yet have firearms: the pike and saber were no match for the more disciplined firepower of the janissaries. Masses of horsemen could be, and were, easily routed by determined volleys of the janissary muskets. In the seventeenth and eighteenth centuries, the tribesmen did get guns, but they still fought from their horses and still relied on undisciplined mass attacks. The Turks met them with fire from light artillery and usually were able to drive them off with considerable losses. This superior firepower, the establishment of fortifications on the highways, and the maintenance of garrisons in the beyliks made it possible for the regency government more or less regularly to collect tribute from the entire area, but not to interfere seriously with the lives of the tribes.

So brief an analysis of the social organization of the regency can cover only the surface of this complex story, but it should convey a picture of a society in which deep traditional social patterns of great diversity made it difficult, if not impossible, for any ruler to create a homogeneous community. Even the traditional Mohammedan religious order was not enough to give unity to a society in which so many diverse streams of blood and culture combined with primitive means of transportation and communication to negate the futile attempts of the Turkish overlords to give political unity to the society. The Algerian regency began as an imposition of power by an army of occupation over territory with a fantastically diverse political and social background. Since this ruling class of Levantines and renegades was never able to integrate the Berber and Arabic peoples scattered over mountain, plain, and desert into a homogeneous unit, with common words for good and evil and a common conception of social order, the regency reign retained throughout its history the character of an army of occupation rather than of a state.

VII *The Corsair Reis*

ORSAIRS OR PIRATES: what was the difference? The pirate was a freebooter, recognizing no rule above his own will; he attacked indiscriminately the ships of any nation; his sole object was loot. The corsair reis, on the other hand, were privateers; they made war only on the enemies of their prince or his god. Like the pirate's ship, the corsair's vessel usually was a private venture rather than a public charge, but the corsair carried a commission that legitimized his activities, and he disposed of his prizes in a manner regulated by his prince. In the sixteenth and early seventeenth centuries, when the Crescent stood opposed to the Cross in the Mediterranean and the Danubian basins, the corsairs fought either a crusade or a jihad. The Knights of St. John established themselves at Malta, the Knights of St. Stephen at Tuscany, and the Christian corsair-privateers commissioned by the viceroys of the Spanish king and the grand master at Malta fanned out in the eastern Mediterranean to capture commercial vessels and their passengers and crews. They made the sea unsafe for pilgrims as well as merchants who traveled the waters of the Levant, and they knew that their actions were justified by God. The same was true of the corsairs from North Africa, the Balkans, and the Levant who preyed on Christian commerce and ravaged the Christian coasts. Both the Bible and the Koran forbade piracy; both justified holy war, and obviously the Christian God and the Moslem Allah approved, for the corsairs were showered with wealth in this world as well as promises of salvation in the next. At the end of the sixteenth century when so-called round ships with tall sails—the *bertones* from the north—entered the Mediterranean, the fanaticism and greed of Protestant Europe was added to that of the Catholic and Moslem peoples of the Mediterranean basin, and it became sometimes difficult to know whether the raiders were corsairs or pirates. Though they might cloak their activity under a flag of religion or their prince, many of them were, in fact, simply pirates recognizing no law above their own will. In this history we are primarily interested in the activities and behavior of the men who flew the flag of Algiers, the green banner spangled with stars, but we should not forget that they were only one part of the corsair warfare that made travel in the Mediterranean hazardous for Christian and Mohammedan alike.

When we first think of the early Moslem corsairs, our minds leap to the vision of an Aroudj Reis, Kheir-ed-din Barbarossa, or Dragut who commanded flotillas of ten to twenty-five galiots, brigantines, fusts, and galleys so that their armadas could cover a large section of the sea and intercept any ships that might try to run through their nets. The earliest corsairs with whom this study had to deal, however, were men whose names mean little in the larger processes of history or even in the annals of their own community. They were the refugees from the Spanish mainland who refused to convert to Christianity. As we have seen, when they first arrived at the North African ports, there was little for them to do to support themselves. Some could find a place in the limited economy of the coast: they might set up workshops for the manufacture of arms, cloth, leather goods, or some other commodity that they had manufactured in Spain. Some became mercenaries in the service of sultans of Morocco or Fez, and some took to the sea as corsairs anxious to revenge themselves on their erstwhile oppressors. In the sixteenth century these men sailed frigates[1] similar to the ones they had known in Spain, powered by six to ten oarbanks with the oars pulled by the same men who fought the ship. Their victims were the small fishing vessels, the little coasters, the unimportant merchant ships carrying grain, wine, fruit, and cloth from one coastal port to another.

We have already seen that their depredations did not cause the Catholic kings to react vigorously until the first decade of the sixteenth century when Spanish armadas captured harbors on the North African coast and established presidios or peñons in the more important harbors from Valez to Tripoli to control the "pirates." These presidios probably prevented the petty corsairs from doing great damage to Spanish commerce for Spanish guns deprived them of the use of the best harbors on the coast. They might capture a fisherman or a small coaster or even raid a village, but they probably would have been little threat to important Spanish shipping inter-

1. The oar-driven frigate should not be confused with the eighteenth-century frigate that carried from twenty to forty guns and was powered by sail. The earlier one apparently provided the model for the hull of the latter.

ests. Even after Levantine corsairs joined the jihad with more powerful ships, these little frigates were not much more than an annoyance
to the rulers of the Spanish kingdoms. Haëdo tells us that as these
"small-time" corsairs became wealthy, they moved from their little
frigates to brigantines or even galiots, but his own list of the reis of
his day belies this assertion, for there were very few Tagarines or
Moudejares (Moors from Andalusia, Valencia, and Catalonia) among
the reis who commanded the important corsair vessels of Algiers.

When the Levantine corsairs appeared in the central and western
Mediterranean, a new situation developed. These men brought larger
ships, brigantines, and fusts with ten to sixteen oarbanks and more
powerful armament, and they were better trained in the arts of naval
warfare. They understood the use of artillery and the arquebus as
well as the bow and arrow and cold steel. Furthermore, in Aroudj
they had a leader whose daring was matched by his skill, as he
demonstrated very early in his career by the capture of two big
papal galleys. As his wealth grew, Aroudj and his brothers added
larger ships to their flotillas: galiots with twenty to twenty-two oarbanks that had power capable of matching the large galleys of the
Genoese or the Sicilian fleets. We have already noted that as his
fame spread eastward, it attracted other daring men to join him.
Many of them, like Aroudj himself, had done time at the oars of
Christian galleys (Knights of St. John) where they learned about sea
warfare; others were trained as subalterns of Aroudj and his brothers.
Some of the earlier reis may have been renegades; we do not have
good evidence about most of Aroudj's or even Kheir-ed-din's first companions. These early sixteenth-century corsairs, who knows whence
they came? The lives of the most famous are shrouded in mythology,
hero worship, or hatred, depending upon the source, so that no real
estimate of their origins can be made. However, by the latter sixteenth century, when Haëdo was in Algiers, renegades furnished
about two-thirds of the commanding personnel in the corsair flotilla;
twenty-two of the thirty-six reis commanding ships with more than
fifteen oarbanks were renegades. A closer look at them reveals that
many became renegades as children. This accounts for some renegade
reis. There were, however, others, like the famous Euldj Ali; he was
a galley slave who converted as a full-grown man in order to be able
to revenge himself by fighting a Turk who had insulted him. However, most of the men whom Haëdo and Dan saw in Algiers were an
international lot who hid their origins in myth and fable. We do
know that the renegades, while drawn from all over Western Eu-

Algiers and the bay from Cape Matifeu to Point Bescade. BELL LIBRARY, UNIVERSITY OF MINNESOTA

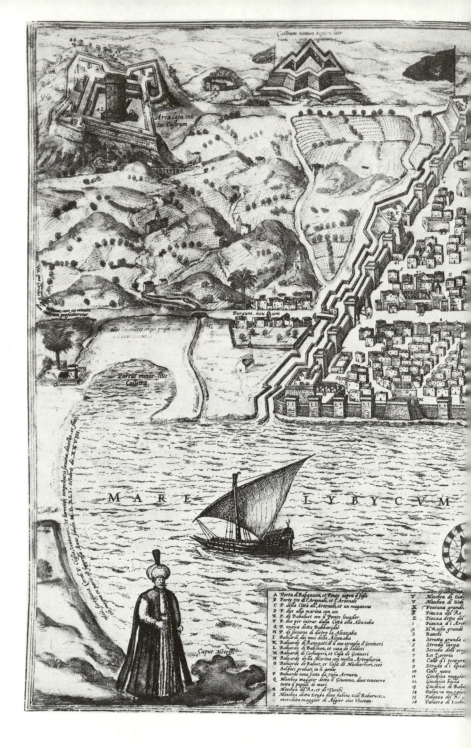

*Castrum nouu sept. late
rium nuncupatum.*

*Arca lata iux
ta Castrum*

Burgum nou Cum

*Portus minor siue
Caletta*

MARE · LYBYCVM

Caput Mõtelli

A Porta d'Babazzan, et Ponte sopra il fosso
B Porte tre d'l'Arsenale, et l'Arsenale
C P. della Città all'Arsenale, et un magazeno
D P. due alla marina con un
Z P. di Babaluet con il Ponte leuador
F P. che per intrar dalla Città alla Alcazaba
G P. nuoua detta Babbaxifit
H P. di soccorso di dietro la Alcazaba
I Baluardi dui nuoi della Alcazaba
K Baluardi de Renegati et a suo seraglio d'Genizeri
L Baluardo di Babason, et casa de Soldati
M Baluardo de Cochupzen, et Casa de Genizeri
N Baluardo de la Marina con molta Artegliaria
O Baluardo de Baduet, et Casa de Mocharzen, cui
Soldati probati in le armi
P Baluardo nouo fatto da yaya Arraes
Q Moschea maggior detta di Giumma, doue concorre
tutto il populo di mori
R Moschea di Re, et d'Turchi
S Moschea detta Reija doue habita zidi Babaruex,
moralita maggior di Algier cioe Vescouo.

T Moschea di Sidi
V Moschea di Sidi
X Fontana grande
Y Piazza del Re
Z Piazza detta del
1 Piazza di Arc
2 Il Rocho grande
3 Banchi
4 Strutta grande e
5 Strada delli serg
6 Strada della Gio
7 La Zereria
8 Calle d'i tentori
9 Strada d'i spata
10 Calle aqua
11 Giudecca maggior
12 Giudecca bassa
13 Giudecca di Babe
14 Piazza maggior
15 Palazzo del Re g
16 Palazzo di Luchi

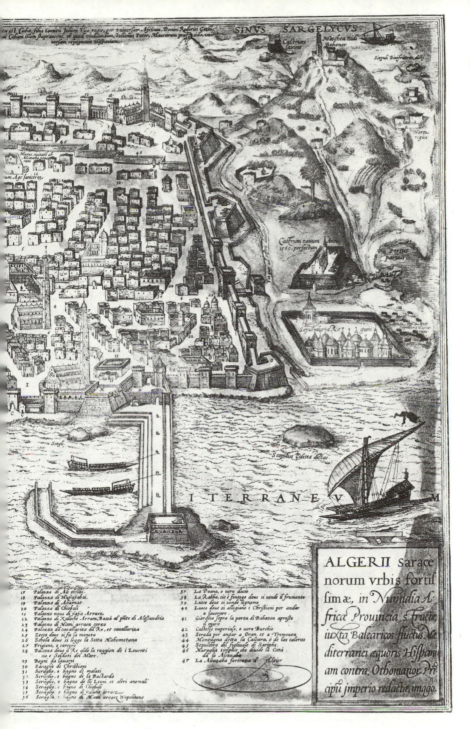

Algiers, a print from a German manuscript c. 1550. COLLECTION VIOLLET, PARIS

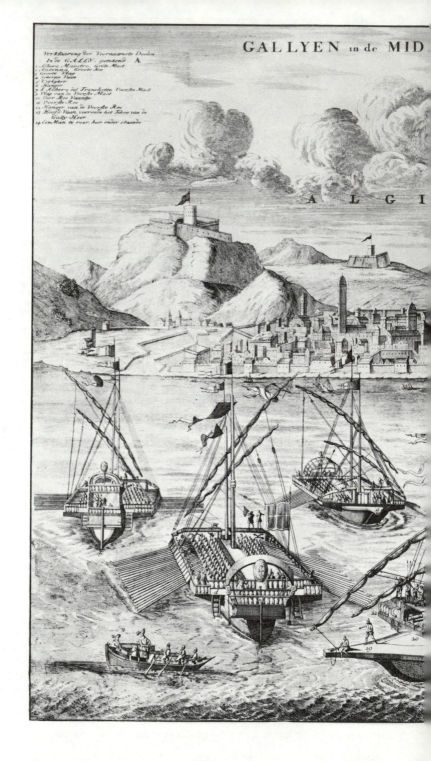

GALLYEN in de MID

ALGI

Verklaaring der Voornaamste Deelen in de GALLY, getekend **A**

ANDSE ZEE.

R S

Algiers, taken from a Dutch print of the early seventeenth century.
The war galleys in the foreground were still "capital ships" in 1600.
BIBLIOTHÈQUE NATIONALE, PARIS

A . t Kasteel vande Moelie
B . De Poort vande Moelie
C . De Nieuwe Batery
D . Het in komen vande Moelie
E . Poort van Babaisson
F . Poort van Babbaxilit
G . Poort van Babaluet
H . Het nieuwe Kasteel gemaeckt
      int Iaer 1569
I . Graf-steden der Koningen
K . Graf-steden
L . 2 Kastelen door de Spannyaers
      gemaeckt

ER

ASGIER .

Algiers, taken from a Dutch print of the early eighteenth century.
The ships with tall sails have become the dominant warships of this period.

Pedro Navarro.

Andrea Doria.

Kheir-ed-din Barbarossa.

Mezzo Morto Dey.

A brigantine, the standard corsair vessel of the sixteenth century.

A royal Spanish galley.

A polacre, typical French merchantman of the sixteenth through eighteenth centuries.

A pinque, Mediterranean merchant vessel occasionally used for corsair activity —both Christian and Moslem.

Warship of first class, early eighteenth century.

Tartane, widely used as merchantmen by all Mediterranean commercial agents.

Ultimo disegno delli forti di Malta uenuto nuouamente. Doue si vede la batturia che fanno li Turchi per li arteglieria posta In diuersi luoghi. Appresso si mostra il luogo de doue li Turchi hanno transportato li schifi e Barche per Terra in Mare, per dare l'asalto d'Jnpeouoso à San Michele, I come sono state Affondate dalli ss.ri Caualieri et soldati I si vede il porto di Malta musetti doue hoggi sta l'Armata del Turca segnata per lettera A. I se il tutto non è così limato, come si douria Imputase alli turbolenti tempi, che non lassano fare à quelli che sonno in malta (quali hanno mandato il disegno) le cose con quella Comodità che se recerca, et quello che si fà, tutto è, acciò li gentili spiriti habbino Continuo Cose nuoue:

Ant. Lafreri Romæ formis 1565 de mese Augusti:

Italian map illustrating the siege of Malta, 1565. NEWBERRY LIBRARY, CHICAGO

L a notte del vltimo di Febraro 1570 hauendo il motto Il sig. Don Alfonso Pimentel Capitani Gñal de la Goleta inteso per le sue spie, che Vsuali teneua xviij barchoni a la Porta di Tunise che risponde à la Goleta fabricati per venir con essi per lo stagno à leuarli l'acqua, et che teneua sopra la Porta di Tunise dui pezzi d'artegliaria, & cinquanta archibuggieri per guardia in detti barchoni, & un corpo di guardia de Turchi va li barchoni et lo stagno. Si risolse mandare xx. barche che tiene nella Goleta et metter dentro 300. archibuggieri Spagnoli con il nº de Castijo, Segura et il Cap. Salazar ordinando che il detto Capitano sbarcasse dui miglie discosto con 70 archibuger et che per una trauersa riconosciuta ben prima da S. S. assaltassero detti Turchi & mettessero foco à li barchoni et che per la diritta se retirassero poi 200. passi discosto dal loco doue ordinò che si trouassero le barche per riceuerlo, et che sbarcassero 40. archibugieri con l'alfiero per farli spalle al retirarse. la qual cosa successe felicem.te per che prima amazzorno le Zentinelle che loro fussero scoperti & appresso li Turchi de li barchoni et il Corpo di guardia & brugiorno detti barchoni & se retirorno senza perdita ne darno alcuno anzi per le medesime spie. s'è inteso poi che le palle de li moschettoni che sparorno li x. barcho-ni al partire con tutto che fusse à mezza notte colsero tutte nel Castello & amazzorono cinque homini, et sparandoli da la Città et Castello poi all'incontro molta artegliaria & archibugieria che tutta passò per aria.

Italian map illustrating Don Juan's capture of Tunis and La Goulette, 1573.
NEWBERRY LIBRARY, CHICAGO

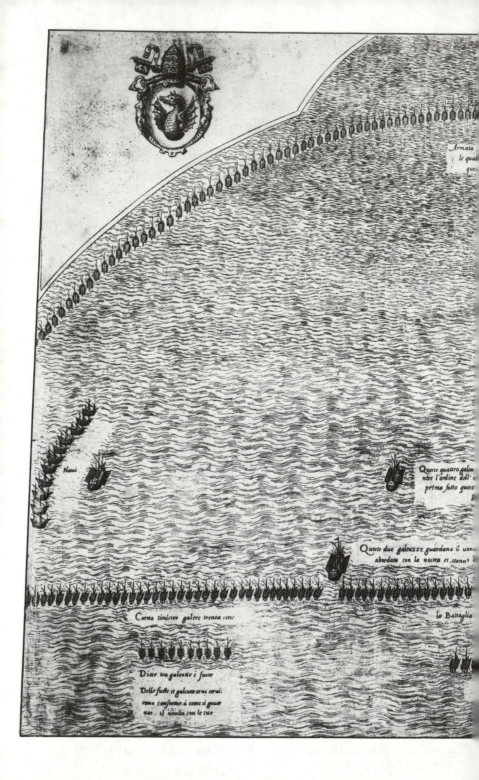

Armata
le qua
que

Queste quattro galee
ntre l'ordine dell'
prima fatto ques

Queste due galeazze guardano il uan
abordata con le nostra et stann°

Naui.

Corno sinistro galere trenta cette

la Battaglia

Dire tra galeotte e fuste

Delle fuste et galeotte ce ne serui:
remo conforme à come il gouer
nar . il nemico con le sue

Ora è col quale Ill. et ecc. S.r Marr'antonio colonna insieme con l'Ecc.mo General Venetiano, partirono dalle Gomenizze alli 29. di Luglio 1572. per caminar inazi à trouare, et combattere l'Armata Turchesca, la quale in numero di 140. galere si ritroua uerso Negroponte, come è stato referito da tre galere nostre, ch'erano ite innanzi à pigliar lingua. e quando si caminaua con quest'ordine, non era ancora arriuato il Ser.mo Sig.r don Giouanni d'Austria, il qual senza dublio sarà poi gionto à congiungersi col presato Sig.r Marcantonio alli 8. ouer 10. del presente d'Agosto. et alli 30 di Luglio doueuano unirsi 12. galere di quelle erano in Candie, le quali saranno ripartite à proportione nella bat-

taglia et nelli corni. Di modo che il S.r Marcantonio hauerà in tutto galere 140. Naui 22. galeazze 6. et 2. o tra fuste galeotte: Inomi et l'insigne dele g.li tutte, et de i S.ri Ca.ni che con sito medesimo ordine, sono stampati dagl'heredi d'Antonio La-fredi Stampator Generale

anta galere
mer

miglio. auanti per dissi:
et deurauno quanto
ro. et aiutare la

per fianco l'armata inimica mentre sta
quanto è due uolte lunga una galeaza

Naui

Corno destro galere trentasette

Diece tra galeotte è fuste

Roma ex Antonij Lafrary
formis MDLXXII

dadieri

Italian chart illustrating the first position of the battle of Lepanto.
NEWBERRY LIBRARY, CHICAGO

En! sculptor Naualis pugnæ ad Echinadas undas
Illustres acies, ut confluxere cruento
Marte simul. Desiderium que pagina possit
Tollere multorū dum gesta hic omnia cernit.
Describant numerū hec singula rite poete.
Historici pangant, et magna uolumina artis
Cūcts tamē satis hec parua tabella resignat.
Extitit Octobris Nonis victoria parta
Diuino nutu quam fecit dextera Christi.
Quando fuit Millenus, Quingentesimus annus
Septuagenus item primus, descendit olympo
Aluo virgineo Verbum sine labe pudoris.
Fædere coniunctæ Trinæ certamine classes
Turcarum Sostilem superant, captiuis trucidat.
Austriadæ Eximiæ primo Ductore Ioanne
Catholici iussu uenit Qui Regis Iberi.
Pontifici, Pij Quintū pro parte Columna
Te, Marce Antoni, columē qui hoc tēpore certū
Romulidum et veterum cui iam debet honores.
Tertius inde fuit Ductor Venerius, Alma
Vrbs virgo Adriacæ misit letissima ab undis.
Aeterno Elogio hoc uestra sit laude dicatum.

Martinus Rota sibinicensis Venetijs faciebat.

Italian picture of battle of Lepanto during the melee. NEWBERRY LIBRARY,
CHICAGO

rope, were preponderantly from the Mediterranean basin; on the other hand, those corsair reis who were born Moslems, came from Egypt, Albania, Anatolia, and the islands of the eastern Mediterranean. Very few of them were of Turkish ethnic origin. We do not know how many ships were in the sixteenth-century corsair navy at any given time. Aroudj Reis started with three or four small fusts; by 1510 he had nine to eleven fusts and brigantines belonging to him and his brothers, and another six to eight belonging to reis who had come to place themselves under his command. He also had some artillery, but these guns were of small caliber quite unable to batter down the walls of the presidios of Bougie or Algiers. Some twenty years later, in 1529, when Kheir-ed-din did have artillery heavy enough to take the Algerian presidio, tradition has it that he commanded eighteen "stout galiots" as well as a number of smaller vessels. In the four decades or so during which the Algerian flotilla operated as a part of the Ottoman navy (1535–78) the corsair squadron seems to have been composed of fifteen or so galiots and small galleys, but in that same period there also was a steady flow of commerce raiders operating out of Algiers and other ports under the beylerbey of North Africa. Since some of these ships belonged to the beylerbey and some to other reis rather than to the government of the regency or the sultan, it is not clear how their owners were recompensed when they sailed with the Ottoman naval establishment. Euldj Ali, who commanded the corsair squadron at Lepanto, not only escaped the holocaust of the battle in possession of the great battle flag of the Knights of St. John (Malta) but was rewarded with the highest post in the Ottoman navy. Presumably he and his reis were also well paid for their services.

After Euldj Ali's death, the corsair flotilla did not decay. Haëdo tells us that in 1581 it contained thirty-six galiots and brigantines, plus numerous smaller vessels. These numbers, however, are fragile; many of the smaller ships and occasionally a larger one were "snapped up" by Spanish or Maltese warships, and all of them suffered from the hazards of wind, weather, and natural decay.

This sixteenth-century corsair fleet was composed of oar-powered galiots, brigantines, frigates, chebecks (zebecs), or other smaller ships.[2] These oar-driven vessels continued in use until the end of

2. The names of ship types often will create confusion. Some of them like the chebeck, caravalle, and frigate were originally small oar-powered vessels, but in the seventeenth and eighteenth centuries their hulls provided models for sailing ships of considerable size. All three of the above were to be transformed into vessels carrying thirty or more cannons, two to three tall masts, and broad sails.

the eighteenth century, but on the turn of the seventeenth century they became a minor part of the Algerian armada, for around 1600 the northerners began to teach them to use the "bertone" and other versions of the round ship that had been developed in Europe.

Père Dan, in the fourth decade of the seventeenth century, counted only two galiots (twenty-four and twenty-two oarbanks), one brigantine with fifteen oarbanks, and eight small frigates (five to six). His count however, must have been faulty, for when the Venetians surprised the Algerian and Tunisian fleets at Valona on the Albanian coast a few years later, they captured four and sank twelve galiots and two brigantines. We do not know how many of them were Algerians, but the Tunisian contingent was small and the Algerian admiral's losses were said to be great. The Algerian corsairs continued to use the galiots and smaller oar-powered vessels, but their number and their size declined. In the eighteenth century the largest was an eighteen-oarbank galiot while most of them had less than ten oarbanks. These latter were obviously commanded by the heirs to the earliest tradition of the Algerian corsair community, descendants of the refugees from Spain who took to the sea for revenge. They preyed upon the small coasters and fishing vessels that could not stand up to their one to three small cannons or prevent the janissaries from boarding when the corsair closed on its victim. The dangerous corsair reis were those commanding the sail-driven ships carrying from twenty to forty cannons.

The good priest may have miscounted the number of oar-powered vessels, but his estimate of seventy heavily armed, sail-powered ships corresponds reasonably well with the figures supplied by the English and French consuls and the English ambassador to Spain. In the next decade, the 1640s, the corsair fleet probably reached its greatest development. The Algerians ranged the Mediterranean from the Adriatic to the Straits; they broke through to the Atlantic and operated from the Canary Islands to Newfoundland's fishing banks. They landed and took prisoners and loot from Ireland, England, Denmark, Portugal, and Spain. The fleet was a far cry from the tiny flotilla that Aroudj brought to North Africa at the opening of the preceding century.

We have a good deal more information about this Algerian fleet after 1660, when both the English and the French rulers ordered their consuls to supply invoices of the potential enemies whenever they contemplated sending a naval squadron against Algiers. These consular lists, however, do have some problems. The French nearly always estimated the number of men aboard any one ship much larger than did the English, nor do the two always agree on the number of cannons carried by each ship. One other problem emerged from the fact that the Europeans persisted in naming the Algerian vessels by the picture on the rear deck; this provided colorful names: *Lyon, Two Antelopes, Orange Tree, Seven Stars, Pine Tree, Red Rose, Golden Sun,* and the like. These were not the names used by the Algerians, and there is some evidence to suggest that the same ship might carry different pictures at different times. Another problem arises from the designation of ships by the number of guns, but usually no indication of the caliber. Thus it is hard to judge the firepower of these ships rated twenty, thirty, or sixty guns. We do know that the English admiralty must have had better information, for the English expeditions to Algiers usually had no ships larger than third-raters. This reinforces the assumption that most of the cannons were five- or six-pounders; one account for 1663 does tell us that the fleet had over five hundred guns, but not more than twenty were nine-pounders or heavier. We also do not know what percentage of the Algerian guns were bronze (*fonte*) and what of iron; the former were much to be preferred. The consular reports before 1737 also do not consistently list the number of pierriers[3] on the ships, but there is good evidence that at least until the middle of the eighteenth century, these lighter weapons outnumbered the cannons.

The French consular lists of the actual embarcations of the corsair vessels for the years following 1737 provide us with precious information about the size of the ships as well as the armament. The majority of the embarcations were ships carrying less than sixteen cannons, and only for a very few years at the midcentury were there any ships with more than thirty. Furthermore, the ships carrying between sixteen and thirty cannons were almost always caravelles, chebecks, or, later, frigates: all ships with shallow draft, sleek lines, and two to three masts to carry a maximum of sail. In the mid-eighteenth century, and again during the great wars of 1792–1815, the regency acquired a few ships carrying fifty to sixty cannons. One of them, the *Dantzik* (58), was obviously either a capture or a gift, but the *Gazelle* (50) and the *Chateau* (50) were built at Algiers. Curiously enough these ships were either lost or retired after very few years of service, while the chebecks, sixteen to thirty cannons,

3. As the name suggests, the pierrier launched a stone projectile; the naval pierrier was usually mounted on the railing of the vessel and was used to repel boarders or sweep enemy decks; by the seventeenth century, iron projectiles had for the most part replaced the ones of stone.

remained in use for years. Another fact that emerges from these consular records is that small oar-powered ships, mostly with less than twelve oarbanks, continued in use throughout the eighteenth century. There were often only two galiots with sixteen or eighteen oarbanks, and four to six smaller vessels, some with as few as six oarbanks. Their firepower was low and obviously not intended to confront either a warship or a well-armed merchantman; they were the classical "pirate" or "corsair" ships that the Mediterranean had seen for hundreds of years.[4]

If the armament of the corsair vessels was relatively weak, the numbers of men aboard were always large. The twenty- to forty-gun corsairs would normally carry from 300–450 men—sometimes more. The "marines" were normally janissaries who signed up for the cruise for a share in prize money; the ships also usually carried several men capable of piloting a captured ship back to Algiers and extra sailors to help them manage it. On several occasions when the corsairs did not have enough men to bring in a capture and the Christian sailors were forced to help manage the ship, the latter overpowered their captors and "rescued" themselves and their ship. Such "mishaps" taught caution and the need for a large crew. But the largest contingent on any corsair vessel was made up of janissaries, who, with cutlass or pistol, supported by their fellows with fusils or pierriers, were expected to storm aboard any ship that had the temerity to resist. Most of the merchantmen who could not run away from the corsairs were wise enough not to allow this dangerous contingency to develop. When it did, the fighting was rude and vicious; those who lived through a boarding by the Algerian corsairs never forgot the experience.

All this leads to a conclusion that we naturally would expect: namely, that the Algerian fleet was built for commerce raiding rather than for confrontation with other warships. There were very few years between 1600 and 1830 that the Algerians had any ships with more than forty cannons, while the classic Algerian raider was a caravelle or a chebeck of eighteen to thirty cannons. These ships were even more maneuverable than the frigates that were the classic

4. The French consular archives in Algiers contained lists of the corsair vessels that applied for passes and copies of the passports that French merchantmen were supposed to carry to avoid capture. The documentation for the years 1737–1827 is a bit sterile, but it does contain the number of ships embarking each year and usually both the type of vessel and the number of cannons it carried, so that some valuable information can be culled from it. Albert Devoulx, "La marine de la régence d'Alger," R.A., 77, pp. 384–420.

eighteenth-century privateers operating out of Le Havre, Dunkirk, Liverpool, or Boston. When these raiders were used as warships, the Algerians often suffered heavy losses. For example, in the 1680s after the Turks were driven back from Vienna, a new Holy Alliance— the Holy Roman Emperor, Venice, Poland, and Russia—confronted the Ottomans at the Danube and the Morea. The Sublime Porte appealed for help, and the Algerians responded by sending nearly all their warships and by building five more: two with forty guns, one with thirty, one with twenty-four, and one with sixteen. When they engaged in battle with the Venetians, their losses were severe, and included their biggest vessels. The English consul saw this as "the common end of all illgotten gains!" Again in the early nineteenth century, when the Greek rebellion harassed the Sublime Porte, Algerian contingents were sent to the Aegean, and again suffered serious losses.

As we have already noted, the Algerian navy was an affair for "private enterprise" during most of its history. The ships were owned by the reis or by wealthy moneymen in the city either as individuals or as a corporation of shipowners, who pooled their money. The dey or pasha might also be an owner, but in his own name as a private investor rather than as representing the state. The pasha, agha, dey, and divan did have a measure of control over the navy in that they regulated the sharing of the profits, gave commissions, attempted to force the reis to obey treaties, and required the owners to replace any ship that was lost for whatever cause. They also might order the reis to go to the aid of the sultan—after 1650—on payment of a subsidy by the Porte. The reis also was held responsible by the regency government for the ship at sea. If he failed to take a prize by reason of cowardice or serious mismanagement, the dey or pasha could order punishment that might include bastinading. If he lost a ship, he had to have a satisfactory explanation; even so famous a captain as Hamidou Reis was put on trial and escaped only when he could produce a chart showing that the anchorage where he had lost his ship to a storm was indeed marked as a suitable anchorage. Without this he might have suffered severely. In the eighteenth century this pattern of ownership was changed; the dey's government became more stable and gradually the deylik (or the dey and his ministers) assumed ownership of most of the corsair vessels and placed them under a minister of marine. In 1717, of the nineteen ships in service (not including the small oar powered vessels), only one belonged to the republic. At the end of the century almost the entire fleet was owned by the deylik, the dey, and his "powers"; it was controlled by the minister of marine.

There were many reasons for this change, but most important of all was the decline in the profitability of the corsair cruise. After the War of the Spanish Succession, with the British firmly established in the Mediterranean at Gibraltar, Vico Bay, and Mahon, and the French bases at Toulon and Marseille, it became unsafe to attack English or French commerce, while the Dutch and some of the lesser trading nations bought immunity from attack by tribute in the form of money or naval supplies. Even the young republic of the United States of America signed a treaty (1795) that provided for tribute to Algiers. This left precious little for the corsair reis to capture. Undoubtedly as a direct result there was a sharp decline in the quality of the men who could command. Fewer renegades capable of commanding a naval vessel appeared at Algiers, and since the Turks did not develop a merchant marine of any consequence, few natives of the regency were trained to command. Naturally under such conditions, private capital did not find investment in corsair cruises to be so profitable; the dey and his government apparently had no serious difficulty in taking over complete control. But let us return to the problems of the corsairs in the heroic periods of their activity.

Where did the corsairs get their ships? Aroudj and his brothers and probably most of their lieutenants sailed ships built in the Levant and the same may have been true for most of the ships that Kheir-ed-din owned when he captured the Spanish presidio in the Algerian harbor. By the mid-sixteenth century, however, there were shipyards in Algiers that could build a galiot of twenty-two oarbanks, and in yards in the smaller ports fusts, pinks, and other small ships were constructed. Like warships of any period, the larger vessels reflected the best technical achievements of the society, but in this case the "society" was perhaps more European than Algerian. A closer look at the actual ship construction shows us that the master craftsmen, the laborers, and perhaps even the ship architects were either renegades or slaves who learned their trade on the northern coast of the Mediterranean. This is not surprising. The Turks and Moors were not usually seafaring people, the janissaries were largely recruited from peasant families rather than from fisherfolk, but the men captured in raids on Christian soil and commerce were nearly all sons of seagoing fathers. We learn that the reis had an important input into the process of construction, for they knew what was expected from a corsair's ship, and here again, the renegades were important, for as we have seen, a surprisingly large percentage of the reis were renegades.

Part of the wood for the ships had to be imported into Algiers from Bougie, Cherchell, or one of the other small North African harbors where timber was available; the rest was "salvaged" from prize ships that were not serviceable as raiders but had wood already shaped for ship construction. The sails, cordage, pitch, tar, and other necessary supplies came from many sources. The refugees from Spain brought many skills that were useful and the Levant continued to supply naval and military stores. In the sixteenth century, after France's entente with the Ottoman empire, French merchants smuggled or openly imported these supplies into the North African ports in open defiance of the papal prohibition, and, in the seventeenth century, English and Dutch merchants competed for this trade. After the mid-seventeenth century, treaties with the Dutch and with many of the lesser princes or city-states provided for "gifts" of masts, sail, cannon balls, cannons, cordage, and other such merchandise in return for immunity from attack. If consular reports are correct, masts constituted the biggest problem: there were no considerable forest areas in North Africa that could supply suitable masts, so they had to come from either the Levant or European sources. Cannons first came from the Levant, then the French and Dutch supplied them, and finally, with French aid, cannon foundries in Algiers also provided these weapons.

From the sixteenth to the eighteenth centuries, there was one common observation about the Algerian corsair ships: the galiots as well as the ships with tall sails were built for speed and easy maneuverability. They could overtake Christian merchantmen, or they could run away from Christian warships.[5] The only easy way to get at the corsairs was to catch them in the harbor and destroy them there. The corsair ships were always built with as shallow a draft as possible, with sleek lines, no unnecessary decorations, and on models of easily maneuvered ships. Their bottoms were scraped often and the ship was maintained in excellent shipworthy condition. The caravelle, modeled on the Arabic *chabbak,* the frigate, which became almost the "standard" privateer of the eighteenth century, modeled

5. The Intendant at Toulon wrote to Colbert: "It is not the fault of our ships that they do not sail as well as those of the Turkish corsairs, but the difference is that ours are loaded with cannons, victuals and baggage; instead, these barbarians use light artillery, carry only six to eight weeks' supplies and no baggage. Thus French captains, even though very good, cannot compete with these robbers." Delarbre, *Tourville,* p. 13.

on the Italian *fregata,* and others like the brigantine were all adopted from small craft that evolved in earlier periods, some from oar-powered, others from sailing vessels. The ships with tall sails were usually armed with eighteen to forty guns of relatively small caliber. At several periods, however, when there was a general war in Europe, 1688–1715, 1744–63, 1793–1814, we find the Algerians with warships of fifty to sixty guns. Some of them were built at Algiers, several were captured Portuguese, Danzig, Venetian vessels,[6] but these were not all as useful for commerce raiding as the smaller more maneuverable chebecks or caravelles. Another characteristic was the spare cargo space; the corsairs carried a minimum amount of supplies and, in contrast to some European warships, no space for the captain to smuggle merchandise for sale. It is not surprising that these raiders earned a reputation for excellent seamanship even if their ability to "slug" out a battle with a third or fourth rater was something less than effective.

When a vessel in the Algerian shipyards was ready to come off the ways, there was a celebration: everybody, from the master architect to the lowest slave laborer joined in a feast of lamb and the "trimmings" (undoubtedly couscous) usual for the period, to the accompaniment of trumpets and drums and speeches. When the ship was ready to sail, its reis hoisted his flag and his scribe enrolled the volunteers and the crew. If the ship was a galiot, the slaves would belong to the reis, to the shipbuilders, to the dey, or even to private patrons who "rented them out" for the voyage. There were elaborate rituals connected with the departure and the return of the corsairs. Since the Koran forbade piracy, every show of piety possible was necessary, particularly after the "holiness" of the corsair raids had long since become a minor aspect of the total activity. The reis usually consulted his favorite marabout to see if the omens were good, and to ask for divine assistance. The blood of a sheep was poured over the prow of the ship to recall that it was on a jihad voyage to kill Christians. As the ship sailed out of the harbor past the shrine of a very holy marabout, the flags dipped and the reis said a prayer. When the vessel returned victorious, either towing or sailing in its wake captured vessels with their flags inverted, the guns of the ship and those of the harbor and the mole thundered salutes. Then with drum and trumpet the victors paraded through

6. One Algerian frigate was the gift (tribute) from the young republic of the United States. The Algerians wanted to buy at least one other one, but President Jefferson stopped the sale.

the town with their newly captured slaves and loot to present themselves to the pasha or the dey. Christians writing about these activities tell us of the shockingly superstitious practices of these quasipirate reis; they were surely correct, for in these years the sea was still largely not understood and their ships were fragile before its terrors. Christians as well as Moslems called on their God and His saints for protection and sent prayers and incense to heaven to thank Him for His favors.

Once at sea the reis was in command; it mattered not that he might be a negro or even a Moor, his word was absolute. The agha high in the janissary hierarchy or a slave at the bottom of the social scale were both bound to respect his authority. The complement of officers aboard included a second in command, a pilot, a navigator, a surgeon, a scribe to keep the log and to invoice the prizes, a master of the hatch, and a crew of sailors to manage the sails and help run the vessel. The military personnel of the ship included an agha and his lieutenant to command the volunteers, and a master cannoneer and his assistants to handle the guns. When the ships with tall sails came to carry twenty or more guns, the men who fired them assumed a larger role in the crew. Several accounts tell us that the sailors were often renegades or slaves, and indeed, several of the treaties with the naval powers contained an article forbidding the forcing of an English or French slave into the role of sailor, which suggests that it was not an unusual practice. Slaves and renegades were more likely to have had experience at sea than the Anatolian or Syrian peasant boys in the militia. These latter were volunteers; they enrolled for the cruise with the expectation of sharing in the prize money along with the other personnel of the ship.[7]

The corsair ships carried only the most necessary supplies. On the galleys both the slaves and the volunteers were fed biscuits, vinegar, and oil, but the latter were allowed to supplement that diet by

7. The scale for division of the profits of a cruise is instructive. In the 1630s the pasha took 12 percent in Algiers, 10 percent in Tunis, the repairs for the mole 1 percent; the marabout, 1 percent. Of the remaining 88 or 86 percent, half went to the shipowners, and the other half to the crew and soldiers. Of the second half the reis received 10–12 parts, the agha 3 parts, the janissaries each 2 parts, master cannoneers 3 parts, other cannoneers 2 parts, the pilot 3 parts, navigator 3 parts, sail master 3 parts, master of the hatch 2 parts, surgeon 3 parts, sailors 2 parts; if there were Moors aboard, they were given only 1 part "because they are people on whom one does not count much." If any of these people were slaves, the patron took their shares and sometimes gave part of it to the slaves. (Père Dan, pp. 265–266.) Dan's account of the division corresponds approximately with those of other informants. See Albert Devoulx, "Le régistre des prises maritimes," R.A. XV, 70–77; XVI, 146–159.

bringing their own supplies of dried fruit, cheese, and other food in their baggage. The crews of the sailing vessels were issued about the same diet that was given to the galley slaves, but, like the volunteers, they were allowed to supplement this on their own. The volunteers on the galleys slept on the same benches with the slaves, but were allowed to move more freely when the ship was cruising or at anchor. The janissaries on both galleys and sailing ships were armed with scimitars and daggers; spears, firearms, bows, and arrows were locked in special closets and issued only when the corsair closed on a victim or had to fight an armed foe.

As much as possible, the corsair reis wisely avoided conflicts that might damage his ship or reduce his crew.[8] They often flew flags of the northern nations until they managed to come close enough to a victim so that resistance was impossible. When they did have to fight, they closed with trumpets blowing, clashing of arms, salvos of cannon, or pierrier fire, and shouts of "Yield, Dogs, Yield!" Most of the engagements were soon over. In many cases when the victim was sailing close to the coast—as was the custom for much of the traffic in the Mediterranean—the crew of the ship simply dived overboard to save themselves from capture. The French consuls' accounts are filled with stories of ships brought into port with no crews: if the ship was captured in the Atlantic, there often was a suggestion that the crew had been murdered; in the Mediterranean, it was almost sure that the crew had escaped by swimming. Whatever might have happened, from all that we can learn, it is not surprising that seafaring peoples of these early centuries feared the corsairs as they feared the devil, perhaps even more so, since some of them had seen the corsairs in action and others had been slaves in the Maghrib, while few had ever seen the king of hell.

As the rising power of English, French, and even Dutch naval forces made capturing nationals of those states hazardous, treaties with Algiers provided for passports of one kind or another. This meant that a boarding party had to be sent to check the passenger list and cargo of ships stopped at sea. Since many of the corsairs, indeed most, could not read European languages, the usual practice was to compare the number of lines, and the length of lines in the

---

8. They were not always so wise. The English consul Martin wrote in November 1675, that the dey's son had been made admiral and given command of a new ship, *The Golden Horse*. Cruising with five other corsairs, he met a Portuguese man-of-war and closed for a fight. The Portuguese escaped capture and in the process killed about four hundred Turks and Moors and properly "banged" the corsair ships. The dey's son was removed from his position and Canary reis was made admiral. PRO. Sp 71–1, fol. 89.

passport with the copy provided by the consul at Algiers. But this did not always satisfy the corsairs: they had the right to take the passengers who were nationals of their enemies as slaves and their goods as contraband if they could prove that they actually were enemies and enemy goods. The only condition was that the corsair must pay the freight of the goods that he confiscated. There were many unfortunate results: the corsair would try to force the crew to point out enemy passengers, and they would use any method, including violence, to prove that the cargo was in fact enemy owned. Both the corsairs and the European consuls in Algiers had many headaches; the seamen often accused the corsairs of violence, torture, bastinadoing, and the like; the corsairs insisted that the captains hid the truth. The English and French rulers felt that the honor of their flags was involved, but there was no easy solution. One further problem: the corsairs often were flying flags not their own, but this was also true of the pirates from Salé.[9] A tough-minded captain did not want to wait until it was too late to determine whether the ship that approached him was from Algiers or Salé, and often enough, when he could hope for success, the merchantman would open fire. This of course was forbidden by treaty, and if the merchantman could not beat off the corsair, the act of defense cost the captain and his crew both liberty and ship.

We have already met some of the most famous of the heroic sixteenth-century reis: Aroudj, Kheir-ed-din, Dragut, Euldj Ali. These men with their friends and lieutenants established the regencies of Algiers, Tunis, and Tripoli as corsair communities and gave them their political and military characteristic forms. But the actual command of the swarms of corsair vessels was usually in the hands of men less well known than the ones who became beylerbeys and admiral pashas in the sultan's service. One of the more famous of these was Morat Reis (Morato Arraes), an Albanian renegade, who first went to sea under Kara Ali and rose to command a squadron under Euldj Ali at the time of the siege of Malta. His capture of a Sicilian galley with the duke of Terranova, captain general of Sicily, on board, and a little later, a papal galley, made him a hero among his peers. His most daring adventure, however, was to take a squad-

9. Salé was a "pirate republic" located on the Moroccan coast. It was governed by a board of fourteen captains with a president who held the rank of admiral. The community was made up almost entirely of Dutch and English seamen; its ships operated in both the Mediterranean and the North Atlantic throughout the seventeenth and part of the eighteenth centuries. (Antonio R. de Armas, *Piraterias y ataques*, vol. III, p. I, pp. 59 ff.) There are other accounts of the community of Salé, and many contemporary references to its activities.

ron of four galiots through the Straits to Salé, where he was joined
by three pirate captains, and then on to the Canaries. The corsairs
sacked Lanzarote, captured the wife and daughter of the governor
and hundreds of people of lesser importance. After a cruise around
the islands and several further landings for more booty and
prisoners, they hoisted a flag for parley and allowed the ransom of
their more important captives. The rest were carried back to Algiers or Salé as slaves. The Spanish, forewarned of the corsairs' return, tried to intercept them at the Straits, but Morat Reis successfully evaded Don Martin de Padilla's armada in a storm and
brought his little flotilla into Algiers. It was a daring raid made more
daring since the galiot was not really a suitable vessel for the Atlantic. Christians liked to believe that God punished Morat Reis by
causing his son to die just before his return, but the story, told in
the testimony about the raid made before the Inquisition, may not
be completely correct.

Other corsair reis were less fortunate. Once captured by the
Spanish there was no question of ransom; if he was a renegade,
he usually was either hanged or burned. Occasionally a Mustapha
Armaud, who was in prison in Naples for twenty years, and fourteen of his fellow reis, did manage to free themselves (1591) probably
with the aid of fellows who had slipped into Naples disguised as
Christian sailors. They broke out of prison, stole a small ship, captured a larger one, and made for Biserta. Their exploit was so rare
that it became folklore.

Many of the renegade corsair captains had checkered careers. We
will see Simon Danser return safely to Christendom only to create
new problems by his gift to the duc de Guise of the two cannons
belonging to the Algerian regency. Suleiman Reis, from La
Rochelle, found salvation and a chance to continue his career by
becoming a Knight of St. John (Malta). The English pirates Ward,
Samson, and Edward earned the right to live splendidly in Algiers
by their prizes and by teaching the other reis to sail the tall ships that
could easily brave the Atlantic.[10]

10. As we have noted, many of the reis as well as their lieutenants were
renegades, and their fate was grim if they were captured. At sea they usually
shared the fate of the English renegade lieutenant of the *Halfmoon* captured
by the English *Sapphire* in the summer of 1681: he was summarily hanged.
(Clowes, *The Royal Navy*, II, p. 457.) The Inquisition in Italy and Spain
burned renegades; no treaty would stop this for it "does not obey the king; its
jurisdiction cannot be limited . . . by treaty." (Marcel Emerit, "Une Marchande
marine barbaresque au XVIII siècle," *Cahiers de Tunisie*, III, p. 364.) It is
small wonder that renegade reis were unwilling to become captains of a
merchant vessel that might touch at a European port.

The richest and the most famous of the corsairs who spanned the great period of Algerian activity (c. 1630–60) was undoubtedly Ali Bitchnin. We met him in other chapters of this book, but he deserves more attention than we can give him. He was an Italian, some say a Venetian, named Piccinio, who arrived in Algiers in command of a pirate ship that he had sailed from the Adriatic; he converted to Islam and quickly rose to prominence in the taiffe through his daring and bravery. His prizes made him rich, and he reinvested in new corsair vessels until his own flotilla earned him the title of admiral of Algiers. He owned two palaces in the city, a villa in the suburbs, several thousand slaves, jewels, plate, and great wealth in merchandise. He built a sumptuous public bath and a great mosque in Algiers as a gift to the city. He had his own bodyguard of footmen as well as cavalry, recruited mostly from the Koukou tribesmen whose sultan became his father-in-law. In the 1630s the redemptionist fathers writing from Algiers looked to him rather than the pasha as the real ruler of the city. Francis Knight, who was one of his slaves, called him a great "tyrant" who respected no man, not even the Grand Seigneur. However, not all his slaves regarded their lot as "exquisitely miserable" or their master as a tyrant. One story tells of a Mohammedan fanatic who, wishing to gain paradise by killing a Christian, begged Bitchnin for the privilege of killing one of his slaves. The corsair agreed but armed a muscular young man with a sword and then invited his petitioner to meet him in an orchard; when he fled, Ali Bitchnin laughed derisively at him. Another slave returned a diamond that he had "found"; Bitchnin remarked about the folly of not taking advantage of a chance for freedom!

Ali Bitchnin probably had ambitions to usurp control over the regency. His alliance with the sultan of Koukou, his bodyguard of hundreds of soldiers, his personal navy, his relations with the coulougli leaders all point to political ambitions. He suffered a serious reverse at Valona, where he lost eight galleys (Knight secured his freedom from him in that battle; he was a slave on board of one of the ships that was captured) and two thousand slaves. A few years later, when the sultan planned an assault on Malta, Ali Bitchnin refused to allow the Algerian naval forces to go unless the sultan would pay a subsidy in advance. The Sublime Porte sent a *chaouch* (messenger or emissary) to Algiers to secure Ali Bitchnin's head; both the chaouch and the pasha had to flee to a mosque to escape the wrath of the corsair admiral's followers. At that point, however, the pasha refused to pay the janissaries' salary, and the corps demanded that Ali Bitchnin provide the money. Apparently, he had not yet prepared his men for a coup. He fled to his father-in-law's territory, and the janissaries sacked his city homes as well as the Jewish quarter. What would happen next? The Sublime Porte obviously feared that Ali Bitchnin might return to Algiers with a Kabylie army; it sent him money, pardon, and honors just short of making him the pasha, but when he returned to Algiers with the sultan's chaouch, he soon sickened and died. His funeral was celebrated with near royal pomp, but many suspected that he had been poisoned on the sultan's orders.

Another reis, Beker Bacha, who appeared in the canonization papers for St. Vincent de Paul, was well known for his gluttony and drunkenness, his cruel and vindictive behavior, his mistreatment of his slaves, his torturing and bastinadoing of those who displeased him. Or at least that was the record that comes down to us. Our informant was obviously pleased to announce that Beker Bacha was shipwrecked, and at the very moment that he believed himself to be saved, he was struck by a wave with a big piece of wood in which there was an iron "cheville": "He had employed wood, iron and water to kill Christians, and God employed wood, iron, and water to kill him. When he died a great number of crows—perhaps devils in disguise—threw themselves on his corpse but did not touch the great number of other bodies that were on the shore." Patently many of the corsair reis had an unsavory reputation in the Christian community—some of these may have been deserved.[11]

Perhaps the last of the great corsair captains was Hamidou Reis, whose career spanned the wars of the French Revolution and Napoleon. Unlike most successful corsairs, he was neither renegade nor Turk; the son of a Moorish tailor, he went to sea as a cabin boy and, by intelligence and bravery, worked himself up to be captain and finally admiral of the entire Algerian navy. His career had its ups and downs. Once, he lost a chebeck belonging to the dey; another time, he was on the wrong side of a political upset, but each time his luck was with him, and he managed to land on his feet. His most spectacular capture was that of a Portuguese frigate, which was renamed *El Portikiza* and, when joined with *El Merikana*[12] (The American) and his own vessel, gave him a squadron of three forty-four gun frigates that were, in fact, the most dangerous Algerian naval flotilla that had been seen for over half a century. His

11. A.N., K1334, No. 6.
12. This ship was a "gift" from the young republic of the United States.

prizes and the captives that he made by landing marines on the coasts of Portugal, Sicily, Naples, and the islands of the Mediterranean made him fabulously rich and respected. One memoirist after another tells us that he had charm as well as intelligence and bravado. He was lucky that his career coincided with the disorders of the era of Revolution and of Napoleon when it became difficult for the naval powers to keep order, but he seems to have been a man of considerable genius who would have made a mark in any case. His end came quickly in 1815. The young republic of the United States had a treaty with Algiers signed in 1795 by which the United States paid tribute in return for the safe conduct of its ships, but when Thomas Jefferson refused to continue the tribute, Yankee commerce offered fat prizes and since there was no U.S. navy available at the moment, the Algerians only partly kept their side of the bargain. Thus in 1815, as soon as the Treaty of Ghent ended the disastrous war with England, President James Madison sent a squadron under Commodore Stephen Decatur to the Mediterranean to punish the "pirates." Near Cape de Gatt the Americans met an Algerian frigate flying English colors; they too flew the English flag until they were almost upon their victim. In the ensuing fight, the Algerian was forced to strike: its reis, Hamidou, had been cut in two by a solid shot from a cannon. There was never again to be an "heroic" corsair; the next year, Lord Exmouth's attack on Algiers gave a death blow to the Algerian naval establishment.

VIII *The Slaves*

S INCE NO CENSUS was ever taken, any count of the number of
slaves or freemen in North Africa during these centuries is
at best an educated guess. Père Dan tells us that there were
about twenty-five thousand male and two thousand female slaves in
Algiers in the 1630s; the figure of twenty-five thousand seems to be
one that most observers in the mid-seventeenth century can agree
upon, but this does not say anything about the many slaves that
were owned by the inhabitants of other towns of the regency or by
the country peoples and the nomadic tribes. Perhaps the twenty-five
thousand figure was too high for Algiers alone and too low for the
entire slave population. One reasonably trustworthy observer tells us
that 500,000–600,000 Christian slaves were sold in the markets of
Algiers between 1520 and 1660, but this figure may be too high, for
it would require the capture of about four thousand slaves a year,
and yet it is surely probable that at least four hundred thousand
slaves were sold during this period. In any estimate of the figures for
the years between 1660 and the French occupation in 1830, we
must remember that the numbers fell off sharply in the eighteenth
century; still it is probable that somewhere between two hundred
thousand and two hundred fifty thousand slaves were taken in this
latter period. While these figures admittedly are loose, they do reflect
the size of the problem. Our evidence clearly shows that in some
years many more slaves were captured than in others, yet it is possible to estimate that the figure would average out to about three
thousand a year during the first period (1520–1660) and perhaps
something less than two thousand a year in the second (1660–1830).
Since most of the captives were men, it is hard to estimate the effect of these captures on the demographic structures of the slaves'
homelands. The largest drain obviously was on the Spanish and
Italian populations, and it probably was a factor in the demographic
crisis that those people experienced in the latter seventeenth century;

both lost 300,000–500,000 persons. However, these were losses that mostly affected the supply of sailors rather than the total population.

Who were these people who were sold like chattel at auction? They spoke all the languages of Europe: most of them came from the shores of the Mediterranean or the approaches to that sea from the Atlantic, and yet they also came from Russia, Germany, the British Islands, Scandinavia, the Netherlands, and northern France. Perhaps most of them were sailors taken at sea; but there were thousands of villagers captured in raids and hundreds of townsmen and others who were passengers on vessels and who were taken as prizes. Thus they ranged from high noblemen, royal officers, ships captains, merchants, and bourgeois travelers to common seamen and poor peasants. The wealthy and important were ransomed; the rest mostly remained slaves for the rest of the years of their lives. For these latter, their fate could be a terrible ordeal or a relatively pleasant situation that might be better than they could have hoped for in Europe. For the Algerians and their city, the center of the wars, the slaves of both high and low status represented an important aspect of their prosperity and well-being: the institution of slavery was necessary for the economy of the regency, for slaves provided both hard metal money (foreign exchange) by their ransoms and labor needed for the economic and social prosperity of the Moslem community. The corsairs who captured them, as they sailed against the enemies of Allah in the holy war that assured salvation as well as considerable profits, were the heroes and the benefactors of the regency.

Most of the captures at sea were made without much struggle. If the victim was not close enough to the shore for the crew to go over the rail and swim for safety, a vessel without cannons and well-armed men had no chance to save itself or its crew. When a ship was armed, there sometimes was a fight, but the corsair vessel carried more men than any merchant ship, and when it came alongside and grappled, pierrier fire blasting from its side guns and men pouring over the rails armed with daggers, scimitars, and pistols quickly overcame resistance. Voltaire's description, in *Candide*, of the cowardice of the papal soldiers when their ship, carrying the old woman, was attacked is undoubtedly a canard, illustrating Voltaire's dislike for both popes and soldiers. In fact, the defenders usually had the undesirable choice of death, or slavery. Captures on land were not less dramatic and terrifying: armed bands of men, sometimes hundreds of them as on the raids on the Canary Islands, would suddenly overwhelm a peaceful village or a small town and carry away men, women, and children unfortunate enough to be in the attackers' path. The defensive villages located on the hills or on cliffs, the walled towns, the signal towers, and the mobile defensive units created to combat the invaders helped to check the depredations of the corsairs, and yet the markets in North Africa saw thousands of peasants sold into slavery.

When a ship was captured, the first thing to be done was the making of an invoice of its cargo and a list of its crew and passengers. The captives were questioned to discover their importance and possible wealth. What gave away status were the lack of callouses on a man's hands and the manner of his speech, his grammar, genteel vocabulary. Naturally every one of the captives wished to downgrade his status to avoid large ransom demands, but the corsairs questioned the crew, and renegades among the former tried to get information from the captives by pretenses of kindness or the offer of small services. Sometimes violence became the rule; crew members were beaten when they refused to give information or gave unsatisfactory answers to questions.

When the ship reached port, the captives were marched to the *jenina* or "king's house," for the pasha or dey to assess his legal right to between ten and twelve percent of the captives. After he had chosen his share, the pasha-dey also reserved the right to purchase from the first buyer any slave at the price that he had brought at auction. The remaining slaves were then marched to a bagño and the next morning were exposed for sale at the *bezestan*, or public market. Dr. Underhill tells us that he was stripped to his loincloth and exposed along with "camels, mules, goats, hares, dromedaries, women, men, and other creatures whether for appetite or use . . ." The mornings were devoted to the examination of the captives' hands, teeth, general health, probable age, and possible value in terms of ransom money. The sale came after midday prayers when the guardian led the captives one by one to the dock and gave the audience an account of the true or pretended worth of the person, who was then sold to the highest bidder. Everyone who went through this experience and later wrote about it leaves us no doubt concerning the trauma and humiliation of the situation.

While seeing oneself being sold at auction must have a shattering effect upon a person, twentieth-century men should remember that slavery in Algiers was not the same thing as slavery in the Americas. Algerian slaves, on the whole, had a different fate from those sold at Charleston, New Orleans, Kingston, or Havana. Mediterranean

slavery since ancient times had always involved men of the same
color, sometimes even of the same race and culture as the owners.
The slave was an unfortunate creature who had fallen into his condition by the chance of war, poverty, or birth. His owner knew that
a turn of the wheel of fate might sometime place him in the
same condition. Thus, while there were brutal patrons, revenge-seek-
ing Morisco refugees from Spain, and onerous labor duties to perform, the condition of slaves in North Africa was not that of the
negro fieldhand on an American plantation. The Moslem religion
tended further to soften the position of slaves: it taught that all men
are brothers and that differences in creed, color, or race did not de-
mean men. While redemptionist monks who traveled from village to
village begging alms for ransom monies gave their auditors harrowing
tales about the lives and conditions of the slaves in the Barbary, the
facts did not completely support these stories, except under the unusual situation where the slave became the property of a cruel, perhaps even psychopathic, master or found himself chained to the
oarbank of a galley.

Even though the monks' tales were probably exaggerated, slavery,
as we shall see, was a devastating, sometimes horrible experience for
most of the men and women who were carried to the Barbary Coast
against their wills. The worst trauma seems to have been caused by
the separation from friends and family and the fact that they found
themselves in a land where language, customs, and religion were
strange. Although many of them were accustomed to being at the
bottom of the social scale in their own communities, their status as
slaves added insult to their general misfortune.

The social status that a slave enjoyed in his homeland was most
important in fixing the treatment he would receive in North Africa.
One witness after another tells us that men of culture or men with
skills were rarely put to menial work. The slaves who were the carriers of loads, the tillers of the fields, the power for the oars were
almost always men whose lot in Europe would also have been hard
labor. There were exceptions, to be sure, particularly in the early
sixteenth century, when famous captains were put to the oars, but
by the seventeenth century such men were too valuable as a source
of ransom money for their lives to be risked in the galleys. Men who
could bring technical skills to North Africa that the natives lacked
were also too valuable for such a risk. While there were stories, undoubtedly true, of the mistreatment of priests by Morisco refugees
from Spain, for the most part the priests seem also to have been al-

lowed to continue their missions—at least, those who took their calling seriously. The pious Moslem recognized and respected piety and good works wherever he found them, and we have much evidence to support the assumption that priests were usually treated with due respect for their calling. Rare and shocking were the cases where Morisco refugees brutally mistreated or murdered priests in revenge for similar treatment of Moriscos in Spain.

Those slaves whose obvious status warranted the assumption that they could raise ransom money were the most desirable purchases. Since it was to the advantage of the victim to minimize his worth and the probable amount of ransom that could be expected, the bargaining between captive and patron had some of the same excitement that is found today in the commodity market.

The dey-pasha who had the first pick of the slaves and the right to buy others at the market price was, of course, able to secure some of the "best merchandise," but wealthy reis and merchants as well as the most affluent members of the Jewish community also made considerable money in this traffic. On a lower level, less important and less wealthy patrons also bought slaves on speculation that their king, relatives, friends, or the redemptionist fathers would find money for their ransom. Sailors were believed to be particularly valuable in the later seventeenth century, for northern kings needed to ransom them to man the new fleets that were coming into being.

For those whose family or friends could provide ransom money the negotiations fixing the amount that should be paid were often long and difficult. During that period the slave was usually closely guarded, sometimes even loaded with irons to convince him that he must reach an agreement satisfactory to his patron. After a sum for the ransom was agreed upon, it was usual to allow the slave much freedom of movement and no obligation to labor. It was not difficult for the slave to give his word that he would not try to escape, for escape was much too hazardous to be worth the effort if ransom were assured. How much money was involved? Sometimes the sums were enormous. Don Martin de Cordova, Marquis de Cortez, for example, paid Hassan Pasha 23,000 gold écus; a Catalan nobleman, Glaceran de Pinos, settled for 100 pieces of silk, 100,000 doubles of gold, 100 horses, and as many cows; the bishop of Govea paid 16,000 ducats; the nephew of the governor of Brazil paid 4,000 ducats, the governor of Mazagan, 10,000 ducats; Father Antoine de la Croix paid 5,000 livres. An artisan or a common sailor might be ransomed for about 500 livres. What is the value of these coins?

Only a moneylender from those times could tell us what these "doubles," "ducats," "livres," "pieces of eight," and other coins were worth in terms of money that a twentieth-century person understands. We note that many of these huge ransoms were paid in part in foreign coins—gold or silver—and in part in the "plate" money that circulated throughout the Mediterranean basin at varying values. By the latter seventeenth century, "clipping" of gold and silver coins had reached a point where the money was valued by weight rather than by the piece; few coins had "minted" edges to guarantee the virtue of the coin. The one thing that we do know is that pashas, reis, wealthy merchants, Jews, Morisco refugees, and their children were engaged in the traffic of ransoms, and that this traffic was an important aspect of the total economy of the North African regencies, particularly of Algiers, since that city had little other commerce to generate exchange either in the city or in the hinterland.

There were several methods for the payment of ransoms. Jewish merchants with correpondents in Italy, France, or Amsterdam were often agents for payment. English or French merchants with agents in London or Marseille served the same purpose. The several European consuls also acted with agents sent from their homelands, and, of course, the orders of redemptionist fathers acted for private persons as well as supervising the funds that their priests had collected in Christendom. The actual exchange from slavery to freedom could be effected in the consular compounds in Algiers when there was a ship in the harbor that could be persuaded to carry the freed slave to his homeland, or the slave could be sent to Livorno (Leghorn to the English) where the duke of Tuscany, whose forefather had established the crusading order of St. Stephen, maintained a "slave prison" in which the slave could be kept until the transaction was completed. The duke, of course, took his percentage for the services. A similar "slave prison" was available at Ceuta just across the Straits from Spain under comparable conditions.

Obviously the rich and the well-born could expect to be ransomed unless there were reasons affecting the well-being of the state or of their patrons that might prevent liberation. Even though it probably would require at least a whole year to accomplish, these favored ones did manage to leave North Africa as free men. What about people who had no money, no family, no friends with money? An Englishman, a Frenchman, a Netherlander, at least after the mid-seventeenth century, might expect that he would be freed by a treaty between his ruler and the regency; there were problems of finding money and making the exchanges, and plague or accident could take him before liberation, but the Englishman, Frenchman, or Netherlander did have a chance for freedom. Yet what became of the poor Spanish, Portuguese, or Italian slave? It was a brutal fact that most of them remained slaves throughout their lives. While the regencies were often anxious to make peace with the powerful commercial states, there was no peace with the king of the Spanish empire, there were no consuls to look out for the interests of the Spanish king's subjects. The redemptionist fathers of the Order of the Holy Trinity and the Redemption of Captives (Trinitarians) and the Order of Our Lady of Mercy (Fathers of Mercy) tried to fill the gap left by the endemic war between the Spanish empire and the regencies of North Africa, but the "gap" remained wide indeed.

These two orders had a long and honorable history that predated their activity on the North African coast in these centuries following 1520. The Trinitarian order was founded in 1198; the Mercy order in 1232. The former, while all Western European in scope, was largely French; the latter was almost entirely Italo-Spanish until the seventeenth century when Marie de Medici introduced it into France. Both orders had a long history of redemption throughout the Moslem world, and in the seventeenth century both orders operated in the Levant as well as in North Africa. Some notion of the size and wealth can be gained from the fact that in 1789 the Trinitarians had some two hundred and fifty chapters scattered from Portugal and Spain to France and Italy with almost half of them in France. These chapters were monastic foundations with varying degrees of wealth. Unquestionably two orders controlled a vast holding of lands and houses that supported their activity. Naturally there was considerable rivalry between them, and when the Order of Mercy came to France in the second quarter of the seventeenth century, the crown divided the provinces between them for the purposes of collections in order to reduce the conflict that had developed.

Members of the orders went from village to village, from town to town, collecting money for redemption. Tassy, as well as other observers, insists that they told stories that were exaggerated, paraded ex-slaves "in solemn procession . . . with uncut beards and . . . terrible miens . . . loaded with chains that they had never worn . . ." They commanded the compassion of the public "who threw silver and gold into the plates . . ." The monks may well have been as guilty as Tassy asserts, but there is good evidence that there were also charlatans masquerading as monks, not actually members of the redemptionist or any other order, who played on the gullibility of the people. Their "ex-slaves" carried more irons and had more terrible tales to tell than those accompanying the "legitimate" orders. How much of the money collected was spent for redemption? The Trinitarian and Mercy fathers had their chapter houses to support as well as slaves to ransom; the charlatans had only themselves and their "ex-slaves." Since twentieth-century "charitable" and "mercy" collections for "this or that good cause" often use over fifty percent of the money collected for "administration," it should not be surprising to find that the monks did not use all their collections for the liberation of slaves.

The redemptionist fathers were always welcomed at Algiers. The dey-pasha received them immediately on arrival, apparently to discover how much money they brought with them for ransoms. The first order was always that the good fathers should be treated honestly and fairly and given no offense. The regency needed the money that they brought; it would be unwise to spoil future ransom payments by mistreatment of the fathers or their retinue. The first slaves to be ransomed were those belonging to the pasha and other important people, usually the old and the infirm slaves no longer useful to their patrons. No others could be ransomed until these were taken care of; this requirement, naturally, was not blatantly proclaimed, but the priests clearly understood it. When they left the palace, the monks were surrounded by slaves begging to be the first freed. It was painful; all seemed worthy, and yet the amount of money at the disposal of the good fathers was strictly limited. The actual redemptions often took weeks of negotiation, and, when it was all over, there were gratifications for the pasha, the agha, important members of the divan, and officers of the port. These ranged from a pittance to a port official to a substantial sum for the pasha and agha. In some cases the French consul who was an "unofficial" protector of the priests held an "open table" for the reis and janissary officers who happened to be in the city; many were renegades who appreciated French wine.

The redemptionist fathers also acted as agents for private redemption of important prisoners. This service was particularly welcome, since the fathers could bring specie money into Algiers without the danger of capture that other shipments might have, and they could "export" the freed slaves with safe conduct to a Christian port. There seems to be no evidence that the fathers received a commission for these services, yet they probably did since the consuls and merchants living in Algiers always were paid for acting as agents.

Royal bounty was slow in coming to the rescue of captives. The first Stuart kings in England could not afford to ransom their subjects and they justified inaction with the argument that if they did rescue Englishmen they would convince the corsairs that the capture of Englishmen was a good commercial venture. In other words ransom would only encourage the depredations. Thus at first the charity of English bishops or wealthy individuals was the sole resource of the poor captives who had no friends with money. In the 1640s the English parliament placed a tax of one percent—soon reduced to one-quarter of one percent—on commerce for the redemption of English slaves. But by the end of the 1640s there was only one mission to Algiers for rescuing Englishmen, and in the next decade the money was appropriated for the use of the navy. The French kings, too, were slow to provide funds for ransoms. King Louis XIII gave a small amount to Sanson Napollon and ordered French towns to pay for the ransom of fellow townsmen, but between 1635 and the 1660s the expenses of war and the problems of peasant tax rebellions ended royal bounty. The Estates General of the United Netherlands was the first European power to regulate ransoms and immunity from attack by a treaty that provided for payment of "tribute," an act that French and English consuls considered to be craven and shameful in every way, but the Dutch decided that it would be cheaper to "buy" protection than to enforce it with warships.

Cromwell was the first to use naval power effectively for both the protection of commerce and the ransom of prisoners; yet only after 1660 did both England and France send powerful naval squadrons to force regencies to respect their commerce and free their enslaved subjects. As we shall see, these expeditions were successful as long as the naval pressure could be maintained, for the regencies had no comparable naval power. However, the European powers were also often at war with each other and were obliged to use their navies against each other, leaving the "punishment" of the Barbary regencies for a peaceful interlude in the European conflicts. Even when successful, there were problems. Slaves not yet sold could be freed, but slaves purchased by individuals had become "private property," and both the English and the French kings respected "private property" even though it happened to be an Englishman or a Frenchman. Thus the treaties that followed successful naval action against the Barbary corsairs provided for the "repurchase" of the captives, usually at a fixed price. The provision often caused trouble for the consul since the kings were unable to raise enough money to ransom all their subjects. In the case of the French another problem developed from treaties requiring the exchange of Frenchmen for Turks and Moors chained to the galleys in France. As we shall see, the French, unwilling to give up useful slaves, sent aged, sick, and infirm men, and not infrequently men who had never even been in Algiers or in the Algerian service.

There is another "footnote" to the problems of English slaves in the Barbary. Some were freed through the efforts of merchants who required the slave to agree to pay part or all of the ransom money when he returned to England. In this way a merchant with money from the bishops or the king could free more slaves, since the ransom money would go further when the slave also promised to pay a part. But often enough the wretches could not raise the money when they returned to England, and their lot in a debtors prison was probably worse than it had been in Algiers, where at least they had freedom to go about the town.

How effective were the efforts to ransom? Grammont attempted to estimate the numbers of slaves ransomed by charitable institutions, royal bounty, and individual payments, and then to count the number of slaves freed by efforts of European navies. The galleys of Malta and Venice captured and freed thousands of Christian galley slaves; the navies of England, France, and the Netherlands also added other thousands to the list. In addition, Maltese, Spanish, and Italian corsairs, landing off North African coasts, captured Christian as well as Moslem slaves for the slave markets in Christendom. Grammont came to the conclusion that naval action released more slaves than Christian charity managed to free.

However, in fairness to the monks and others who labored in the service of redemption as well as to the goodly number of them who gave their liberty and their lives as martyrs to the cause, we must point out that the years between 1550 and 1750 were not good ones for the collection of money. In the last forty years of the sixteenth century the French economy was seriously disrupted by civil and religious wars, while the reformation of the church cut large sections of Europe off from the Catholic community, and thereby ended the collection of money in some of the richest provinces heretofore available to the monks. In those same years Castile and parts of Italy were drained by the taxes that Philip II had to impose for his wars in the Mediterranean, the Netherlands, the English Channel, and the Atlantic approaches to the Iberian peninsula. The seventeenth century was even less favorable for collections.

Spain and Portugal were both in a serious economic and demographic decline while the needs of the king grew apace. But more important, the devastating climatic conditions that brought drought, frost, floods, and, with them, famine and pestilence affected all Europe. An agricultural community that suffers famines about every decade has little money to spare for distant charity. Added to crop failures was another equally serious problem: war. The great German war that became an all-Western-European struggle, now called the Thirty Years War, filled the first half of the century, while the wars now usually known as those of Louis XIV spanned the second half. Indeed, from 1618 to 1713, Europe knew few years of peace. Taxes and the exactions of relatively undisciplined soldiers competed with the redemptionist fathers and other charitable institutions for the available surplus money in Catholic Europe. The Protestant Netherlands and the kingdoms of the English throne also suffered from the same agricultural crisis resultant from unfavorable weather, while civil as well as international war demanded money and manpower that might otherwise have been in part used for redemption of slaves.

Not all captives could be ransomed. Anyone who might be useful in the shipyards, or later in the cannon foundry, was too valuable to lose through ransom. The same was true of some officers from sailing vessels who might be persuaded to become renegades, or who might be useful aboard ship even as a slave. These people were told that they need not hope for rescue or ransom, that they never could return to Christian Europe, but if they would only renounce their religion, they were assured of an honorable and lucrative place in the regency's society. If they refused, master carpenters, shipbuilders, iron founderers, and the like were put to work at their trades as slaves—slaves that were very well treated, indeed, even pampered. There was another class of captives that could not be ransomed. Just as the European naval officers hanged any renegade reis and imprisoned any Moslem reis they might capture to reduce the number of competent officers available to the corsair navy, so also some of the Spanish officers were denied ransom for fear that they might return with vengeance or because their behavior had angered the regency authorities. Kheir-ed-din even refused to allow the cadaver of Don Juan de Portomondo, leader of an unsuccessful slave rebellion, to be ransomed for burial. Others were kept in Algiers for personal reasons. Ali Bitchnin Reis, for example, kept two knights of Malta as "honored" prisoners as insurance for his own ransom in case he

might be captured in a sea fight. However, these cases were unusual, for the capture and ransoming of Christians, especially in the
seventeenth century, was an important commercial activity for a
community that had very little other commerce with the outside
world.

Escape was another but difficult route to freedom. In the early
sixteenth century when the Spanish still held Bougie, a few managed to find their way overland, but it was dangerous: Unfriendly
natives, wild animals (with lions, hyenas, and cheetahs abounding),
and little to eat or drink made it a nightmare for those who attempted
it. Others escaped by sea. Hardy Spanish or Majorcan sailors made
rendezvous with slaves on the coast, but this, too, was hazardous,
for the Algerians tried to keep careful watch. At least one or two
successful escapes were made in boats constructed secretly at Algiers
and launched at night; the escapees arrived at Majorca half dead
from exposure. In the latter seventeenth and the eighteenth centuries the most successful method of escape was effected by swimming to an anchored warship. It was almost impossible to use this
route on a merchant vessel since the Algerians forced the captains to
land their sails and tillers so that the ship could not leave port without permission. Warships suffered no such indignity, but they were
required to anchor out in the harbor so that only the strongest swim-
mer could reach them. If the escapee was not caught by a patrol
boat, the outraged patrons often descended upon the dey to demand
action. Then the consul was in trouble: indeed, not only the consul,
but the entire community of the flag of the offending warship. As
a result, naval officers were sternly forbidden to carry off escaped
slaves. Sometimes they obeyed; sometimes the crews of the ships
would raise the money to pay for the poor wretches' ransom; sometimes the slaves were taken to freedom in spite of protests.

Escape was dangerous. If the slave failed, he was beaten, sometimes mutilated, sometimes brutally executed as an example to others.
While a few did manage, the vast majority of the slaves apparently
considered escape too uncertain to make it worth their while to try.

The other question that inevitably arises is: Why did the slaves
not revolt and take over the city? In the summertime a large number
of the janissaries were either at sea with the corsairs or on "sweeps"
in the hinterland to collect tribute; very often there were not more
than 5,000–7,000 possible defenders in the city. There were twenty-
five thousand slaves. Why did they fail to overwhelm the defenders
by revolt? As a matter of fact there were rebellions; several of them
came close to success; others, like an early one inspired by the son

of a Spanish admiral in 1531, were nipped in the bud as a result of betrayal. However, in 1559, in 1662, in 1753, and in 1763 serious uprisings led to much bloodshed and fighting in the city, but in each case the defenders were able to suppress the rebellion and brutally to punish the poor fellows who tried to lead it. Like similar slave revolts on the island of Malta, the advantage was with the defenders who had better weapons and were accustomed to fighting together as units rather than as individuals. In Algiers there was an additional advantage on the side of the defenders; the Christians not only belonged to different confessions and thus distrusted each other, but they also spoke many different languages and honored many different customs and folkways. Furthermore, not all of them were sufficiently dissatisfied with their lot to risk the violent death that would follow failure. In any case, neither the Moslem slaves on the island of Malta, where they greatly outnumbered the knights and their mercenaries, nor the Christian slaves in the regencies, were able to mount a successful rebellion during all the three centuries that they were enslaved in those lands.

What of the lives and fate of those who did not escape, who were not ransomed? The monks who roamed Europe seeking alms for the ransom of these unfortunates, and, indeed, the petitioners who wrote to their king begging for relief, gave a dismal, desperate picture of the lives of the unransomed slaves. They were loaded with irons, beaten, worked beyond human endurance, often hungry and ill-clad, and their captors sought to steal their immortal souls by urging them to renounce their God! These were tales to bring tears to those who heard them, and, it was hoped, to draw money from their pockets to support the charitable business of ransoming the unfortunates. As a matter of fact, however, the actual conditions in North Africa were much more complex than this simple picture would have us believe. As we have noted, a few of the slaves were purchased as a speculative business venture; others presumably were purchased for a variety of services that they might be able to perform in the fields, the shops, the homes, or the ships, shipyards, and public works of North Africa.

Few of the above services could be more effectively performed if the unfortunate Christian should give up his religion, and some of them would become impossible if he did. Richelieu, St. Vincent de Paul, Père Dan, and many others echo the monks' tales of forced conversion; indeed, Richelieu's interest in saving souls from hell loomed so large in his writing that it almost seems more important than the return of French sailors to their proper tasks on French ships. There were cases in which patrons, apparently out of affection for their slaves, did urge them to renounce their religion, but, for adult male slaves this practice seems to have been the exception rather than the rule. The Moslem patron, tolerant of the Christian religion, often remarked that a "bad Christian would make a bad Mohammedan," and indeed the behavior of many renegades in Algiers seems to confirm this opinion. Furthermore, when a slave converted, he was on his way to freedom: he could not be sent to the galleys or to hard labor, and it was easy for him to throw off his obligations of servitude. His only problem was that a horrible death awaited him if he ever tried to return to his Christian faith. Some patrons, however, not only did not try to convert their slaves but also forced them to remain Christians even though they might ask for conversion. The famous example is that of Ali Bitchnin, who even used violence to prevent this practice. It is clear that the patron derived no economic advantage from it, so that we find most patrons discouraging—even forbidding—conversion.

And yet there were thousands of renegades in Algiers during these centuries, and many of them must have arrived as slaves. Who were they? The most conspicuous at the turn of the seventeenth century were ex-privateer captains whose professional careers ended when the kings of France and England and later the Estates General of the United Netherlands made either peace or a truce with the king of the Spanish empire. For many of them it was a short trip from privateer to pirate to corsair reis and renunciation of their religion. But from the stories we have, the conversions were obviously not all the results of religious experience. It was simply easier to dispose of their booty as prizes in the war than it would have been to sell the same if they had captured the ship and cargo as pirates. There were naval officers in the corsair naval establishment who had been captured and then renounced their religion in return for honor and wealth in an adopted society; some of these reached high places in the corsair navy, and later even in the Ottoman naval establishment. Favorites of their patrons, they had renounced their Christian religion, and had risen to power through influence, hard work, great ability or just plain luck. Often over half of the seventeenth-century corsair fleet was commanded by renegades; in the eighteenth century, when the profits from the corsair activity declined and the state or the dey came to own most of the ships, the percentage of renegades, indeed the number of good captains, fell off drastically.

There were also renegades in the janissary corps. By the eighteenth century the numbers became impressive. Where did they come from? If we are to believe Christian observers, who probably are not too generous in their judgments, many of these men were refugees from their own past. We do not know how many arrived at Algiers as free men nor can we be sure that all or even most of them were "black sheep," criminals, or wastrels; some surely were simply dissatisfied with their opportunities in their homelands. As for the janissaries who came to Algiers as captives, renounced their faith, and finally were accepted in the janissary corps, again we have little real evidence. In the eighteenth century when the recruits from the Levant declined in numbers, there may have been some recruiting that persuaded men to renounce their religion in favor of a position in the corps; one account even suggests that an ex-slave janissary was obliged to give part of his income to his patron.

There were renegades elsewhere in Algerian society. We have already noted that most adult slaves were not urged to renounce their faith; nonetheless master carpenters, shipbuilders, founderers, and the like were often persuaded to do so. The same was true for officers on the captured ships whose skills were needed in the corsair navy. Captured Spanish and Italian soldiers, even high officials, were also recruited; on one occasion a whole regiment was persuaded to become Moslem and to join the Algerians against the Tunisians. However, our Christian authorities were usually happy to announce that few soldiers or sailors succumbed to Moslem blandishments.

There were other sources of converts: children, friends, and women. It was not at all uncommon for a child, captured and sold, to be treated like a child of his patron's own family. The baldi were easy-going, and, we are told, affectionate toward their children; it was common for a child-parent relationship to develop, and easy for a child to forget his own home and religion. There are many cases in which these children became the heirs of their patron. Another source: friendship. In a Moslem household where there were several wives, the husband often had to defend himself against the intrigues of his own family. His sons could benefit from his death, but a slave had much to gain from his living, and an attractive slave could become a friend. There were enough cases of this relationship for us to assume that many of the renegades passed through this frame: some became ship captains, some merchants, some inheritors of their patrons' fortunes.

Marriage between freed slaves and their patrons also resulted in apostasy. The wife, or wives, in Moslem homes kept in close confinement often had a natural curiosity about the outside world. Even today in villages on the upper Nile we see women trying to get a glimpse of "the foreigner" while their men shout for them to get in the house—even throwing rocks at them to force them to do so. Several memoirists have told us of the women's interest in slaves, and the development of close relationships. As long as the husband was alive, these had to be proper or the slave risked a horrible death, but there were cases when the husband died and the slave, renouncing his Christian faith, became a Mohammedan and husband of the widow.

The relationship went the other way as well. Most women captured in raids on the coast were peasant women, while passengers captured at sea were women of high status. Opinions differ about their fate. Voltaire's "old woman" would have us believe that female captives were raped by all and sundry, but Molière presents a woman who, after ten years as captive on the Barbary Coast, was a suitable marriage partner in a good bourgeois family. Obviously she had not been molested. The available evidence would suggest that there was some justification for Voltaire's opinion, but very creditable witnesses support the opinion that women were well treated, even when they became slaves. From what we know about men and women, we are not surprised to find that there were many women who renounced their religion and married their patrons. Surely not many of them married the corsair reis who captured them, as did the young Italian noblewoman Marie de Gaëtano, who married Kheir-ed-din (when he was nearly fifty), but there were enough intermarriages to call attention to the possibility; for example, the wife of one of the deys was an English renegade. Presumably it was not too difficult for a young woman to conclude that marriage in Algiers might not be too different from marriage in Europe and surely preferable to a life as a house slave.

We cannot know how many renegades and slaves contributed to the gene pool of the Algerian community. One writer suggests that there were at least twenty-five thousand renegades in the three centuries that figure in this account; the figure may even be low. However, it is clear that there were enough Europeans who bred offspring in the Barbary communities to influence the genetic structure of the community. As we have noted, today in the cities of Algiers, Tunis, and Morocco we can recognize in the characteristic features, eye, hair color, and body build of the people in the streets the fact that many races have contributed to the composition of these communities.

What was the fate of the vast majority of Christian slaves? Obviously no simple answer can cover the variety of situations in which we find these people. Cervantes, who had been a slave himself, wrote: "[Their lot] is sad and miserable . . . a harsh and rude slavery in which labors were long and happiness short and fugitive . . . purgatory in life, hell in the living world . . ." And yet elsewhere he speaks of kind and generous patrons. Tassy, who was never a slave and yet knew Algiers, suggests that all pictures of harshness are overdrawn, but even he cannot conceal the fact that there was hard work to be done and there were hard masters to be endured. If we look at the household slaves of the wealthy reis, bourgeois merchants and shipowners, and important officials, we see men clothed in fine garments, well fed, fairly comfortably housed, and with light labors to perform—some of them pampered friends and confidants of their owners. Some of them would be freed and inherit their patron's fortunes. Slaves of the janissaries had to keep their owner's few goods in order and prepare his table, but they dressed about as well as their patrons, they ate from the same dishes, they usually were good friends. One janissary remarked that it was hard to know "whether you are my slave or I yours." There is no need to romanticize the relationship, and yet observers do confirm the idea that most of the janissaries were generous with their slaves, that the slave ended by being one of the family. There are also suggestions that homosexual relations were not uncommon. Most of the janissaries were not married.

Slaves of the dey and the reis might have very different lots: some would be chained to the oarbench of a galiot, some were forced to labor in the stone quarries and transport stone for the mole and other building enterprises, some worked in the gardens and fields surrounding the country homes of the wealthy outside the city, some were carriers of water and other burdens: not all were pampered house slaves or life guards for their masters. The most wretched, by all accounts, were the poor fellows who were purchased by the farmers who supplied Algiers with breadstuffs and vegetables. Very often they were overworked, underfed, and badly housed, besides being driven to hard labor from sunup to sundown—veritable work animals. The most fortunate were those purchased by indolent, wealthy baldis or coulouglis; their lives were often much better than they would have been in Europe.

There was another group of slaves whose lot was also varied, but quite different from the above. Many patrons bought slaves as an investment. They housed them in a public—or private—bagño and either rented them out as laborers to anyone who needed workers or expected them to care for themselves and pay their masters a weekly stipend. These men were "pools of labor" available if more oarsmen were needed, if workers were required to unload a ship, or any other labor. Others of them were artisans who either worked for a master artisan or themselves maintained their own atelier where they made clothes, shoes, barrels, or other commodities. Their patron took a share of their earnings and expected them to look out for their own food and clothing. Some of the most successful of this latter group maintained wineshops where they sold the wines that the corsairs captured.

As we noted, these slaves were housed in bagños, some belonging to the regency or the pasha, others to wealthy reis who provided bagños for their own as well as other patrons' slaves. There were a number of these bagños; they differed somewhat in size and structure, and yet they were enough alike to be discussed together. The bagño was a compound that could be closed and locked at night. In the mid-seventeenth century only one of them was a true prison, locked at all times: It was used for captives whose ransoms were not yet negotiated and others who had to be kept in close confinement. The bagños were for male slaves; women and children, when not housed by their patrons, were kept in other establishments, separated from the men. Each bagño consisted of one or more open courtyards, surrounded by a two-story housing with a balcony, letting out on the court. The rooms were oblong and usually depended for light on the courtside openings; each room housed from ten to twenty men who slept on mats with blankets provided either by their patrons or themselves. Most of the living was done in the large courtyards where, as today in many African homes, the cooking was done, food eaten, cards played, fights or arguments carried on, tall tales and general social intercourse took place. All accounts tell of the colorful disorder, the noise, the dirt, the crowded conditions. In the larger bagños there were wineshops managed by slaves, purveyors of food (flat breads, couscous, and other easily cooked foods), and, once the gates were closed, a thieves' market where all sorts of commodities were available cheaply.

The governor (guardian-bachi) was responsible for the security and at least part of the food of the inmates and for the maintenance of order in his domain. This officer was usually a renegade, and, if the accounts are even nearly correct, he was usually more anxious to line his own pockets by cheating on food and exacting small "presents" than in any other aspect of this position. His aids were also venal; like the governor, they preyed on the men under their charge. The only serious problem in these bagños was the occasional outbreak of violence. The most spectacular case in the literature arose from a conflict between Muscovite and Spanish slaves that seems to have originated in the differences of religion, language, and customs of the two groups. The fighting started in the daytime and was checked by the interference of the governor, but when the doors were closed for the night the bagño witnessed a classic riot in which several were killed and others injured before order was restored.

The other area for disorder emerged from the wineshops that slaves operated in the bagño, as well as on some of the streets of the city. These wineshop owners could buy the wines captured by the corsairs at reasonable prices so that their customers could drink excellent vintages inexpensively (the best wine was exported, and only exported wine was captured). Many of the slaves took to wine to lessen their pain, and, while good Moslems were not supposed to drink alcoholic beverages, there were enough of them who did, and we are told, enough renegades whose religious fervor was something less than complete, to fill the wineshops in the afternoons and well into the evenings. Inevitably there were disputes and clashes of personality when the wine flowed freely. In the bagño, as well as on the street, the owner of the shop was "responsible" for peace and good order, but what could he do if the offender was a janissary? If a slave raised his hand against a soldier he could be beaten—even killed—for his action. The wineshop patrons solved the problem by providing their "assistants" with a ladder; when a customer became offensive, they managed to insert him inside the two middle rungs and march him out of the shop onto the street. The system sounds easier in the accounts of ex-slaves than it must have been in the wineshops themselves, but somehow a modicum of order was maintained.

The other source of entertainment in the bagños was the telling of yarns about the world beyond Algiers. Most of these men were sailors: there were few parts of the world that no one of them had not seen. In the evenings stories about women, strange places, strange customs found in the New World from the fishing banks in the north to the Straits of Magellan, in Asia from Japan to India, and in the Afro-European world from the extreme north to the Cape of Good Hope. In one way or another the entire world became the subject for tales and questions put together somehow in the strange

lingua franca of the Algerian slaves. It was a cosmopolitan society—
at least a cosmopolitan "port" society.

The thieves' market in the bagños provided money for "extras"
as well as for necessities and offered a wide variety of commodities
that the slaves or others might desire to purchase. Stealing was a way
of life for many of the slaves. In some cases their patrons did not
adequately provide for their sustenance; in others it had become a
"trade" that took care of many needs. Apparently the Algerians
accepted the fact that slaves would, and perhaps had to steal, and
since much of the depredation was aimed at the Jewish community,
thievery was tolerated to an astonishing degree. Some of the stealing
was shoplifting, cutting purses, or break-ins; some of it seems to have
been "confidence" games that involved the moneychangers. This latter has been mentioned so often that it appears to mean that it was
either very common or that, when a slave managed to shortchange
a money lender, it became an event worth talking about. In any
case, the thieves' market that opened as soon as the guardian-bachi
closed the doors for the night was a common institution of the
bagños.

Wineshops and the gossip and storytelling in the courtyards may
have provided amusement and some consolation for many of the
slaves. Others found relief in their religion. By the end of the seventeenth century, every bagño had a chapel (the first one had been
founded by Father Duport in 1551 in the bagño belonging to the
coulougli that the Turks named the "Drinker's Tavern"). Masses
were said every day in most of these chapels either by priests who
were themselves slaves, or by members of the redemptionist orders
who had thrown their lot in with the slaves for the latters' salvation.
Some of these priests were very popular; their sermons and their willingness to listen to the plaintive stories, as well as to console the
weary and despairing, brought acceptance from Protestants, Greek
Orthodox, and Roman Catholics alike. The Turks, too, respected
these men both for their piety and good works and for their effect
on the behavior of the slaves (only here and there a greedy guardian-
bachi exacted a small fee for attendance at a religious service). There
were only a few priests, slaves like the rest of the occupants of the
bagños, whose life patterns brought disgrace and discredit to their
religion. There were very few Protestant ministers among the slaves
for the good reason that Protestant villages were not often raided,
but Protestant slaves could attend religious services in the English,
Dutch, and later Swedish and American consular compounds without interference from their Turkish masters.

The redemptionist priests also maintained hospitals and even pharmacies in or near the bagños where the sick slave often received better care than was available to his master. These hospitals were in part supported by a small voluntary tax on goods sold by European merchants in Algiers, a tax that became obligatory by a decree of Chaban Dey in 1794. In Algiers custom was easily translated into law. These hospitals were small affairs at first; at the opening of the seventeenth century we find one of them maintaining eight beds —four bunks on either side of the room—with a small altar on the far wall between the bunks. It was served by a barber-surgeon and an attendant. This does not seem much to twentieth-century men, but in the Algiers of that era these hospitals were impressive. As Father Monroy wrote in 1612: "Turks and Moors often visit here [the hospital] . . . It was a strange marvel for them to see Christian slaves having such an establishment in the city of Algiers . . There was nothing comparable for their sick . . ." In the eighteenth century, when these hospitals were much larger, it was not uncommon for Moslems to seek admission.

The redemptionist fathers also maintained a Christian cemetery outside one of the gates of the city (Bab-el-Oued) where slaves could be buried in holy ground even though they might die far from their homeland. At times the number of deaths made single graves impossible. For example, we are told that in 1740 the plague killed an average of three hundred slaves a day for three months! Although this figure was obviously exaggerated, there can be no doubt about the size of the crisis. In at least seven other years in the latter eighteenth century, the plague killed thousands more of the slaves, a fact that accounts for the decline in the slave population perhaps at least as much as did the decline in the corsair naval activity during that half-century. It is now impossible to make any estimates of the number of burials in the Christian cemetery, for the harbor at Algiers has been extended to include that piece of ground.

While the problems of Moslem slaves in Malta, Italy, France, and Spain does not really come within the scope of this book, it seems important to mention that Christians were not the only ones in this era to have the misfortune of falling into slavery. Perhaps a majority of the Moslems in slavery were captured in sea fights or as crews and passengers of Moslem vessels taken by Christian corsairs. Maltese and Italian corsairs ranged throughout the Levantine waters, and the slave market in Malta was about as active as the one in Algiers. The warships of the western naval powers also captured and sold Moslems when they were at war with the Barbary. Another source of Moslem slaves came from the raids that Christian corsairs made on Moslem villages. Like the Spanish and Italian shores of the Mediterranean, the North African coast also was largely deserted by its population except for fortified harbors, because it was unsafe to live close to the sea. An even more shocking source of slaves shows up at regular intervals in the correspondence from Algiers: Christian captains would take Moslem passengers, pilgrims perhaps on their route to Mecca or simply travelers going to one of the Levantine ports, but instead of landing them at Alexandria, they would turn in at Syracuse or Messina, or some other Christian port, to sell them in the market. Other cases recount that the Christian vessel would be stopped by a Maltese or Spanish corsair, and the unfortunate Moors and Turks aboard would be confiscated as legitimate prizes, while the Christian vessel was allowed to go on with its voyage. The Algerians were often convinced that the captain and the corsair were in collusion with each other. Other Moors and Turks became slaves as the result of an accident at sea; on several occasions a ship carrying pilgrims had the misfortune of being wrecked on the Sicilian coast and its passengers and crew promptly sold as slaves by their "rescuers." As a result of these various routes to slavery, a considerable number of people—women as well as men—who were either important in the naval and janissary communities or wealthy baldi society found themselves in slavery, and their friends and family could and did bring pressure on the dey-pasha for their release.

Just as there were Christian captives whom the Moslems were unwilling to release, there were Moslem captives for whom the Christians would not accept any ransom. As we have noted, it was usual for Christian naval officers to hang any renegade who fell into their hands, especially if the man should happen to have been originally a subject of their king. The Spanish, Maltese, and Italian authorities imprisoned "for life" any Moslem corsair reis who fell into their hands. The reason was simple: they understood that the Barbary navies never had a plentiful number of competent commanders, so that any one that they might capture and imprison would be one less capable officer available for the corsair fleets. In the sixteenth century, there were striking cases (Dragut, for example) in which an important naval officer was ransomed at very high prices, and often the subsequent career of the freed corsair reis gave his late captor much reason to regret his bargain. In the seventeenth century important corsair captains might hold high noblemen or knights of Malta as captives who could be exchanged for themselves in case fortune should turn against them. Such exchanges had the same quality that exchanges of important superpower spies or other personnel have in our own day.

There were few other Moslem slaves in Spain or Italy either ransomed or exchanged. There was no Islamic redemptionist order; there were no Barbary consuls in the domains of the king of Spain, no regular means to lubricate either ransoms or exchanges. Occasionally a Moslem slave would be exchanged for a Christian slave either at Ceuta or Leghorn when the two families managed to reach an agreement either through the good offices of the French consul or a Jewish merchant, but this was not common or usual.

Some writers have insisted that Moslem slaves in Christendom were not as well treated as Christian slaves in the African regencies, but the evidence available can only be inconclusive. It is unlikely that Christian slave owners could be categorized any more easily than owners in the Barbary regencies: obviously the life of slaves was hard, the lives of those chained to the oars extremely hard, and since we know more about Moslem galley slaves than about Moslem slaves in Christian homes or on Christian farms, it has been possible to assume that slavery on the south side of the Mediterranean was a lighter burden than it was on the northern side. Such an assumption, however, must be suspect.

Some of the most useful historical data about the conditions in North Africa come to us through the writing of ex-slaves: some like Cervantes were ransomed, others like Thomas Knight were freed when Christian naval units captured Algerian galleys. As a general rule we find that the ex-slave has a story to tell about his own captivity that justifies the assumption that slavery on the Barbary Coast was at best an unfortunate experience and, at worst, a terrible one; and yet it is from these accounts that we can also cull the fact that many patrons were reasonable, humane men who actually sympathized with their slaves and treated them well, while others either neglected or misused them. The letters of Christian slaves in the Barbary, and, apparently, of Moslem slaves[1] in Christian Europe all show one thing in common: a desire to be free and to return to homes and families.

1. We do not have letters from Moslem slaves to their parents and friends, but in the correspondence of the deys with the ministers of the kings of France there is ample evidence that such letters did exist and that they uniformly urged friends and family to do everything possible for their release.

IX *Algerian Regency and Europe: First Phase, 1600–1630*

THE LONG ENDEMIC WAR between the rulers of the Spanish and the Ottoman empires burned out in the 1580s, but the truce established between the principals did not extend to their vassals. The Knights of St. John at Malta, of St. Stephen in Tuscany, and the privateers outfitted in the harbors of Italy, Sicily, and the other islands of the western Mediterranean continued to attack Moslem commerce and to waylay pilgrims bound for the Holy places of Mecca and Modena, as well as other innocent travelers in the Levantine waters. At the same time the corsair reis operating out of the harbors of the regencies of Tripoli, Tunis, and, above all, Algiers carried on unrelenting war against Spanish, Italian, and Portuguese commerce and coasts. For both Christian and Moslem, it was a jihad, a holy war. The Knights of Malta had their vows as well as their long history of conflict with the Moslem power, and the Spanish and Italian privateers knew that their action brought both wealth and salvation. On the other hand, all North Africa knew that this war was for revenge as well as for the glory of Allah, for the memory was still green throughout the Barbary of the brutal assaults made by Spanish conquistadors who attacked the main harbors from Oran to Tripoli, murdered the population, looted their goods, and imposed huge fines on "vassal" states that were allowed to exist. Nor was that all; as we have seen, North Africa also had become the home of tens of thousands of men and women who had been driven from their homes by Spanish "racial and religious intolerance" and whose relatives in Spain were still suffering (as late as 1610) under intolerant Spanish rule. It was easy to recruit a crew for a corsair cruise against the "enemy" whose cruisers still descended on North African villages to capture slaves and booty, whose soldiers stationed at Oran and Mers-el-Kébir made razzias deep into the countryside behind the Spanish-held port towns. Thus neither the Christian nor the Moslem vassals of the kings of Spain and the sultans of the Ottoman Empire gave up their acts of hostility when the war between their overlords came to an end.

What was the place of the European princes in this Mediterranean melee? Throughout most of the sixteenth century the kings of France had been allies or at the least associates of the sultan; with a common enemy, Spain, it was easy for them to agree upon some common action. It was not always as close as the cooperation between Kheir-ed-din and Francis I that brought the Turkish navy to spend a winter in French harbors, but French sails, powder, and shot, and all sorts of naval supplies had long been at the disposal of the Moslem corsairs on the Barbary Coast. Both the Moslem reis and the Sublime Porte at Istanbul looked with suspicion on the fact that there were so many French noblemen in the service of the Knights of St. John at Malta, but this did not prevent the French ambassador on the Golden Horn from exercising great influence on the sultan's viziers. Indeed, the French ambassador had been able to secure the removal of an Algerian pasha unfriendly to France as well as to remove the head of a reis who had pillaged a French merchant vessel. By the end of the sixteenth century, however, the French ambassador's influence over North African events, like that of the Sublime Porte itself, had begun to wane. Nonetheless, French seamen were still reasonably secure from the attacks of the Barbary reis and welcome in the regency harbors. Furthermore, there was a French consul in Algiers, in Tunis, and in Tripoli, and a French merchant consortium had a concession to hold a fortified trading post, the bastion of France, stationed on an island off the coasts at the border of Tunis and Algiers. This bastion financed a coral fishery and traded with the Berber tribesmen to exchange European goods for their wax, hides, grain, horses, and many less valuable commodities. As long as the kings of France still waged an endemic war against the Spanish empire, this Franco-Barbary entente more or less guaranteed the peace between France and Moslem North Africa. Only after Henry IV made peace with Spain at the very end of the sixteenth century did French commerce begin to be fair game for the Barbary reis, especially for the Algerians.

The English came into the Mediterranean as traders, privateers, and pirates in the latter sixteenth century. Elizabeth secured a treaty with the sultan that gave her traders and seamen privileges about equal to those enjoyed by the French even though the Franco-Ottoman treaties had made the French king the protector of Christian merchants in the Levant and had given French consuls a large measure of legal authority over all Christians in Ottoman ports. English privateers and pirates very early found safe refuge in the harbors of the Algerian and Tunisian regencies. Their war was with the Spanish empire; this made them allies or at least associates of the Barbary reis. During Elizabeth's reign the English Turkey Company (Levant Company) was supposed to be responsible for the appointment of English consuls in the Ottoman port towns; it was difficult to appoint one in Algiers for there was so little commercial traffic in that city "of the war" devoted primarily to the cruises of its corsair reis.

After Elizabeth's death, her successor, James I, announced that the time for war was past and not only made peace with Spain but also gave great influence and prestige to the Spanish ambassador at the English court. Naturally the change was duly noted in Algiers and Tunis. English pirates, however, were still welcome in the Algerian and Tunisian harbors where they, with their counterparts from Flanders and the Netherlands, taught the Moslem reis how to build and sail the tall ships powered by wind. English merchants, on the other hand, were no longer so secure when they sailed through the Mediterranean for trade in the Levant, and the English ambassador at Istanbul, like his French counterpart after Henry IV had made peace with Spain, found that he could not bring much pressure to bear to halt "unlawful" pillaging of English ships by the Barbary reis. The sultan's authority could no longer easily protect the ships of nations presumably friendly with his regime, and also at peace with Spain.

The other north European trading power, the United Netherlands, did not send many ships into the Mediterranean before the end of the sixteenth century, although those Dutch and Flemish seamen who did brave the Straits were usually welcomed in the Barbary harbors as allies against the king of Spain. For the most part, however, the "sea beggars" armed with letters of mark from the Prince of Orange or the Estates General took stations on the Atlantic sea lanes leading to Spain and Portugal, and when Dutch merchants sent forth their ships to trade in the great world, their first targets were South America and the Orient rather than the Mediterranean. Thus the first "Dutchmen" to operate in the Mediterranean were a nice cross between privateers and pirates. They seem to have preyed more or less indiscriminately on the commerce of the subjects of the king of Spain and of the Republic of Venice. Many of them became renegade reis operating out of Tunis or Algiers who, with English and some French sea captains, taught the Algerians and Tunisians to sail ships that could break into the Atlantic and greatly extend the corsairs' field of activity. It was only after 1600 and especially after signing the twelve-year truce (1609) between Spain and the United Netherlands that Dutch merchantmen appeared in the Mediterranean in considerable numbers and many of them soon became prey for the Barbary corsairs.

Thus we see that England, France, and the United Netherlands had little trouble with the corsairs operating from the regencies in the Maghrib as long as these states were also either at war with, or hostile to, the kingdoms of Spain, but when these three states made peace with the "enemy," the corsairs ceased to regard them as allies, and before long arrested merchant ships belonging to their erstwhile friends, and condemned their crews to slavery. As we shall see, protests at Istanbul could reverse the decisions in the first decade of the new century, but before long the sultan's authority could not assure safety to any ships plying the Mediterranean.

However, up to the first decade of the seventeenth century, the kingdoms of Spain were still the prime enemies of the Barbary regencies. Refugees from Spanish intolerance fed this hostility. Many of them became rich and influential; others happily joined the "Holy War." Even had the Spanish become more reasonable in their attitudes toward Islam and the Barbary, these refugee families and the native Moors who well remembered the brutality of Spanish soldiers and marines who had landed on their coast would have had no trouble convincing their neighbors that Spain was still the enemy.

The other problems of Spain at the end of the sixteenth and opening of the seventeenth centuries have some of the aspects of a tragic drama. Charles V and his son Philip II ruled the vast conglomerate known as the Spanish empire for almost a century. They had a political complex that stretched from the Philippines off the Asiatic coast, to the Americas, and the Iberian peninsula and Italy. For a long time this great empire seemed to be supported by gold and silver from the New World, but in fact this treasure would not have been enough for their needs if Charles V and his successor Philip II had not also been able to draw wealth and power from the kingdom of Castile. In many ways the fateful fact about this Spanish empire was its dependence upon Castile for the money and the soldiers to defend the entire complex, for neither Charles nor any of his Hapsburg successors were ever able to force or persuade the other Spanish kingdom (Aragon) and its dependencies in the Mediterranean to carry any considerable part of the expense of the wars that filled the entire sixteenth century. Castile was rich, and Castile had as its dependencies the far-flung empire beyond the seas that also brought wealth into its king's treasury, but Charles's wars with France and the Ottoman Empire, and Philip's wars with France, England, the Ottoman Empire, and his own subjects in the Netherlands, placed terrible drains on that wealth. By 1600 Spain seemed still to be the political military giant that had walked so heavily across the history of the past century, but a closer look at the debts of the Spanish king, at the demographic and economic situation of Castile, and at the situation of the mines in the New World where soon the flow of precious metal would slow up, all suggested that the giant was in serious trouble. When Philip III came to the throne, the Spanish empire was really in trouble. The new king was better prepared to be a monk than a ruler, and the problems that beset his government could not be solved by the inept men who governed his lands. They might strike out to end the war in the Netherlands or to wipe out the "vipers' nest" at Algiers, but they were unable to do either. The hundred years of decline and decay that was to end a century later with the war of the Spanish Succession had begun; even a vigorous statesman, Gaspar de Guzman, Duke of Olivares (1521–43), was unable to stem the process.

The decay that was imminent in the Spanish empire was reflected in the decline of Spanish commerce. There were several factors involved in that process. Undoubtedly the activities of the Barbary corsairs was one of them, but the incursions of their counterparts, the English "sea dogs" and Dutch "sea beggars," and the astonishing explosion of English and Dutch piracy in the Mediterranean basin also had serious consequences for Spanish seaborn trade. These English and Dutch pirates and privateers were welcomed in North African ports where they sold their booty and refreshed their crews and sometimes joined their hosts as renegade reis. These men owed no allegiance to the Grand Seigneur and therefore had no hesitation in attacking the ships of Ottoman allies like the French or friends like England or Venice. Their powerful sailing ships, armed with cannons, were an important factor in the decline of Venice[1] and also of Spain's Mediterranean dependencies. The Spanish considered violent reprisals for the depredations of both pirates and Algerian reis, but plans for an assault on Algiers at the turn of the century came to nothing. The Spanish military had become too cumbersome and beset with internal problems to allow any success.

1. Albert Tenenti, *Piracy and the Decline of Venice, 1580–1615.*

Curiously enough, the decline in Spanish power was paralleled by a decay in the strength of the Ottoman empire. The two giants that had met at Malta, Lepanto, Tunis, and a dozen other battle-fields both showed signs of weakness at the same time. After Sulei-man the influence of the sultanas, the venality of officials, the de-cline in the discipline and efficiency of the janissary corps, weakened the authority of the Sublime Porte and with it the power to control its creatures. The decision not to appoint another beylerbey to suc-ceed Euldj Ali for fear that so strong a figure might completely break away from Ottoman control was symptomatic of the problems con-fronting Suleiman's successors. As we have already seen, the pashas appointed to govern often enough had little experience to equip them for the office. They were neither sailors nor soldiers and they showed little understanding of the complexities of the government of the regency. The result was further weakening of the ties between Istan-bul and Algiers, for the pasha as the sultan's representative could not really govern.

This combination of forces at the end of the sixteenth century fi-nally led to conflicts between the Barbary regencies and France, England and the Netherlands. The long tradition of friendship with France gave French shipping some immunity as long as the Grand Seigneur's writ carried in his empire, but after the long civil wars, French commerce, especially from Marseille, again assumed an important place on the highways of the Mediterranean, and inev-itably attracted the greedy attention of the pirates as well as the corsair reis. The French had the capitulations granted by the sultan, and also the favor of the Sublime Porte to protect their shipping, but once France was at peace with Spain the sultan's protection was less effective. Furthermore, since French merchant vessels made good profits from carrying both goods and passengers from Spain and Italy, there was a question whether the French flag could really protect foreigners on French ships. This was lucrative both to the merchant ships and to the French consuls in the Levant who collected two percent consulage on all merchandise bought or sold by Christian merchants (except the English) in the Ottoman Levan-tine ports. Were they carrying "enemy" goods? Was it contraband? The Moslem reis naturally justified their captures on the grounds that it was. Pirates mostly operating from Tunis raided any shipping indiscriminately. French protests had little effect.

A serious crisis broke in 1604. North Africa, along with much of western Europe, was visited by a famine, and when it was learned that the French concessionaires at the bastion were exporting grain to France that should have fed Algiers, there was a great agitation. The Algerian janissaries aided by the galleys of Mourat Reis, the famous corsair admiral, attacked and sacked the bastion. When Henry IV protested in Istanbul the Algerians responded by violence against the person of the French consul. However, the kingdom of France still had influence in Istanbul and the sultan enough power to remove and strangle the pasha who had failed to stop the assault on the French concession. Sultan Amat and Henry IV made a new agreement that expressly forbade the Barbary corsairs to enslave Frenchmen or to confiscate their goods and ships. In return the North African reis were assured of the right to refit their ships in French ports and to buy supplies in the French market.

The pirates, operating from Barbary ports not bound by this agreement, continued their attacks on French commerce. Henry IV had no effective naval force, but he did commission a condottiere privateering navy under Sr. de Beaulieu to attack the pirates at Tunis. De Beaulieu was most successful when he joined forces with the Spanish Sicilian Mediterranean armada in an assault on the Tunisian port, La Goulette. They sank or burned sixteen warships that mounted over four hundred pieces of artillery. For a short time the pirates were less troublesome. This did not affect Algiers.

The serious breach between France and the regency of Algiers came a little later over the incident of the cannons of Captain Simon Danser. This time it was the French rather than the Barbary regency that behaved questionably. The issue was the result of a pardon that Henry IV awarded Captain Danser, a pirate reis whose daring exploits at sea had earned him the title "Diablo-Reis" among the Algerians. He seems to have been a Fleming, but he had a wife living in Marseille and was anxious to give up his active role in the Algerian corsair community for a more peaceful enjoyment of his great riches.[2] Danser got his French pardon through the mediation of the Jesuits for whom he rescued six of their members from slavery. He managed to get most of his treasure aboard his ship and to sail to Marseille. He was luckier than another northern pirate, Bonel, who was brought to Marseille at the same time and beheaded. Danser, grateful for generous treatment by the French government, presented the duc de Guise, the governor of the province, with two brass cannons, which, unfortunately for subsequent events, were on loan to him from the

---

2. Danser was only one of many such adventurers: Ward, Bishop, Johnson, Glanfield, Graves, Binny Arras, Samson, Denball, and others with English, Dutch, and Flemish names were his comrades. Some of them became renegades; others, like Danser, remained "Christians" regardless of how they lived.

government of Algiers. Naturally the Algerians, shocked at Danser's "treason," demanded the return of the two cannons.

The political crisis moved slowly but surely. Guise refused to give up his cannons, but it was events in France, quite unconnected with Danser, that delayed action. Henry IV was murdered, the regent Marie de Medici had troubles to worry about both in the Rhineland and in Paris. Nothing was done. This was the sort of crisis that the Algerian reis were waiting for: French Mediterranean commerce was plentiful and rich and tempting, and with the refusal of the French king to grant redress, it was an excellent opportunity for the corsairs. The pasha who should have protected his sultan's ally had his own troubles with famine, an earthquake, and rebellions or threats of rebellions by the Kabylie and the coulougli. Thus, Frenchmen were soon seen in the slave market, and French ships with their cargoes were sold at Algiers as prizes. Marseille's losses soon were running into the thousands of livres, French slaves were demanding relief on the part of their king, and Algiers entered a new era of prosperity.

There were protests in Istanbul, but the Algerians were now able to delay or refuse to give answers. The Marseille merchants bought and armed five sailing ships built in Holland to take reprisals on their tormenters; we are told that their commander, de Vincheguerre, had less success than Beaulieu had had, and yet by 1617 there were several hundred "Turks and Moors" serving as galley slaves in France. As a result whether the French wished it or not, France was at war with Algiers, and French merchantmen and sailors were prizes sold at auction in that city.

The English experience at the turn of the seventeenth century was similar to that of the French. English ships were rare in the Mediterranean before the 1580s, but Elizabeth did secure a treaty with the Porte that allowed the so-called Levant (or Turkey) Company to establish consuls and carry on business in the port towns of the Ottoman empire. The Algerian reis at first regarded these English ships as fair game, and the pasha at Algiers refused to give the English ships safe conduct letters; indeed, he told the representative of the Levant Company that he expected his corsairs to make some English prizes. However, there were few, for the English ships were well armed and usually capable of taking care of themselves. Indeed, after five English merchantmen successfully beat off a squadron of Doria's galleys (1586), the pasha at Algiers "showed himself marvelously glad to entertain them in the best sort, and promising abundant relief for all their wants, making a general proclamation in the citie upon paine of death no man . . . should presume either to hinder them in their affairs or to offer them any manner of injurie in body or goods."[3] Even so in 1600 the Levant Company's consul, one Mr. Tipton, had to live in the Jewish quarter and found many reasons for protesting to the pasha about the activity of the reis vis-à-vis English ships and seamen; the latter became slaves when their ships were captured or sunk by Algerian corsairs.

In 1600, however, the shoe was also on the other foot. Two English captains (pirates?) brought in a vessel to be sold as a prize, claiming that it was of Spanish origin. Shortly afterward the real captain of the captured ship appeared in Algiers to inform the pasha that the vessel had been under Venetian registry and he demanded justice. The capture was a simple act of piracy. Before the Algerians could act, the Englishmen had burned the prize, and the fire nearly destroyed all the vessels in the harbor. Suleiman Bey wrote to Elizabeth protesting that this illegal act endangered the harbor, frustrated Algerian justice, and could result in Venetian reprisals. This came at the very end of Elizabeth's reign, and her successor did nothing about it on the grounds that the Englishmen in question were not under his control. Soon the evil behavior of other English pirate-privateers became a scandal. Captains Bent and Buccolli who had evoked the first protest were only the forerunners of the English adventurers and freebooter pirates who operated out of North African harbors after James I made peace with Spain. They and the Dutch sometimes became renegades, sometimes remained Christian, but in either role their lives and patterns of behavior made the pious Moslems sure that Christians were evil and unruly men. However, even while their whoring and drinking and gambling scandalized many Mohammedans, the North African reis welcomed the men who taught them to break through the Straits into the Atlantic, where they captured English ships.

Englishmen did not even have to wait until their new king made peace with Spain to have their ships raided by the corsairs from Algiers. In September 1602 the lord admiral of England wrote to the consul at Algiers and the ambassador at Istanbul to protest the capture of the *Marigold* in the Atlantic and the loss of some 1,730 pounds sterling. While the French at this period were able to have a pasha removed and strangled, the English had no such influence.

3. Philip Jones, *True Account*, 1586.

James I's peace with Spain ended whatever immunity English ships had from the Algerian raiders just at the very time that the reis, aided by the northern renegades and adventurers, were beginning the greatest period of their corsair activity. As we have seen, the corsairs could insist that Spanish merchandise and Spanish passengers were fair game, but this was an excuse when a friendly flag tried to cover enemy goods or persons. When events allowed them to regard English, Dutch, or French ships as belonging to an enemy of Algiers, no excuse was necessary. And as soon as their ships were operating on both sides of the Straits and indeed ranging from the Canaries to Iceland and beyond to the fishing banks off North America, the Algerian corsairs easily found and captured English shipping. If the legality of a capture was questioned, the simple expedient of looting the vessel, enslaving the crew, and sending the ship to the bottom of the sea destroyed most of the evidence. In the first seven years of James's reign the English ambassador in Spain asserted that four hundred sixty-six Englishmen were captured and enslaved by the Algerians, and the king's government could do nothing about it. Its only action was to grant commissions to English captains for cruising against the pirates, which allowed the captain to keep whatever he might capture with no payment to the admiralty.

For its part the Levant Company managed to fight off most of the corsairs by sending flotillas of heavily armed merchant ships in convoy. These big merchantmen were more than a match for the corsair galiots; in fact, one of them armed with nineteen guns stood off five "Turkish" galiots commanded by an English renegade named Walsynham, and forced them to withdraw. But it also went otherwise. In one engagement half of a fishing fleet of thirty vessels fell prey to the corsairs off Newfoundland. Thus by the second decade of the seventeenth century the corsair flotillas operating from Algiers had become a serious menace to the shipping of England and other northern states. There seemed to be no easy redress. Sir Francis Cottingham, England's ambassador to Spain, wrote in 1617: "The strength and boldness of the Barbary pirates is now grown to that height, both in the Mediterranean and the Ocean, as I have never known anything to have wrought a greater sadness and distraction to this court." There were suggestions both in Madrid and London for joint Anglo-Spanish naval action against Algiers. When this operation became possible, however, the Spanish had second thoughts about joint action with their erstwhile English enemies.

James I and his ministers learned of the problem from their unhappy subjects. Before the end of the second decade of the seventeenth century the number of petitions for the king's bounty from Englishmen enslaved in Algiers, as well as requests from English merchants to the Admiralty for protection, demanded some sort of action. Sir William Monson, a sailor with fifty years of service behind him and a considerable knowledge of conditions in the Mediterranean, prepared a memorandum for the king's government. Its basic premise was that the corsair reis could not be controlled without the cooperation of all the Christian European powers, both Protestant and Catholic. Algiers, he noted, was guarded by "desperate rogues and renegades . . . who have renounced God and virtue . . ." All attempts to capture the city had failed; the only hope for success would require cooperation of all the European powers. This observation is interesting in that it was to be repeated by one memoirist after another for the next two hundred years. Monson went on to suggest a stop-gap expedient similar to the proposal of a group of Bristol merchants, who suggested that merchants from the coastal towns of Europe should be commissioned to attack the towns and villages of North Africa to capture men, women, and children to sell in the markets of Spain and Malta. These privateers should also be assured of their possession of everything that they could capture. Monson also insisted that every renegade reis captured should be immediately hanged, and no Moslem reis should ever be freed to return home. It is clear that the corsair reis had no monopoly on ruthless behavior.

Nothing came of Monson's proposals, but bloody battles at sea and more Englishmen in slavery convinced Buckingham and the king that something should be done. They decided, however, not to act in conjunction with the Dutch because of the latters' brutal treatment of English seamen in the Far East. An all-English expedition that might cooperate with the Spanish fleet was their answer. Apparently the Levant Company was persuaded to help underwrite the expenses to the tune of twenty thousand pounds, and the ambassador at Madrid secured promises of Spanish aid. The English armada that finally left for the Mediterranean consisted of six regular warships mounting two hundred thirty brass guns and twelve merchantmen with two hundred forty-three iron guns of smaller caliber.[4] Sir Robert Mansel commanded this fleet from his flagship the *Lyon*,

4. By 1620 England's iron industry was making iron cannons on a large scale. It was the foremost producer of iron guns in Europe. However, the iron gun was dangerous to the crew that manned it because of the tendency to explode; Europe had not yet learned to make iron without considerable impurities. The bronze or *fonte* gun was much better; it did not rust the way iron did, and explosions were rare.

a warship of six hundred tons burden, forty guns, and a crew of two hundred and fifty. Mansel's ships were more than a match in fire-power for anything the corsairs could put against them, but the corsair ships were faster and more easily maneuvered, so the advantage of the English firepower was more or less canceled.

Mansel arrived before Algiers late in November 1620; the visit turned out to be fruitless. The pasha immediately sent honeyed words about his "Emperor's command to treat the English with friendship and respect," but even then, with the English anchored off the city, an Algerian reis brought in two English vessels as prizes. The pasha immediately announced that the captives would be freed. On December 3, a squadron of six Spanish warships arrived and fired seventy-four balls into the city. The harbor guns replied. No damage was done to either side; nor did the English give the Spaniards any help. A few days later, when rough weather threatened, Mansel sailed away. He had succeeded in freeing about forty English slaves, all of them overaged; hundreds of other Englishmen were still in Algiers.

Mansel went to Spain for supplies, and to make plans for use of Spanish galleys to tow fireboats in position to burn the Algerian fleet. There was a comedy of misunderstandings. A Dutch squadron appeared off the coast, presumably waiting for the twelve-year truce with Spain to end; its commander proposed joint action with Mansel against the Algerians. The Spanish assumed that the plan then was for a joint attack on them as soon as the truce ended. In the end, neither Dutch nor Spanish aided Mansel's plans. He did try to burn the Algerians by himself, but the wind was against him and his oar-powered boats were not strong enough to put the fireboats in position. He finally withdrew. The tradition that his mission was a miserable failure is reflected in every account of the expedition except that of Julian Corbett, who exonerates Mansel with the curious remark that obviously was more characteristic of Corbett than of the English government in 1621: "The English government," he writes, "had no intention of throwing away a fleet in rashly attacking the most ruthless enemy of Spain." If that statement is true, why did the government send Mansel to Algiers in the first place?

The English response to the enslavement of Englishmen and looting of English ships does seem feeble, but in 1620–21 the English navy was weak and the English exchequer was quite unprepared for a long or expensive operation far from English shores, especially against a foe so hard to get at. Furthermore, James I was more concerned at this moment about the fate of his daughter, whose husband, the "Winter King," Frederick of the Palatinate, was expelled from Bohemia that very year. He also aspired to marry his son Charles to a Hapsburg princess of Spain. The corsair reis were a menace, but at that moment events in Europe (the Thirty Years War) were more dangerous to a king who wanted above all to keep peace for his kingdom and security for his dynasty and throne. The corsairs responded to English weakness; Secretary Burchell wrote, "Sir Richard Mansel's back was scarcely turned but these corsairs picked up forty good sail belonging to the subjects of his master, and infested the Spanish coast with greater fury than ever."

One incident from Mansel's expedition is an interesting footnote to the situation in both England and Algiers. The pasha demanded that Mansel should appoint a consul, but the admiral had no one "suitable" for the post. So he dressed a "common man" in gentleman's clothing and put him ashore with one hundred pounds in his pocket. We do not know what actually happened to Richard Foorde. The Public Record Office has letters from him in which he tells of the wretched state of English slaves, of his spending the one hundred pounds to rescue some of them, of his own precarious position without money or friends. He faced the hostility of the pasha, hunger, and an existence "scarcely better than that of the slaves." There is, however, no evidence that the English government did anything for him; a "common man" was obviously expendable. The next year, however, the English government did decide that a treaty must be made and an English consul was appointed to look after English commerce, to attempt to secure freedom for slaves, to prevent Englishmen from becoming renegades, and, finally, to keep Algiers from joining England's enemies in case of war.

Sir Thomas Roe, England's ambassador to the Sublime Porte, made a treaty with "those of Algiers" in March 1622 that presumably established peace between the two states on a firm basis. An English consul was to be appointed to Algiers, and English merchants were to bring cloth and other commodities (war supplies) to Algiers for sale. The English king agreed to repurchase seventeen "Turks" that Mansel had sold in Spain in exchange for a similar number of English slaves in Algiers. Other English slaves could be freed by purchase. James I confirmed the treaty and appointed James Frizell to be the consul. His salary, to be the responsibility of the Levant Company, was paid for only two years. Frizell's letters for over a decade after 1626 indicate that the company did not pay, and that the king somehow failed to make it do so. Nor were Frizell's demands for the appointment of another consul more successful. The reason for the company's neglect seems to have been the fact that merchants not connected with the Turkey Company intruded into the trade at Algiers, so the consul was left to support himself with the consulate fees.

Frizell's road was not an easy one. The Algerians had made peace with England, as the pasha explained in a letter to James I, because the sultan had ordered it, and they were obliged "to obey the orders of Allah, His Holy Prophet, and their lord the sultan." But they soon had complaints. English merchants, contrary to the treaty, transported enemy goods and passengers from port to port and refused to surrender either of them on demand from the corsairs. English sea captains captured and sold Turks and Moors into slavery, and the seventeen Turks and Moors whom Mansel had sold in Spain were not returned. The Public Record Office documents never solve this problem. Were these men ever repurchased? We do not know. The pasha wrote to James that "had it not been for the intelligence and discretion of your faithful servant James Frizell . . . it would have had a more troublesome end." Even so the king's government gave Frizell no recompense for his services although these were to continue for a long time to come.

Sir Thomas Roe's treaty that ended the first war between England and the Algerian regency was to become the basis for all future agreements between the two countries. Sir Thomas, it seems, was highly diffident about treating with the Algerians, whose culture and political sophistication were much below that of the ministers at the Sublime Porte at Istanbul, but to get peace he had to deal "with those of Algiers" and to agree on the establishment of a consul who was as much a representative of his king as of the interests of the merchant company trading in the Levant. His treaty was the first recognition on the part of the English government that Algiers was in fact, if not in the legal fiction of the day, a quasi-independent society with which the European powers would have to deal even though they might regard negotiations with "such people" as beneath the dignity of a European prince. Other states with commerce in the Mediterranean were also soon to be forced to recognize the real situation in the Algerian regency, and to negotiate directly with the pasha, agha, and divan rather than with the Sublime Porte at Istanbul.

The Dutch did not become deeply involved in Mediterranean commerce until the early years of the seventeenth century so that

they were later than either the French or the English in discovering
the problems that the Barbary corsairs presented to European princes.
The rebellion of the United Netherlands against their ruler, who
happened to be the king of the Spains and Portugal, made the
commerce of the Iberian peninsula a natural target for the Dutch
privateers. Armed with letters of mark, they ranged from the Channel
to the approaches to Europe from both the New World and Africa
and finally sent their ships around Africa to India and beyond. By
the opening years of the seventeenth century, Dutch merchants and
bankers had parlayed their position in the commercial world into a
complex of empire and trade that made Amsterdam the center of all
north European commerce. Goods from the Baltic, from the Orient,
from Russia's White Sea, from French ports on the Atlantic and the
Bay of Biscay, from Germany, and from England were brought to
Amsterdam, graded, sometimes refinished (wine was cut with
water!), and then re-exported—and all in Dutch ships. This empire
forced Englishmen to go to Amsterdam to buy Swedish, German,
Russian, French, and Oriental goods. Likewise Frenchmen, Germans, Russians, Swedes, and others did not trade with each other;
they sent their goods (in Dutch ships) to Amsterdam and bought
the goods of the world from Amsterdam. The price of copper, tin,
wool, bullets, powder, wine, cheese, indeed hundreds of commodities was set at Amsterdam, and the Dutch sea captains carried these
goods to and from the world. With such an empire, it should come
as no surprise that Dutchmen appeared in the Mediterranean basin
as soon as their military power allowed them to break through the
Straits to attack their enemy, Spain, from the rear. Like the English
seamen, the early Dutch invaders of that sea were privateers who
often found it easy to become pirates. Venetian and French shipping
suffered as much from these invaders with their high walled ships as
did the Spanish empire's subjects from Barcelona to Naples. As
pirates, many of these Dutch adventurers discovered that they could
operate out of Barbary harbors in cooperation with the Moslem corsairs.

   After 1609 Dutch merchantmen also came through the Straits to
buy and sell rather than to make war on their erstwhile enemy Spain,
and Dutchmen were soon being sold in the slave markets at Tunis
and Algiers, and Dutch cargoes and ships were taken as prizes. The
rulers of the United Netherlands first tried to neutralize the Barbary
corsairs by a treaty with the sultan similar to those made by the
French and English. The 1612 treaty assured Dutch shipping and

seamen against capture by the North African corsairs (as long as the Dutch did not resort to piracy), and the North Africans were promised haven in Dutch harbors as well as the opportunity to buy naval and war supplies. The treaty specifically forbade the sale of Dutchmen in Greece or Asia Minor; the fact that it did not include North Africa seems to indicate that the Sublime Porte recognized that its authority was less there than it was closer to the sultan's capital city. This treaty with the sultan did not, could not, prevent difficulties between Dutch commercial interests and the Maghrib corsair communities.

The Dutch were no longer Algiers' "allies" against a common foe, and were anxious to trade in Spanish ports. Dutch sea captains were ready to ship Spanish goods and carry Spanish passengers from one port to another. There was no universally recognized international law covering this problem, yet the Dutch regularly insisted that trade should not be interfered with by war. Since they were willing to trade with the enemy or the friend at any time, they wanted their flag to cover all goods and passengers in their ships.[5] The Algerian reis insisted on their right to confiscate the goods and to enslave the subjects of their foes found on any ships whatsoever. Nor was that the only problem: the Algerians did not freely accept the immunity that the sultan's treaty had granted the Dutch ships and seamen. Dutch shipping was too tempting a target, for, unlike the English, whose big merchantmen carried formidable armament, the Dutch usually shipped in small lightly armed freighters that were an easy mark for the corsair reis. Thus, in spite of the treaty, between 1613 and 1622 the Algerians made prize of four hundred and forty-seven Dutch ships. They were mostly small, and they were a tiny percentage of all Dutch ships on the seas, yet they were losses, and the merchants of Amsterdam wanted them stopped.

In 1622 the Dutch by-passed the sultan and made a treaty with the "City and Kingdom of Algiers," but the corsairs, unready to forfeit the opportunity for rich prizes, continued to take Dutch ships. Therefore in 1624 a Dutch squadron appeared in the Mediterranean, captured several Algerian vessels, and then dropped anchor before Algiers. Admiral Lambert demanded that all Dutch slaves must be released and a treaty negotiated that would be respected. In case of refusal he announced that he would hang all his captives. Pasha,

5. In the seventeenth century the laws of war at sea were ill defined. The Dutch wished always to hold to the proposition that neutral ships covered all merchandise. The Algerians, and later the English, insisted on the right to confiscate contraband goods—and to define what was contraband!

agha, and divan decided that this was a bluff and refused to be intimidated. On the refusal Lambert promptly hanged from the spars of his ships the Turks and Moors that he had captured—and sailed away. As soon as he had captured another group of Algerian Turks and Moors, he returned with the same threat. This time the people of Algiers protested so strongly that the government did release the Dutch slaves and the Dutch ships still in custody and declared themselves willing to make a new treaty. The treaty of January 1626 reaffirmed the earlier one with a few additional articles.

The Dutch treaties with Algiers are important documents in that they dramatically highlight the problems that Northern European princes were having with the corsairs. The first question to be "settled" was the rights of neutral ships to carry goods and passengers of an enemy of the Barbary regency. The treaty provided that the corsairs could hail a Dutch ship and, when the merchantman lowered his flag, could send a small boarding party to examine the cargo and passengers. If there were enemy contraband goods aboard they could be confiscated after payment of the freight to ultimate destination; if enemy passengers were aboard they could be taken captive. But neither the crew nor non-enemy passengers nor any goods belonging to neutrals could be taken. The treaty also expressly forbade any rough or brutal treatment of any members of the crew to force them to "confess" to the existence of "enemy" persons or goods on the ship. It was not uncommon for the corsairs to bastinado crewmen to get confessions that would allow them to confiscate or enslave.

The treaty also provided for the establishment of a "consul ambassador" at Algiers with special regard for his status. As we have noted, the Algerians had very often held the consul responsible for the acts of his fellow countrymen no matter whether they were official acts or those of a private person. The consul was sometimes thrown in irons and imprisoned, and in case of an actual breach, his very life was in danger; he was considered as a sort of "hostage" and was not even allowed to board a warship without an exchange of "hostages." In the Dutch treaty, it was agreed that the consul was to be allowed to leave the city freely, that he was not responsible for the debts of his fellow countrymen or the actions of private Dutch sea captains. He was to be allowed to have horses and to travel freely outside the city, and finally in case of a war between the United Provinces and Algiers, he would be allowed to leave peacefully. All these privileges had been accorded—if not always respected—by the Grand Seigneur to European ambassadors. The Algerian-Dutch treaty extended them now to the consul at Algiers. Thus the

Dutch were recognizing the "powers" at Algiers as at least a quasi-sovereign state.

Other articles dealt with the rights and privileges of merchants trading at Algiers. In the first place the Algerians gave up their usual practice of forcing a merchant vessel to send its sails and cordage ashore for "safe keeping" until it would be given the right to depart. Dutch merchants were not to be required to "loan" money to Algerian officials and not to be forced to pay tariff duties except on goods actually bought or sold. They were expressly allowed to exchange their merchandise for local produce, and in case the goods bought did not pay for the goods sold, they were to be allowed to accept specie money and carry it with them. They were also expressly allowed to import "forbidden items": powder, lead, shot, white and grey iron, tin, bullets, cannons, oars, sails, cordage, and cables. These were of course "forbidden" to be exported but very welcome as imports. Dutch merchants were allowed to deal in herring, cheese, butter, beer, and other foodstuffs, and the merchants and their crews were not to be mistreated by any persons while they were in Algiers.

Another problem covered by these treaties concerned the status and possible use of Dutch slaves. The treaty prohibited the practice of freeing a slave on condition that he would go on a cruise with an Algerian reis, unless at the same time the slave renounced his religion. Dutch seamen were obviously more skilled in handling the ships with tall masts and big sails, and these skills were in demand for the corsair ships. At the same time, the treaty forbade the landing of Dutch slaves or Dutch renegades in case a corsair ship should take refuge in a harbor under the jurisdiction of the Prince of Orange. This measure was protection for the patrons who owned slaves, and for the life of the renegade, who probably would be executed were he to come under Christian jurisdiction.

The treaty of 1626 reaffirmed that of 1623 made with the Sublime Porte, with an interesting formula guaranteeing its observance. The pasha and high officers of the Algerian regency insisted that they were entering this treaty without "treason or tromperie in their hearts" and that any infractions would be "upon their heads." For their part, the subjects of the Prince of Orange were expected to "swear before their God" that they were not carrying Spanish goods or passengers. This was easy for the Dutch at that moment for they were again locked in another desperate struggle with the Hapsburg princes that was to last until the middle of the century.[6]

6. These treaties are reproduced in Dumont, V, II, pp. 413–415, 485–487.

Like the English, the Dutch discovered that they could not secure any redress for their complaints at Istanbul. The regency already had come to a point where it controlled its own foreign policy, and therefore any successful negotiations had to be carried on at Algiers.

As we have already noted above, at the same time that the English king and the Dutch regents discovered that their treaty with the Grand Seigneur did not guarantee the safety of their ships and seamen against the depredations of the Barbary corsairs, the French too fell at odds with Algiers over the two brass cannons that Captain Danser presented to the duc de Guise. Marseille merchants had had trouble with the inroads of pirates and corsairs even before Danser arrived in their port, but when the duc de Guise refused to return the two guns, the situation drifted into open war between the kingdom of France and Algiers. This was very satisfactory to the Algerian reis; French shipping between Marseille and the Levant provided fat prizes, relatively easy to capture since the French vessels were small and rarely sailed in convoy. Marseille's cries for help were soon heard in Paris, but Marie de Medici had too many other problems troubling her regency to give great attention to Algiers. (After the murder of Henry IV, in 1610, Marie de Medici became regent for her young son, Louis XIII.)

Yet Marie's government was not the only one with problems. The pasha at Algiers who should have protected the French from the inroads of the reis had to listen to his corsair captains rather than to the viziers at Istanbul, for Algiers was suffering from famine, earthquake, and a rebellion of the Kabylie tribesmen, and the pasha had to concentrate all his efforts simply to maintain his wavering authority. Thus he authorized the reis to take French prizes and to sell Frenchmen in the slave market of Algiers even though the French had a friendly treaty with the sultan.

All at once the problem of freeing French slaves in Algiers became much larger and more complex. Danser's cannons brought France into a war with Algiers even though France was the favored nation in Istanbul. It was serious, for the corsair reis began to take French commercial shipping on a large scale. As their losses mounted, the merchants of Marseille lost confidence in the power of the little fleet commanded by Jaques de Vincheguerre and demanded that the king's government must come to their assistance. The men in Paris could find no other route than an attempt to secure the aid of the Sultan. The French ambassador at Istanbul begged for relief from the incursions of these unruly Ottoman subjects on the Barbary Coast. Evidently the sultan was willing to listen, and, as it turned out, he still had some influence in Algiers, for when a Turkish emissary carried orders that the pasha at Algiers must negotiate with the French for peace, the pasha and divan agreed to do so. The pasha's powers in 1617 were still sufficient to allow him to discuss terms of peace with a representative of the king of France. However, the royal government in Paris that had secured the intervention from Istanbul would not deal directly with the pasha, agha, and divan of Algiers. These "powers" in the corsair city simply represented a provincial government; thus only French provincial authorities could negotiate with them and not lose face. The duc de Guise, as governor of Provence and concessionaire at the Bastion of France, sent Baron d'Allemagne to work out a treaty at Algiers. This was actually a frank recognition of the fact that Algiers had a policy and powers that might not be the same as those of the Sublime Porte at Istanbul, but the king of France did not thereby recognize the corsair regency as equal. The negotiations moved slowly and did not yield fully satisfactory results; moreover, the first token return of Turkish slaves was bungled by the French naval commander. He failed to keep the captives under his control, and they simply disappeared in the crowds at Algiers. French protests drew a blank. Both sides assumed bad faith. However, by 1619 the Algerians, urged on by the sultan, assured the French king that they were ready to negotiate and "had every intention of guarding as inviolate the terms of the capitulations . . ." The duc de Guise was less sure; he wrote: "His Majesty finds it difficult to have confidence in their words . . . they have badly used the orders of their emperor." Nonetheless, since some way must be found to make the sea secure for French commerce, His Majesty "will find a way to end the problems between them."[7]

At last a treaty was written, and an Algerian delegation went to France to put a final seal on the peace, but an irrational act again led to hostilities. An Algerian reis with a reputation for violence stopped a French square-sailed ship (*polacre*) loaded with a very rich cargo. Its papers were in order and peace had been announced, but the reis could not resist the chance for riches. He pillaged the ship and murdered the entire crew, except for two young sailors who somehow managed to hide, and after much hardship, to reach Marseille with their story. Captain Drivet and the thirty-odd members of the murdered crew had friends and relatives in Marseille who demanded

7. B.N., Ms. Franc. 16141, fols. 256ff.

revenge. Unhappily also at Marseille at that moment was Caynan Aga and some forty other Algerians who had come as a peace mission. A wild mob attacked the hotel where the Algerians were staying, and in spite of efforts by calmer spirits to save them, the entire Algerian mission was promptly massacred. In the seventeenth century cities did not have police forces able to control a mob. The pamphlet *Histoire nouvelle du Massacre des Turks fait en la ville de Marseille en Provence* (15 pp. Lyon, 1620) is only the most colorful of several contemporary accounts of this unhappy event.

When the men in Algiers heard nothing from their emissaries in France, the pasha and divan asked: "What has happened to Caynan Agha?" He was both popular and powerful in the janissary corps. When the truth came to light, the Frenchmen in Algiers were almost in as much danger as Caynan Agha had been: the consul and the entire French community were thrown into prison and threatened with horrible deaths while the reis, who had not liked the peace with France, happily put to sea to make the French pay for their crime. Within six months twenty-one French prizes were sold in Algiers, five of them had cargoes valued between twenty to twenty-five thousand livres, and only eight were worth less than seven thousand livres. The French consul set the loss at two hundred eleven thousand and nine hundred livres. Only one hundred twenty-eight French sailors had been captured since many of the crews saved themselves by jumping overboard and swimming ashore.

M. Caix, the French consul in Algiers, warned the governors of Marseille that France must either make a real peace with Algiers or a "good war." For the moment the French government could do neither. Louis XIII and his favorite, Charles d'Albert de Luynes, were engaged in hopeless conflicts with both the Huguenots and the great nobles who supported the queen mother; they were unable to do anything constructive about the problems of Algiers and Marseille. In January 1621 Caix wrote that new ships were being prepared for raids against French commerce; he added that his own life had been spared only because he was lavish with his gifts. In March he announced that three hundred janissaries and fourteen warships had attacked the Bastion of France and killed or enslaved all its population, including Guise's representative, the Baron d'Allemagne. He added that there were one thousand Frenchmen enslaved in Algiers, and French losses now mounted to 1.2 million livres.

The king's government during the first years of the 1620s was nearly paralyzed by internal problems that loomed larger in Paris than the depredations of the Algerian corsairs. The chorus of complaints about losses and demands for assistance came to nothing. The French ambassador at Istanbul was able only to persuade the Porte to send letters to Algiers demanding an end to the hostility, but the divan, under pressure from the reis and also satisfied that the war with France was a just conflict, as well as a profitable one, managed to ignore the sultan's orders. By 1624 when Cardinal Richelieu was more or less firmly established as the minister in charge of foreign affairs, the situation had become a full-scale crisis. The corsairs had extended their activity into the Atlantic, and the coasts of France—even Picardy, on the Channel—as well as the Atlantic commerce were exposed to the same dangers that threatened France's Mediterranean provinces. Richelieu realized that something had to be done.

The problem was still complicated by procedural questions. The king of France had long negotiated with the sultan of the Ottoman empire as an equal, and any problems concerning the king's government and Algiers had always been discussed at Istanbul. The consul at Algiers did not report to the king; he was an agent of the authorities at Marseille. But negotiations at Istanbul were unable to affect the behavior of the Algerian regency. The English and Dutch had faced up to this problem by direct negotiations: Sir Thomas Roe dealt with "those of Algiers"; Admiral Lambert sailed into the roadstead at Algiers and dealt directly, if brutally, with the pasha, agha, and divan of the regency. Richelieu's first impulse was again to make the duc de Guise as governor of Provence responsible for the negotiations, but in February 1626, he decided that they could more effectively be carried on by an agent of the king acting under royal instructions. Richelieu may have seen this as another step in the process of bringing more and more of the affairs of the kingdom under his control. The fact that the men at Marseille later criticized and fought the action of his agent, Sanson Napollon, may be evidence of their opposition to this intrusion of royal authority into an area that had heretofore been their concern.[8]

Richelieu's agent, Napollon, was a Corsican with wide experience in the Levant, where he had been consul, secret agent, and merchant; he spoke fluent Turkish, understood Moslem customs, and had great skill as a negotiator. He first went to Istanbul and secured a letter

8. The documentation for Richelieu's intervention does provide interesting reading, but it also leaves many questions unanswered. AAE Alger Mem. et doc. XII, fols. 14–21; B.N. Ms. Franc. 16164, fols. 76–81 *et passim;* R.A., XXIII, pp. 96–112; Grammont, *Négociations, XVII Siècle,* pp. 28ff.

from the grand vizier empowering him to negotiate with the pasha, agha, and divan of Algiers. When he arrived in that city, his reception was mixed, but a generous distribution of gifts and his engaging personality overcame much of the opposition to him and a treaty, but not before the divan sent its own agent to Istanbul to establish the authenticity of Napollon's letter from the vizier. Napollon's own account of the negotiations tells of almost endless discussions, elaborate circumlocutions, long-winded speeches, and secret talks. It is the same story that diplomats and naval officers were to tell for the next two hundred years: negotiations with Algiers were always long, involved, and greased with gifts.[9]

The peace (1628) was costly, and Marseille had to foot much of the bill. Danser's cannons were "recovered" by buying them from the duc de Guise, and Napollon's gifts to members of the divan and important reis finally were paid for by the city. What about the property and slaves that the Algerians had captured? The merchandise had been sold, already eaten, or used beyond recovery; the ships had been sold or broken up for the reuse of the wood, which meant that they too could not be recovered. The slaves? There were "Turks and Moors" in slavery in France and Frenchmen in slavery in Algiers. The Turks and Moors, however, were nearly all the property of the king of France, chained to the galley oars, while the Frenchmen in Algiers were nearly all the private property of individuals, and private property, unlike state property, was sacred. If these Frenchmen were to be freed, their patrons must be compensated and allowed a "little" profit. Napollon finally agreed to the redemption price: two hundred livres for each slave belonging to individuals; the Turks and Moors in French galleys to be exchanged for French slaves belonging to the Algerian government.

We should note that this provision for repurchase soon became a serious problem. French slaves were no longer resalable in Algiers since the price was set and repurchase was presumably soon to be accomplished, but the king's government had no such an amount of money available for repurchase. Richelieu decided that the communities where the slaves had been born should pay for redemption, and the families forced to reimburse them. This would take some of the burden off Marseille and the other Mediterranean towns, but, of course, it did not work. When money was not forthcoming fast enough to satisfy the owners in Algiers, there were angry words and

9. B.N. Ms. Franc. 16141, fols. 284ff. and 294–324.

threats of new reprisals: Napollon's skills were tested to the limit. However, as long as he lived, he was able to prevent a new rupture between France and the Algerian regency.

Richelieu apparently was unhappy with the fact that he had to negotiate with the "rabble" that controlled Algiers, but his naval forces were simply incapable of imposing French will, and thus negotiation was his only solution. "It has been impossible," wrote Richelieu of himself, "for the Cardinal to repair the faults of a century." A navy that might "increase the reputation of the king and purge the seas of the corsairs . . . who had so long preyed on the subjects of Christian princes, stealing their substance and reducing their subjects to slavery could not be built in a short time, but it would be a worthy effort" for the king to build a fleet "that would force the corsairs to hide." Until such a fleet could come into being, even the Christian king of France had to deal directly with the pasha, agha, and divan of Algiers.

By the 1630s the three treaties that the Algerian authorities had negotiated with the three European states having important commercial activity in the Mediterranean signaled the opening of a new era for the regency. Heretofore the sultan at Istanbul made agreements with European princes and ordered his pashas to see that they were recognized; as late as 1604 a pasha lost both position and life for failure to do so. By the 1620s, however, the Algerian reis and janissaries had become powerful enough to ignore or refuse orders from the Sublime Porte; thus, if European princes wished to come to terms with the corsairs and the corsair community, they had to negotiate directly with Algiers. This was a development fraught with many problems and dangers, for the regency was not exactly a stable political community, and the princes who negotiated with it had little respect for this society that they came to regard as a "republic of cutthroats and thieves." Thus any agreement between the regency and a European prince was always in danger of fracture by one side or the other, and the sultan at Istanbul could no longer be relied upon to put things right.

X Algerian Regency and Europe: 1630-60

THE YEARS bounded by the crisis in Bohemia (1618) and the Peace of the Pyrenees (1659) were filled by war and revolution that affected all Western Europe from the Atlantic to the frontiers of Poland and Russia. German historians call it the era of the Thirty Years War; French historians know that the war did not end for France for another decade after peace came to Germany. English historians are interested in it as the era of the Civil Wars and the Commonwealth. It also might be known as an era of peasant revolts against tax collectors, of the Fronde in France, and of the rebellions in Barcelona, Naples, and elsewhere. These were often short but violent explosions of wrath against encroachments of royal authority. As if this were not enough to try men's ways of life, nature itself contributed to the disorders, for these were years when harvests failed and the price of bread often quadrupled to bring famine and the maladies associated with malnutrition. Meteorologists may call it the "Little Ice Age," but contemporaries knew it as stark tragedy. Small wonder that woodcuts depicting the Four Horsemen of the Apocalypse were popular with a population besieged by war, famine, pestilence, and death.

These were also years when princes and their ministers made great strides in the establishment of royal authority over baronial and municipal powers. The "absolute state" that Louis XIII spoke of as his was a political power that did not share its authority with the great nobles, town councils, or other corporations; Richelieu and his king tried to establish that power in France, and other princes were following a similar program with more or less success elsewhere in Europe. The bureaucratic-military state did not really triumph until the next generation, when princes could dispose military power overwhelmingly greater than that available to those of their subjects who might dispute with them, but the efforts of these "princely revolutionaries" added to the turmoil of the era, when great nobles or towns or religious groups or other corporations sought to curb the successful development of the "absolute state."

SPAIN 1630–60

The rulers of Spain were particularly involved in the many difficult European disorders: The rebellion in the Netherlands, the hostility of France that finally led to open warfare in 1635, rebellions and civil conflicts in Italy and Barcelona—all combined with a faltering income from both the New World mines and the tax harvest in Castile to shake the foundations of the empire that Charles V and Philip II had left to their less able descendants. From the early 1620s until the peace of the Pyrenees in 1659, the demands of soldiers fighting on a dozen fronts exhausted the treasury and the credit of the kingdoms of Spain. Added to these troubles was the endemic conflict with the Barbary regencies. The naval patrols from Alcanti and Barcelona, from Naples, Palermo, Messina, and the system of watch towers and coast guards gave some protection against the sea rovers. Perhaps the dramatic decline in Spanish commerce and particularly Spanish shipping made the corsairs a little less dangerous since there were not so many Spanish prizes available to them. As long as the larger European problems remained vitally important, however, Spain could neither prevent the corsairs from passing through the Straits nor drive off their flotillas that watched the sea lanes on both the Atlantic and Mediterranean sides of those waters.

Nonetheless, the Spanish did fight back. One Spanish historian, after explaining that the many problems limited Spanish naval activity, tells us that they did engage the corsairs: "Today it will be Fajardo who fights the Algerian ships at Cape St. Vincent, tomorrow it will be Queside on the coast of Portugal or Jaun de Canas who strikes them fiercely. At the same time the Marques de Villafranca and Santa Cruz fights them in the Mediterranean." He admits, however, that the battles were indecisive. The Spanish did capture an Algerian admiral galley, and they did destroy a good number of corsair vessels, yet the total effect was small. The fact was that between 1521 and the peace of Westphalia (1648) the most important obligation of the Spanish naval establishment was to guard the lifeline from Spain to Genoa, the first leg on the long tortuous route that connected Spain with both the Rhineland and Austria; it was a large task that often overtaxed the declining naval forces of Spain.

If the armadas of the king of Spain were unable to curb the North African corsairs, it was also true that the armadas of the sultan of the Ottoman empire could not halt the depredations of the Knights of St. John at Malta. Although the knights were vassals of the kingdom of Sicily, their obligations to the Spanish empire were nominal; their important activity was the "holy war" against Islam. This included war against the Barbary corsairs, but more importantly, war against Islamic commerce and pilgrims in the eastern Mediterranean. Malta was even better suited as the base for a corsair community than Algiers. The latter had only its man-made mole to protect the anchorage from the seas, while Malta had several good ports, including the magnificent situation at La Valette, where two deep harbors side by side were easily guarded by impressive fortifications. Moreover Malta was located in the central Mediterranean; from its harbors, ships could reach both the Turkish Levant and the Spanish Ponant.

The deep harbor at La Valette made Malta a natural stopping place for French merchant ships on their route to the Levant. Wood, water, and other supplies were available there, especially after a number of French merchant houses had established factories (warehouse compounds) to facilitate their Levantine trade. The harbor also had long been a base for Christian corsairs who secured letters of mark from the Grand Master and flew the Maltese flag. In the early seventeenth century there were sixty to eighty corsair ships of various sizes operating from Malta. The fact that most of these sea captains were Frenchmen made both the sultan and the North African regency rulers wonder whether France was not really their enemy even though the French ambassador at Istanbul assured them that these corsairs were in no way connected with the king of France.

With both merchants and corsairs using its ports, the island developed an important slave market as well as opportunity to dispose of captured ships and their cargoes. By the end of the sixteenth century these enterprises, plus the activity of the corsairs, demanded some organization. So in 1605 the Grand Master created the *Tribunale degli armamenti* as a board with the power to regulate the corsairs flying the Maltese flag. Every corsair captain took an oath to respect these regulations.

One of these forbade the molestation of Christian commerce as well as any infidel ship armed with a pass from a Christian prince. This fact created problems. The captains of these corsair ships took an oath not to molest Christian shipping or Moslem shipping armed with a pass from a Christian prince. But what in fact was "Christian shipping"? The courts at Malta were plagued with cases that arose out of the fact that the Greek Orthodox and other Christian churches in the Levant were both Christian and subject to the Grand Seigneur. Were they possible prize victims when they went to sea? Were they schismatics, or were they heretics? They were a headache for the court and the corsairs who hunted in the Levant for prizes, for they would come to Malta and sue their tormentors in the Grand Master's tribunals. These eastern Christians, however, were not the ones upon whom fell most of the pressure from the knights and the Maltese corsairs. North African villages suffered at their hands the same sort of tribulations encountered by the villages on the coasts of Spain, the Islands, and Italy. Malta was a Christian Algiers in more ways than one; it had a slave population almost equal to that found at Algiers, and revolts or dangers of revolt there were as real as at Algiers.

However, by the middle of the seventeenth century, the naval power available to the Spanish kings in Spain and their Italian possessions, even when supplemented by the flotilla of "the Religion" at Malta, was not strong enough to prevent the corsairs of North Africa from marauding their coasts and capturing their merchant shipping. About all that the Spanish navy could accomplish was to keep the sea lanes between Barcelona and Genoa reasonably secure for the transport of soldiers and supplies destined for Central European battle fields. Even after 1648, when a peace made in Westphalia ended Spansh conflict with the United Netherlands, this line of communications was still important for maintaining Spanish armies fighting the French in the southern Netherlands. The Moslem corsair reis could not be contained as long as this was a primary responsibility, and after the war with France ended in 1659 (Peace of the Pyrenees), the rapid decay of Spanish military power precluded any important naval action against the North African tormentors.

FRANCE 1630–60

Like the Spanish, in the 1630s the French king also did not have naval forces capable of controlling the Algerian corsairs in 1620. Although, as we have seen, Richelieu was not completely pleased with the treaty that Sanson Napollon negotiated with the pasha, agha, and divan of Algiers, he agreed to ratify it. His thoughts in a memoir on the problem reflected the situation of France. Richelieu recognized that the French kingdom needed a naval force that could check both the Spaniards and the Barbary corsairs. He not only understood the need for a navy but also actually began the construction of one capable of defending French interests. However, with a war in Germany to fight and peasant rebellions against taxation to suppress, it was slow work, and in his memoir to the king he was forced to admit that the naval forces available were inadequate. He wanted to defend French commerce against the corsairs, and to deprive the Spanish of the Mediterranean as a highway for soldiers and supplies. He also was worried about the souls of the poor unfortunates who were slaves in the Barbary; their salvation was as much in danger as were the goods of Marseille merchants. Richelieu believed that a squadron of ten galleys in the summer and six to eight in the winter patrolling the seas "between Corsica, Sardinia and Barbary" would force the corsairs *"to hide or to expose themselves to the same evils that they now do to us!"* This sentence is underlined in the manuscript, perhaps by Richelieu. The memoir ends declaring that this "design is worthy of a Christian king . . . to defend the lives, goods, and souls [of his subjects] from the cruelty of the infidels." A little later Richelieu returned to the subject: "The greatest reproach to our nation," he wrote, "is that the king who is the eldest son of the church is inferior to the pettiest prince in Christendom in his marine power . . ." In an effort to change this, Richelieu suppressed the offices of the two admirals of France, consolidated them in his own ministry, and developed bureaucratic control over the naval establishment on both coasts. In his insistence on a Mediterranean galley flotilla, he admitted that, while it might not keep the Spanish in check, "Algiers, Tunis and all those on the Barbary will respect and fear our presence in place of their present scorn." One of his commanders was the first to capture and enslave the crew of an Algerian corsair after the peace of 1626, and by the late 1630s the French galley fleet in the Mediterranean, often powered by "Turks and Moors" at the oars, was becoming a respectable force.

Since he was unable immediately to build a navy[1] capable of

---

1. Richelieu did build a French fleet, but, needless to say, it was not solely the activity of Algerian corsairs that prompted his decision. The preponderant English naval power during the siege of La Rochelle and the Spanish naval superiority guarding the line between Barcelona and Genoa were probably of much more moment in his thinking. His decision to build a navy, however, set

controlling the Barbary corsairs, Richelieu was anxious to maintain the advantages that Napollon's treaty of 1628 assured for the kingdom. There were problems, however. The French consul who returned to Algiers was not a royal appointee; the office belonged to the Vias family, who nominated the man who actually filled the post. The consul in residence reported to Marseille rather than directly to the king. The treaty of 1628, however, also provided for the reopening of the Bastion of France, which was a profitable factory (fortification, offices, warehouses, and so on) for coral fishery as well as for the commerce in wheat, hides, wax, horses, and other commodities available on the coast. Napollon managed to insert an article in the treaty naming himself the factor as long as he lived. This meant that much of the trade in local commodities as well as in naval supplies, cloth, and other things from France escaped from the control of the Marseille merchants, who named the consul at Algiers. Inevitably this fact led to conflict, but Napollon's position with the regency government at Algiers was secure, first because of his personal popularity, and second, because he had agreed to a substantial annual money payment to be made by the Bastion in lieu of taxation. This subsidy became such an important source for the salaries of the janissary corps that Napollon believed that the Bastion would always be safe even if relations between France and Algiers might become strained.

It is hard to guess what might have happened had Richelieu listened to Napollon's advice about the policy the kingdom of France should have in North Africa. Richelieu, however, apparently shared the common opinion that the Algerian regency was governed by an untrustworthy lot of renegades and unprincipled infidels. He dealt with them out of necessity since the sultan was unable to defend French interests from Istanbul, but he obviously found these nego-

---

off a naval race between the kingdoms of France and England. By 1631 the French had a total of forty ships ranging from 200 to 900 tons. That year the English built four of 800 tons, two of 500 tons (an 800-ton ship carried between 34 and 40 guns). The next year Richelieu built one of 1,400 tons, but the English laid down the keel for a three decker of 1,500 tons, *The Sovereign of the Seas*—with 102 guns. The French responded with the *Couronne*, 2,000 tons; it had only two decks and 72 guns, but was 28 feet longer than the big English ship. The next advance was the development of the frigate; the first one, the *Dunkirk*, was only about 300 tons, but carried 20 to 30 guns and was very maneuverable. This started a new naval race building frigates that were not only useful on patrol but also made the most successful privateers. (Julian Corbett, *England in the Mediterranean,* vol. I, pp. 180–82.)

tiations distasteful and completely distrusted the honesty and good faith of the men at Algiers. The facts were, however, that the Algerians showed better faith than the French. Almost immediately after the signature of the treaty, a French merchantman was brought into Algiers on the pretext that it had resisted verification of its papers. There was a clamor for condemnation since the corsair captain was very popular and his ship belonged to influential people. Nonetheless, the divan released the ship and its cargo. A few days later, another French merchantman was brought in as prize, and immediately released. Then the divan ordered the reis to end molestation of French ships under pain of execution. Sanson Napollon called the attention of the consuls of Marseille to these incidents as proof of Algerian compliance with the treaty; we do not know whether Richelieu ever learned about them.

In any event, the French were less punctual in their observance of the treaty. There was the case of the sixteen Algerian sailors who were picked up after their ship sank near the French coast. They were brought into Marseille and immediately massacred! A little later the *Saint Jean* of Arles captured an Algerian tartan and sold its entire crew to the Spanish. While Napollon was trying to explain these acts to the divan, a French warship under the command of Sr. de Lanney de Razelly attacked and captured an Algerian corsair vessel and put the entire crew to the oars. The reis, Mohammed Ogia, was both popular and influential, and de Razelly was a naval officer commissioned by the king. Emotions ran high in Algiers; this was no act of an irresponsible private sea captain. De Razelly offered to allow his captives to be ransomed at three hundred livres each—except six renegades whom he refused to free at any price. Napollon was incensed. Was it really worth while to imprison six renegades "who have already lost their souls anyway" and thus cause the death or imprisonment of one hundred fifty Frenchmen and perhaps many more who might be captured in the future? Napollon was sure that this act by a naval officer of the king would provoke another war. Events were soon to prove that he was right.

Emotions ran high in Algiers with each new "outrage" committed by the French. When it was a French naval vessel that broke the treaty, the French vice consul was put in irons and thrown into prison, where, apparently, he died. Napollon went to Algiers and somehow prevented the pasha and divan from declaring war on France, but he could not prevent depredations on French commerce. The reis sailed to avenge their colleagues, and very soon French prizes and French slaves were again commonplace in Algiers, even though there was no formal declaration of war. La Roncière tells us that the Algerians kept the peace of 1628 badly: he quotes Père Dan's statistics that they took over eighty ships with cargoes valued at five million livres and enslaved twenty-three hundred Frenchmen in 1629–31, but our patriotic historian of the French navy seems not to have noticed that the French broke the treaty first, and then refused to release the Turkish and Moorish galley slaves in the chiourmes—galley teams—of the royal navy. This was to be the story of the entire century: French galley captains were unwilling to break up a chiourme that had learned to function effectively, and the captains especially did not want to give up their "Turks" who made the best oarsmen. When the divan demanded freedom for the Turkish and Moorish slaves in France, the French captains returned only the old and infirm, pretending that these were the only ones they had, this in face of the fact that letters from the galley slaves in Marseille regularly reached Algiers.

On the other hand, the Algerians also could be difficult. They refused to exchange slaves one for one and insisted that the patron who purchased slaves should be able to sell them at market prices rather than at initial cost, and, as Francis Knight explains, the "market" price went up with every discussion of exchange. Both sides may have had responsibility for the breaches of the Franco-Algerian treaty of 1628.

The fact that Napollon's holdings at the Bastion were undisturbed while the French ships were being made prizes at Algiers convinced the Marseille merchants that he was really a Mohammedan, or at least a renegade, working against them. They had not been pleased to have him become factor of the Bastion for life; it had always been the property of the Duc de Guise as governor of Provence and the exclusive preserve of the Marseille merchants. Napollon was an outsider in their opinion. The intrigues against him had started immediately after the signing of the treaty of 1628. They attempted to undermine his coral-fishing operation by an intrigue with Tunis; they wrote letters condemning him to Paris. Once the Algerian reis again were taking French prizes the chorus against him could not be ignored in Paris.

By this time Richelieu's position as the king's minister was quite secure, and he had already begun the programs that were to strengthen the authority of the king in all sections of the kingdom. As early as 1629 we find him explaining that the Bastion should not be the property of any private person; it should be under the king of France and governed by a governor appointed by the king with the power to provide for the security of the coral fishermen and merchants trading there. At that time Richelieu meant the Duc de Guise, when he spoke of a private person. The duc, governor of Provence, had enjoyed the revenues from the Bastion before it had been sacked at the opening of the century, and he, with the merchants of Marseille, were trying to reestablish his ownership. Richelieu's general policy for the extension of royal power was aimed at undermining all such private governing enterprises; he was bent on depriving the "great nobles" and the towns of their special privileges and powers. When the problems of the Bastion reached crisis proportions, Richelieu sent the Abbé de l'Isle on an inspection trip with power to decide the fate of both Napollon and the Bastion. De l'Isle went over the records, interviewed officers, and finally decided that Napollon, who had been sent to Algiers by Richelieu in the first place, should remain there. After a parade of the soldiers of the Bastion, de l'Isle announced his decision and formally installed Napollon as royal governor of the Bastion (April 1632).

There is some evidence to suggest that Napollon's appointment was also inspired by Richelieu's desire to secure a strong point for entrance on the North African coast. Napollon built the Bastion into a fortification and an espionage base where he could "learn what comes to pass in Barbary." The coral fishery and trading post may even have been "blinds" to the design of conquest, for he saw the Bastion as an island base for soldiers who might be used for establishing a foothold on the mainland.

Clearly there was more to Napollon's establishment as a royal governor than merely justifying his actions up to that time. The very next year he prepared a plan for driving the Genoese from the island of Tabarque, where, as a result of the agreement between Kheir-eddin and Doria a century earlier, the Lomellini family had a factory and a coral fishery. Napollon thought that he had bribed his way into an easy victory, but the man he thought he had corrupted told the governor of the Lomellini factory the whole story. The Genoese were ready for Napollon and his men when they landed. Napollon was killed, and his men were driven off. Nothing more was done.

After Napollon's death on May 10, 1633, Richelieu sent a new mission headed by Samson le Page to end the conflict if possible. From the point of view of historians the most important thing that le Page did was to take a redemptionist priest, Père Dan, with him to ransom slaves. Père Dan stayed in Algiers long enough to accumulate the data for his histories of Algiers.[2]

It is not surprising that Richelieu was unable to do more about the Franco-Algerian conflict. The years following the first breaches of the treaty were filled, in France and the rest of Europe, with the Day of Dupes, the exile of the queen mother, the civil conflict with the duc d'Orléans, the trial and execution of the duc de Montmorency, Gustaf Adolph's invasion of Germany, his death and the disintegration of the French-supported Protestant coalition from the battle of Nördlingen to the Peace of Prague. These were events more pressing on Richelieu's calendar than the problems of the Barbary. He finally was convinced that France must declare war (1635) on the Hapsburgs, only to discover that the kingdom was quite unprepared to stop the invasion that threatened Paris itself. The surprising thing is not that he was unable to do much about the Barbary, but that by 1636 he did succeed in creating a Mediterranean fleet that could show the flag of France in those seas.

How should these new French galleys be deployed? The depredations of the Algerian corsairs led one faction in the royal council to advocate using the navy to invade and destroy Algiers; obviously they were oblivious to the problems that would be encountered. Another faction, fearful of the costs and possible failure as well as of the reaction that might develop in Istanbul, suggested an attempt to secure a treaty with the sultan that might end the Barbary incursions. They probably were anxious to secure the sultan's favor if or when France went to war against the Hapsburgs. Another faction suggested direct negotiation with Algiers.[3] This latter proposition was adopted, yet le Page went to Algiers only to discover that a treaty was difficult to negotiate. However, even as a failure, his mission was evidence of the growing influence of the king's council in this area that heretofore had belonged politically to Marseille.

The new fleet was little more influential than the diplomats. In 1636 under the command of the sailor-archbishop de Sourdis and

2. Like Father Haëdo before him, Père Dan was a sincere Christian, much disturbed by the sight of his fellow Frenchmen in slavery, and very hostile to the Mohammedan religion and customs. If one understands this bias, Dan's history is a most valuable document, which throws light on this period before we have good consular reports to tell us the many details that are necessary to understand a complex problem. Historians are grateful to men like Père Dan, the ex-slave Francis Knight, and others who have left us interesting and useful accounts of their stay in Algiers during these years.

3. Grammont, "Relations entre la France et Alger, 1633–40," R.A. XXIII, p. 417.

the Duc d'Harcourt it put to sea and quickly captured five corsair ships. At Algiers there was fear of invasion, and Joussouf Pasha ordered a special levy to strengthen the city walls; as a second thought, however, he merely put the money in his pocket and sailed home to Istanbul, leaving another reason for depriving the pashas of power. In 1637 Richelieu ordered the fleet to sail into the Algiers roadstead and demand a treaty; a storm scattered the fleet, and only two ships arrived with the demand. The divan scoffed at the threat and added that any warlike activity would result in the death of all Frenchmen living in Algiers. The two ships sailed away; one day later another squadron arrived with two corsair vessels it had captured. The Christian slaves had been freed and the Moslems chained to the oars. One of the captured vessels belonged to Ali Bitchnin, the richest and most influential member of the taiffe. A riot broke out in the city; all the free Frenchmen, including the vice-consul, were thrown into prison in chains and threatened with death. The divan urged the burning of the consul, but Ali Bitchnin insisted that he was the wronged one, his ship had carried 7,000 pieces of eight. He merely asked for and received permission to attack the Bastion to teach the French a lesson. "The damage," he said, "was done to me as the sole owner of the vessel . . . I desire no revenge, but I am yours . . . and I suggest the taking of the Bastion, . . ." which he did at considerable profit to himself.

Bitchnin's raid on the Bastion had unforeseen results. He had no trouble surprising the French fortification, capturing or killing 317 Frenchmen, including the governor, and carrying off the loot. Still when the Bastion no longer paid an annual subsidy, the treasury in Algiers suffered, and then when the Kabylie tribesmen refused to pay their tribute because they lacked the money that they usually acquired by selling their produce at the Bastion, the treasury in Algiers was in crisis. The bey of Constantine tried to collect the tribute by force only to have his janissaries severely defeated. The Kabylie tribesmen now had firearms that they had purchased at the Bastion.

This crisis resulting from the Ali Bitchnin's raid was followed by another that seriously hurt the Algerian admiral and many of his captains. The Grand Seigneur ordered the Algerian fleet to join his armada for an attack on the Venetian positions in the Adriatic. A bad storm forced the Algerian-Tunisian contingent to seek shelter in the little port of Valona. The Venetian admiral Capello surprised them there in a position that made their artillery useless. They lost sixteen galleys, four sunk and twelve captured; three thousand slaves were liberated and a host of Algerian and Tunisian janissaries killed. Ali Bitchnin suffered the greatest loss, since most of the ships were his personal property. It may even be that the Valona disaster was in part responsible for his failure to seize the government of Algiers at this critical moment.[4] His death, perhaps from poison, came soon afterward. There was another interesting sequel to this battle. The sultan assured the Algerians that he would take revenge, but Venetian gold smoothed his anger: the Grand Seigneur appeared to be as avid for money as the triennial pashas that he sent to Algiers. The next time he asked for aid from the corsair fleet the reis demanded a subsidy paid in advance.

The divan sought to recover the prestige lost at Valona in 1638 by a foray against the Koukou tribesmen, who had so soundly defeated the bey of Constantine, but in place of victory, the janissaries found themselves surrounded and forced to surrender. This defeat redounded to the French cause as well, for when the agha made peace, he agreed to abandon the effort to collect tribute, to give an amnesty to the coulouglis who had fled to the Kabylie strongholds after their disastrous failure at rebellion, and to re-establish the Bastion of France. It is interesting and instructive to note that the disaster at Valona and the defeat of the janissaries in the Kabylie mountains, rather than the pressure of the French fleet, disposed the divan to listen to new proposals for a new treaty with France.

When the divan indicated willingness to negotiate, Richelieu sent Sr. J.-B. de Coquiel with a naval escort to make a peace that would free French slaves, re-establish the Bastion, and write a solid treaty of peace. The naval escort, however, was little more than a bluff. The building and support of the Mediterranean navy had been interrupted by the needs of the war in Germany and the Netherlands. Indeed, Sourdis was most apologetic when he wrote to the pasha explaining that he could not send his whole fleet because it was needed to contain the Spanish. He added only that "if you think my presence is necessary . . . I will come with the rest of our armament." In the ensuing discussions, the Algerians, under pressure from their Kabylie "vassals," agreed to re-establish the Bastion, but they were less flexible on other points for a peace treaty.

The treaty that M. de Coquiel signed on July 7, 1640 gives much insight into the problems that were involved. The governor of the

4. See Chapter VII, pp. 148–149.

Bastion was henceforth required each year to pay twenty-four thousand doubles to the pasha for the janissary corps' salaries and ten thousand doubles into the treasury of the Casaba for reserves. In return, all ships going to the Bastion enjoyed freedom from molestation, and the coral fishermen were assured of haven from storms in any Algerian harbor. The governor of the Bastion could build sentinel posts around its fortification and could rent buildings for storehouses of dwellings in the port towns of Bone and Cole. The Bastion had the right to bake bread, give French nationality to everyone working on its premises, bury its dead, and regulate contracts with local merchants. The treaty also fixed custom dues, conditions for trade, even the right of the Bastion's ships to keep their sails when in port. And finally it was agreed that even in case of war between France and Algiers, the Bastion would remain free and unmolested and would continue to pay its annual subsidy.[5] Neither the merchants nor the powers in Algiers wished to see a repetition of the destruction of this trading post since both had suffered as a consequence of Ali Bitchnin's attack a few years earlier.

It was more difficult to write a general treaty of peace and friendship. The discussions broke down over questions of the release of French slaves, the visitation of French merchant vessels, and several other less important points. Bad weather forced the French naval vessels to return to France and de Coquiel went with them. He returned the next year (1641) and managed to reach an agreement, but Richelieu refused to ratify the treaty. His objections were the same as those that French ministers would have to future treaties. In the first place he wanted more guarantees for the physical and spiritual well-being of Frenchmen who were slaves in Algiers. He also objected to the Algerian demand that the crew of any ship that would resist "visit and search" parties with weapons could be enslaved. The cardinal was aware that the Salé pirates often flew the Algerian flag until the moment that they had boarded the unsuspecting merchantman. Thus if the Algerians did not want the French to resist they should stop this Salé practice. Richelieu went on to insist that the demand for "visit and search" was contrary to the French treaty with the Grand Seigneur, and yet he had to admit that he could not object to the confiscation of goods and the capture of persons belonging to the Algerian regency's enemies. It was a nice point, for French privateers also demanded this right. Richelieu finally decided that de Coquiel had not followed his instructions; the treaty

5. A.A.E., Algérie XII, fols. 101–3.

was not ratified. A similar treaty, however, was made after the Cardinal's death the next year.

The situation demanded a treaty. There were almost five thousand Frenchmen in slavery and the losses incurred by French merchants were intolerable. The French naval power that could be deployed against the corsairs was a feeble effort: the five or six galleys attempted to patrol a huge area at a cost of 15,000–16,000 livres a year. It took few prizes, and failed to protect French shipping. A memo presented to the council indicated the futility of the French patrol: it pointed out that the Algerians with forty-six warships and a number of galleys were in fact a dangerous enemy that could not be coerced without much greater expenditure of force. The council noted further that since the Grand Seigneur no longer could control the regency, the French would again have to negotiate directly with Algiers just as the English and Dutch had been obliged to do. These arguments prevailed, and another French mission went to Algiers and signed a treaty almost exactly like the one that Sanson Napollon had negotiated fifteen years earlier.

The Algerian reasons for ratifying this agreement are less than clear. It may be that the crisis in the regency government that was in the act of depriving the pasha of all his power made peace with France attractive. Or it may be that the reis, who had considerable power in the government, needed access to the French market for naval supplies; or it may simply have been that, since France was again at war with Spain, the Algerians recognized the French as allies against their enemy. Unfortunately the documents to solve the problem are not available.

Richelieu died in 1642; Louis XIII followed him a few months later, leaving the kingdom to a child, Louis XIV. The government of his mother, Anne of Austria, as regent, and her first minister the Cardinal Mazarin, was confronted with a costly foreign war with Spain and also with domestic problems inherent in a weak regency; it had little time for the Barbary corsairs. However, although neither Mazarin nor the queen regent gave much attention to Algiers, they made a fateful decision by placing the consulates at Algiers and Tunis in the hands of the Lazarist fathers.

The background of this decision is not entirely clear; this was a period when the counter-Reformation was strong in France, and a pious cabal often interfered in the political process. However, it seems that Father Vincent (known to us currently as St. Vincent de Paul) was shocked when he learned how little of the money collected by the redemptionist fathers for the freeing of slaves was actually used for that purpose. He resolved to do something about it. St. Vincent was an intimate in the royal household; he had prepared Louis XIII for death; he was close to Anne, whose piety was a model for the ladies of the court; and he was a member of Mazarin's council of conscience. The good priest was a pious man, and his contemporaries believed the story that he had been a slave in Tunis and thus knew much about the problems of Barbary slavery. The story was a "white lie," perhaps told to cover a distant part of Vincent's past, but it gave the good priest leverage in the court.[6]

It is not clear whether Father Vincent persuaded the Duchesse d'Aiguillon or she him, but in any case she bought the consulates in Algiers from the Vias family (1646) and presented it, and the one in Tunis (1648), to the Lazarist fathers.[7] At the moment the king's council was deeply concerned both with the course of events that led into the Fronde and the negotiations at Munster for a treaty to end the German war. The Algerian consulate could not have been of great importance in 1646–48, or indeed in the decade that followed, when Mazarin, after a short exile during the Fronde, bent all his efforts to finding a solution for the war with Spain. Father Vincent de Paul enjoyed the confidence of Queen Anne and it is probable that Mazarin was happy to have him interest himself in the problems of Algiers rather than to become involved in further intrigues in the court. Mazarin apparently paid little attention beyond asking whether it might not be possible to capture a base on the Barbary coast that would allow France to control the activities of the corsairs, a question that may have been responsible for Louis XIV's action shortly after Mazarin's death.

The transfer of the consulate from lay to clerical hands had several unexpected results. On the one side the merchants were to discover that clerical consuls did not excuse violations of the papal bull *In Caena Domini*, which forbade the sale of any kind of war equipment to the infidel. Laymen as consuls looked the other way when French

6. It is amusing to see how tenacious is the myth of St. Vincent's captivity in Tunis: even Tapie continues it in the U.S. edition of his *France in the Age of Louis XIII and Richelieu* (p. 141), long after Grandchamp's essay "La prétendue captivité de Saint Vincent de Paul à Tunis" (*La France en Tunisie au XVII siècle*, vol. VI, pp. 1–20) had demolished the story.
7. MM. Chaix, Ricou, Blanchard, and Picquet had acted in turn as vice consuls at Algiers. They created a consulate with archives and chancellor, and a compound where the business of French merchants could be cared for. Their correspondence largely concerned commercial affairs and was directed to the authorities in Marseille rather than Paris.

merchants brought all sorts of naval and military supplies to the Bastion and the ports of Bougie and Algiers. These supplies continued to be sold, but the clergymen-consuls made difficulty wherever they could. On another level, the arrival of French priests of the Lazarist order was not welcomed by the Spanish and Italian priests of the Trinitarian, Mercy, and Capuchin orders, which had heretofore had control over the spiritual life and the repurchase of the slaves. To make matters worse for these priests, Father Vincent and the duchess d'Aiguillon succeeded in persuading the pope to make the French consul a titular bishop and apostolic vicar for all the Barbary. The Spanish Trinitarians, who had long labored at the problem of release of slaves, who had built and managed a hospital in Algiers, and who had been the principal support for the souls of the miserable ones in captivity, saw this as an affront and refused to obey the orders of the new vicar. The new dignitary was proclaimed in 1650, the time when Mazarin and the queen were deeply involved in the Fronde. The government had nothing to do with it or, for that matter, with the difficulties that the clergymen-consuls managed to get themselves into through their mismanagement of finances and softhearted reactions toward the problem of slavery.[8] Vincent tried to find someone in Marseille to buy the consular office from the priests, but, since he insisted that the priests continue to exert "moral authority," no one was willing to buy it.

ENGLAND 1630–60

As we have seen, Sir Thomas Roe's treaty "with those of Algiers" was signed a few years before Napollon's treaty, and attempted to regularize the relations between England and the Algerian regency. As with the French, the first fractures of the terms of the treaty were made by Englishmen rather than Algerians. Early seventeenth-century princes had trouble controlling the behavior of their subjects, even of their commissioned naval officers. The bureaucratically or-

8. One of the first Lazarists to take office, Père Barreau, spent all the money that was available and then went into debt in his efforts to save slaves. The French government had no money to give him, and even Father Vincent could not find enough to cover his debts, amounting to 7,000 piasters. The unfortunate priest was loaded with irons and thrown into prison. A generous pasha secured his freedom, because the father had been of great assistance to victims of the pestilence, but within a short time he was again in financial trouble, this time for 6,000 piasters. For a second time he escaped a horrible death because slaves came forward with money to clear his obligations.

ganized state that was to come in the course of the century was still in embryo form. Commissioned privateers easily became pirates whose behavior at sea could not be supervised. But it was not simply the actions of a merchant captain turned pirate that disturbed the peace with Algiers. Regularly commissioned English warships also broke the peace. As in France, English officials had a generalized contempt for the "renegade and riff-raff" communities on the North African coast with the result that official contacts between Europeans and the regency government often offended the latter. Several incidents illustrate the problem. During Buckingham's war with Spain (1625), an English privateer forced an Algerian reis to surrender a Spanish ship that he had taken as prize; naturally the reis protested. When Buckingham came to the aid of La Rochelle against King Louis XIII of France, another English privateer "captured" a French ship that had already been captured by an Algerian corsair and was sailing under the control of the Algerian prize crew. The English admiralty court awarded half the prize to the English privateer, half to the Algerians, but the Algerians, unfamiliar with the language or the laws of England, were swindled by a "Dr. Hart," who pretended to be a "great lord" and persuaded them to let him handle their case. They came off with nothing at all. Then there was the Algerian official mission sent to London to "kiss the hand of the king," (Charles I), and present him with "horses, lions and tigers," in addition to trying to get redress for the willful violations of the treaty by English seamen. They fared little better. The king, Charles I, left their "entertainment" to the Levant (or Turkey) Company: it was careful not to spend too much; the king's gifts were niggardly, and the mission was a failure. Buckingham suggested that the king should send another "gift" to Algiers, which apparently did not help much.

In Algiers there was also a problem. The corsair reis and the owners of their ships were not happy with a treaty that prevented the capture of English ships; by the 1620s the English flag was often seen in the Mediterranean. The reis always reminded the pasha, agha, and divan that the business of Algiers was war and that the capture of enemy ships and seamen brought riches to the regency. A good excuse for breaking the treaty and declaring war on England came when an English warship attacked and burned an Algerian corsair vessel. Poor James Franzel, the English consul, was put in irons and thrown into prison: small wonder that in his next letter, he again begged the king's government to send a replacement and allow him to return home. The papers in the Public Record Office leave the clear impression that English actions were alone responsible for the Algerian declaration of war; there is, however, no evidence to suggest that the Algerian reis were not pleased with the renewed opportunity to attack English commerce.

In the war between England and Algiers that followed, the latter had advantages: Even though the Turkey Company's ships were usually heavily armed merchantmen more or less immune from corsair attack, there were other English ships in the Mediterranean, the Atlantic, the Channel, the Irish Sea, and off the banks of Newfoundland that were easy targets for the reis. The most daring attack was a descent on the English coast itself at Baltimore by which the renegade Morat Reis managed to carry off hundreds of English men, women, and children for the slave market in Algiers. There were other landings on the English and Irish coasts that were less dramatic and yet caused emotion in England. Charles I's new navy was quite unable to guarantee English shipping or even English coastal towns against the nimbler corsair vessels.

It was not long before the king, high officers in the church, and the Levant Company were deluged by letters from slaves in Algiers, or from their families in England, begging help. Many of these letters have a piteous ring: the misery of fathers in slavery, the hunger and distress of wives and children. The king had no money to use for the redemption of slaves even though his ministers were impressed by the need to rescue badly needed seamen for the navy and merchant marine; he could only authorize others to collect money for the relief of these wretched people.

The government did, however, take counsel to see what should be done. A committee made up of Sir Thomas Roe; a Mr. Leathe, a merchant doing business at Algiers; Kelham Digbye, an English merchant, and Alderman Garraway prepared two important reports on the problem. As for redemption, aside from the fact that the king did not have money for this purpose, the committee feared that any public policy of redemption would merely inform the Algerians that Englishmen were profitable merchandise. It would only stimulate them to further efforts to make captives for redemption. The families and friends might undertake to free some of the captives, but even this had disadvantages, since by freeing some, the others might sink into discouragement, perhaps even renounce their religion. Nor was diplomacy an answer, for the committee agreed that the word of the North African rulers could not be trusted; they would always consider "infidel goods and persons" to be fair game. (Nothing was said about English failures to live up to the treaties.) This left continuing the war as the only viable solution, but even that presented obstacles. The committee was not in agreement about the amount of military force that would be needed to impose England's will on the regency. One proposal argued that four warships, two of five hundred tons and two of three hundred and fifty tons, could force the Algerians to sue for peace in less than two years. The cost would be £15,000 a year. The less optimistic estimate suggested that a flotilla of eight ships operating over three years at a cost of £50,000 a year might be needed to bring the "pirates" to reason. However, the price tags of £150,000 or even £30,000 were more than the king's treasury could afford.

Obviously if ransom, diplomacy, or war were all unacceptable, some other alternative had to be discovered. The committee fell back on another time-tested recipe: establish the war against the Barbary as a private enterprise for adventurous sailors and businessmen. This might expand the war to include the entire Ottoman empire, so the English ambassador at Istanbul must explain to the sultan that the behavior of his North African subjects was forcing the English king to take reprisals in the form of letters of mark for English privateers, allowing them to attack all commerce bound for Levantine ports. The ambassador could express "regrets" that the sultan's failure to control his subjects had led to so drastic a measure and hope that war with the sultan could be avoided. But even this proposal could not be recommended to the king, for the merchants of the Levant Company undoubtedly would suffer; their markets would be captured by French and Dutch interlopers. The idea, however, was one that would appeal to English sea captains who remembered the profits that were made in the past by privateers. Nothing came of the commission's report, and the number of Englishmen in captivity continued to increase.

There were two interesting books published in England just before the conflict between Charles I and his Parliament beclouded other problems. Francis Knight (*A Relation . . . 1640*), who had been a slave in Algiers had two suggestions: one that a treaty with the divan and pasha would be honored by the Algerians if the English lived up to it; he noted that English captains found it too easy to move from the position of merchant to that of pirate. His second proposal—a war of conquest—appealed to the English predatory behavior by telling of the riches of Algiers: gold, silver, jewels, gold chain, silver plate were plentiful. The city, he believed, could be captured and sacked by an army of thirty thousand men supported by a fleet. On the other hand, he pointed out that trade might be more profitable than war; he noted that it might be possible to supplant the French at the Bastion. The trade there was worth two hundred thousand ducats a year and under English management it could easily be increased. The second author, Henry Robinson (*Libertas or Reliefe to the English Captives,* 1642) argued for an all-out war against the Algerians. Any proposal for a blockade would fail, for it would take years to wipe out the corsair fleet, but a land attack could force them to recognize England's rights. Robinson insisted that the sultan would have to agree to allow this attack on his vassals since he had no seapower capable of supporting them. If he objected, Robinson was willing to make war on the Ottoman empire, as well as on Algiers.

In the period after 1634, the number of Englishmen in slavery continued to grow. Henry Robinson put the number at five thousand by 1640; this figure may be a bit high, but the lowest estimate was three thousand, enough to generate a constant stream of petitions to the king and Parliament. It was in these same years that Charles I made a serious effort to build a royal navy that could make the English flag respected at sea, and one petitioner after another pointed out that these slaves were mostly seamen who might serve the king better on his ships than in Algerian bondage.

When the Parliament came to discuss the problem of Englishmen in slavery, the house set aside, for the relief of slaves, the fines imposed on members for being late to prayer, which, of course, produced little money. In January 1641–42 a more substantial program was suggested: the House of Commons imposed a one percent tax on imports and exports to provide a fund for redemption. The Lords passed the bill May 5 the same year. This was the first recognition by any prince or parliament that money raised by royal taxation might be used for redemption; in other countries the burden was placed on municipalities or the church, but mostly on charity.

The first attempt to use this money for redemption came in 1645, when Edmond Cassen left England with a ship loaded with goods and money to redeem slaves in Algiers. He also was commissioned as consul and empowered to make a treaty of peace and security with the Algerian regency. His ship went aground in a storm off Spain and burned; some of the money was transferred to another ship, the *Diamond,* which promptly went down near Cadiz. Some thought that it was God's way of telling them something, but Cassen returned to England and prepared another expedition for the relief of English slaves. He arrived in Algiers in 1646 with money for redemption and the rank of consul; the pasha and divan received him graciously and assured him that Algiers was ready to make a peace with England that would last "to the end of the world." The troubles between the pasha and the divan made them both ready to treat with England; they needed no new difficulties.

Cassen made a new treaty that was hardly more than a reaffirmation of the one that Sir Thomas had made some twenty-five years before. English ships were to be welcomed at Algiers, and their crews were not to be molested by "bad words or deeds." The tariff duties were fixed at ten percent, and the property of an Englishman who died in Algiers could not be confiscated. No Englishman could be made a slave and no English ship a prize. The warships of the two nations would henceforth salute each other at sea. The Algerians were also assured of welcome in English ports. The problem of the English slaves then in Algeria was more difficult; they were private property, and both England and Algiers respected the rights of private property, so freedom depended upon purchase of the patron's rights. Cassen discovered that slaves came high: he sent home the names of two hundred forty-six Englishmen that he had freed (October 1646), but admitted that he could not repurchase more than a fraction of the total number in slavery.

Cassen (also spelled Cason and Casson) apparently remained at Algiers until his death in 1651 or 1652. These were stormy years in England: civil wars; the trial and execution of the king; finally the establishment of the Commonwealth with Cromwell as lord protector. The Commonwealth government was firmly supported by the merchants of London, who approved of the Navigation Acts and the Anglo-Dutch war aimed at breaking the monopolies of the Netherlands. They were also interested in Mediterranean trade. The establishment of sound English representation in the commercial ports of the world was obviously necessary to promote English trade. Thus at Cassen's death the English consulate at Algiers was placed on a firmer basis. The new consul, Robert Browne, was not a dependent of the Levant Company: he had a fixed salary of £400 a year plus money for "gifts" that were necessary to create good relations—all to be paid by the Treasury. His instructions, too, were more direct and sterner than those of his predecessors: If any person or merchandise be taken from an English ship or any other violence contrary to the

treaty be offered to an Englishman *"you will forthwith demand restitution"* (underlined in document). If no action follows these demands, "you will write to London and also to the Mediterranean
fleet so that it may present itself before the said city and do whatever further it shall have directions for . . ."

At the moment it was not Algiers that annoyed the lord protector;
that regency had its own troubles, and as the crisis over the role of
the pasha heightened, it did not wish to add conflict with England
to its problems. The Tunisian corsairs, on the other hand, with no
such restrictions on their activities, were taking English prizes and
enslaving English sailors. As a result, Cromwell sent Admiral Robert
Blake into the Mediterranean to punish them and force a recognition
of English rights, and then to see that Algiers also recognized English rights. His orders are indicative of a new note that was to develop in the relations between the Barbary regencies and the princes
of Europe. Upon arrival before Algiers, he was instructed to take the
consul aboard and discover the true state of affairs; also if there were
reason to do so, he must demand restitution of any persons or ships
or goods illegally captured. Any captive that he might free was to be
taken aboard his ships and sent home by the next merchant ship
available. He was also authorized to conclude "such articles of peace
as you see fitt and necessary." In case of refusal, Blake could use
force ". . . to assault them either by land or sea and fight with, kill
and slay all such persons as shall oppose you." His orders also included the watching of French and Spanish forces as well as quiet
aid to the Venetians in their war on Crete. He by-passed Algiers and
made directly for Tunis.

His first stop at La Goulette produced frustrations; the Tunisians
put him off with evasive words. A second visit shortly afterward
found them "more willful and untractable than before, adding to
their obstinacy much insolence and contumely, denying all commerce
and civility." They refused him water and fired on his boats. Blake's
supplies were low, so he withdrew to watch from the sea and sent
part of his fleet to Italy for bread and other supplies, but he had no
intention of letting the matter stand. "Their incivility," he wrote,
"did so work on our spirits that we judged it necessary for the honor
of the fleet, the nation, and religion . . . to make them feel us as
enemies." Blake's letters show clearly that he was a seventeenth-
century man; he believed that God's intentions were obviously supporting his actions. So when the fleet reassembled, he sailed into the
port of Porto Farina, where a large section of the Tunisian corsair

ships was anchored under the guns of the fortress. Blake tells us that "The Lord, being pleased to favor us with a gentle breeze which cast the smoke on them . . . facilitated our attack." In hot action nine Tunisian ships were either sunk or burned at a cost to the English of twenty-five dead and forty wounded.

Blake admitted to having some doubts when he saw the full effect of his attack; did his instructions allow him to punish insolence that vigorously? "I confess," he wrote, "because of the ambiguity of my instructions . . . I did much hesitate . . . until the barbarous behavior of these pirates did turn the scale." His doubts vanished completely by the time that he reached Algiers, where the news of his vigorous, decisive action had preceded him.

At Algiers, his instructions that permitted the use of force paid handsome dividends. As Blake wrote, the "pasha and divan welcomed [Blake] . . . with professions of esteem . . . and readily agreed to negotiate the enlargement [freedom] of English slaves." He did have a slight problem: while his ships were off Algiers a number of Dutch slaves swam out to them and were taken aboard by the sailors. This was absolutely contrary to the treaty and immediately brought protests. The sailors, unwilling to surrender the poor wretches, took up a collection—one dollar from each sailor—and bought their freedom. The Algerians were obviously satisfied, for they reaffirmed the treaty that Cassen had negotiated a few years earlier.

In the middle-years of the seventeenth century, Cromwell was not much more successful than Charles had been in controlling the behavior of English priates, privateers, and merchant sea captains. England's peace with the Dutch was tenuous, and, in an alliance with Mazarin's France, Cromwell briefly went to war against Spain. The Algerians, however, had complaints: English ships were carrying enemy goods and passengers and refused to surrender them to the Algerian reis. An English captain took Moslem pilgrims as passengers aboard his ship—including an envoy of the sultan, and then sold them to a Venetian merchant. "We are certain," wrote the pasha, "that they were made slaves and their goods divided up. We pray you to bring the captain to justice." The pasha went on to threaten that the Algerians would take revenge for "we cannot abandon our beloved king's *chiaus*." While Algerians had reason to object to English behavior the reis were also not above breaking the treaty provisions. Consul Browne wrote to Secretary Thurloe: "These people are very earnest to have justice done them, but care for doing none themselves . . ." He explained that they have detained Englishmen taken from a foreign ship, they have confiscated goods from a shipwreck, and they have "confined" the English consul. "It is some months," he wrote, "that I perceved theire treatment of us has beene farr different to what it was wont to bee . . ." Blake's intrusion into the Mediterranean obviously had been only a temporary measure; if the English rulers could not control their sailors, the Algerians were not willing to control theirs; perhaps the internal problems in Algiers made it impossible to do so. The next moves were to be made by a new government in England after the restoration of the Stuart dynasty to the throne.

The last years of the decade 1650–60 saw the resolution of many problems that had been troubling the princes of Europe for more than a century. The confessional wars that came out of the Reformation of the church were ended. The Peace of Westphalia (1648) had brought an end to the German War, the Peace of the Pyrenees (1659) temporarily settled the conflict between the kingdoms of France and of the Spains, and the Treaty of Olivia (1660) brought peace to the Baltic. It was Mazarin's dream that his diplomacy would pacify Christendom, and as the young king Louis XIV looked over the Europe of 1661 when he assumed full control of his state, it seemed that Mazarin had really accomplished his mission before his death. Since that decade also ended with the Restoration in England that returned the Stuarts to their "rightful" throne, it seemed that the problems that had troubled the island kingdom for two decades were also finally settled. The difficulties of that decade, 1650–60, had been so pressing that the annoyances caused by the Barbary reis were often simply overlooked or allowed to continue because there seemed to be no suitable response. Only Cromwell's England came down hard on the corsairs whose activities incensed the merchants of London; this vigorous action, however, was to provide a new pattern for European relations with the Barbary. The next generation, that of Louis XIV, Charles II, and William of Orange had to find ways of containing the violence that these disorderly communities did to their merchants and their subjects.

XI *Algerian Regency and Europe: 1660-88*

THE QUARTER-CENTURY following 1660 produced striking changes in the political and military institutions of Europe that eventually were to have an important impact on the corsair communities of North Africa. The regime of the young Louis XIV, who assumed control of his kingdom when Mazarin died, was in fact a continuation of the work of the two great cardinal ministers who had governed France in the preceding decades. The war ministry, and with it a standing army dependent on the king that Richelieu had envisaged when he merged the offices of admiral and constable of France into his ministry, emerged as the strong arm of the royal government. The rise of a powerful French navy was paralleled by naval construction in England and the United Netherlands, a naval race that produced navies with which the corsair regencies could not compete. The North Africans were also quite as unable to develop a "modern" bureaucracy as they were to build warships on the size and scale of the European naval powers. This meant that the commerce of the three most important European states would become dangerous "game" for the reis, except when these states were at war with each other.

The Algerians, however, had little room for maneuver; unlike Tunis, where there was considerable legitimate commerce and an extensive agricultural community, the Algerian economy was largely dependent on prizes. With Spanish commerce and shipping in decay, this meant that Algiers had to be "at war" with other Christian powers to survive. The seventeenth-century European consuls often remarked that unless Algiers was at war with England, France, or the United Netherlands, the community could not exist. During the "great years" of the Algerian corsairs, this fact did not create any serious problems; Algiers could be at war with one, two, or even all three of these powers with relative security, for wars and civil rebellions prevented European states from responding effectively, but after 1660, the problem became more difficult with each passing decade.

The three important commercial powers had already established characteristic patterns of behavior toward the Algerian corsair state. The Dutch, pragmatic realists that they were, came to believe that whenever possible the best solution would be a treaty to guarantee their vessels from attack even if that meant paying a sort of "tribute" to the "pirates." It might well be less expensive to buy off the corsairs than to attempt to fight them. English and French consuls regarded this as "shameful," "cowardly," "disgraceful": in effect the Dutch were supplying the Algerians with war materials to attack the commerce of other nations, for masts, guns, sails, powder, and shot were always part of the "tribute." A "contemptible way" to secure immunity for Dutch ships. However, even this sort of "tribute" did not completely assure the Dutch of the safety of their commerce; the government also required that any Dutch ship trading in the Mediterranean must carry at least twenty-six guns and a crew of at least forty to enable it to resist piracy. The penalty for failure to obey was confiscation. The greater part of the Algerian navy carried fewer guns.

The English also depended upon naval power and treaties to secure safety for their ships, but these treaties did not entail the payment of "tribute." The ineffective naval force that James I had sent to impress the Algerians in the early 1620s did little, but in the 1650s Cromwell's warships and an admiral willing to fight persuaded the Algerians that England really could have a dangerous navy. English Mediterranean commerce was carried either in well-armed merchantmen belonging to the Levant Company or in small coasters that made their living by carrying English merchandise as well as foreigners' goods and passengers from port to port. These small ships, as Sir John French noted, "were a constant temptation to the Barbary . . . and consequently an expense to His Majesty and a loss to his subjects . . ." He added that "we do not make a tryall of their valour but of their honesty." However, only when the corsair community was convinced that it was too dangerous to be at war with England was the "honesty" evident.

During most of the century and a half that preceded 1660, the French had been tacit or even open allies of the Barbary corsairs against a common enemy: Spain. In the years after Henry IV made peace with the Spanish king and when Marie de Medicis allied the two crowns in marriage contracts, the immunity that French commerce had previously enjoyed faded into oblivion. A clever negotiator like Napollon was able to breach the differences that grew between Algiers and France, but his influence hardly survived him. French commerce was particularly vulnerable because much of it was carried in small coasters that could not defend themselves. There was an additional problem. The French captains going to the Levant used Malta as a first port of call to secure supplies and depot goods. As a result, French merchants dominated Maltese commerce and gave the island the appearance of being almost a French colony. As we have noted, when the Algerians remembered that the majority of the Knights of St. John were French, it did not seem unreasonable to regard the French as allies of their most dangerous enemy. Thus, both the comparative weakness of their ships and their association with Malta gave the Algerians "reason" to question French loyalty to treaties. To counter their depredations, the French government tried several times to persuade the merchants to send their ships to the Levant in convoys, but this was always resisted because if all the merchantmen arrived at the same time, the prices of their cloth and other commodities would be depressed, while the prices of local produce that they wished to bring back to France would be higher. Thus, when the treaties broke down or the reis felt free to be bold, French commerce was the most profitable source of prizes.

In 1660 all three of the important commercial powers were in trouble with the Algerians. There were 20,000–25,000 slaves in the regency; most of them were Spanish, Portuguese, or Italian, but the number of English, Dutch, and French slaves also ran into the hundreds, perhaps even thousands. It is not surprising, therefore, that as soon as relative peace "broke out" in Europe, the commercial states moved to end the drain both on the manpower for their ships and the capital of their merchants and shipowners.

As long as the kingdom of France was at war with the Spanish Hapsburg rulers, Mazarin was unable to apply military force to the problems of the Barbary, but even as the treaty of the Pyrenees was being negotiated, he suggested that the king might capture a harbor on the African coast that could be used for naval patrol of the area. After Mazarin's death in 1661, the young Louis XIV returned to this idea. The next year when Charles II's Portuguese princess brought the port of Tangiers under English control as her dowry, the French were further convinced that they must secure a harbor to balance the English position. Louis ordered a naval sweep along the North African coast, and his council discussed several possible areas for a landing. The man most responsible for the plan was Colbert, Mazarin's trusted agent, and now the king's minister for finance, naval, and commercial affairs as well as a host of other aspects of the king's government. Colbert had suggested one of his relatives for the concession of the Bastion in 1652, and he had many other personal financial investments in commercial ventures to the Levant; he was also interested in returning to Richelieu's program for the construction of a naval arm that would bring prestige to the king and security to French commerce. Once Colbert took over the direction of French policy toward Algiers, the softer regime, with its religious overtones that Father Vincent de Paul and his Lazarist consuls had adopted, was changed for a policy closer to Admiral Blake's "cannon diplomacy." Curiously, the merchants at Marseille opposed Colbert's hard line; they believed that it would be cheaper to make diplomatic concessions than to use force and invite the counterattacks from the corsairs.

Colbert and his master, however, had both contempt and hatred for the "pirates, renegades, and ruffians" who governed Algiers, an attitude, in part, well deserved at the time when Colbert paid attention to the Barbary, for this was the period when the divan had successfully pushed the sultan's pasha into the background and managed to murder every agha who attempted to govern the community. The French regarded them as *scelerats* (nefarious, perfidious ones). Thus, Colbert saw nothing unreasonable to demand that the Parlement of Aix "find" a law that would require the death penalty for Suleiman Reis, a French renegade, and that his master could order a brutal bombardment of Algiers simply as a policy of terror. This same king and minister might worry about the physical and spiritual health of French slaves in North Africa, but at the same time, they would cynically refuse to exchange Turks and Moors, slaves in French galleys, unless they were too old or too sick to pull an oar.

The first adventure by the government of the young Louis XIV, like several that followed it, was a catastrophe. Chevalier Paul, a French Knight of St. John who commanded the French galleys, had warned the king that the Algerians had forty to fifty warships carrying between twenty-five and forty guns each, "all with good sails . . ." They could be very dangerous, but Colbert also knew that the pestilence of 1663 had caused so many deaths that the Algerian "countryside has become deserted." Thus the Algerians did not appear to be dangerous, and Louis XIV's ministers decided to implement Mazarin's suggestion that France should obtain a usable harbor on the Algerian coast both as a commercial port and as a base for the control of the Moslem corsairs. They understood that the Berber population would welcome them as mutual enemies of the Turks. After a false start, Colbert managed to assemble a fleet from both the Mediterranean and Atlantic naval bases that carried an expeditionary force to the little port of "Gigery" (Djidjelli). Unfortunately for the French efforts, the command was divided and most inefficient. Under a flag of truce, the natives asked why the French were landing on their soil. "To attack your Turks," was the response. The Berber replied: "I am astonished that rich men, well nourished, well clothed come to a land where there is nothing good, where you have nothing to gain. Half naked, scarcely enough to eat and yet we are men of war . . . you will not get peace. Leave . . . seek another country where you can make war more advantageously." The French should have listened. Instead they landed cannons and supplies but failed to construct defensive lines. This provided time for the janissaries to transport their guns and equipment from Algiers to Djidjelli. When they arrived, the Berber natives preferred to fight beside the Moslem Turks rather than join the Christians against them. The French were driven into the sea. They lost all their cannons (thirty-five brass and fifteen iron guns), all their baggage, and some four hundred men left as prisoners, many of whom "turned Turk" to escape the worse fate of slavery. The English consul almost gleefully reported the celebration that followed in Algiers, and the French in Tunis were followed by cat-calls: "Gigery! Gigery!"[1] Louis XIV's letters to his commanders at sea, Chevalier Paul and the Duc de Beaufort, are eloquent testimony to his interest in the expedition, but characteristically he took no reprisals on the men responsible for its failure.

Gigery was not the only conflict between French soldiers and Moslems that year, for when an Ottoman army marched up the Danube to attack the German empire, Louis XIV, acting as landgraf of Alsace rather than as king of France, contributed an expedition that took a decisive role in the defeat of the Turks at St. Gotthart. The Grand Seigneur was unable to react either in defense of his North African vassals or to take revenge for the French intervention on behalf of the German emperor. The French, however, did want revenge for their defeat at Djidjelli, and for the next two years Chevalier Paul and the Duc de Beaufort cruised the Mediterranean

1. Some of the French cannons left there in 1664 were found after 1830 in the possession of tribes forty miles from Djidjelli.

against the Algerians and succeeded in burning or sinking eight to ten of the regency's warships. The naval campaign might have gone to a conclusion satisfactory to the king had not the English attack on the United Netherlands (1666) forced Louis XIV to declare war on England in support of his Dutch allies. To pursue that war, the French Mediterranean squadrons were ordered to sail to the French western Atlantic ports with all speed. It is true that they got there too late to act effectively in support of the Dutch, but their departure made further campaigning against the Algerians impossible. The Dutch, whose naval arm was badly used by the English, believed that Louis deliberately failed to support them; the evidence is contrary to this notion.

While the Anglo-Dutch war was in progress, Philip IV died in Spain leaving a sickly child, Charles II, as his heir. The French king believed that his queen, Marie Theresa, the eldest daughter of Philip IV, had a right to part of her father's estates. His case for the "devolution" of part of the Spanish Netherlands may not have seemed valid to many men in Europe, but Louis XIV had a fine army to support his claims. When the Spanish refused to recognize Marie Theresa's rights, war was inevitable. The Algerians could wait to be punished; Louis XIV sent Sr. Trubert to Algiers with instructions to make a new treaty that would confirm those of the past and add the condition that two Algerians of important rank should be sent to live in Marseilles as hostages for the French consul and others living in Algiers. Trubert assured the rulers of the regency that the French king would loyally respect the treaty and that he expected the Algerians to honor it punctually. His instructions authorized "gifts" to a "people who only follow self-interest" as bribe for an Algerian declaration of war against England. After negotiating this treaty, he had orders to try to enlist the king of Tafilette, a Moorish chief in the hinterland of Tangiers, to join France in an assault on that port. He could offer the "king" up to one hundred thousand francs if he would attack by land when the French blockaded Tangiers by sea. Trubert did succeed in writing a treaty with Algiers, but the proposal for an assault on Tangiers melted as another political dream of the era.

The treaty of 1666, however, did not end the difficulties. This was the period when Colbert was making a determined effort to build a French navy. When he took over the direction of naval affairs in 1661, it consisted of thirty warships of all kinds; when he died two decades later, it numbered one hundred seventy-six, of which thirty-two were galleys. It was the galley fleet that caused difficulties with

Algiers. Convicts made poor oarsmen; they lacked physical strength and familiarity with the sea. There were not enough freemen willing to take service at the oars, so the galley fleet had to depend upon slaves. As early as 1662, we find Colbert and the king ordering French naval commanders to land on the North African coast to capture slaves, and when this did not yield enough men, the French purchased slaves in the markets of Malta and Florence. Most of these men were either Moors or Turks, and many of them had friends and relatives in Algiers or were members of the Algerian janissary corps. They managed to send letters home begging the regency to find some means of relief. The treaty of 1666 provided for the return of these unfortunate Moors and Turks in exchange for French slaves, but as usual the galley captains were unwilling to see their chiourme disrupted; once a "team" of slaves was taught to row together, it became imperative to keep the team together. As a result, when again the French returned "Moors and Turks" it was always only the old, the infirm, or the sick: the able-bodied slaves were "not available" when there was a collection for redemption. This practice caused new difficulties between France and Algiers, and the contemptuous attitude of the king and his ministers did not make the difficulties easier.

The kingdom of England also had problems on the Barbary coast after 1660. When Charles II was restored to the "throne of his ancestors," there was a sheaf of problems that needed solution. There were several hundred English sailors in slavery, and the money collected by the tax on imports for the redemption of these poor wretches had been spent for other purposes. Another crisis developed when Lord Enchequin and his whole party, including his son, fell into the hands of the Algerians and were sold. Enchequin had shared the king's exile and risen high in the French army; since he was the king's friend and needed at home for the English military, his release became a primary object. Charles sent a friendly letter to the governors of Algiers saying that "since God had restored him to his rightful place," he wished to secure a treaty with Algiers. As we have seen, he appointed Robert Browne to be consul and ordered his ambassador to the Sublime Porte, Lord Winchelsea (Inchelsea) to negotiate a treaty that would both restore the conditions of earlier English treaties with Algiers and add several new conditions.

Lord Winchelsea's account of the negotiations underlines the fact that Algiers at this moment was not easy to deal with. The meeting of the divan with the English negotiators was an incredible experience. He wrote, "it is a ridiculous method of consultation . . . not paralleled in the whole world, nor is it possible that this form of deliberation can ever produce any mature or solid results." "These barbarians intoned" their decisions: "Do we wish to enter into negotiations?" called the agha; "We do," responded the entire divan. It cost the ambassador a bribe of £50 to get a treaty about the same as the earlier English-Algerian agreements, but he had no faith in it. He advised the king that war alone would force the Algerians into line, and war, he believed, would be easy since the corsair fleet had low fire power and the city fortifications were weak.

The ambassador's pessimism was well founded. The reis insisted on their right to board any ship to discover "enemy" passengers and goods; they extended the right to allow them to use violence on the crew to obtain information. Consul Browne protested: English captains pointed out that they had to carry Spanish goods and passengers to make their voyages profitable, and if they could not guarantee safety, this traffic would dry up. When there was no redress for the consul's protests, an armed intervention seemed to be the only hope to settle the question. An English fleet was prepared to go to the Mediterranean area to collect the Portuguese princess who was destined to become the bride of Charles II. It called on Algiers, failed to secure any satisfaction, and bombarded the city. Contrary to Winchelsea's optimistic prediction, the fleet did little damage. However, shortly after the English ships had departed, a great tempest wrecked most of the best Algerian ships and damaged the mole. What the fleet failed to achieve, this storm did; and the Algerians, now fearful of English naval forces, signed a new treaty (1662) that met most of the English terms; they were willing to respect it as long as the corsair fleet was weak.

The new treaty created a system of passes that the Algerians agreed to respect, and limited to two the number of men who would be allowed to board an English ship to inspect its cargo and passenger list. It also attempted to regularize the repurchase of English slaves. However, if Consul Browne is to be believed, "these people" were intransigent and the treaty was soon in trouble. "They make prizes as they please," he wrote, "abuse our commanders and seamen to make them confess"; they assume that a bill of lading written in Italian signifies "enemy goods"; they cannot read passports. They "will believe nothing but what is in their interests." He admitted that there were some people of "better sort" who were ashamed of these "perfidious proceedings" and that the agha might wish to do something else. But the agha became dangerously ill, and consul Browne died of the plague. In one of his last letters, he apologized for filling his reports with complaints—"There being little else to be reported from these perfidious people . . ."

Soon Browne was not alone in making complaints. Charles's new bride brought as her dowry the harbor of Tangiers. The port could not be supplied from the hinterland, and it was far from England, so most of its provisions and other needs came from Spain across the Straits. This traffic was carried in small ships, flying the English king's flag, and commissioned by the governor of Tangiers, but the sailors all spoke Spanish, and indeed, were Spaniards, yet subjects of Charles II of England. The Algerian corsairs regarded these ships as fair game and their crews as candidates for slavery. Naturally the governor protested. The Algerians had at least one "counterprotest," when an English captain put in at Tangiers with a group of Turks and Moors as passengers and immediately put them to work loading stone. The English government was not interested in the incident.

Even before Browne's death, the English decided to act decisively. The Algerian naval establishment was still weak, and most of its cannons were of small bore; their three galleys did not even take to sea during the summer of 1663. Charles sent the pasha a letter to inform him that Sir John Lawson was being sent to Algiers to get satisfaction for the breaches of the treaty. To assure Englishmen that this mission was a proper one, Charles announced in a public proclamation that, at great expense, he was sending a naval force to the Mediterranean to protect foreigners in English ships, for "it would be a great blemish if persons received unto their English captain's protection should . . . be delivered into the hands of their enemies."

Admiral Lawson arrived at Algiers (1664) with a copy of a treaty of 1662 that had been ratified by the sultan. The Algerians immediately released eighteen English ships, but Lawson became convinced that "until it please God to make them feel some smart, no peace can be made with them, but that is worse than war." Lawson could not stay to see what would happen, since the Anglo-Dutch War that broke out required his presence in Atlantic waters. However, Captain Thomas Allen took over command and continued the negotiations. After a short sharp naval encounter with the English squadron, the Algerians signed a treaty agreeing to cease "meddling" with passengers on board English ships and to live up to the treaty of 1662. Allen left Captain Nicholas Parker to take Browne's place as consul and returned to England believing that the treaty would assure an era of peace.

Thomas Allen's treaty was written in 1665. The next year the

Algerians renewed a treaty with France. As the new English consul, John Ward, noted, the tempest of 1662, the plague, the losses to the French in 1665 severely weakened the Algerian navy and made the divan reasonable. Yet by 1667 they were building a new fleet; six frigates with up to forty-four guns would be ready by 1668. Consul Ward was sure that once these ships were off the stocks, Algiers would probably declare war on either France or England. There were very few prizes available; on every sea the reis met English and French ships everywhere protected by treaty; they took a few Dutch ships and even those "not without apprehension of the Flemings coming to these seas . . . to pay off old scores." Ward explained that if there should be a peace with the Dutch, Algiers would surely break with England or with France. It could not be at peace with all three of the major commercial powers.

French involvement in the War of the Devolution in 1667–68 momentarily paralyzed French ability to act effectively in the Mediterranean. This fact combined with the controversy over the return of Turks and Moors in the French galleys persuaded the English consul that Algiers would soon declare war on France. But Louis managed to extricate himself from the dangerous position created by the so-called Triple Alliance (England, the Netherlands, and Sweden) that offered mediation but threatened intervention. The Treaty of Aix-la-Chapelle ended the war, freed French forces, and allowed Louis to send a squadron to Algiers to demand a reaffirmation of the treaty of 1666. The English consul was right even so: Algiers could not remain at peace with both England and France. With some urging on the part of the French consul and French merchants at the Bastion, the reis began to interfere with English shipping, especially with those vessels that carried grain, oil, fruit, and other foodstuffs from Spain to Tangier. Then victory at Crete released the new Algerian frigates that had been assigned to service with the Ottoman fleet, and English ships were stopped and searched more frequently. The government in London decided that a naval demonstration should be enough to bring the Algerians to recognize English rights. It was soon to learn, however, that England was far away from Algiers; the French might impress the dey and divan with a small squadron of warships, for France and the French fleet were just across the sea. England would need greater force to become threatening.

In the late summer of 1668, Sir Thomas Allen arrived at Algiers in command of a small squadron to demand redress. "I hope," he wrote, "in a short time to be able to give some good account of that treacherous people who are so shamelesse that though they keep noe promises . . . they acknowledge that wee keep ours . . ." But he had only a small unimpressive squadron, the Venetians had surrendered at Crete, the French admiral Beaufort had been killed, and Islam was riding high. When Allen and one of his captains spoke at the divan, the agha insisted that they must be "drunk to talk that way," and the whole divan chanted Algerian complaints against the English. They would not listen to rebuttals; they demanded the appointment of an English consul who would be reasonable. They then sent one Mohamet, a renegade priest, to Allen's ship with a letter in elegant Latin listing their "complaints." When Sir Thomas pointed out that these complaints were made of "whole cloth," Mohamet agreed. They had been prepared simply to prevent English demands on Algiers.

When it became evident that they were getting nowhere the English captains decided to send fire ships into the harbor to burn the Algerian fleet anchored there. The project failed for lack of a suitable wind, but the Algerians found out about the plan and immediately pretended to be willing to negotiate. They agreed to a reestablishment of the Treaty of 1662 with additional clauses, but hardly had Allen sailed away when an English ship, the *William of London*, was stopped by the Algerian *Orange Tree*: forty Spanish travelers were sold into slavery, and all the goods, even those belonging to the crew, were confiscated. By April 1669, Ward had a sheaf of similar violations. Obviously a small squadron was not enough to impress the Algerians.

It was clearly war. The Admiralty in London sent orders for an invoice of the Algerian naval forces. There were twenty-five warships available to Algiers; they carried between sixteen and forty-four guns; total firepower of the Algerian naval forces was seven hundred and forty-eight guns, mostly of small caliber. Sir Thomas Allen's new armada consisted of twenty-three ships of the line, mostly third and fourth raters (third-raters carried forty to fifty cannons), obviously with firepower much greater than the Algerian navy plus the guns on the mole. It also had fireships, ketches, and supply ships. Only a little over a half century earlier, James I had sent Mansel to Algiers with the first English naval demonstration before the city; it had turned out to be a pitiable affair. This new armada was better prepared to impose its will.

James, duke of York, wrote Sir Thomas's instructions to "master by force" any Algerian ship that he might encounter en route to Algiers, and when he reached the city, to demand the release of Spaniards as well as Englishmen captured on English ships, and in addition the return of all goods confiscated. Finally the guilty reis must be punished. If the Algerians agreed, Sir Thomas could renew the treaty and assure them that English captains would not transport for sale any Algerians or Turks who were slaves. If no agreement was reached, Sir Thomas could attack and sink their ships in the mole, and any shipping in the harbor. James's orders were bold compared with the timid ones that his grandfather James I had given to Mansel.

Sir Thomas arrived September 1, 1669; he saluted the city and received a ship from the mole but did not send his letter ashore for he hoped to burn the Algerian fleet that night. No seventeenth-century captain had a monopoly on ruthlessness. The wind, however, was not right, so that on the next day he sent his demands for the return of the Englishmen and Spaniards taken from English ships. He also started to stop all ships entering Algiers and held them and their crews and passengers. When the Algerian reply to his demands was unsatisfactory, he burned a recently captured Algerian warship of twenty-four guns. He then offered an exchange of prisoners. The answer was again unsatisfactory—and England and Algiers were at war.[2]

This time the Algerians merely confined the English consul to his house rather than throwing him in prison because, wrote Ward, "ye king and chief governor is my friend." However, the Algerians announced that they were not afraid of the English: their ships were faster and they were sure that England was not prepared to fight an inconclusive war. Sir Thomas's fleet did sail away without a treaty, but the next spring, Sir Thomas returned with ten warships of the line. He joined the Dutch Admiral van Ghent to hunt down the corsairs. The war went against Algiers: in August the English sank one of the biggest corsair vessels, and in September the Anglo-Dutch naval forces managed to force a fight near Cape Sparrel in which they sank or burned seven of the biggest Algerian ships, including four with forty-four guns. The Algerians lost twenty-two hundred men and several of their most skillful commanders. Sir Thomas brought

2. One of the Spaniards in Algerian hands was Don Lorenzo Santes de Pedro, an important and very wealthy nobleman. When his friends ransomed him for 30,000 pieces of eight Sir Thomas was much annoyed since he was "making warr occasioned chiefly for their sakes." (Pro. Ind. 13395 f. 573.)

the news to Algiers. The governors realized that it must be true, for their fleet was long overdue, but the divan ordered the death penalty for anyone who suggested ending the war. There were five new warships on the stocks almost ready to sail, and the Algerians were sure that Sir Thomas would have to leave the station as the season progressed, which indeed he did.

However the English returned the next year; in the spring of 1671 Sir Edward Spragg arrived before Bougie where he found seven of Algeria's best ships anchored behind a protecting boom. Two young lieutenants managed to cut the boom so that the fireships could enter the harbor. The attack was a complete success: seven ships, including three less than a year old, were completely destroyed. A Dutch slave swam out to the fleet with the news that thirty-one hundred men had died, and all the "churagean's [surgeon's] chests" had burned completely so that, with no medicine, many more would probably die of their burns and wounds. Spragg lost seventeen killed and forty-one wounded. When the news reached Algiers, there was a revolution. The agha was killed, and a new regime, under the aegis of the reis, began with the installation of the first dey.

The revolution in Algiers brought a wealthy reis to power with the title of dey and assurance that he could command the respect and obedience of the city. His first act was to invite the English to negotiate a new treaty. Spragg insisted upon the reinstatement of the terms of earlier treaties with additional clauses confirming the right to ransom English slaves at the original sale price, as well as stronger guarantees for the safety of the traffic between Tangiers and Spain. He was not, however, able to stay before Algiers very long for Charles II called him back to the Channel waters in preparation for the combined Anglo-French attack on the Netherlands. He left John Ward, the consul, to take care of the details. This was typical of the period: conflict in Europe always took precedence over any action of the Maghrib coast whether it was punishment of the corsair-Turkish communities or negotiations with them.

The 1688 Treaty of Aix-la-Chapelle ended the War of the Devolution and, as we have seen, gave Charles II enough freedom of action to be able to send his fleet into the Mediterranean to punish the Algerians. It also gave Louis XIV freedom to consider revenge for the French debacle at Djidjelli. Almost the same time that Sir Thomas Allen brought the English squadrons into the Mediterranean, Louis XIV ordered Sr. de Martel to take to the sea and burn their corsair ships in the harbors of Tripoli, Tunis, and Algiers. "His majesty," wrote Colbert, "expects you not to return without some action of vigour that will make these barbarians feel the punishment that their lack of faith for treaties brings on them . . ." Even so the squadron did not get to sea until the following spring. Colbert wrote: "I would have great joy to bring the King news of some striking action . . . like the burning of ships . . . a descent on the land . . . taking a ship at sea . . ." He received no such "good news." The next year, 1671, Jean d'Estrées was in command. Colbert wrote, "The King would be pleased if you would attempt something considerable against Algiers." But—it was the English Admiral Spragg who burned the Algerian fleet. Louis XIV wrote: "I am weary of hearing of English naval action when the French fleet does so little." At the moment, however, the kingdom of France was concentrating its wealth and power for the massive *Blitzkrieg* against the Dutch; the navy could not be used against Algiers, for there was to be a long war that would absorb French resources and energy from 1672 to 1679.

The French and English naval efforts between the peace of Aix-la-Chapelle and the outbreak of the Dutch war were harbingers of the future. After 1665, competitive naval construction in England, France, and the United Netherlands had begun the first really significant naval race in modern times. In the succeeding years, the fleets of these three nations grew by leaps and bounds, not only in numbers but also in size. In 1650 a ship with forty guns was a powerful weapon; by the 1680s ships with one hundred ten guns— veritable floating fortresses—had reduced those of the 1650s to third-raters. No petty state like the regency of Algiers could hope to construct such ships, nor could it hope to stand up against a determined assault by the sea powers. However, the situation was not simply a petty corsair state versus the sea powers; during these same years the latter were matched against each other. In 1672 the English and French kings turned their naval forces against the Dutch; they had no spare ships with which to punish the Algerian corsairs. The day was yet to come when royal sea power could assure the tranquillity of the seas in the way that the emerging royal armies were in the process of guaranteeing tranquillity within the kingdom.[3]

3. In another book I have pointed out that the development of armies wearing the king's coat, supplied by the king's commissioners, and commanded by officers under the control of the king's war minister ended the long period when a great nobleman or a powerful city could defy royal commands and contest power with the king. Cf. J. B. Wolf, *The Emergence of the Great Powers, 1685–1715* (1952).

Admiral Spragg's treaty created problems. It provided for the ransom of English slaves at the original sale price, but in fact there were only £4,441 6d in the Chamber of London for ransoms, while there were two hundred eighty-three slaves valued at £22,369 24s 6d ready to be ransomed, and this figure did not include all the English slaves in Algiers. The treaty, however, "froze" the price of these slaves: their patrons could not sell them, and there seemed to be little chance that the English government would find enough money to ransom them. There was a riot by the protestors, and the English consul, Ward, was killed. His successor, Martin, almost suffered a similar fate, but somehow he shamed the dey into protecting him. In July 1674, the dey wrote to Charles II to urge the king to send money for ransoms: "[If you] do not redeem them wee shall send you back your consul . . . and soe it shall bee occasion to break our peace with you." At the moment, Sir John Narborough was on his way to Algiers with money for redemption, but his orders allowed him to make peace or war "according to your best judgment."

Sir John did not have enough money to ransom all the slaves, but he was able to satisfy the "important" patrons—those capable of raising a riot—by using the king's money and persuading some of the slaves to add their own money to the royal subsidy. Some, he discovered, did not wish to return. Captain Hamilton writes that "they are tempted to forsake their God for the love of Turkish women who are generally very beautiful . . ." He forgave the poor wretches their weakness, for these women "are well versed in witchcraft . . . captives never get free." Narborough sent home a list of the one hundred thirty-nine slaves that he ransomed at a cost of 56,248 pieces of eight in November, and Brisbane, the chancellor of the consulate, added another one hundred and thirty-five in December. Brisbane was careful to note that the king was "obliged to ransom only those slaves who were there in 1671"; later captures were not included in the treaty. When it was completed, the dey and his officers expected something more: Martin wrote that "they are in great expectation of a present from His Majesty . . . and to deserve it they . . . [compelled] the patrons to take half plate and half aspers for their slaves." It is not clear whether they were properly "gratified."

In 1674–75 the political situation for England changed considerably. Charles II had gone to war against the Dutch in 1672 as an ally of his cousin Louis XIV under terms that were kept secret from most of his advisers (Treaty of Dover); two years later the pressure for his withdrawal from the war had become too much to resist, and

Charles, who wished above all to die in his bed as king of England, was wise enough to yield. Why not? Louis's assault on the Dutch Netherlands was bogged down, and his withdrawal from the entire lower Rhine inevitable; Louis now was deeply involved in a war with the Hapsburg ruler in Spain and the Hapsburg emperor in Germany, as well as with the Dutch Netherlands and several of the most important German princes. This was not the same war that Charles had been willing to fight to punish the Dutch; it was a general European war, a war largely directed against France. The Dutch, moreover, had experienced a revolution when the French attacked, and William, Prince of Orange, a cousin of Charles II, who was married to Charles's niece, Mary, had become the virtual ruler of the United Netherlands. England made peace, a separate peace, in 1674.

The French armies had to withdraw from their advanced position on the Rhine, but in 1675 Colbert's navy defeated a combined Spanish and Dutch fleet off the island of Sicily, and the French army managed to establish itself on that island. Withdrawal from Louis XIV's Dutch war had been profitable for English merchants. They managed to "grab" a lion's share of the trade that the Dutch could no longer carry on and still fight a war. They also got much of the former French trade since France, too, was deeply engaged in the war. But when the French installed themselves on the island of Sicily, the English became unhappy, for that would have placed French naval power exactly on the center of England's communications with the Levant. An English naval squadron under Narborough was in the Mediterranean with orders to teach the Turks at Tripoli that they must respect English rights; his squadron remained in that sea to watch the French and protect the fabulous development of English seaborne commerce.

It was not long, however, before this extension in English commerce created problems with Algiers. English ships sailed with "strangers" in its crews; English ships sailed with forged passports from the admiralty; English captains refused to give up passengers who were enemies of the regency. Result: Englishmen became slaves, English ships were condemned as prizes; the English consul made himself unpopular in Algiers. In July 1676 Charles II again sent Narborough to Algiers to demand restitution and punishment for past, and assurance about future, offenses; he need not be "too rigorous in these demands for some little things can be overlooked," but he should consult with the consul. If there was no satisfaction, Narborough had the right to declare war.

Narborough did not sail immediately. In October he got a list of the Algerian warships: two with fifty guns, five with forty, one with thirty-eight, two with thirty-six; three with thirty-four, three with thirty, one with twenty-four, and a number of smaller vessels with ten to twenty guns each. The consul had been warning for a decade that the Algerian fleet was a little smaller than formerly, but more heavily armed. The shipyards at Algiers were now able to build frigates with fifty guns. However, it was not the size of the Algerian navy that detained Narborough in England; on April 9, 1677, he married Miss Elizabeth Colmady. Secretary of the Navy Pepys did not give him time for a long honeymoon before asking pointedly, "How soon the state of your new affairs will allow your looking after and carrying out the old?"

Perhaps inspired or emboldened by his recent marriage, Narborough, armed with the rank of admiral, sailed into the Mediterranean in August 1677; his fleet was presumably strong enough to inspire respect. He arrived at Tangiers to find the port under siege by neighboring Moors, but rather than tarry there, he announced his intention of going to Algiers to demand "satisfaction for . . . the many abuses and injuries done to His Majesty's subjects . . ." He did not wait to be given "satisfaction": in September, operating from Tangier, he captured four Algerian corsair vessels carrying seventeen to twenty-two guns and fought several others that escaped with considerable damage. Then on the way to Algiers, he overwhelmed the *Rose of Algiers* (forty-six guns) and captured its German renegade captain.[4] All this without a declaration of war; and yet he was surprised when the Algerians were "resolute and surly . . . would not treat . . . nor harken to anything of peace, but shot at my boat when she approached the shore . . ." With such response he left Algiers after four days on the roadstead and sailed off to Leghorn to sell his captives. Pepys had ordered that the Christians be freed, renegades hanged, and Moslems sold.

It may be that some of the Algerian reis welcomed this attack

---

4. These encounters at sea were not easy victories for the English. Captain Herman of *Sapphire* was killed in the fight with the *Golden Horse*. In the fight between the *Guernsey* (52 guns) and the *White Horse* (50), the Algerians tried several times to board but were driven off at considerable losses to both sides. One Algerian two-deck ship with fifty-four guns was captured more or less intact and became the English *Tiger* (46). Three of Narborough's ships drove the *Citron Tree* (32) and the *Calabash* (28) ashore: the ships were burned, but the crews escaped. Clowes, *Royal Navy*, II, pp. 451–53; Dyer, *Narborough*, 165–69.

without declaration of war. As consul Martin pointed out at the end of October 1677, the French corsairs had driven Dutch and German shipping from the Mediterranean, and the sea "swarmed with English shipping . . . with the goods of all nations under our banners." The reis were "beginning to grow desperate for lack of prizes." Now they were bringing in English ships. When consul Martin tried to free them under the treaty, he "narrowly escaped with [his] life." He was distressed: war, he noted, costs hundreds of pounds and slavery, while peace, with bribes, costs little. He had every reason to believe this for he was put in chains and escaped only with "house arrest" by virtue of his friendship with the dey and the dey's son-in-law, while in the next year and a half, one hundred fifty-seven English merchantmen were made prizes and nearly four thousand men, slaves. By spring 1678, Martin's letters were pitiful protests: he was treated like a criminal; the plague threatened everyone; his friend Babba Hassen, the aged dey's son-in-law, was off with an army toward Oran; and no word or money from London to reward and console him for his loyalty and service.

Part of Narborough's failure to secure peace was the result of the spread of the plague at Algiers (Martin seems to have been one of its victims). But of equal importance was the arrival of a Dutch mission anxious to make peace at almost any price. Dutch commerce had been practically driven from the Mediterranean by French privateers after 1672, and after the defeat of the Hispano-Dutch naval forces off Sicily in 1675, Dutch naval prestige was at its lowest ebb. Any Dutch ships that might escape the French were prey for the Algerians. By 1678, however, the European situation began to change: everyone knew that the French must negotiate an end to the so-called Dutch war or face the prospect of English intervention on the side of their enemies. A Dutch squadron again appeared in the Mediterranean, and Dutch negotiators, with honeyed words, suggested peace with Algiers. The French and English consuls suddenly found themselves as allies trying to prevent such a peace. When they learned that the Dutch were willing to "bribe" the Algerians with "tribute," their indignation knew no bounds. The English and French, each anxious for his king's prestige, and armed with greater naval power, could assume a more predatory attitude toward the "pirates, cutthroats, and other riff-raff" of Algiers, but Dutch merchants had reached the conclusion that it would be cheaper to "buy" protection than to establish it with naval power. They were less dependent upon "codes of honor" and better able to strike a balance between the costs of a naval expedition of questionable success and the profits of trade uninterrupted by the Barbary reis.

In April 1679 the Dutch made their first treaty agreeing to pay the "tribute" that the French and English consuls called "shameful." The treaty of 1679 was the most complex peace yet negotiated between Algiers and a European power: its twenty-one articles were concerned with all manner of problems including even the Jews who dealt with their fellows in Algiers and Amsterdam, but the core of the treaty was an agreement to give the Algerian dey cannons, masts, cannon balls, muskets, bullets, powder, cables, sails, and other naval supplies both as a gift to secure the treaty and as a continuing annual gift. The conditions of the Algerian-Netherlands treaty were completed by additional agreements of 1680 and 1681, which further shocked the English and French consuls, but the French could take some satisfaction in the fact that the Dutch were not allowed to repurchase their nationals from slavery at the first sale price; they had to deal individually with each patron.[5]

The Algerian treaty with the United Netherlands complicated the problem for the English. It removed Dutch shipping as possible prizes and thereby made more important the opportunity to take English prizes. It also provided a new model for treaties with European princes, one that the English would not consent to sign as long as their naval officers believed that force could bring the Barbary regencies to accept an agreement on English terms. On the other hand, the dey in Algiers had his problems. Pestilence raged in the city and killed soldiers, sailors, baldi, and slaves indiscriminately; both the janissary corps and the naval establishment suffered from its ravages. Babba Hassen, who really governed in his father-in-law's name, found himself caught between the "hawks," who needed war with England to maintain the prosperity of the regency, and the "doves," who feared the impact of the English navy. At first, the "hawks" seemed to be right, but when in 1680 Admiral Arthur Herbert took command of the Mediterranean fleet this changed. He managed to capture two small Algerian vessels and to drive another

5. In the eighteenth century, the Dutch treaty was to become the model for other small powers that wished to trade in the Mediterranean without interference from the corsairs; the young republic of the United States of America, when its ship captains no longer flew the English flag that guaranteed immunity, were to learn that either this system of "tribute" or vigorous naval action was the price for safety in the Mediterranean. Dumont, VII, I, pp. 404–6.

(fourteen gun) ship ashore, but he was unable to force the main Algerian ships to stand and fight. The English bottoms were foul and the Algerian frigates nimble. The next year, however, with his ships cleaned, the admiral captured in succession the *Golden Horse* (39 guns), the *Rose* (22 guns), and the *Great Genois* (36 guns),[6] with almost nine hundred Turks and Moors and two hundred Christian slaves. The admiral wrote to London that the soldiers in Algiers were inclined to peace, but the reis did not want it. Babba Hassen, who might be in danger of his life if he made peace, proposed a treaty like the one concluded with the Dutch but which the English would not consider.

Herbert believed that he might have gotten a treaty at once had several English merchants in Algiers not advised the dey that England would not sustain the expense of a long naval demonstration. However, in 1681 the situation changed, and the dey was ready to renegotiate. Yet it was not just the English naval presence that secured the peace. The Algerians' conflict with France was coming to a head, and the dey did not want to be at war with two naval powers at the same time. The new treaty was to become the axis for Anglo-Algerian relations for the next hundred years. Its stability, however, was undoubtedly the result of the fact that after the 1690s England emerged as the first naval power in the world, and after the treaties of Utrecht, English presence in the Mediterranean was assured by the establishment of English naval bases at the Straits and in the western Mediterranean. The kingdom of England did not need to pay tribute to secure protection of its commerce.

Admiral Herbert left one of his lieutenants, Captain John Neville, in Algiers as consul. About one year later Neville wrote a long memorandum for the instruction of the ministry in England. His suggestions and those of Samuel de Paz laid out basic plans for English Mediterranean policy vis-à-vis Algiers. The first requirement was the maintenance of a permanent naval squadron to cruise at the Straits and visit the North African ports. It will "give reputation . . . to His Mjst's naval power and deter breaking of the peace by the corsairs." The next requirement was appointment of a consul who would not engage in commerce but would be well paid and

6. Algerian warships were not named like those of the Christian navies. Europeans gave them names to correspond to the figures painted on the stern of the ships. The *Great Genois* was a Genoan frigate that the Algerians had captured; its stern had two lions and a crown as symbol; this made the name too complex so that Herbert gave it a simple one.

provided with "small sums of money" for bribes: "a small gratuity may hinder another nation's making peace with them" and later prevent much greater expenditures for war. The consul must choose his own interpreter; at present the dey had provided the English consul with a Dutch renegade for this service, and he helped the Dutch rather than the English. Both memos urged that the consul encourage the dey to make war on both France and the United Netherlands. Finally, both memos suggested that English sailors should not be allowed to take service in foreign merchantmen and thereby cause problems for the consul. At this point Captain Neville's wife petitioned the king for his return: he had been absent on ship and as consul for four years, and she wanted him home. Apparently Charles felt that his servant had done his duty, for Philip Rycaut replaced Neville, whose suggestions were taken seriously when the Anglo-Algerian treaty was renewed with the accession of James II to the throne of England.[7]

Even while Admiral Herbert's warships were anchored on the Algerian roadstead, the dey and divan decided to declare war on France. It had not been an easy decision. There was a proverb in Algiers that the French could make soup at Marseille in the morning and eat it at Algiers that very evening. France was close enough to Algiers to be dangerous, even when its naval power was relatively weak. But proximity was not the only reason: As long as France had been an ally or at least a friend against Hapsburg Spain, France had been a convenient source for naval and military supplies, and the Algerians still needed access to French markets. Furthermore, the Bastion as a trading post not only imported supplies for the reis but also provided a market where the Kabylie tribesmen could sell their produce to secure merchandise as well as the cash needed to pay tribute to the regency government. At the same time the Bastion paid the regency an annual "tribute" much needed for the salaries of the janissary militia. All this made the regency overlook the fact that a majority of the Knights of Malta were Frenchmen, and that the French navy had many of them as officers. All this could have been forgiven had the French king been willing again to become an ally of the corsairs, or even willing to live up to the obligations of the treaty between them. But Louis XIV and his ministers were not

7. The duke of Grafton, writing 6 October 1687, suggested that at that moment the English treaty was safe because the Algerians would not make peace with France, but, if such a peace were ever made, "I believe a war with us would closely follow." (Pro. Ind. 13396 fol. 425.)

Berber or Arab horsemen in battle order. COLLECTION VIOLLET, PARIS

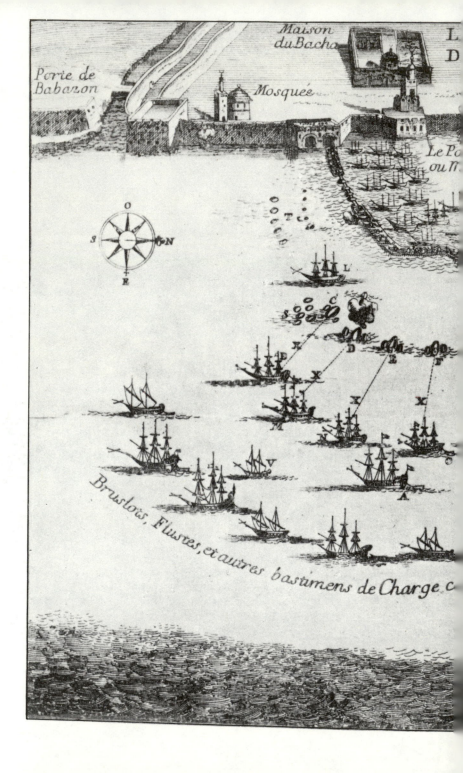

Porte de
Babazon

Maison
du Bacha

Mosquée

L
D

Le Po
ou T.

O
S   N
E

T

L'

C
S

E   D   E   F

X

M   X   X

O

V   A

Bruslots, Flustes, et autres bastimens de Charge. c

Porte de Babalouet.

ER
R

our du Fanal

Magasin et Hospital

A· Mr. le Marquis du Quesne Lieutenant General·

B· Le Marquis du Quesne fils Capi-
taine commandant le Laurier

C· Mr. du Quesne Mounier, neveu
du General commandant la
Galiotte Lardente·

D· La Menaçante, commendée par
Mr. Goëton

E· La Cruelle, par Mr. de Pointy·

F· La Bombarde, par Mr. de Combes·

G· La Bruslante, par Mr. de la Motte
Heran, ayant pour Lieutenant et
pour Enseigne le Chevalier de Fri-
cambaut son frere·

H· La Foudroyante commandée
par Mr. de la Piaudiere·

I· La Fulminante, par Mr. de Chevig

K· Mr. le Commandeur Desgouttes
commandant l'Estoille·

L· Le Cheual Marin commandé par
Mr. de Belle - Isle·

M· Mr. le Marquis d'Amfreville Chef
d'Escadre, commandant le Vigilant

N· Mr. de Septeme, command· l'Aimabl·

O· Mr. de Lhery, Chef d'Escadre, commandant le Prudent·

P· Mr. le Comte de Sebbeville, commandant la Sereine·

Q· Mr. le Chevalier de Tourville Lieutenant General, commandant le
Ferme·

R· Mr. le Comte d'Estrées, commandant le Fleuron·

S· Deux Corps de gardes de Chaloupes
armées pour le Secours des Galiotes, en cas d'Attaque·

T· Canots de garde a l'Entrée du Port·

V· Barques armées en guerre·

X· Marque les Amarres, Traïes ou
Cordages sous l'Eau, servant a
tenir les Galiotes et les faire aller
des Vaisseaux a l'Ancre, et de
l'Ancre aux Vaisseaux·

Representation of Duquesne's bombardment of Algiers.
COLLECTION VIOLLET, PARIS

Representation of Duquesne's bombardment of Algiers.

On the facing page, above: Execution of a priest in retaliation for Duquesne's bombardments. COLLECTION VIOLLET, PARIS

Below: Battle between the *Mary Rose* (A) and four smaller English ships and six Algerian corsairs. The 30-to-40-gun corsairs were driven off. BELL LIBRARY, UNIVERSITY OF MINNESOTA

Battle between two corsairs and an English merchantman. COLLECTION VIOLLET, PARIS

Lord Exmouth's bombardment of Algiers, 1816. BIBLIOTHÈQUE NATIONALE, PARIS

Above: Careening a brigantine. In the distance men are boiling the pitch for application to the hull. *Below:* The Bablason Gate at Algiers. We see a man convicted of a crime hanging from the hooks on the wall. When there were no victims the gate was believed to be "hungry."

A. De Poorte Bablason.
B. De Haeex daer in fy de
    Misdadigen smyten.
C. Poortje Aen de drooge graft.
D. Huifes in de graft.

TOT AGIER,
in Barbarye.

POUR ALGER,
en Barbarie.

A. La Porte Babason.
B. Le crochet ou l'on le
    les crimines.
C. La Porte du fossé see
D. Maisons du fossé.

Above: The courtyard of one of the *bagños,* or prisons, for slaves; an etching made in the late eighteenth or early nineteenth century. COLLECTION VIOLLET, PARIS. *Below:* Algerian dress at the end of the seventeenth century. The bearded man is a Turkish officer with his wife; the younger couple are Algerian *baldi,* or natives; in the background, a peasant and his wife. BELL LIBRARY, UNIVERSITY OF MINNESOTA

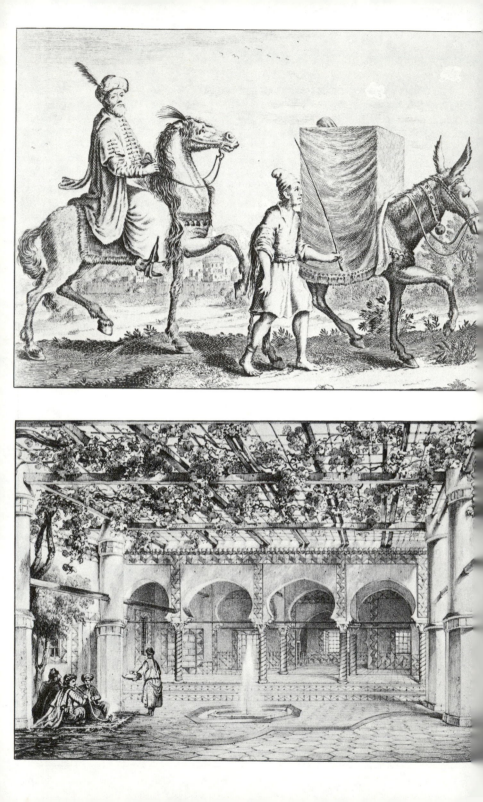

On the facing page, above: An Algerian *baldi* traveling with his wife and a slave. *Below:* The interior of a wealthy home in Algiers, eighteenth century. BELL LIBRARY, UNIVERSITY OF MINNESOTA PHOTOS

Street scene in Algiers, eighteenth century. BIBLIOTHÈQUE NATIONALE, PARIS

willing to become allies, nor were they willing to return able-bodied Turks and Moors who were slaves in their galleys. Those whom they did send to Algiers under terms of the treaty were not only old and infirm, but most of them were not even members of the Algerian community. The French did not want to return any slave that might tell about others who were chained to the oarbanks. Nor was that all: when the Algerians complained, the king and his ministers did not answer. When the Algerians sent an ultimatum, it was ignored. Louis XIV and his ministers could not conceal their contempt for the "Republic of brigands," for the "ox-drivers," and "renegades" who were the "great and powerful seigneurs of Algiers." This contempt finally drove the dey and divan to declare war: within a month, twenty-nine French ships became prizes and over three hundred Frenchmen, slaves.

There were many people in France who had wished to come to an agreement short of war: the governors of the Bastion regularly urged their opinion that the Algerians were loyally keeping to the terms of the treaty, and, indeed, the terms were useful in that they made it dangerous for a French sailor to take service on a foreign ship. Furthermore, they interfered with the commerce of French rivals. One merchant of Marseille suggested that the few miserable galley slaves who might be returned were surely less valuable than the French ships and sailors who might be captured by the corsairs. But these voices of moderation and compromise were not to be heard. The French deliberately provoked Algiers into hostilities; as Colbert wrote to the intendant of the marine at Toulon: "It is His Majesty's intention to make war on the Algerian corsairs." He ordered the dispatch of a spy to map fortifications, harbors, and other installations around Algiers. There were many factors behind this policy. The devout in the court believed that the Christian king should drive back the infidel and succor Christians in bondage. They had not forgotten Father Vincent, soon to be canonized as Saint Vincent de Paul; his priests were still on the Barbary Coast. However while the priests in Algiers urged moderation, there were other pious people who wished the king to make war on the infidels. There were other pressures for war with Algiers: Colbert's growing naval establishment needed an opportunity to prove itself and thereby attract the attention of the king. And finally there was a conviction shared by all Louis's ministers after 1679 that French prestige demanded violent reaction to any objection to or frustration of French policy. This was the era when the image of the French in Europe became "grotesque, distasteful, and fearsome." Colbert affirmed his belief in violence: "The terror of His Majesty's arms in the Levant and that which His Majesty will do to punish the insolence of Algiers," he wrote, "will put the commerce [of the Levant] . . . almost entirely into the hands of His Majesty's subjects . . . terror will oblige all parties to execute the treaties punctually . . ." He obviously meant "all parties except the kingdom of France," but no matter, this attitude ruled out the voices of moderation. On his minister's advice, Louis XIV decided to send a mighty fleet to accomplish the deed that his Hapsburg ancestor, Charles V, had failed to achieve. He would obliterate the "pirate nest" at Algiers.

The men of moderation had lost; in 1682 Admiral Duquesne, commanding a powerful fleet, proceeded to Algiers with orders to destroy the city to its foundations. The French depended upon a new weapon, a mortar designed by S. Renau d'Elicagaray; it launched a huge explosive shell at least 700 *toises* (approximately 1,350 meters) that presumably would wreck any buildings that were near the center of the explosion. This weapon was soon to be used in the Spanish Netherlands and at Genoa to impose French will by terror and to punish any disobedience to the French king. Duquesne's flotilla arrived off Cherchell on July 25; he bombarded the little town and burned two ships. July 29 he was before Algiers, and refused to negotiate; he had come to punish Algiers for its temerity in declaring war on France. August 20–22 and again on the 26th the bombardment caused little damage; the shells fell short due to "powder defects." On August 30, the mortars launched one hundred forty shells that struck in the town. On September 3, the Algerians tried an attack on the mortar ships but were repulsed. The dey asked for terms, but Duquesne refused to talk. On September 12 the French fleet sailed away with the intention of returning the following spring; the bombardment had killed about five hundred people and destroyed some fifty buildings. Both Louis XIV and Colbert were distressed that their mortars had not been more effective and ordered that more care be taken for the next year's attempt. As for Duquesne, the king recognized his services at Algiers and at Chios, where he burned a part of the Tripolitan corsair fleet in the harbor; Duquesne received a gratification of 100,000 livres and the elevation in rank to that of marquis under the name "du Quesne."

The next year when the French returned, Duquesne was as brutal as before. He refused to give the aged and ill Père Vacher a seat when the vicar priest came aboard with offers from the dey for negotiation; indeed, he even insulted him by saying that he was more Turk than Christian. To which Père Vacher simply replied: "I am a priest."

The bombardment that followed was more effective than the previous year: Babba Hassen offered to meet any terms. He sent hostages to Duquesne, returned hundreds of French slaves without payment of ransom, but when Duquesne escalated the terms by demanding a huge money payment as reparations (700,000 livres) Babba Hassen protested that he could not find that much money. In the "mismanagement" that followed, Mezzo Morto, one of the hostages and a most influential reis, offered to "settle everything" if he were only sent ashore. He did: he rallied the reis and part of the militia, murdered Babba Hassen (the aged dey escaped to Tunis) and had himself elected dey. He then announced that he would shoot from the mouths of cannons all Frenchmen in Algiers if Duquesne continued his bombardment. When the French took Algiers in 1830 they found the "consular cannon"; it had been forged by a Venetian in 1572 and could fire a ball 2,500 *toises* (about 4,800 meters) with "excellent exactitude." Père Vacher and other French priests and nationals were tied to this cannon and blown to bits when Duquesne reopened his bombardment.

The French had great hopes for another new weapon. Two huge bombs weighing 9,000 livres each and armed with eighty-four quintals of powder, almost an atomic bomb before the fracture of the atom, were prepared for launching. However, the mortars failed to deliver these monsters; their mission was a failure. Yet the bombardment with bombs weighing twelve to fifteen pounds each did great damage to the flimsy houses of the city; over five hundred were destroyed along with several mosques and a bath. The death toll, however, was not so great because the mass of the population fled the city for the suburbs before the bombardment was started. Fewer were killed by bombs than by the pestilence of the preceding summer. The damage was done, largely, to the homes of the baldi; the dey and his officers, the reis and janissaries suffered less, and saw no reason to allow the bombardment to bring them to terms. Mezzo Morto defied the French suggestion that the time had come for a treaty.

Duquesne's position was difficult. Mezzo Morto as dey would not treat, and more bombs led to more executions of the unfortunate Frenchmen in Algiers. Colbert had written to Duquesne that the king "wishes to make them pay dearly for the peace that they ask for . . ." But they would not ask! Colbert had gone on to say that the king "will be much pleased by the glory that he will gain and the profit that all Christendom will receive by the entire destruction of that city . . ." His bombs were doing damage, but the city would not be destroyed. We are told that Duquesne took to his bed and left direction of the action to his officers, who soon lost confidence in his leadership. He could not destroy Algiers; he had neither the infantry nor the artillery needed for a landing and an assault. He finally sailed for France, leaving Algiers with smoking ruins, but unbowed. The English consul Rycaut wrote to Lord Dartmouth: "See how little these people value French bombs of which I compute the number to be about 6000 . . . the best information that I can gett about 800 shops and house beat down!" A Turkish account placed the number at three hundred fifty houses destroyed and "many people killed." The great mosque had been badly damaged the year before.

At this moment the situation in Europe again dictated French policy toward the corsair community of Algiers. Duquesne's abrupt bombardment of Chios and the Tripolitan corsair vessel in that port had practically led to a breach between the Sublime Porte and Versailles when the Grand Vizier Kara Mustapha summarily threatened to put the French ambassador in prison. The sultan's government was unwilling to do much to help Algiers, but Chios was much closer to the center of his realm; for the moment it looked as though Louis XIV would soon be fighting a naval war against both Algiers and the Ottoman empire. However, Kara Mustapha's politics were not sea centered; he was planning a massive assault up the Danube against the Austrian lands of Emperor Leopold I. Over 200,000 men were being assembled on the lower Danube ready to break the twenty-year truce that had been agreed upon after the Ottoman defeat at Saint Gotthard in 1664. At that time Louis XIV, as Margrave of Alsace, had sent a French contingent to aid the German armies; both the accounts of the battle and the terrible losses suffered by the officers of that French army testified to the fact that the French were the most stubborn as well as the most effective of the Christians who won that battle.

However, when Louis XIV learned of Kara Mustapha's plan to revenge the earlier Ottoman defeat, his political orientation was quite different from that of two decades before. Sr. de Vauban and the Marquis de Louvois had convinced him that he must ring his kingdom with a system of fortifications that would guarantee victory in any future war with the Dutch, the Germans, and the Spaniards. The recent Treaty of Nymwegen, however, had not given him all the territories that he needed to complete this system, and he was in the process of acquiring these lands by a highly irregular method: annexation in full peace on the grounds of feudal interrelationships of the near and distant past. The "reunions" and annexations of counties, towns, the city of Strasbourg (1681), and other territories along the eastern and northern frontiers of France were unquestionably naked aggression against the German princes and the Hapsburg rulers of both Spain and the German empire. In Germany leagues and alliances were beginning to form to check the progress of this French aggression, and Emperor Leopold was obviously preparing for war. When Louis learned of the planned Ottoman invasion of the Danube basin, a grand plan of action seemed realizable that would bring recognition of his conquests as well as prestige and glory to the kingdom and king of France. The kingdom of France would stand by as a neutral when the Turkish hordes overran Austria and threatened to engulf the whole of central Europe. Then at the right moment the king of France could appear as the shield and sword of Christendom, save the Germans from Ottoman slavery, and accept for himself or his son the crown of the Holy Roman Empire, thus displacing the Hapsburg rivals of his house and lands on a throne that, united with the kingdom of France, could again recreate a united Christian Europe. It was a grand idea, and Louis suddenly stopped all plans for war with the sultan and ordered his ambassador to assure Kara Mustapha that no French soldiers would stand in his way on the route to Vienna.

Although it was a splendid idea from the point of view of the French king, it did not work out quite as he had expected. The Turkish armies reached Vienna and placed the city under siege, but Vienna did not fall. Karl of Lorraine with a German army and Jan Sobieski with a Polish one joined hands, relieved the city and drove Kara Mustapha's forces down the river. No French army aided the relief of Vienna, nor was a French army needed. Louis XIV, however, was not checkmated by the German-Polish victory; when it was obvious that Vienna would not fall, French armies invaded the Spanish Netherlands and Luxembourg, launching their new mortar shells on the cities to terrorize the Spanish and imperial authorities into an agreement that would recognize the legitimacy of the recent annexations and transfer Luxembourg to the kingdom of France.

By the time that Duquesne returned from his second bombardment of Algiers, the kingdom of France was in a crisis. The Hapsburg king of Spain had declared war, and the Hapsburg emperor in Germany was debating whether to fight France in the west or the

Ottoman empire in the southeast. The fortified city of Luxembourg fell to French arms, but the emotion that ran through Europe left open the question of war or peace. Under such conditions, the French government decided upon a conciliatory policy toward the corsair community of Algiers; the navy might well be more useful and more needed elsewhere. On 5 January 1684 the Marquis de Seignelay, minister of marine affairs, wrote to Admiral Tourville that the "present situation [war with Spain and perhaps with the Emperor] makes it absolutely necessary to make a treaty with Algiers."

As a result, on April 2, 1684, while Europe waited to see whether the German empire would be at war in the west or in the southeast, Admiral Tourville arrived at Algiers accompanied by a *capidji* from the sultan who could explain that France and the Ottoman empire were in good understanding and that he wished the Algerian regency also to be friends with the French. Tourville was as flexible in his negotiations as Duquesne had been rigid. In twenty days a peace was written to last "one hundred years." It provided for mutual surrender of captives, exonerated the consuls for any bad debts by fellow nationals, arranged for passes, and practically restated the previous Franco-Algerian treaty. One stipulation required an important Algerian to visit the French court to make peace with the king. On July 4, 1684, Hadj-Djafer Agha had an audience with Louis XIV, and the next spring Hadj-Mohamet brought two handsome horses as gifts to his majesty. Both the English and the Dutch consuls tried to prevent the completion of the peace, but the bombardments had convinced the Algerians that they should make peace if the conditions were at all satisfactory.

Events in Europe, however, soon made the French king and his ministers more confident in their policy of terror. The German emperor decided to make peace, or rather a truce, with France, and to make war on the Ottoman empire. When the emperor agreed to a twenty-year truce, the king of Spain had no alternative to peace with Louis XIV. In France this truce of Ratisbonne seemed sure evidence that the annexations of the past years were to be confirmed in the future; Europe could not stand up against the power of French arms. But first the Genoese had to suffer for their assistance to the Spanish in the recent little war: the mortar ships, accompanied by a mighty flotilla, destroyed a large section of that city, and then the duke of Genoa was forced to humiliate himself at the court of the French king. The "face" of France in Europe after bombardments at Algiers, in the Netherlands, Genoa, the siege and capture of both Strasbourg and Luxembourg, the brutal imposition of violence on the

Protestants in the lands of the duke of Savoy was one to make men tremble—or to prepare themselves to confront French power with power of their own.

The Algerians were soon to learn that the contempt that French statesmen had shown them in the past had not changed: the king and his ministers still regarded the Algerian government as a rabble of thieves and ruffians with whom one need not treat seriously. They had agreed to peace only because of the situation in Europe. The same old problem emerged: Turks and Moors chained to the French galley oars. Many of them were janissaries whose friends and families clamored for their return; others were reis or other naval officers with important contacts in Algiers. Some of them had been chained to the oars for fifteen to twenty years. There were others in the galleys in addition to these men with connections close to the regime; some of the Moors were from wealthy or important families who also had some ability to make their desires known to the dey; he could not really ignore the demands that these people should be freed. But the French simply would not release them. In instructions to his negotiators, Louis ordered that they should avoid, if at all possible, any agreement to return able-bodied men. When Tourville could not avoid agreeing to the mutual return of slaves, it was the same old story: the French sent aged and sick men, many of them not even "Turks" from Algiers, rather than the janissaries that the dey expected. Protests that these slaves had never been in Algiers, and that their return placed a burden on Algiers, were blandly turned off or not answered. Nor was this the only problem: a French squadron under Admiral Jean d'Estrées bombarded Tripoli with mortar bombs, and by threat of a similar mortar attack, forced the Tunisians to sign a new treaty that gave French merchants special privileges heretofore reserved for the English. Another squadron of French warships arrested five Algerian ships. The crews of two of them managed to get overboard and ashore, but three crews were captured, and the dey was unable to get them released.

For two years after Tourville's renewal of the treaty the dey and divan tried in vain to persuade the French to honor their commitments. Colbert was dead, but his son Seignelay, who shared his father's contempt for the "cut-throat" republic, was his successor and refused to answer the dey's letters or to do anything about the Turks and Moors in the French galleys. Finally in desperation the Algerians again declared war on France, and the reis began to bring in French prizes. This action was not universally popular in Algiers; the French bombardments had cost heavily both in property and lives, but the greatest weight had fallen on the baldi, who had little or no influence on policy. The taiffe of the reis favored the war, and it had powerful influence in the dey's councils. As long as Algiers was at peace with England, the Netherlands, and France there were few prizes. The dey, himself a member of the reis corporation, owned at least one of the corsair ships; the report was that he cared little for a bombardment as long as there were rich prizes. French merchants, and particularly those of the Bastion, were appalled at the prospect of a new war, but when Denis Dusault, the governor of the Bastion, wrote to the dey urging peace, the Algerians disdainfully replied that he should tend to his commerce and leave politics to men who governed. Obviously, although the war came about because the French refused to live up to their treaty commitments, it was not regretted by everyone who lived in Algiers.

The Algerians declared war in August 1687, and the reis began to bring in French prizes. The first French warships arrived before Algiers on June 13, 1688; by the 16th there was a mighty armada of galleys, *polacres,* tartans, bomb-galiots, and warships. Admiral d'Estrées floated a message ashore for the dey; Mezzo Morto asked an English officer to reply that "if he [d'Estrées] has aught to say, he can send a flag of truce ashore which shall not be injured." He added that if there was a bombardment the French consul, the vicar general, and other Frenchmen would be put to the cannon. D'Estrées reportedly told Captain Hobman that, "if he were not an Englishman he would hang him for bringing such a message." On June 22 the French bombardment began "with great prejudice to the houses and shops" of Algiers. Three Frenchmen were placed on the mouths of cannons, but the consul escaped this first execution. As an English merchant described it: "Ye consul was ready to be made a sacrifice . . . but Ali Rais begged his life, and he was returned to the bagñes" —but only temporarily. The Algerians offered to parlay, but d'Estrées refused; they were still to be punished. On the 23rd, the bombs began to "play with aboundance and vigor . . . 3000 in all. The Turkish cannons did little damage . . . but at 4 P.M. the consul was fired away with four other Frenchmen." D'Estrées ordered the execution of three Turks whose bodies were floated ashore on a raft. On the 25th the vicar general and four other Frenchmen were fired at the mouth of the cannon, and the next day there were three more Turks floated ashore on a raft! On the 27th bombs again: seven Frenchmen were brought out to be executed, but they were given the option of becoming Jews, which they quickly accepted. There was a side issue of money for the pasha-dey before they were "sent to learn the Mosaic Law." The Algerians now refused any suggestion for parlay. The dey remarked that the French would leave when they had fired their last shot. Early in August d'Estrées received orders to return to France. Plans were being made for a French invasion of the Rhineland, and the fleet might well be more useful at home, rearmed and equipped, than at so distant a post with most of its powder and shot expended.

A French memorandum prepared for the king's council expressed dissatisfaction with the French wars against Algiers. The English had been able to destroy thirty corsair ships in a fourteen-month war; the French captured only five. The English had made war secretly, quietly; the French with much noise. The French warships could not draw up to the more nimble Algerians because they were "heavy wooden ships, loaded with heavy cannons . . . they have twice as much spare parts . . . they are loaded for a voyage to Siam . . . large amounts of wine, water, and all kinds of food." The Algerians carried biscuits and olives, and only a three weeks' supply. The memoirist, however, did not seem to know that the bombardments had done damage "far greater than was expected [after the first relatively ineffective experience]; a third of the town in ruins . . . it will never be built to its former splendor."

Mr. Cole, a merchant of Algiers, remarked: "They have already done yt prejudice . . . 20 years wont make ye towne soe beautiful as it was before . . ." What was also unknown in 1688 was the fact these bombardments had engendered so much fear and hatred of the French that the good will that Frenchmen had acquired over the preceding centuries was never again to color Algerian policy. In the Netherlands, Germany, and Italy as well as in Algiers, Louis XIV's policy of terror left a heritage of hate that colored attitudes for generations to come.

D'Estrées was called home on the eve of a French invasion of the Rhineland that was supposed to deter the Ottoman empire from ending its war with the emperor and to force the Germans to make the truce of Ratisbonne into a permanent treaty of peace. It did block the Ottoman peace talks, but Philippsburg held out longer than had been expected, the Germans did not "fold up" in face of French power, and as soon as the French army was committed to the Rhine, the prince of Orange, William III, was able to sail for England to "protect English liberties and the Protestant religion"—as well as to bring England into the alliance against France (the "Glorious

Revolution" of 1689). Like so many of Louis XIV's projects, this one turned out differently from what was expected. The Algerians were the gainers: in April 1689 a French agent secretly arrived at Algiers; May 13th a French warship arrived with an officer prepared to negotiate on Algerian terms.

The new treaty was largely based on the former ones, but the French now agreed to return the five ships taken before the war began and to pay a huge sum for a ship belonging to the influential Memet Reis that they had burned. They also agreed to furnish the Algerians with nine thousand bombs, four mortars, and a master cannoneer for a siege of Oran; this presumably would also aid the French war effort against Spain. They further admitted that the Algerian reis could enslave "foreigners" found aboard French ships and that French warships would not cruise along the North African coast. For their part the Algerians agreed to ransom slaves held by the French at 150 reals for Turks, 100 for Moors, to restore the merchandise taken from French ships when the war began, and to allow the repurchase of French slaves, but at prices to be set by the patrons. The French had ninety days to ratify the treaty and to deliver the bombs. It was characteristic of Louis XIV's relations with Algiers: the French first showed contempt, then bombarded the city, and finally, under pressure of events in Europe, renewed their treaties with new concessions to the corsairs. However, the experience of the three bombardments had serious results on the course of Algerian corsair warfare; the future was still to be blurred by European wars, but the corsairs were never again to enjoy the prosperity they had known for so much of the seventeenth century, for the Europe that emerged from these wars was quite different from its earlier patterns.

The real significance of the English naval warfare that had effectively checkmated and sunk Algerian corsair naval units and the French bombardments that so heavily punished the city of Algiers did not become fully apparent for another quarter century. In the years between 1689 and 1714, there were two great wars involving the military forces of all Western Europe; when they were over, the Mediterranean basin and the peoples living on its shores were under a new and vastly different politico-military situation, and a new balance of power was responsible for new orientations in the corsair communities of North Africa.

XII *The Great Wars:*
1688–1714

I
N THE LATE SUMMER OF 1688, Louis XIV ordered his son to
lead an army into the Rhineland to besiege the great fortress
of Philippsburg. This was a move to prevent the Ottoman sultan
from making a separate peace with Emperor Leopold and the Holy
League.[1] The French did not want this peace; it would release a
battle-tested German army that could be used to reverse the French
annexations—the so-called reunions—in the Rhineland. As we noted
above, when the German imperial and Polish troops defeated the
Turks at Vienna, Emperor Leopold signed a treaty with Louis XIV
that was merely a truce. It did not recognize the legitimacy of the
"reunions." Thus, when it appeared that Leopold's armies could be
released from Hungary, Louis XIV decided that the time had come
to force the Germans to recognize his annexations. However, the invasion did not go as the French had expected. Philippsburg was more
powerful than they believed it to be, and autumn rains turned the
siege area into a sea of mud. The fortification did fall, but by that
time German troops were already well on their way back to Germany
from Hungary, and the French could think of no better response
than to burn and destroy all towns and villages in a broad belt of the
German Rhineland. This action did not persuade the Germans to
make peace; on the contrary, it was the act of terror that gave birth to
German nationalism.[2]

1. The Holy League of the German empire, Venice, Poland, and Russia came
into being in 1683–84 after the defeat of the Turkish siege of Vienna. By 1688
the League's victories had driven the Turks from Hungary, and the German
imperial armies were besieging Belgrade (captured in September 1688), the
Venetians were in full control of the Peloponnesus, and were threatening
further invasions of the Balkans. The Sultan and his ministers were ready to
make peace.
2. The French invasion of the Rhineland had another very serious result. Once
the French army was committed to the siege of Philippsburg, the Estates
General of the United Netherlands gave William of Orange permission to

The Sublime Porte, upon learning of the French invasion of the Rhineland, did not make peace with the Holy League, but Louis XIV soon found himself at war with a coalition of powers that included the German emperor, most of the German princes, the kingdoms of England and the Spains, and the duke of Savoy. The fortresses with which Vauban had ringed the kingdom of France guaranteed against an invasion, but the coalition was powerful enough to prevent a serious French incursion into Germany or the Netherlands. As a result Louis was at war for nine years, a war of attrition that made dreadful demands on his kingdom and his people.

No war of this magnitude could be fought without affecting Algiers. As we have seen, in the summer before his invasion of the Rhineland, Louis XIV had sent his bomb-ketches, supported by a powerful naval force, to bombard Algiers into submission. The effects of the bombardment were devastating to homes, marketplaces, and mosques, although the loss of life was slight. The French sailed home, leaving in Algiers a profound hatred for France and its king. On the other hand, when the French became involved in war in Europe, they were ready to let bygones be bygones in North Africa. This was the familiar pattern; each time that Louis XIV became involved in war on the continent, his ministers sought to make peace with the Barbary community; they wanted no miniscule conflict on their flanks when they had a real war elsewhere. Thus the French ambassador at Istanbul secured the appointment of Ismail Pasha to be pasha of Algiers and to make peace. However, Ismail, a self-proclaimed creature of Louis XIV, was not allowed to land at Algiers; indeed, he was told that his life would be in danger if he tried to do so. His letters to Louis XIV give us a lugubrious picture of a man rejected, as well as a mirror of the hatred that the terror bombardments had aroused.

There could be no peace in the fall of 1688, yet early the next year the dey, Mezzo Morto, had good reason for coming to an agreement with France. He had returned to Algiers from a punitive expedition on his western (Moroccan) frontier just when the French naval forces ended their bombardments. In January the next year he discovered that he was facing an alliance of the sultan of Morocco and the bey of Tunis that would engage his forces in a desperate

move his army to England in defense of the "Protestant" cause. King James II, his queen, and his newly-born son fled the kingdom, and as a result of this so-called Glorious Revolution, William and his wife Mary (eldest daughter of James II) became king and queen of England.

conflict. This made peace with France seem to be a reasonable proposal. However, when he received a letter from the French king suggesting peace, the divan responded in stony silence. The dey and his ministers might be ready for peace, but the divan was still hostile. Nonetheless, Mezzo Morto continued the negotiations in secrecy and finally agreed to a treaty that was essentially the same as the last one; it was signed September 24, 1689, just before Mezzo Morto led his soldiers eastward to fight the bey of Tunis.

The expedition proved to be a disaster, and, as so often happened in such cases, the janissaries demanded the dey's head. He escaped and ended his career as admiral pasha of the sultan's Black Sea fleet. Hadji Shaban, a tough-minded soldier, then became dey of Algiers; he was the first of the long series of soldier deys who ruled the communities in the eighteenth century. The era of the deys drawn from the reis had ended.

The new dey was confronted with the same problem that had harassed his predecessor: the Tunisian frontier. The bey of Tunis had again become allied with several Kabylie tribes, with the result that they no longer paid tribute to Algiers. Since this tribute money was absolutely necessary to meet the pay of the janissary militia, the dey had to concentrate his undivided attention to the recovery of his control over the Kabylie tribesmen and the punishment of the Tunisian bey. Hadji Shaban had to persuade the divan that the treaty with France was necessary. He explained to Louis XIV and to Seignelay in separate letters that the treaty was unpopular, because a large segment of the divan believed that Mezzo Morto had lined his own pockets when it was concluded. However, obviously the treaty had to be made. After finding several acceptable minor alterations, he announced that France and the regency of Algiers had concluded a treaty that would last a hundred years. This rhetoric was commonly used, but in this case it proved to be astonishingly correct, for the treaty did remain in force until the era of the French Revolution.

The conclusion of a treaty between France and Algiers posited a problem for the new king of England, William III, who was also stadtholder of the United Netherlands. Algiers could not afford to be at peace with more than two of the three important commercial powers, and the reis were better pleased when Algiers was at war with at least two of the three. Since England and Algiers were at peace—for the moment, anyway—and now that France had managed to secure a treaty, William understood that it was unlikely that the United Netherlands could also make peace with Algiers. Nor was the plight of his Dutch compatriots the only one; the Algerians had a treaty with James II of England and the passes recognized by the reis were signed in James's name. The "Glorious Revolution" that put William and Mary on the throne had resulted in James's exile to France, and that worthy monarch quickly wrote to both the sultan of the Ottoman empire and the dey of Algiers[3] pointing out that William was a usurper and that he was an ally of the German emperor whose armies had captured Belgrade, as well as the ally of the Venetian senate whose armies and naval establishment had conquered part of Greece and were oppressing all Moslem Levantine commerce. James urged that no pass signed by William III should be accepted by the Algerian reis. The English consul at Algiers was in a curious situation. With regard to the question of a peace between Algiers and the United Netherlands, he knew that peace with the Netherlands might mean war with England. Moreover, the consul's problems were increased by the fact that while the king of England in his role of stadtholder of the United Netherlands was urging an Algerian-Dutch peace, English policy in the past had been to encourage the Algerians to be at war with the Dutch, and even after William became king of England, there were many people in England who were not unhappy to see Algiers at war with their most formidable commercial rival.

Both the English and the Dutch had long since decided that a policy of firmness, oiled by bribery and, in the case of the Dutch, outright donations amounting to tribute, was more effective and less expensive than the French policy of terror. Naval action against so elusive an enemy required the maintenance of a considerable squadron at sea for an extended period of time, and naval bombardments that were obviously only marginally effective, were terribly expensive. As a matter of fact, both the English and the French consuls at Algiers urged bribery as a suitable substitute for naval action. In 1683, after the savage French bombardments, consul John Neville wrote to his English superior: "Sir, for money these people will do anything you would have of them . . . the dey would cut off any head on request . . . for a fee." Indeed, the dey did ask how much the French bombardments cost, and on hearing the figure, remarked that he "would destroy Algiers himself for that sum." However, a policy of bribery could also be difficult. Consul Rycault's "gifts" in 1684

3. The English consul informed his government that King James's letter could be purchased for fifty dollars.

totaling 442 Dutch dollars in purses ranging from sixty dollars for the dey's principal advisers to a few piasters for menials became a "precedent"; once given they were "expected." Subsequent consuls had difficulty explaining that they were not to be regular affairs. A similar situation arose a few years later when a shipment of powder and shot arrived at Algiers in the hold of a warship. The English thought it was for sale, but the dey assured them that it must be a "gift" following the precedent established by Admiral Herbert several years before. When the consul protested, the dey cannily remarked that it would be easy to get a peace with the United Netherlands if the English so wished it. Such a tradition made the consuls wary, but, once war developed in Europe, all of them were eager to expand the policy of bribes or tribute (call it what you will) to enlist the Algerians against their enemy.

When their respective governments urged them to secure the action of the Algerian corsairs against the national enemy, both the English and the French consuls privately or separately insisted that money would be the crucial factor in such an effort. After 1690, the English consul assured his government that about 10,000 Dutch dollars would be enough to secure a new breach between Algiers and France. This was a large sum and not easily transferred in cash, for the Mediterranean swarmed with French privateers and warships. Nonetheless, the money finally managed to find its way via Livorno. In the meantime, the French consul was complaining bitterly about the niggardly actions of his government in comparison with the generosity afforded to his English rival. When the cards were down, however, both sides failed to obtain Algerian intervention in the war. The English consul explained that just when he had the necessary money to bring off the coup, French engineers arrived with dredging equipment capable of clearing sand from the Algerian harbor behind the mole. The Algerians, like politicians in other places and times, took the bribes but failed to deliver the *quid pro quo*. In 1691 Hadji Shaban had good reasons for taking the money from, but avoiding difficulties with, either England or France.

The dey's major problems were the continued hostility of his Tunisian and Moroccan neighbors. Mezzo Morto had attempted to set a puppet prince on the Tunisian throne; his efforts failed and finally he lost his own throne when his soldiers rebelled against him. Hadji Shaban was soon involved in the same conflict. His first military efforts were directed against the sultan of Morocco, whose armies had invaded the western beylik. Shaban defeated him and secured the information that there had been a project to partition the Algerian regency between Morocco and Tunis. Shaban quickly turned on Tunis with Tripoli as his ally. The Tunisian Mehemet Bey was defeated and driven into exile, while the victorious Algerians placed a new puppet on the Tunisian throne. On his return to Algiers, however, Hadji Shaban found the city in rebellion against his government and dangerously threatened by another epidemic of the plague. The janissary militia crushed the rebellion, but the plague took a serious toll on the city. Indeed, it is quite possible that the endemic visitation of the bubonic plague was a principal cause for the decline of Algiers in the eighteenth century.

The victory over Mehemet Bey in Tunis proved to be short lived. The political and military scene in North Africa was fluid and irrational. In part this was the result of the inadequate military technology available to these people. The janissary militia was anything but a well-organized disciplined force. Its members had little or no drill. Its battle tactics depended upon more or less close, ill-formed squares or lines of musketmen who fired at random, aided by some very small-bore artillery that needed protection from the infantry. The same tactics were used by the Tunisian Turkish militia, but it was considerably smaller than that of Algiers. For the rest, the swarms of Berber and Arab horsemen depended almost as much on their vocal tumult as upon the lances and muskets that they carried. These horsemen, apparently undisciplined, were easily demoralized by cannon and musket fire. A battle often had some of the tragic drama that had characterized the attacks of French feudal cavalry against English bowmen or Flemish pikemen in the latter Middle Ages. Perhaps the difference was that the Berber and Arab horsemen were quicker to flee than the feudal cavalry had been. This tendency to escape from an impossible battle left the tribesmen free to join in the next one, where there might be a chance for more success and booty. They were probably wise to leave the scene of defeat as quickly as possible, for the usual pattern was for the defeated Turkish janissaries in the Tunisian army to join the victors in capturing Arabs or Berbers. Any of them who could not produce a good ransom were put to the sword and their heads carried away in triumph.

The political life in the Maghrib was always fortuitous. Within a very short time Mehemet Bey returned to power in Tunis and again easily found allies in the Kabylie tribesmen, who hated their

Turkish overlords in Algiers. The sultan of Morocco, anxious to redefine his relations with Algiers, was quick to join the Tunisian against the common enemy. This turn of events again cost Hadji Shaban some forty thousand écus, the tribute that should have been paid into the treasury from the eastern beylik. It was money badly needed to pay his soldiers. There was no alternative. Again, the Algerian militia invaded Tunis, this time as allies of the bey of Tripoli, who also had a score to settle with Mehemet Bey.

By 1695 Shaban had "pacified" North Africa and had developed new visions of his role.[4] From a series of letters that he wrote to Louis XIV and his ministers, we see Hadji Shaban, the soldier dey, struggling toward a conception of a North Africa again united under the direction of a beylerbey pasha; he saw this western sanjac as an outpost of the Ottoman Empire, a "pear to refresh the sultan" and assure his Mediterranean frontiers. Shaban regarded the "Arabs" (a term that obviously lumped Arabs and Berbers together) as the real enemies that must be controlled to assure Turkish overlordship as well as financial support for the janissary militia. He clearly believed that he was the man who could rule the congeries of towns, tribes, and other political entities. The new bey of Tunis was his vassal, the bey of Tripoli his ally; his vigorous campaigns proved that he was a soldier capable of maintaining his rule. However, before the sultan actually got around to making him beylerbey, Hadji Shaban was the target of a murder plot. He managed to frustrate this

4. Hadji Shaban wrote to Louis XIV March 6, 1695 to tell him of his victory over the Tunisians. Even though they had superior numbers, "The all-powerful God, without regard for this advantage, gave us victory . . . When the two armies met, each of our soldiers faced 200 men [probably a gross exaggeration] . . . one battalion of Algerians had [to fight] four battalions of enemies . . . more than 40,000 men, cavalry and infantry. However, thanks to Heaven . . . they lost courage and strength . . . and we secured a complete victory. We took possession of all their goods and riches, their artillery, muskets, tents, pavilions, and munitions of war . . . the traitor Mehemet Bey fled and took refuge in Tunis. The Pasha had already sought his safety in a French vessel . . . This victory took place on the plains of Kef, and we cut to pieces 10,000 rebel Arabs who followed the Bey. We gave quarter to 2,700 Turks who joined our party . . ." He went on later to point out that "It is I . . . whom God has wished to serve as the instrument to deliver the city of Tunis from tyranny and to punish the wicked . . ." He reported that the sultan had honored him for his victory by the gift of a "magnificent robe of honor which he has given me to show the world his satisfaction . . . At the same time he has made me prince and general commander of the three republics, his lieutenant in the Empire. Thus today I see myself as prince, governor, general and absolute commander of the three states of Barbary." (Plantet, *Correspondance des Deys d'Alger*, I, pp. 451–52.)

first project, but his savage reprisals alienated a considerable section of influential janissaries. A second plot succeeded: he was carried off to prison and strangled. It is ironical that Hadji Shaban had, a few years before, explained to Louis XIV that his spheres of action were limited because the dey was simply the "creature" of the militia, a "creature" who could not act without its support. A decade or so later, the deys changed that feature of the constitution so that they could at least govern without worrying about the divan. His immediate successor, however, a less adventuresome man, did not follow up the projected unification of the North African regencies. His principal objectives seem to have been good food and a desire to live to enjoy it.

While the Algerians were at war with their neighbors, they obviously wanted no conflict with as dangerous an enemy as the French king whose bomb-ketches were only a few days away from Algiers. Nonetheless, relations with France did not go smoothly. The perennial problem of Turks and Moors, slaves on the French galley benches, continued to haunt the dey and his ministers. These poor wretches were sometimes the sons or relatives of reis or other important people in Algiers, while others were simply janissaries who had friends in the militia; still others were often related to Moorish families in the city who also had some influence. The galley slaves managed to send letters home telling of their fate and giving names of others on the benches; these letters were carried to the dey with demands for action. On the other side of the picture, we find the French galley captains with important roles as coast guards or couriers. They did not want to have their rowing power disrupted by the removal of their best oarsmen. The criminals and Huguenot dissenters[5] sent to the galleys from mainland France were usually too weak, too unused to the sea, to be good oarsmen, while the Turks and Moors were usually men who knew the sea and were capable of pulling at the oars. There were always "good" reasons for refusal to release slaves from their benches, reasons that made no sense at Algiers.

Hadji Shaban sent one of his most eloquent men, Mehemet Elmin, to France to try to persuade the king to implement the treaty clauses providing for the release of the Moslem slaves, or at least

5. After the revocation of the Edict of Nantes in 1685 a steady flow of Huguenot dissenters was directed toward the galley fleet; these unfortunate men were guilty only of practicing their religion. There is much evidence to suggest that most of them, especially the preachers and teachers, were physically unfit for the labors on a war galley, but, since they were sent there as punishment, their lack of physical strength was not a consideration.

those with connections in Algiers. Mehemet Elmin arrived at Versailles at an unfortunate moment. The war in Europe was obviously a sticky affair that was costing too much and promising too little for the kingdom; it absorbed much of the king's energy and time. Even more important for the Algerian emissary was the fact that Seignelay, the minister with whom he should deal, was sick, terminally ill; he died soon after Mehemet Elmin returned to Algiers. Since the minister had reports from his intendant at Toulon indicating the importance of the galley slaves to the successful operation of the Mediterranean naval effort, Mehemet Elmin found himself always in the antechamber; he never got a chance to see Seignelay. His letters are pitiful complaints of a man whose time, money, and energy are frittered away without any chance for a successful conclusion of his mission. Finally the ministry ordered him to leave Versailles and go to Toulon, where the intendant would consider his case. He had no more success there than he had had in Versailles.

While his emissary was in France, Hadji Shaban wrote to Louis XIV and Seignelay to urge the French to abide by the conditions of the treaty. These letters are interesting more for the insight they give us into the mind of the dey than for an understanding of the problem. The dey's arguments were laced with ponderous theological propositions, discussions of moral rights, and long-winded repetitive statements of the Algerian case. Hadji Shaban obviously dictated these letters in the same spirit in which he lectured or addressed sessions of the divan. It would be interesting to know how they were received at Versailles.

After Seignelay's death in 1690, the new minister of marine, Pontchartrain, proved to be a little more pliable, especially after 1692, when he also had responsibility for managing the royal efforts to combat the famine in France. Even so, de la Croix *fils,* who had been translator of the Algerian letters and dragoman for many of the negotiations, explained in a memoir that the treaty of 1689 had been a good treaty, one that the Algerians largely adhered to, but that it was broken by intrigues of individual officers in France, who "do not know the country, do not speak the language or know the customs and manners of negotiations, or past history . . ." After reading the letters from Algiers, it is hard to understand why the dey did not break off all relations with France, but since much of the corsair fleet was on duty with the Ottoman navy and the greater part of the Algerian land forces occupied in wars on the frontiers, it is likely that the need of the subsidy from the Bastion of France as well as the potential danger involved in war with France decided the issue in favor of peace. We have no documents to decide the point.

In 1692 the famine in Europe[6] made the North African grain markets an important factor in the conduct of the war. The English consul at Algiers recognized that cutting off the flow of grain, especially from Tunis, could have a serious impact on the French war effort. At the same time, Pontchartrain, as minister in charge of fighting the famine, also recognized that Tunis had become a vital source of grain for the south of France. Both the famine and the uncertainties of the war in Europe produced a more accommodating French posture, and yet the number of Algerian Turks and Moors on the oar benches of the French galley fleet continued to be a problem for the relations between the two countries.

While Hadji Shaban had been engaged in his wars with Morocco and Tunis, the European conflict seemed to have no probable conclusion: it was a stalemate. The war at sea, however, did finally produce results that affected the corsair communities. The battle of La Hougue (1692) at first appeared to be an indecisive victory for either side; indeed, the French ordered Te Deums while the English and Dutch both proclaimed victory. In Algiers it was far from clear, and yet within a year it became obvious that La Hougue marked the end of French superiority at sea. Colbert's fleet suffered from storms after the battle, and with Seignelay's death, there was no one to urge Louis to spend his money on the fleet. By 1695 the French were restricted to privateering in the Atlantic and close coastal patrols in the Mediterranean. Furthermore, the establishment of an English naval base at Cadiz gave the Anglo-Dutch navy control over the Straits, over the Atlantic approaches to Europe, and the possibility of exerting preponderant naval pressure in the Mediterranean. Since most of this latter power was used to control the sea on the southern and eastern coasts of Spain,[7] English naval power was recognized in Algiers, but to the chagrin of the English consul, not as a preponderant force, strong enough to persuade the dey to break with France.

Indeed, the Algerians must have recognized that neither side could really claim victory. French Te Deums sung for the conquest of Namur were all well and good, but obviously their Anglo-Dutch

6. Patrice Berger's Ph.D. thesis on this famine (University of Chicago Library) is an excellent presentation of the problems involved.
7. This could not prevent the catastrophe that befell one entire English naval expedition when a heavy storm destroyed an entire squadron.

enemy was not really disheartened nor were the French in any position to force them to seek peace. On the contrary, it was the king of France who tried to form a "third party" from the neutrals to intervene and bring about an end to the hostilities.[8]

This situation suited the dey and his ministers. They were quite willing to listen to suggestions for intervention in the war from both sides—and to do nothing about it. The fact that they were courted by both, however, had practical advantages. The consuls and foreign merchants showered them with gifts: brilliantly dyed fine cloths, watches, guns, clocks, rings, mirrors, dried fruit, fine wines, fancy confitures. The English consul was careful to remind his government that the wives of the Algerian *poweres* (ministers) were greedy as well as influential; they, too, needed "gifts." Money also changed hands, but neither Hadji Shaban nor his successor, Hadji Ahmed, would break with either the English or the French.

The war in Europe was finally ended by the treaties of Ryswick and an earlier treaty between the king of France and the Duke of Savoy without Algerian intervention. Indeed, Hadji Ahmed managed to die a natural death of the plague (1698) without becoming involved in warfare on any of his frontiers. His successor, Hassan Chaouch, also a janissary officer, was not so fortunate. The problem was Tunis. There were several families vying for control in Tunis. In 1699 one Mourad Bey emerged as victor. His career had already been a stormy one. At one point his uncle had ordered that he should be blinded, but a friendly French physician managed to carry out the operation without actually depriving him of his sight. When the tables turned and Mourad won power, the uncle's head garnished a pike. Once in power Mourad returned to the policies that Mehemet had followed a decade earlier: interference with the tribute paid in the Algerian beylik of Constantine. In the spring of 1700 there was a battle between the forces at the disposal of the bey of Constantine and the Tunisians. Mourad Bey emerged victorious and massacred his prisoners, including some five hundred janissaries. He sent their ears to Tunis as evidence of victory, and opened negotiations with the sultan of Morocco for joint action against Algiers.

The news of the massacre brought hundreds of the janissary militia to the dey's palace demanding vengeance. Hassan Chaouch immediately resigned his office and Hadji Mustapha, a vigorous soldier, became dey. The new dey organized an expedition to break

8. Richard Bingham's Ph.D. thesis, University of Illinois, Chicago Circle, explores this problem extensively.

Mourad's siege of Constantine. His forces were inferior to the Tunisians, but he attacked their camp at night; it was a complete surprise—a fact interesting in what it reveals about these armies—and a decisive victory. Mustapha massacred all the Arabs and Moors that he captured; the Turks were allowed to save themselves by enlisting in the Algerian janissary corps.

Mustapha's problems were a repetition of those faced by Shaban a decade earlier: the Moroccans next invaded the western beylik with a huge army, mostly horsemen, supposedly strong enough to crush the Algerians. The Algerian militia, however, were better disciplined, and their firepower was better directed. The tribesman melted away under this fire, and again Mustapha carried off a victory. He returned to Algiers with some three thousand heads as well as fifty live Moroccan chieftans who could be expected to find handsome ransoms.

The dey announced his victory to Louis XIV by sending him several of the beautiful horses that were part of the booty. This gift arrived in France just when the king was in the act of accepting the throne of Spain for his grandson Philippe, an act pregnant with importance for Algiers since this brought the French and the Spanish crowns under the Bourbon family. The one had been traditionally a friend of Algiers; the other its most persistent foe. Henceforth, of course, the king of France could no longer be counted on to welcome Algerian raids on Spain or Spanish shipping.

The acceptance of the Spanish thrones for Philippe did not necessarily mean that war would follow, and yet it did. The reasons are complex and outside the scope of this account. Mustapha had other problems than those confronting the great powers in Europe: Mourad, bey of Tunis, who had escaped when the Algerians broke the siege of Constantine, recovered from his defeat and planned a new invasion of the Algerian territory (1702). However, before he could get his forces under way, Ibrahim Cherif, one of his own officers, engineered a coup d'état, and managed to place Mourad's head, along with those of his four relatives (two were children) on pikes; they were exposed from the balcony of the palace at Tunis.

In 1703 and 1704 Mustapha Dey and Ibrahim Cherif, now bey of Tunis, were allies in a projected attack on Tripoli, but before it could materialize, Mustapha discovered that the Tunisian was also plotting with the Tripolitan bey to slaughter the Algerians when they landed on the shores of Tripoli. The Algerians evaded the plot, and the Tunisians were immobilized because an outbreak of the plague that daily killed hundreds of victims struck their city and encampment (1704).

The sequel to the story is almost a baroque drama. Hadji Mustapha invaded Tunis to punish Ibrahim Cherif for treachery. The Tunisian was defeated and a new bey elected, who immediately insisted that the Algerians were fighting Ibrahim Cherif, who was their captive. Therefore, the war should stop and the Algerians should go home. Mustapha, however, had other ideas; he wanted a treaty and reparations to be able to pay his soldiers. In an effort to impose his will, Mustapha overreached himself, failed to dislodge the Tunisians, and finally was himself overthrown by his own disgruntled soldiers, who returned to Algiers with a new dey (1705).

In the meantime the war in Europe became more and more violent; two brilliant commanders, Prince Eugene of Savoy and the duke of Marlborough, were battering the French armies in Europe, and, at Malaga Bay in 1704, a naval engagement gave the English the opportunity to establish themselves at Gibraltar. The naval engagement itself was not really a decisive victory. The two fleets battered each other for hours; both were badly mauled and almost out of powder and ball by the time they disengaged, but the English went on to land at Gibraltar and establish a base, while the French celebrated victory with Te Deums but did not again seriously challenge the English control of the Straits. Indeed, in the years that followed, the English navy managed to sweep deep into the western Mediterranean. It captured Port Mahon on Minorca, patrolled the Italian coasts, and supported an abortive invasion of southern France itself.

This shift in naval power, added to the curious political structure in Spain, paved the way for a successful Algerian assault on the Spanish-held bases of Oran and Mers-el-Kébir. These two were among the earliest Spanish conquests on the North African coast. They were captured shortly after Isabella's death, and their powerful fortifications had defied one assault after another in the succeeding two centuries. Oran and Mers-el-Kébir provided the Spanish navy with a base for its patrol of the Mediterranean approaches to the Straits as well as for patrols to the east toward Algiers itself. The fortifications also dominated the hinterland for miles around. Some of the native peoples were encouraged to bring their produce and other goods to the market outside of the walls of Oran, and a few Moorish people were allowed to live in the city, but, in fact, Oran was a Spanish town, a garrison city, and a base for both the naval action and *razzias* against the native tribes. These periodic raids were a persistent trial for the nomadic and semi-nomadic tribes living within a hundred miles of Oran and an embarrassment for the bey of the western beylik. If it were not so trite, we could say that Oran was a "bone in the Algerian throat!"

The shifting naval power and the structure of the conflict over the succession to the Spanish thrones created a situation that encouraged an assault on the city. Two princes claimed the thrones of Spain: one the Bourbon Philippe V supported by his French grandfather's kingdom, the other the Hapsburg Karl (Carlos) III, supported by his Austrian grandfather, the kingdom of England, and the United Netherlands. Both claimants put soldiers—foreign soldiers—on Spanish soil. While Philippe's French supporters were Roman Catholics, Karl's armies were made up of English and Dutch protestants, French Huguenots, and German Lutherans as well as a few German Catholics. The Protestant soldiers in the Hapsburg armies were often scandalized by the religious practices they saw in Spain where the shrines and churches seemed to them to be pagan rather than Christian. As a result, their behavior often scandalized the Spanish people to the detriment of the Hapsburg pretender's cause. The problem spilled over into North Africa where the Roman Catholic governor refused to have anything to do with the heretics who were attempting to place Carlos III on the throne. Unfortunately for him and his soldiers, the supporters of the Hapsburg pretender were the only ones with naval power that might have saved Oran.

The attempt to capture Oran began shortly after the battle of Malaga Bay. The Algerian dey, Hadji Mustapha, was in Tunis at war with his eastern neighbor, when the bey of the western beylik, Moustafa-bou-Chlar'em, decided that the time was ripe for an attack on the Spanish position. He was an aggressive, ambitious soldier, but the forces under his command were hardly enough to bring Oran to surrender. He began the siege late in 1704 but did nothing more than draw the siege lines. In 1705 his blockade became more effective as the Berber and Arab tribesmen came to join his forces. By the end of that year Oran was cut off from the land and dependent upon sea lines for its supplies. That was the year that Hadji Mustapha was deposed. His successor resigned the next year. The siege of Oran continued to be an action of the western beylik and to be indecisive. It was 1707 before the government at Algiers decided that Oran could be captured. The dey recognized that victory there could fill his treasury while the siege would occupy a large number of his soldiers far from Algiers, where they would not be dangerous to him.

He rounded up all the forces that he could spare and placed

them under the command of Ozen Hassan, a relative [9] who had shown some skill as a soldier. The siege guns were transported by sea, the army moved by land and, on the way, managed to pick up hordes of Berber mounted tribesmen who scented the possibility of loot as well as a holy war against a hated enemy. When Ozen Hassan arrived, the investment of Oran became an active assault. The Spanish governor's requests for support became frantic, but Philippe V could not give him much aid, and he refused to have anything to do with the "heretics" who were supporting Carlos III. He said that he would rather deal with the devil; unfortunately for the Spanish this was not a viable alternative.

Oran, however, was a well-fortified position that would not yield without a fight. To capture the city, the besiegers had first to reduce four outlying fortified positions, each independent of the other but in easy communication with the city behind the walls. Once these forts were captured, the city and its citadel still remained. And even then there could be no conclusive victory until the fortifications guarding Mers-el-Kébir were also taken. Small wonder that one assault after another had failed in the past, for as long as supplies and reenforcements could arrive by sea, Oran and Mers-el-Kébir were nearly impregnable.

The Algerians had with them several renegade engineers, or at least renegades who understood mines and explosions that could breach the walls. The first fort, San Ferdinando, fell on September 8, 1707 after an explosion opened a breach. This gave the Moslem gunners a better place from which to fire on Santa Cruz; that fort fell the last of September following another explosion that opened its walls. The next position, Saint Grégoire, was more difficult, but by the end of November a mine blasted a hole in its walls and the fort was taken by storm. Their stubborn resistance provided the janissaries with the excuse for massacring the survivors. The last outlying fortification, La Moine, fell a few days later, and its defenders suffered the same fate. If the treatment of the vanquished seems brutal—even barbarous—it should be noted that the Spaniards often behaved in the same way; warfare between Moslems and Christians in North Africa had long been a bloody, brutal affair.

The assault then turned to the city itself. The citadel of Oran fell January 2, 1708. The fortified harbor of Mers-el-Kébir held out until the middle of April. By this time the war in Europe had

9. It is not clear whether he was a cousin or a brother-in-law, but he was at any rate a trusted friend.

built up to a crisis that occupied all attention; Oran meant little or nothing to those engaged in that conflict. The Algerians, however, had a great victory to celebrate. After a siege of four years that had bogged down to a stalemate, the Algerian janissaries had taken the position in a ten-month campaign. The number of casualties on both sides was great, but when the Algerians returned to their city with two thousand prisoners—many of them people of quality: officers, some French Knights of Malta, some important Spanish families—the rejoicing was great. There also was considerable booty in the baggage trains, and the tribesmen who participated in the siege and sack had some revenge for past Spanish depredations.

The dey sent the keys to Oran to Istanbul with the request that Ozen Hassan should be made a pasha. The request was never granted. By 1708 Oran must have seemed far away, far distant from the Golden Horn, and relatively unimportant. The sultan's government was still reeling from the defeat at the hands of Prince Eugene and the treaty that Emperor Leopold had imposed upon the Porte. The Greek advisers who rallied to the sultan's government when Italian merchants and Jesuit priests threatened their religion and their commerce, were uninteresed in expansion in the western ocean. After 1700 the big problem for the Ottoman empire was not expansion; the sultan's ministers were fighting for its survival. As far as the sultan's viziers were concerned, the victory at Oran came one hundred and fifty years too late.

When the victorious soldiers returned from Oran, the French consul presented the dey with a fine piece of cloth, although, as he wrote, his English rival outdid him with gifts costing at least 500 piasters. These were hard years for the French. They saw their English rivals rise to a position of dominance in the Mediterranean, the Anglo-Dutch army fighting for the Hapsburg pretender in Spain got horses, grain, and fodder from Algiers, and when French privateers chased English ships, at least forty of them in two years managed to find safety in Oran, now held by the Algerians. When the terrible famine at the end of the first decade of the century threatened to compel Louis XIV to accept any terms his foes would give him, the English managed to stop much of the importation of grain into France from North Africa. The dey did not even protest when an English warship sank a French ship under the cannons of Bône on the grounds that the ship was sinking, due to cannon fire received before it arrived at Bône. The French consul confided with his government that "the real reason is that the dey does not wish to become embroiled with the English whose seapower he fears . . ."

Be this as it may, the English consul also had his troubles with the Algerians during these last years of the war. There were endless disputes about citizenship as the English flag covered more and more Italian and Spanish seamen, sometimes in ships that did not have a single Englishman on board. A serious crisis came in 1711, when an English privateer, after unsuccessfully ordering an Algerian corsair to lower his flag, opened fire. The ensuing fight was uneven: the Englishman had forty-four guns, the Algerian twelve. The Algerians lost half of the crew killed or wounded, and the ship nearly sank. The consul warned his government that the incident could result in the execution of Englishmen in Algiers or even a declaration of war against England. Result: Sir John Jennings sent Captain Balchen to Algiers with a letter promising that Mr. Norris, the privateer captain, would be punished for his unwarranted attack. There also was a considerable "present" involved, and the dey "seemed well pleased."

Even the possibility that France might be weakened so severely that her commerce could be attacked with impunity did not persuade the Algerians to declare war on that kingdom. The documentation is scanty, but there is considerable evidence that the flow of "presents" for the dey, his ministers, and the more important reis had much to do with Algerian neutrality. Both England and France paid for "protection," not in the way the smaller states did with "tribute" money, yet the "presents" that soon became "traditional" had the same effect. In 1712 the United Netherlands managed to end the long period of war between the Dutch and Algiers. The treaty of 1712 provided for regular payments in the form of war supplies as well as money to guarantee the safety of Dutch commerce against Algerian raids. Dutch naval power had declined during these hard years of war; the United Netherlands was in no position to use force comparable to that of France or England; indeed, in the years following 1714, the United Netherlands increasingly became dependent upon English power and protection. The days when this little republic could plan peace or war on a par with the kingdoms of France, England, and Spain had come to an end. Dutch power, in the eyes of the Algerians, could be equated with that of Sweden or Denmark; peace with the Dutch could not last long.

These last years of the war were also difficult for the Algerian government. The conquest of Oran did not guarantee the dey and his commander immunity from Algerian political problems. During the last years of the war in Europe, the corsair reis found it increasingly difficult to bring in prizes. French commerce was almost swept from the seas, and the allies, fearful of the French privateers, convoyed most merchant voyages of their own and neutral shipping. As a result the sale of captured vessels declined; in a three-month period only two were brought into port. The militia, however, still expected to be paid, and the dey was constantly scraping the bottom of his treasury. As we have seen, one important source of money was the tribute, or taxes, paid by the tribesmen in the three beyliks. The bey of each beylik was expected to bring the money that he collected in person; in actual practice the beys usually avoided this mission by sending a substitute with the money. It was better to remain in the beylik, protected by troops that could be depended upon, than to risk safety and freedom in Algiers. The governor of the western beylik established himself in Oran after the capture of that city, and he regularly remitted the tribute expected from his province. The bey of the eastern beylik was slow to remit his tribute; in 1710 the dey ordered him to bring the money to Algiers. He failed to obey; instead he gathered up all the treasure that he could lay hands on and quietly departed for points unknown! Without money, the dey could not pay his janissaries. He tried to explain, but a revolt erupted, and the dey and Ozen Hassan, hero of Oran, were both murdered.

The ruffians who led the assault placed one of their own on the throne. For five months the city of Algiers knew only anarchy. The new dey, Ibrahim (called "the Mad") was not a wise man; he attempted to seduce the wife of one of the janissaries, and the outraged woman called for help. Slaves rushed in, fired on the dey as he fled, and called out the scandal for all the city to hear. The palace proved to be no refuge for the would-be seducer; he had a host of enemies who were only too glad for the opportunity to butcher him.

A new dey was elected. Ali Chaouch emerged as the strongman with support from the more reasonable elements of the militia. He sought out and beheaded the friends and supporters of the late dey, and altered the structure of the government to give his ministers the authority to govern. His reign began the process that gave the dey more power and weakened the divan to the point that it later became a "rubber stamp." When a pasha appointed by the sultan arrived in the harbor, Ali Chaouch refused to allow him to land on the grounds that Algiers did not need a "stranger" to assist in its government. The sultan finally accepted this decision and agreed to install Ali Chaouch as pasha.

After the treaties of 1713–14 ending the war in Europe, Ali

Chaouch did everything he could to build up the corsair fleet so that he could either find money to pay his troops by the sale of confiscated ships and cargoes, or from the "tribute" paid by the smaller powers, to assure free passage of their merchantmen. He also was able to force the remission of tribute by the beys, and he began the creation of strong points, or fortifications, in the beyliks that would a little more effectively guarantee Turkish control over the tribesmen.

The strong dey was not universally liked. In 1713 there was an attempt on his life by soldiers who wished to check the erosion of the powers of the divan. The plot failed; the guilty ones were strangled. In 1715 an earthquake wrecked a large part of the city of Algiers and created much confusion, looting, and potential political disorder. The dey not only survived the crisis but also managed to die peacefully in his bed three years later.

The two great wars of the latter seventeenth and early eighteenth centuries marked the beginning of a new era of naval power that was to have decisive impact upon the North African regencies. The new warships at the disposal of the kingdoms of England and France were far beyond anything that the Algerians could muster. Carrying more than one hundred guns, the first-rate battleships were veritable floating fortresses, while the bomb-ketches that could launch missiles of great destructive force added another dimension of terror. In the eighteenth century, third-rate battleships were all that were needed to contain the corsairs. The Algerian fleet managed to capture several of these warships (frigates) but most of their ships carried less than fifty guns and were no match for the warships belonging to the European naval powers. Naval technology, nurtured by the naval race of the 1680s and the great wars, was in the process of making the traditional Algerian corsair fleet almost an anachronism. The reis would no longer prey on the commerce of the important commercial powers.

XIII *The Eighteenth Century:*
The Dey's Government

ONE OF THE MOST INSIGHTFUL documents dealing with the government of Algiers is a memorandum written by the French consul LeMaire in the mid-eighteenth century. He points out that by 1750, the political structure of the regency had become somewhat more stabilized both in the exercise of central authority and in the government of the beyliks. This does not mean that all eighteenth-century deys could die in their beds nor that the Berber and Arab tribesmen regularly submitted to the orders of their Turkish overlords; indeed, the contrary was true. And yet, the anarchy that had dominated the middle seventeenth century, when the divan and the taiffe exercised a rampant sort of democracy flavored with assassination, was curbed by the development of the authority of the dey as absolute ruler.

This situation did not develop overnight. When Mezzo Morto was forced by his soldiers to surrender his office, a popular officer of the janissary corps was elected dey, the first of a long series of deys drawn from the ranks of the soldiers rather than from the taiffe of the reis. The regime functioned haltingly at first; however, early in the eighteenth century, when Ali Chaouch became dey after Ibrahim the Mad was murdered, the office acquired a strong man who knew how to govern. He survived several plots against his life; he forced the sultan to name him pasha; he lived through earthquakes and pestilence that "holy men" attributed to his policies offensive to Allah; he governed the regency and managed to die in his bed. His successor, Mohammed Dey, was not so lucky; he was murdered by sailor plotters, who objected to his naval policies, but they in turn were rounded up and beheaded or impaled by the dead dey's ministers, who then named one of their own number to the high office.

The new dey, Abdi, agha of the spahis, was an even more vigorous ruler than Ali Chaouch had been; he also was much wiser. LeMaire tells us that he was the man who stabilized the regime of the regency. As we see him today, his reign somewhat resembled that of the big city boss in the United States, considering, of course, that the janissary corps and the taiffe composed his constituency. He started his reign by assuring the ministers in his inner council and those who served him of their lives, their property, and their right to pass their estates on to their children. He himself was honest and free from graft or corruption, but he looked the other way when his subordinates filled their pockets as long as the state was not thereby endangered. This made the council of the "powers" (ministers) into a cohesive and structurally solid force. These men realized that their offices, power, and wealth depended upon the dey, and that the dey depended upon them. LeMaire tells us that Abdi never removed an officer as long as he was doing his duty, but when one of them died, he always managed to replace the dead man with a relative or a friend who came from Menemen, the same district in Anatolia where the dey had been born. This started the so-called Menemen dynasty that ruled Algiers during most of the eighteenth century.

Perhaps the most important result of this new situation was the decline of the power of the divan; nevertheless, freedom from the "democracy" of the divan did not mean freedom for the dey to act without consideration of consequences. Indeed, as the dey became more absolute, he lost the right to be capricious. His predecessors could act violently, tyrannically, irrationally; they were checked only by the assassin's bullet or the knife. Abdi and his successful successors rarely gave a decision when first confronted by a problem. Like Louis XIV or other "absolute" rulers, he replied evasively to requests; problems and policies were referred to the council of ministers, the "powers," for decisions. If they could not reach an agreement, each member sent his "trusted friends"—perhaps the word should be "spies" —to check the attitude of the soldiers. Thus, even though the divan no longer controlled policy, the opinion of the janissary militia still carried weight. Algiers continued to be governed by the leaders of an "army of occupation."

After Abdi's elevation to the office, the dey's relations with the Sublime Porte also became formalized. Ali Chaouch had persuaded the sultan to nominate him as pasha, but when Mohammed was murdered, the sultan sent an official from Istanbul to assume that honorary office of pasha. Abdi refused to allow him to land. After some negotiation the sultan agreed to send the kaftan, or insignia of office, to the dey, thus uniting the title of dey and pasha in one person. This may not have been the best solution from the point of view of the sultan's ministers, who thereby lost an appointment that could have been given to friends or sold to the highest bidder. The solution, however, may not have been unacceptable to the Porte, for the sultan's government often could—and did—secure naval aid from the corsair fleet, and in return for favors of one kind or another, the viziers at Istanbul were able to collect "presents" from Algiers. The deys, for their part, were proud to wear the kaftan sent from the Sublime Porte, and they needed the right to recruit new troops in the Levant to fill up the janissary militia. A curious relationship developed: eighteenth-century Ottoman sultans were assured that the dey-pasha of the western sanjac "was always ready to obey as a serviteur of the one who by the most high is the most powerful of emperors . . . the shadow of God on earth." And yet, whenever the sultan's orders conflicted with the desires or will of the dey, they were ignored. This scene, created early in the eighteenth century when the corsairs had captured a rich Ostend prize, is typical. The sultan, at peace with the Hapsburg emperor who was also ruler of the Austrian Netherlands, demanded that the prize be restored to the Ostenders. The comedy was carried out in the divan, where the dey pretended to be its agent. The chant in the divan ran: "We are at peace with England and France . . . no other Christian powers. We want no part of the sultan's peace with the Holy Roman Emperor!" They did not fear Charles VI and Prince Eugene quite the way the sultan and his ministers had learned to fear them. On another occasion Morgan tells us that they insisted that they would "burn their ships and become camel drivers" rather than give up the right to decide which of the sultan's orders to obey. In the eighteenth century the ties between Algiers and Istanbul were even more slender and tenuous than they had been in the preceding period, and yet they were not broken.

Even with the kaftan and title of pasha-dey, the office was not an unmixed blessing. The dey was still prisoner in his palace, always under threat of assassination. His salary was that of the highest-paid officer in the militia, including daily bread allowance. His table was paid for by the government and his living quarters were free, but if he had a wife, she could not live in the palace with him. The office did have opportunities for amassing wealth: presents of all kinds from consuls, beys, caids, the Jewish community, and merchants seeking favors as well as a share of the spoils from the corsair prizes.

But what if the dey amassed a fortune? If he had heirs, they usually dissipated it quickly, or the new dey might confiscate most of it. As a result we find that, for their honor and prestige, the most successful deys built new mosques or baths or refurbished old ones, developed a cannon foundry or strengthened the fortifications. Since it was impossible to pass the office from father to son, as was the case in Tunis, dynastic interests did not dominate Algerian politics. Bishop Juan Cano summed up this melancholy situation: "Thus lives this rich man without being master of his revenues or his treasures, a father without children, a husband without a wife, a despot without liberty, king of slaves and slave of his subjects." The situation was perhaps even worse, for the dey's life was often in danger. Of the thirty deys who ruled between 1683 and 1818 only sixteen died a natural death; fourteen were murdered. As Father Fau wrote in 1729: "The dey does not go out often . . . it [may happen] that outside his palace he is saluted by a musket shot that relieves him of his title of dey and his life."

LeMaire was reasonably sure that, by the mid-eighteenth century, the system was strong enough to protect the dey from assassination; he was wrong. Only a year or so after he had prepared the mémoire, the "Albanian" clique did manage to murder the dey and his treasurer; they in turn were systematically killed by the high cook and his slaves. The new dey, Abdi, nominated by the surviving "powers," was hailed by the divan with the formula: "It is the will of Allah!" An interesting sidelight to the murder of the dey and his treasurer emerges from the fact that in the dead treasurer's papers it was discovered that he had had great plans to murder the dey himself and establish his own family as hereditary rulers of Algiers. His plot ran deep into the beyliks as well as in a clique in the janissary corps. This was the last time that anyone tried to create an hereditary office of dey; the new dey, suspicious of everyone, managed to execute the plotters and, in the next year or so, many other high officers, including the high cook who had killed the Albanians and refused to accept the office of dey when it was offered to him.

The successor to these eighteenth-century deys was one of his ministers, usually the khraznagi, or treasurer, although other officers also could aspire to the throne. The only formal requirement was that the dey must be a native Turk; renegades and coulougli were excluded from this high office in order to protect the power and supremacy of the janissary army of occupation. The man aspiring to be the dey could be semiliterate, he could be the son of a peasant or, as in one case, the son of "a vendor of beef tongues." As a result the men who became deys brought with them a great variety of experiences, abilities, and personal characteristics. Several were generous, understanding rulers; others were suspicious tyrants, trusting no one and ruling badly.

Despite its disadvantages the system evolved in the eighteenth century did provide more stability than the reigns had known in the preceding period, for it resulted in the development of a sort of bureaucracy. The real authority in the regency was exercised by the dey and the "powers." The latter were ministers appointed by the dey to serve at his pleasure; they were usually his friends, but they were truly also his "creatures." The first officer in this "cabinet" was the khraznagi, who was both a sort of prime minister and the natural successor to the high office of dey. The military power was divided between the agha of the janissaries; the cogea, or commander of the cavalry; the agha of the Moorish troops; and the vek-al-khardji, or minister of marine. The major-domo of the household was the beytulmalji, or great cook, and the receiver of the tribute (secretary of the horse) was the khujat-al-khey. In addition there were secretaries, police officers, messengers, and others needed to carry out orders. Many of these people came from the "pool" of talent drawn from the janissary militia, the codeas. These were men who could read and write and buy the office of codea. They were in fact the cadre from which civil servants could be drawn. They managed the sale of horses, grain, leather, and other items under the control of the government. They also went to sea on the corsair ships as scribes to register the capture of prizes, the amount of the merchandise, and the number and quality of slaves taken. Several of them became reis themselves; others became "powers" in the dey's government.

The "powers" usurped traditional authorities. For example, the agha of the two moons continued to act as judge in crimes committed by members of the militia, but the power to command the corps, as well as the auxiliary troops, was vested in ministers or "powers" in the dey's inner circle. The same was true of the marine. The taiffe continue to elect an "admiral," but in the course of the eighteenth century most of the ships in the fleet belonged either to the deylik or to individuals who also were "powers" in the dey's government rather than to individual reis or combines of merchant adventurers. The real power in marine affairs thus was usurped by the government; the vek-al-khardji came to control the corsair fleet.

A concomitant of this development was the gradual decline of the corsair fleet. There were many reasons behind this. In the first place, the number of competent reis declined seriously in the course of the century, partially because there were hardly any renegade captains to join the taiffe, but probably more likely because English and French commerce was off bounds for the corsairs during the entire century, and the Dutch, Swedes, Hamburgers, Danes, Americans, even Venetians managed to buy protection. At the very end of the century even the Spanish secured a treaty. This left fewer opportunities for prizes; the regency could and did occasionally break relations with one or another of the smaller powers, but since most of the commerce was carried in English, French, or Dutch ships, the corsair reis had increasing difficulties in securing prizes.

Another factor in the decline of the eighteenth-century corsair fleet can be noted: there was a progressive shift toward light chebecks carrying between twenty and thirty guns as the standard corsair vessel. While these chebecks couldn't possibly stand up against European warships, even of the third class, they were shallow-draft, easily maneuvered, fast vessels that could outrun the warships that carried heavy armament, and thus could capture the small fishing and local commercial vessels plying the Mediterranean coasts but not the heavily armed merchantmen. The Algerian fleet in the mid-century boasted of several frigates, but in each case they were ships that in one way or another had been captured or bought rather than ships built at Algiers for the corsair navy.

A second problem emerges in the eighteenth century: why did the dey allow almost the entire international trade of the regency to fall into the hands of European or Jewish merchants? Part of the answer can be found in the increasingly important role of the Jews in the government of Algiers. As the dey's regime became more bureaucratized, Jewish financiers assumed a larger role. The Turks regarded themselves as soldiers and rulers, not as financiers. Thus Jewish merchant houses with contacts all over Europe became more and more important for the ongoing business of the regency. With influence, came power and greater importance in the commercial society. The dey's government was the principal agent for most of the commodities that Algiers sold to Europe: wool, hides, horses, wheat, and other such primary goods were the virtual monopoly of the deylik. But the dey could not market these goods himself; he had to depend upon the foreign merchants—mostly Frenchmen— and the Jews to manage his business. Why did the reis not step in and take part in this profitable business? The answer is simple when we look at the rules and regulations that Christian powers and Christian harbors placed on Moslem commerce. There were dozens of rules, of tariff, of regulations all aimed at keeping Moslem traders out of the European market. And reis who happened also to be renegades had the added hazard that their lives would be in danger if they landed in a Christian port.

Thus, although the dey's government seemed to gain in stability, it did not really move toward a position of commercial equality with its European neighbors. The redemption of slaves was still in the hands of the redemptionist fathers, or consuls, or Jewish or Christian merchants. The commerce of the regency was in the hands of non-Moslem merchants. The dey might have a monopoly on the export of many basic commodities, but he was still dependent upon others to manage his affairs.

When one left Algiers for the beyliks, the problems of complexity grew apace. Rinn's study of Algiers under the last dey points out that the government had much in common with the kingdoms of medieval Europe in which kings ruled and involved a complex of lords, vassals, and corporate towns, "subjects" who often enough were more powerful than the king himself. This was the situation in the regency: the kings and sheiks who ruled the Arab and Berber peoples in the hinterland maintained polite relationships with the beys, who pretended to govern the beylik for the dey in Algiers. The bey's power often rested on his personal or family relations with the people he "governed," or on the system of "blockhouses" garrisoned by janissaries, which more or less dominated the more important routes of communication.

Unquestionably the political situation in the beyliks by the mid-eighteenth century was more stabilized than it had been earlier. This in no small part was due to the the abandonment of the practice of recalling the beys after a term of two to four years. Moustafa-bou-Chlar'em, for example, the man who started the siege of Oran that captured that city, ruled his beylik for almost twenty-five years; he was destined to see the Spanish recapture the prize, Oran, that he had taken in his youth. But the important thing seems to have been that, in those twenty-five years, the bey was able to learn how to govern and, perhaps equally important, to establish relations with the sheiks and towns in his beylik that allowed him to establish his family almost as hereditary beys of the west. It was enough to be a son-in-law of the bey to give prestige and place in this beylik. Where so many of the sheiks and emirs ruled tent villages that were hard to control, personal contacts were most important in the political process.

In the eastern beylik, Keliane Houssein, surnamed the "man of the poignard," ruled at Constantine for almost twenty-five years. He too learned from his mistakes. Early in his career he was ambushed in the high plateau by a Kabylie "army" when his plans for a "sweep" had been too hastily prepared. He learned to prepare carefully for his military activities, and he developed the "blockhouses" needed to secure the routes. These fortifications resembled the nineteenth-century frontier outposts in the western plains of the United States; the Kabylie tribesmen may have had much in common with the North American Sioux Indians.

From all accounts both of these two beys and their more successful successors governed by a nice mixture of force, guile, intrigue, bribery, and friendly persuasion. The fact that the Arabs considered themselves superior to the Berbers as well as to the Turks allowed the beys to practice a "divide-and-rule" policy, especially since the Berber Kabylie tribes were themselves far from united. Again the situation has much in common with the mid-nineteenth-century American West.

It is also interesting to note that coulougli could aspire to the office of bey. Indeed, in both the western and the eastern beyliks, sons followed their fathers in office. The founders of the dynasties were native Turks; their children were the sons of "native" women. The tradition was not broken in the nineteenth century, when, for example, Osman Bey, the son of Mohammed el Kébir, "inherited" his father's position in the western beylik after 1815. His father was the soldier bey who reconquered Oran in 1792. Likewise Hassen Bey, who ruled at Constantine in the early nineteenth century, was the son of Salata Bey, who held the office before him. One observer after another tells us that the coulougli officers "hated" the Turks, oppressors of the Berber people, but when they ruled the beyliks they collected the tribute and ruled the land much as their Turkish fathers had done before them.

It was no simple matter to govern the nomadic and quasi-nomadic tribes as well as the more stabilized villages and towns on the coast and in the interior of the land. A Turkish garrison of fifty to several hundred janissary militia men could usually control a town, and yet Tlemcen as well as several other towns or small cities managed to drive out the garrison and to establish a patrician government that could last for years, even for a decade, before the Turks could re-establish their authority. The open countryside was even more difficult, since a very large part of the Algerian regency was situated on the high plateau and mountain lands or on the fringe of the desert. The fertile lowlands made up only a small part. Many, if not most, of the inhabitants of these mountainous regions were nomadic peoples following their herds from place to place. There were some well-established towns or villages in which the inhabitants mixed agriculture with some hand or craft work producing marketable commodities. The tent villages or down-ars were ruled by a sheik, or several of them might be joined under an emir; the towns had a patrician government, usually carefully watched by a Turkish caid who commanded a garrison. All of these people lived under Koranic and customary law, law administered usually by their own natural or hereditary officers. All of them resented the tributes exacted by the Turks as taxes, and evaded payment whenever possible. It is small wonder that on the frontiers the rulers of both Tunis and Morocco found ready allies among these tribesmen. The beys needed all the wisdom and skill they could muster to rule.

In many cases the tribute was paid only when a Turkish camp commanded by a caid, or even by the bey, made a "sweep" to collect it. In the latter seventeenth and the eighteenth centuries, these "sweeps" became more difficult because the native tribesmen possessed firearms. However, they did not learn more effective battle tactics. They may have been brave enough, but the bands of horsemen were unable to face the concentrated fire of the Turkish soldiers, especially when the latter also had small cannons. There were times, however, when the Turkish column was trapped or ambushed in the mountains and badly defeated. Control of the towns was somewhat easier since it usually depended upon a Turkish garrison established under a caid, in the town's fortification. The garrison acted to protect as well as to dominate the community. It was a reminder that the entire territory was ruled by an army of occupation.

In the latter eighteenth century the Turkish authority in the beyliks eroded because the supply of soldiers from the Levant began to dry up. The janissary militia, no longer strong enough to fulfill its responsibilities, had to be supplemented by auxiliary troops recruited from the Berber-Moorish populations. These were never as trustworthy as the janissaries, but there was no alternative. When the French arrived in 1830, there were few janissary militiamen in any of the beyliks. Even in the Dar-es-Sultan, the territory ruled directly by the dey, Berber and Moorish troops, commanded by a caid and the agha of the Moorish auxiliaries, were the only soldiers garrisoned in the towns. The entire beylik of Titteri had only fifty janissary spahis and one hundred and twenty janissary foot soldiers, and in both the eastern and western beyliks the janissary militiamen were no more than a token force. Indeed, in the entire regency, there were not more than twenty-five hundred janissaries, and many of them were unfit to fight.

Thus it is probably true that the regime, based upon an army of occupation drawn from beyond the frontiers of the regency, was already in ruins when the French invasion occurred. The fact that the deys of the nineteenth century had not cured the endemic revolts by the Berber and Arab tribesmen and by the better-established townspeople is evidence that the dey's government had not evolved from the pattern of any army of occupation to that of a rule based on indigenous support. Perhaps no such government was possible in a land with the cultural patterns we find in the central Maghrib of the early nineteenth century.

XIV The Eighteenth Century: Algiers and Spain

N o matter which Christian power might be at war with Algiers, Spain and the domains of the Spanish king were always the enemy. There could be no peace with Spain; Spanish fishermen and coastal shipping provided the reis with a "natural prey." When other prizes were unavailable, the unfortunate Spaniards were always there. The watchtowers along the Spanish coast, the villages perched on the hillsides or on rocky promontories, the fortifications of the harbor towns were all mute evidence of the threat from North Africa, while the hundreds—even thousands—of subjects of the Spanish king enslaved in North Africa could testify to the fact that all precautions could not prevent raids on both land and sea.

In the last years of the reign of Charles II, the power of the Spanish thrones was so decayed that little could be done to protect the king's subjects. When Charles II died (1700) and a European war broke out to determine the right of succession to the thrones, the European war became a civil war in Spain with partisans of the Austrian Hapsburg Charles III fighting partisans of the Bourbon Philippe V. Spaniard fought Spaniard, and French, English, German, and other European soldiers added to the melee. This war provided the Algerian Turks with the opportunity to capture Oran and Mers-el-Kébir. No help was available for the defenders. The loss of Oran, however, was a serious blow both to Spanish pride and to the Spanish naval position in the western end of the Mediterranean. It also was a defeat for Christendom, the last of the important Spanish sixteenth-century conquests in the war with the Mohammedans. Thus the urge to reconquer Oran was a religious as well as a political irredenta, as real as the nationalistic irredentas of the nineteenth century.

The decisions of the battlefield left Philippe V in control of the thrones of Spain and a shift in English policy prepared the way for a compromise that would give him possession of the Spanish crowns, while his rival secured the crowns in Italy and the Spanish Netherlands. But Philippe was not quite free to act immediately to recover Oran. His problem was the unification of the Spanish kingdoms through the development of a French-type bureaucratic government. His regime produced, for the first time since the union of the crowns of Aragon and Castile, an administrative and fiscal structure that gave a unity to the kingdom. He did not actually incorporate the several crowns of Spain into a moral union with Castile, but he did impose Castilian institutions on all of them and thereby provided the kingdom with new economic and political vigor. These new forms did not, of course, make the power of Spain equal with that of England or France, but they did alter the balance of power that had existed between Spain and the North African Moslem states. The Spanish army, stiffened with French discipline, became a more effective instrument, and the Spanish navy recovered some of its former power. Although the king and his ministers had too much to do in the years immediately following 1714 to give North Africa serious attention, by 1721 they were able to relieve the siege of Ceuta and by 1730 they were ready to plan the reconquest of Oran.

In June 1732 a mighty armada of five hundred and twenty-five sails ranging from powerful battleships to supply and courier vessels, carried an army of thirty thousand men to Oran. In addition to the guns on the warships, there were almost two hundred siege guns to batter down the defenses of the city. The Comte de Montemar, the commander of the expedition, was ably supported by competent officers and trained men. There was hardly any fighting. Moustafa-bou-Chlar'em, the bey who had directed the Turkish siege that had captured the city a quarter of a century earlier, was in command, but he had practically no support, and the mortally ill eighty-eight-year-old dey, Abdi Pasha, was unable to make up his mind to send aid from Algiers. Abdi died in September. The new dey, his brother-in-law, tried to assemble an army, but it was too late. Both Oran and Mers-el-Kébir fell to the invaders almost without opposition. It was a bitter pill for Bou-Chlar'em; he had to surrender the conquest of his youth without being able to put up a real fight.

When aid did arrive from Algiers, Bou-Chlar'em attempted to besiege the city, but this time the Spanish were not weakened by civil war and the Turks were not as strong as they had been earlier. A

Spanish sortie put most of the Algerian siege guns out of commission, massacred a large number of the Moslem soldiers attempting the siege, and overturned the siege works. The sortie cost the Spanish fifteen hundred men, but the Algerians lost more, including the possibility of mounting a successful siege.

The Spanish ruled Oran from 1732 until the French Revolutionary era when they were again obliged to turn it over to the Algerians. The eighteenth-century occupation, however, was different from that of the sixteenth and seventeenth centuries. The Spanish no longer sent deep razzias into the hinterland. Oran became a Spanish city, garrisoned by Spanish troops, and supplied from Spain by sea. There were a few Moslem families living in Oran, but the city was Spanish and completely oriented toward Spain. There seems to have been no program for extending Spanish control into the territories beyond the immediate areas of Oran and Mers-el-Kébir.

The installation, however, did give the Spanish greater power to resist the incursions of the Algerian reis. Oran and its harbor became an important base for the naval patrol of the western Mediterranean. The warships of Spain, Malta, and Naples could operate with bases from Oran to Malta. They patrolled the sea and raised the villages and towns of the Algerian and Tunisian regencies. By the end of the eighteenth century, the North African coast was practically denuded of villages—indeed, of people, for the inhabitants, like the Spanish villagers, had abandoned the coast as too dangerous a place to live. Algerian corsair warfare and the measures developed to combat it were both cruel, brutal, and expensive; the peasant populations on both sides of the sea probably had more in common with each other as a consequence of this warfare than they had with their rulers who were directing it.

In the years between the reconquest of Oran (1732) and 1775, the Spanish government was forced to concentrate attention on wars and threats of wars in Europe rather than on a plan to force Algiers to cease its attacks on Spain and Spanish shipping. As we shall see, on the several occasions during these years when the French considered war against the corsair community, the idea that France should cooperate with Spain in such a conflict was vetoed on the grounds that French and Spanish interests and projections were different from each other and often actually in opposition. The Spanish could desire the complete annihilation of the Algerian community; in the eighteenth century, the French not only did not wish to see such a conclusion, but even admitted that a peace between Spain and

Algiers might not be in French interests since it would free Spanish shipping from the threat of the corsairs, and thereby create a serious competitor for the French. The Spanish did in fact have the ambition to destroy Algiers as a "pirates' nest"; it only required finding the right time and way to accomplish this.

Charles III became king of Spain in 1759. His first problem was to find a way out of the Seven Years War that would not cripple his kingdom, and in the next decade he earned for himself the title of "enlightened despot" through his reforms that injected new life into the Spanish community. By 1774 he was ready to consider Algiers. The plan was for a direct assault on the city by land as well as by sea. Victory would end once and for all the threats from the "pirates' nest."

The expedition was entrusted to the Count O'Reilly, a distinguished soldier, member of a family of Irish extraction that had become well established in Spain. In spite of O'Reilly's reputation the choice was an unfortunate one; he proved to be an officer who could carry out commands given by others, but he was not able to take precautions that might ease surprises, nor did he have the decisiveness needed when events reached a crisis.

The expedition was well supported. It included infantry contingents with almost twenty thousand men, some eight hundred cavalry, and nine hundred artillerymen with their guns. The naval forces carried thirty-five hundred sailors and a large number of slaves for the heavy work. Of the five hundred-odd ships in the armada, fifty were warships with firepower well beyond anything that the Algerians could mount. The expedition was ready to leave in the summer of 1775. It was a formidable array: O'Reilly had every reason to hope that he could repeat the success that his predecessor had had against Oran in 1732.

An expedition of this size could not be kept secret. Thus the Algerians made preparations to confront the Spanish with all the force they could muster. The three beys brought their best troops; the tribal sheiks, anxious for both loot and an opportunity to fight a battle against the enemies of Allah, sent clouds of horsemen; and the dey's ministers mustered all the forces at their disposal. As a result, before the Spanish arrived, the horsemen, camel drivers, and more or less regular soldiers were waiting for them. The dey announced that he would pay ten dinars for each Christian head brought to Algiers. "This measure was wise," writes the author of *El-Zorat-el-Nayerat*, "for the hope of pecuniary recompense obliged the soldier to decapitate all that fell into his hands and carry the bloody proof to the feet of the pasha." It also could have completely disorganized the Algerian defenses had the Spanish not so foolishly overreached themselves, for the disorder resultant from indiscriminate search for heads to remove could have been a disaster.

Allah, or just plain luck, must have been with the Algerians for the Spanish made mistakes even more unfortunate than they did. They landed on the same beach that Charles V had used two hundred and thirty-four years earlier. The debarkation began about four A.M. on July 7, 1775. As the troops landed, they immediately became involved with skirmishers who tried to prevent their landing. The Spanish quickly drove them back only to find themselves under fire by marksmen sheltered in trenches or behind barricades on the hillsides. As more troops landed and tried to expand their beachhead, they also came in contact with horsemen from the beyliks. Rather than withdraw and fortify the landing beach, as more troops came ashore, they were thrown into the fight. Their progress continued to be contested from sunken roads, hedgerows, and other defensive works. The fire was deadly. At this point there was a command to pull back and regroup, but before the order could be obeyed, the Berber tribesmen drove a huge herd of camels over the right side of the Spanish position. Men and horses were frightened by these ungainly animals, and the withdrawal turned into a disorderly rout. One officer later wrote that "without the extreme ignorance of the enemy who did not know how to profit from their advantages, nothing could have saved the Spanish from total destruction." The offer of ten dinars a head may well have saved a part of the Spanish army. The Spanish fell back in disorder to the beachhead only to find that the Algerians had moved cannons to the nearby hills and could enfilade the withdrawal. There was nothing to do but to re-embark as many of the troops as could be saved. The expedition was a failure.

A month after the defeat O'Reilly attributed the disaster to "an excess of unconsidered ardour" on the part of troops who "without sleep, attacked too rapidly and lost their advantages." But it was more than just unconsidered ardor. Each infantryman had only eighty-one cartridges: by the time the rout began, the infantry had used up its ammunition and no additional supplies were put ashore. Even had they not been disorganized by the camel herds, they were in trouble, because the soldiers were put ashore without their supplies, they went into battle without preparing a fortified beach, and their scouts missed the fact that the Algerians had placed cannons on the hill opposite the beachhead. We have a number of excellent accounts of this battle written by men who were there; they all agree that the expedition was botched by bad intelligence, bad judgment, bad planning. A Spanish critic who probably should have the last word later wrote: "The expedition was executed with little knowledge of the terrain, the number of the enemies, or the preparedness for defense." This adds up to disaster.

The debacle was not on the scale that Charles V had suffered, but it was a humiliating defeat that the Spanish army would have liked to forget. They lost all the cannons that they had managed to land, most of the muskets and small arms belonging to the infantry, and all the supplies that were put ashore. Twenty-seven officers and five hundred men were killed, a hundred ninety-one officers and over two thousand men were wounded; we do not know how many of these also died, but the recovery rate in the eighteenth century was much less than that of the twentieth. The Turkish author who hailed the victory tells us that the "Spanish say that the bullets were poisoned because all the wounded died . . . Allah be praised!"

The catastrophe that overtook the O'Reilly expedition did not end Spanish efforts to force the Algerians to make peace with the Spanish monarchy, but the general European war known as the War for American Independence distracted the attention of the Spanish court until an end to that conflict came into view. The Algerian officers, however, again considered the possibility of a new siege of Oran, for during these years when attention was focused on the North American continent, the bey of the western territories, Mohammed, surnamed el-Kébir (the great), managed to bring the tribesmen in his jurisdiction under control. By a careful use of force and persuasion, he succeeded in obtaining more or less regular tribute payments, as well as some military assistance for a new siege of Oran. The Spanish, however, made this siege into a formidable task; they fortified the city more effectively than it had been earlier and provided it with an adequate well-supplied garrison. It is true that the Spanish were largely captive to their own walls, but also true that those walls were a powerful defense. By 1780 Mohammed Bey had managed to blockade the city on the land side, but as long as the Spanish could keep the seas open, the Algerian Turks were far from capturing it.

By 1783, when the American war finally ended, the Spanish court was ready to react both to Mohammed's siege of Oran and to the problem of revenge for the debacle that had overtaken O'Reilly's expedition. Again the preparations could not be kept secret. The dey, fearing the repetition of a recent slave revolt, sent some fifteen hundred Spanish slaves out of the city, and called on the beys for troops to help resist the expected invasion. The Spanish, however, finally contented themselves with a bombardment and naval demonstration rather than a full-scale invasion. A fleet of ten frigates, twenty-five chebecks, and forty *chaloupes* (sloops) appeared before Algiers on July 29, 1783; the bombardment started August 1. In nine days the Spanish threw almost four thousand bombs and a like number of round shot either into Algiers or at the fortifications. The damage was less than had been hoped, and yet it was considerable. Several hundred houses, including the dey's palace, were badly damaged and about two hundred people were killed. The effectiveness of bombardment had increased somewhat since the French efforts a century before, and yet the "progress" was not great; in 1783, it required a little more than half as many ships to accomplish about the same destruction that Duquesne's bombardment had wrought in 1682. We have no way to compare the costs of the two expeditions.

In 1784 another Spanish armada appeared before Algiers and again attempted to bombard the city, but the Algerians, with powder and shot and a few new cannons provided by Sweden, the United Netherlands, and England, were able to prevent the Spanish from anchoring near enough to place their bombs in the city. The exchange of shot between the warships and the fortifications did little damage to either. Obviously bombardments were not going to reduce Algiers.

Nonetheless, the growing Spanish commerce and, with it, the depredations of the Algerian reis demanded that something be done about Algerian-Spanish relations. In 1785, through the good offices of the French consul, the Spanish obtained the right to send a mission to Algiers to discuss peace. The big concession that the Spanish negotiators could make was the return of Oran and Mers-el-Kébir to the Algerian Turks. The Spanish believed that this would not be too much to give if they could secure a trading post with concessions similar to those that the French Bastion had in the eastern beylik. Apparently the Algerians believed the prospect of an annual payment as well as the reoccupation of Oran was a suitable substitute for the continuation of hostilities. With the growth of Spanish naval power, the corsair "trade" was not as profitable as it had been before. In any case, the dey and his ministers agreed to a peace treaty with the Spanish monarchy, the first in the entire history of the two governments. The central point of the treaty hinged upon the cession of Oran.

Shades of Isabella the Catholic, of Cardinal Jiménez de Cisneros, of the heroic Spanish soldiers who had so long defended Oran, these shades of the past joined the outraged pride of living Catholic bishops and noble Spanish patriots. As criticism of the treaty mounted, the Spanish government found one way after another-to delay the evacuation of Oran. Charles IV succeeded to his father's throne in 1788; there was no time to remove troops from Oran. Then in 1789 came the French Revolution; it occupied the attention of all Europe. The Algerian Turks, however, were more interested in Oran than in the "Rights of Man and the Citizen" or the problems of the French monarchy. Mohammed Bey either sent emissaries or went himself to all the dow-ar villages and towns of the western bey-lik; since the Spanish did not deliver Oran, he was seeking aid for a renewal of the "holy war" that would recover it. By 1789 he may have had almost fifty thousand men available for a siege; most of them, it is true, would be useful only to patrol roads and fields to enforce the blockade. Then nature—rather than Algerian powder and mines—came to the support of the besiegers.

In August 1790 there were several small earthquakes in the area around Oran. On October 8 and 9, the earth shook with more force; it was a threat of things to come. On October 21–22 the earth heaved and shook, tumbling down buildings and walls. Oran was in ruins. All the medical doctors in the city were killed, the governor and his entire family were killed, three high officers and thirty-one captains and lieutenants were killed, some two thousand ordinary people and common soldiers were killed. Terrified survivors combed the rubble for friends and relatives; they were weeks burying the dead. The government in Spain sent reinforcements and supplies immediately, but the fact that the earth continued to tremble for a whole month after the violent quakes of October 21–22 slowed the efforts to prepare for the coming of the Algerians and their Berber allies. The quakes had hardly ended when Mohammed Bey arrived before Oran to re-new the siege of the city.

Mohammed Bey and his officers were sure that the earthquakes were the work of Allah, intervening on their side of the conflict. But when they tried to storm the city, the Spanish met them with a mur-derous fire that drove them back in disorder. Mohammed was soon convinced that he must adopt more conventional means for taking

Oran: close siege and mining operations. Oran was undoubtedly doomed, a fact recognized at this juncture by the government in Madrid. The death of the aged and ill dey in Algiers brought the treasurer, Hassan, to the throne; he was willing to listen to Spanish diplomatic overtures. A new treaty, signed in September 1791 and ratified by both parties early in December, again provided for the evacuation of Oran and the establishment of a Spanish "bastion" in Mers-el-Kébir to facilitate Spanish trade with the western beylik and to use the waters off the coast for fishing. In return they were to pay the dey a fixed subsidy. On the last day of February 1792, Mohammed Bey, now called el-Kébir, solemnly entered Oran. By the time he arrived most of the Spanish families resident there had returned to Spain; he assured the seventy or so remaining families that their way of life would be tolerated and unmolested as long as they remained loyal. A short time later the sultan sent his congratulations to the dey and the bey for the return of the city to Turkish control that had so long submitted to Christian domination.

With the second occupation of Oran, the Algerian regency had finally succeeded in driving the Spanish from the central Maghrib; the story that began with Cardinal Jiménez's and Pedro Navarro's conquest of the port cities from Oran to Tripoli was ended. In those nearly three hundred years, Spaniards fought Turks, Berbers, and Arabs in conflicts that were variously called jihads or crusades; they were bloody, cruel wars that sometimes brought wealth to the victors and always promised salvation to men who were killed. The historian must recognize the heroism of the actors, the pathos of the story, the tragic impact as well as the moments of exhilaration of the events. The philosopher may ask if it is simply Shakespeare's "tale told by an idiot," or a lesson that could teach later generations more about the human condition and the problems of governing men.

XV *The Eighteenth Century: The Rest of Christian Europe and Algiers*

THROUGHOUT the eighteenth century, England and France remained at peace with Algiers. The naval power of these two states made it advisable for the Algerians to keep the peace. Keep it they did, but only so far as was necessary to convince their powerful "friends" that war with Algiers would be more costly than the maintenance of so-called "peaceful" relations through diplomacy. Both English and French warships periodically visited the harbor of Algiers to impress upon the dey and his advisers the fact that preponderant naval power was available, while the consuls of the two great powers regularly explained that their governments insisted upon Algerian compliance with the terms of the treaty of peace.

In the course of the century, other European states also managed to make peace with Algiers, thus securing immunity from capture for their ships: the United Netherlands, Hamburg, Denmark, Sweden, the Emperor (mainly for his Austrian Netherlands), Venice, and, at the end of the century, the new Republic of the United States of America. These treaties secured safety for a price: The dey's government could be assured of about the same income from tribute that capture at sea would yield in the form of prize money, although the treaties were not easily negotiated because the reis and merchants involved in profits from prizes were usually unhappy when another flag was granted immunity. It would not be profitable to discuss the various negotiations leading to these treaties, but the story of the problems encountered at one point in the development of the treaty between the United Netherlands and Algiers in the mid-eighteenth century does provide an instructive illustration.

In the years between 1714 and 1720 forty Dutch ships were made prizes and about seventy-five hundred Netherland seamen became slaves. Considering the size of the Dutch commercial fleet, these figures do not indicate major losses; it is possible that losses from tempest and from captains' errors might even have matched the financial drain. However, for the merchants and shipowners who lost their money, and for the families of the men, as well as for the seamen themselves who became slaves, these losses were serious. There was an additional problem that worried Dutch shipowners: as long as Dutch ships were in danger of becoming prizes, foreign merchants were reluctant to trust their merchandise and their persons to Dutch ships. This gave advantages to the English and French shipping.

The first proposal to end these costly attacks was for the building of a Dutch corsair navy to fight the Algerians. A petition to the Estates General insisted that a fleet of six warships, three with fifty guns, three with forty guns, could end the Algerian depredations by a close blockade. The cost: 383,400 florins a year. Nothing came of this proposal, but the next year the Dutch ambassador at Istanbul attempted to enlist the assistance of the Sublime Porte in the securing of a treaty with Algiers, and the Dutch consul at Smyrna made a contact with Bekir Reis, the admiral of the Algerian taiffe, that considerably enriched the latter. As a result the sultan urged the dey to consider peace with the United Netherlands, and Bekir Reis seconded the suggestion. When he agreed to receive a Dutch mission, the dey told the French consul that the Koran required that he must listen to any power "begging" for peace.

Six warships, commanded by a rear admiral, arrived before Algiers. The dey appointed a Flemish slave to be the interpreter. As the negotiations progressed, it became clear that his knowledge of Turkish was elementary; the negotiations were going nowhere. At this point the newly appointed French ambassador to the Ottoman empire, M. d'Andrezel, also appeared at Algiers on a warship to discuss problems between Algiers and France. In exchange of visits, the Dutch admiral asked the ambassador if he might borrow M. Lenoir, the French interpreter. D'Andrezel quickly agreed, and instructed Lenoir to keep him informed about the course of the negotiations. The French understood that peace between Algiers and the Dutch would increase Dutch competition in the carrying trade. Presumably Lenoir's "interpretations" were correct and yet the negotiations broke down. Lenoir, however, was not the only factor in the rupture of the negotiations. There were complaints by both reis and others that peace would destroy an important economic enterprise, namely, the capture of Dutch prizes. Then at a critical moment a cloud of locusts appeared at Algiers: holy men assured the populace that Allah was speaking against any peace with the Dutch.

The collapse of the negotiations finally came over a "misunderstanding" about terms. The dey demanded fifty masts, six bronze and six iron cannons, fourteen thousand cannon balls, one thousand quintals of powder, fourteen hundred muskets, and fourteen hundred sabers. The Dutch admiral, with instructions that did not allow payment in war supplies, thought that he had an agreement with the divan for a gift of four thousand piasters every year for six years. Lenoir, aware of the situation, suggested that the Dutch should explain to the dey that he had misunderstood. The dey pretended to be angry. The Dutch admiral offered to increase the payment to eight thousand piasters. The dey replied that neither he, nor his predecessors, had ever accepted money, that it would be dishonorable to do so. The Dutch admiral sailed away without a treaty, but not before he assured the French ambassador d'Andrezel that the Dutch ambassador at Versailles would thank the French king for French assistance at Algiers. A few years later another Dutch mission did secure peace on the conditions set by the dey—that is, massive gifts of war supplies. The French and English consuls both condemned the Dutch treaty as immoral and disgraceful; the Dutch were supplying equipment for the Algerians to attack other Christian commercial states. We should note that later deys had no problem accepting cash tribute: Venice paid 22,000 gold sequines and an annual tribute of 12,000 gold sequines for peace; the young Republic of the United States paid $642,500 and an annual tribute of $21,600 in naval supplies; Hamburg, Sweden, Denmark, and Naples also paid handsomely for protection.

While the purchase of protection usually gave a measure of safety to the commerce of the country paying "tribute," this was not universally the case. The reis, finding their possible victims reduced to those flying the Spanish, Portuguese, or petty Italian states' flags, sought every excuse to condemn as prize ships those of states technically at peace with the regency. For the petty state, indeed even for the emperor as ruler of the Austrian Netherlands, it was often impossible to get much redress. The Danish king at one point decided to use force, but the little flotilla that he managed to send to Algiers could not get close enough for its cannon balls to reach the city, let alone to do any serious damage, and his warships were unable to close in on any of the light and fast Algerian chebecks. It was a disaster that inspired a satirical poem at Algiers and some mirth on the part of the other consuls in the city.

The experience of the young republic of the United States was happier than that of the Danish kingdom, and thus should have more place in this history since a North American historian writing about Algiers can hardly forget that the Marine Corps of the United States sings about its exploits "on the shores of Tripoli" or that the first navy of the young republic was built with the Algerian corsairs in mind. Shipping from the English colonies flew the English flag, and except for a very short period in the seventeenth century when the Algerians did not understand why the ships from the "American plantations" did not have proper passports, the Anglo-Algerian treaty covered shipping from England's colonies. In 1783, when peace between the confederation of the United States of America and England was being written, the Americans tried unsuccessfully to obtain a clause that would assure them continued English protection for their commerce in the Mediterranean. This failure was only one part of the problem that confronted the commercial interests of the young republic. The markets of England and France, protected by mercantile legislation, were largely closed to them. Even in the West Indies it was not easy for merchants from the new republic to establish satisfactory commercial relations. One area not closed was the Levantine territories of the Turkish sultan, but when the star-spangled banner appeared in Mediterranean waters, it became a legitimate prize for the Barbary corsair reis. In the early 1790s the problem was compounded when both Spain and Portugal made peace with Algiers and thereby allowed the corsair chebecks to prowl in the Atlantic, where again they found U.S. shipping. John Adams, ambassador to London, advised "buying" protection as other small states did; Thomas Jefferson, ambassador to Paris, urged the building of a navy to force respect for the new flag. The confederation was unable to do either successfully.

However, the fact that no navy existed made it imperative to attempt to "buy" protection, but the first commission sent to Barbary to negotiate had only $80,000. The dey of Algiers expressed his admiration of General Washington, and even asked for his picture, although the money was not enough to interest him. When the new constitution for a federal republic provided a government that could tax, Secretary of State Jefferson, contrary to his early advice, placed $800,000 for the ransom of U.S. slaves and the purchase of peace. A treaty in 1795 cost $642,500 plus an annual tribute in naval supplies. The next year this treaty was extended to include the gift of a thirty-six-gun frigate. The price did not seem exorbitant; in 1799 some eighty U.S. ships passed peacefully into the Mediterranean to trade with the Ottoman empire. These ships were excluded from both the English and the French markets.

A curious side note to the gift of the frigate: when it was delivered, the Algerians found that they had no ship with equal sailing ability. The dey ordered two more, at his expense. When Jefferson became president he refused to allow the frigates to be delivered and also refused to send war supplies as tribute. His hostility to the commercial interests in competition with his own agricultural constituency made him hostile also to a navy and to tribute to expand commerce, but when the Algerians attacked U.S. commercial vessels, Jefferson was responsible for the building of the famous frigates that were later to fight in the war of 1812. In the Jefferson-Adams correspondence during the years just before the death of both men, John Adams hailed Jefferson as the father of the U.S. navy.

The most striking naval victory against the Barbary states came after the Treaty of Ghent released the U.S naval forces for action against the "pirate" states. Stephen Decatur with a flotilla of three naval vessels entered the Mediterranean, met and fought the admiral of the Algerian navy in June 1815. When the engagement was over, Admiral Hamada Reis and many of his men were dead and some five hundred Algerian seamen and janissaries were captives. Decatur proceeded to Algiers, where he announced the results of his engagement. The Algerians could not believe that their most famous and most daring admiral could be both defeated and dead, but Decatur released several "intelligent" prisoners who confirmed the story. The result was a new peace between Algiers and the United States, a peace guaranteeing the freedom of U.S. commerce without the payment of a tribute.[1] The next year Lord Exmouth practically wiped out the Algerian naval establishment in a surprise raid. While the Algerians did recover somewhat, they were never again a threat to U.S. commerce.

As a result of the treaties signed with the smaller states of Europe, the consular corps at Aligers underwent an important change. In the preceding century the French, English, and Dutch consuls were the

1. The best short account of the relations between the United States and the Barbary regencies is to be found in James A. Field, *America and the Mediterranean World*, 1776–1882 (Princeton, 1969).

only representatives in Algiers; they often remained in their consular offices even when their governments were at war with the regency, but their lives and living conditions were frequently very difficult. In the mid-eighteenth century, when the consular corps broadened to include most of the European states with commercial contacts in the Mediterranean, the consuls became, in effect, quasi-ambassadors, and an esprit de corps developed among them. At one point the fact that England and France were at war with each other did not prevent both consuls from joining the entire corps in a protest over the treatment of one of their number.

We have excellent pictures of this mid-century consular corps in a memorandum by the French consul LeMaire and later one by the French scholar de Paradis. These observations supported by information gained here and there in the correspondence allows us to see that the members of this consular corps were a diverse lot. Several of them, perhaps in part driven by their environment, were heavy drinkers: one English consul was a man to whom no one could trust a secret for he was usually in his cups. Some were arrogant men who believed themselves brighter and better informed than they actually were; one conceited Dutch consul posed as an authority on "high politics" because he had lived in Paris and continued to read the *Gazette.* He was also the son-in-law of the Swedish consul, a merchant with great influence over the dey because of the favors that he could give to him. Most of the French and some of the English consuls were career men, others were merchants, often not subjects of the king whom they supposedly served. One French consul, the son of a former French consul, had lived in Algiers as a boy and spoke the languages of the regency fluently; most of the consuls, with no such advantage, had to rely upon their dragomen for communication.

By the end of the century the lives of these consular officers had become less onerous. They were permitted to leave the consular compounds where all the business was conducted, and to live in villas outside the city walls where gardens gave a bit of elegance to their lives. There also developed a social life among the consuls and European merchants with a few of the more civilized reis, Turkish officials, and wealthy coulougli and baldi inhabitants of the city. Most of the Turkish officers, however, remained outside this circle.

One of the most interesting members of this group was a merchant called George Logie (Logier, Legier), who first appeared in Algiers commanding a merchant ship flying the Swedish flag. He negotiated the treaty of peace for Sweden and subsequently became the Swedish consul. He managed to buy several prize ships that he operated under the Swedish flag as a merchant and general commercial agent for the dey. At one point in his career, he aspired to become consul for England and had the dey's support for his candidacy. The dey expelled the English consul on a pretext, but when Admiral Cavandish appeared before Algiers with a squadron and Mr. Black, the expelled consul, the dey relented and allowed the Englishman to return. Logier's position was not thereby greatly damaged. The dey relied upon him to arrange much of the commercial business of the regency and to supply the dey and his ministers with appropriate gifts. M. Lenoire tells us that the dey actually disliked and feared the Swedish consul, but that he was too dependent upon his services to break with him. Logier was the father-in-law of the Dutch consul and had several other consuls dependent upon his favors. His power was later only equaled by Jewish financiers, who also made themselves indispensable to the dey and his government.

Logier's efforts to have himself appointed English consul underlines a difference between the French and English appointments. In the eighteenth century the French consuls were regularly people with experience in the consular corps, often men with a knowledge of Turkish gained in the Levant before they appeared at Algiers. The English, on the other hand, were often enough merchants resident in Algiers, or merchants with interests there. This was a deviation from the policy adopted in the mid-seventeenth century after several merchant-consuls were accused of being the cause of war between England and Algiers. As a result of this changed procedure, even the dey sometimes attempted to choose between the available successors to an English consul who died in office, and on several occasions the government in London actually accepted the dey's choice. Perhaps as a result of this the English consul was often at odds with English merchants resident in Algiers who did not hesitate to interfere with the consular business with the dey or to write uncomplimentary letters about the consul to the ministers in London. One English consul remarked that such behavior on the part of a French merchant would result in his immediate return to France. The French ran a tighter ship than any of the other states.

While the life of a consul in eighteenth-century Algiers was more secure than that of his seventeenth-century counterpart, he still had problems with the corsairs and the dey, even though a treaty of peace and protection might guarantee the safety of this kingdom's shipping. One serious problem continued to arise because the

Algerian reis failed to show their true flag until after demanding the right to board the merchant vessel and to check its cargo. The merchant captain could not be sure that he was dealing with an Algerian reis or a Saléan pirate. The latter usually also flew false flags until the last moment. If the captain had firepower enough to hope for a victory, he might answer the request with cannonballs. Result: if he failed to drive off the corsair, he would be taken into Algiers, his consul might be placed under arrest, and the populace might even try to lynch both the captain and the consul. One French consul called this situation a "nightmare" for himself and his staff. Other consuls were under the same hazard. It was no easy matter to smooth the "wounded" feelings of the dey, to buy off the anger of the friends and family of Algerians killed in the conflict, and at the same time to rescue the offending ship and its crew.

There were other problems connected with the right of "visit and search" that was written into most of the treaties. The ship's captain had to carry a passport, but the reis and his secretary often enough could not read English or French, to say nothing of the other European languages. As a result the practice was to compare the length of the lines on the passport with those of the reis's copy. If they did not correspond, the pass was declared to be a forgery and the vessel arrested. Usually the consul could secure the release of the ship when it was brought into port, but often enough some of the cargo was "missing." The Algerians hated to give up a prize, and the dey knew that decision to free the ship would be unpopular. After such an incident, one exasperated consul wrote: ". . . the unstable avidity for money drives these barbarians, makes them forget justice and violate the faith of treaties . . ." He went on to say that the "ferocious dey considered only his own sordid interests."

A problem that carried a special danger for the French consul and his staff arose from the fact that Algerian pilgrims sailing for Mecca, and distinguished Algerians or Turks going to the Levant, often took passage on French vessels. On a number of occasions these ships were stopped by Spanish or Maltese corsairs, and the Moslem passengers along with their possessions were taken into Christian ports where the pilgrims were sold as slaves and their goods confiscated. Whenever this happened the French consul was in trouble. It was not easy to persuade the Spanish to give up Moslem passengers and never possible to secure the return of their possessions. On several occasions the French king repurchased these poor wretches and returned them to Algiers. On only one occasion did the Spanish government "graciously" release captives that it had refused to free on French request. The Spanish had hopes at that moment of securing a treaty of peace with Algiers and their generosity caused the French consul to lose face.

The problems connected with the escape of slaves was a constant during the entire experience of European consuls in Algiers. The slaves, of course, were property, and the European states did not question the legitimacy of this property. Both the consuls and European merchant and warship captains were constantly warned against assisting the slaves to escape, but once some poor devil managed to swim to a ship anchored on the roadstead, it was not easy to turn him over to his former patrons to face an inevitable death. And yet the patrons, the dey and the divan, regarded this as theft, as evidence that the Europeans did not live up to their treaty agreements. Even when a little group of slaves managed to rig up a boat and sail away to Majorca, the French consul came under serious accusations. When another group managed to overpower a small crew left on board while most of their fellows were enjoying the "delights" of Algiers, the French consul was accused of having a part in the whole transaction. These incidents were constantly reviewed and paraded whenever the European consul brought charges that the Algerians were not living up to their treaty.

Another consistent source of eighteenth-century conflict between the dey and the French and English consuls emerged from the fact that many ships flying the flags of England or of France were manned and commanded by men who obviously were not Englishmen or Frenchmen. After 1715, England's bases in the Mediterranean area were important naval and commercial harbors; the inhabitants of these bases were obviously men of Spanish or Italian origin. These men could fly the English king's flag and not speak English. When their ships were stopped by the reis, the Algerians assumed that they were merely trying to avoid capture. The French case was slightly different. Many ships flying the French king's flag were manned and commanded by men born along the Mediterranean coast between Marseille and Leghorn. It was not uncommon for the reis to stop a ship flying the French flag but manned entirely by Genoese personnel. The consuls at Algiers were confronted by the assertion that the flag and registry were merely a subterfuge. These were difficult cases. The French consul often gave up on cases involving Genoese; the English consul sometimes could persuade the dey that residents of Gibraltar or Port Mahon were indeed subjects of his majesty the king of England.

Another problem bothering the eighteenth-century consuls came from the fact that Jewish merchants resident in Algiers acquired great influence with the dey and presented the French merchants with serious competition. The dey came to depend upon several of these Jewish merchants for financial assistance and in turn granted them considerable advantages. These merchants were "European" Jews; they did not have to dress in the manner of their African co-religionists and their culture and economic outlook was formed by contacts with Jewish merchants in Europe. The French consuls resented them almost violently and urged their king to pass ordinances that would prevent these favored Jews from trading in French ports. It was no use; the Jewish merchants had contacts, they dealt in prize goods as well as in more regular merchandise, and they were essential to the dey's government. However, if anyone doubts the antiquity or the depth of European anti-Jewish sentiments, he should read the dispatches of the French consuls in eighteenth-century Algiers.

Christian merchants also caused trouble and conflict. One flagrant case was that of a merchant who accepted a consignment of goods belonging to the dey, and then managed to swindle him of both profits and capital; another, a merchant owing the dey a large sum of money who died without resources. The French king was obliged to make good the losses to avoid further difficulty. In a way it was justifiable, for the French king's government established rules, port regulations, and tariff duties that made it practically impossible for a Moslem merchant to trade in French harbors. Thus the Algerians could not themselves actually carry their own cargoes of wool, hides, wheat, wax, honey, and other such commodities to the French market. The trade was entirely in the hands of Jews or of Frenchmen. This was a legitimate complaint of the Algerians. Port regulations practically prevented them from trading with Europe in their own ships.

Protocol also was the source of difficulties. The Algerians complained that French and English warships often enough failed to salute them properly. By the eighteenth century the salute at sea had become a fixed ritual; failure to follow it to the last detail could be construed as an insult. The same was true in the pattern of saluting for warships, admirals, consuls, and simple ships' captains in the harbor. The warships saluted the town when it entered the roadstead outside of Algiers; the town cannons and those on the mole were expected to return the salute. If the admiral sent a party ashore to negotiate, he had to be sure that the mole properly saluted his men or they would not land. When the flotilla that arrived carried an ambassador, the salute had to be different than for a simple emissary. A consul warranted five guns; the king's ambassador, eleven! It was not always possible to agree on the number of guns that should be fired; neither side wanted to lose face. Once one was in the presence of the dey, other problems arose. One of the most persistent developed out of the dey's insistence that the consul should kiss his hand. This was not the custom in other courts; refusal, however, could and did cause friction. Another question involved the consul's right to wear a sword. In earlier years this had not been pressing since most of the consuls were merchants who did not ordinarily wear a sword, but by the eighteenth century, when the consuls regarded themselves as "semi-ambassadors" and many of them were actually career men, the sword was a symbol of office. Yet the deys wanted no arms in the council room. The Algerians were obliged to leave their arms at the door; so also must the European consul. The consuls usually won the argument over hand kisses, but lost those concerning the right to wear a sword.

In spite of all these problems, neither France nor England nor the Algerian regency actually broke off relations during the eighteenth century. The Algerians did from time to time break with one or another of the petty states that paid tribute for protection, but, even though the French in particular could furnish many prizes for the reis, they refrained from conflict with either of the big naval powers. Undoubtedly it was fear of reprisal that persuaded them to keep the peace. In the eighteenth century, the presence of English naval bases in the Mediterranean basin made it possible for powerful English naval units to operate freely along the North African coast, and the French fleet, based at Toulon and Marseille, was also within easy striking distance of Algiers. The bombardments of the later seventeenth century as well as the overwhelming power of the naval establishments in the eighteenth century made France and England too dangerous to be provoked into war. This interpretation does not credit the Algerians with their often-asserted "faith to their pledged word," and it is true that the deys often spoke of their desire to support loyally the treaties that they had signed. Nonetheless, it seems naïve to believe that a society that had come to depend upon corsair-quasi-piracy in the seventeenth century became piously law-abiding in the latter eighteenth century, especially if we note that by that time European naval power was overwhelming, even considering the fact that the Algerian chebecks were fast and easily maneuverable.

There were diverse reasons for the restraint shown by the English and French governments in face of the pinpricks and petty annoyances they experienced from the Algerian corsairs and the tyranny of the deys. Some writers were sordid enough to suggest that England and France kept the peace with the "barbarians" because they were pleased to have them prey upon the commerce of their petty rivals for world commerce and passenger service in the Mediterranean basin. This may well have been a reason why neither government ever responded to the numerous pleas that Christian Europe should join in an effort to wipe out the pirate nests in North Africa. Indeed, it is possible to document it in the correspondence of the English and French consuls, but there were other, perhaps more important, reasons for Anglo-French failure to end the piracy of these robber republics, and to end once and for all the enslavement of Europeans by Moslem raiders. For one thing, during much of the eighteenth century the English and French fleets were involved either in actual war with each other or in preparation for a new war. Louis XIV always found it expedient to have peace with the Barbary states whenever he was at war; his successors were of the same opinion. This does not mean that they did not consider military action against the Algerian regency, for, as we shall see, they did, but there were always reasons for postponement. Even though the Algerian naval power was not significant, it was difficult and expensive to control; and even though Algiers could be bombarded, there was always a question whether it was worth the costs. The seventeenth-century bombardments had done damage, but most of the population left the city for safety, and the most permanent result had been a severe Francophobia in the Algerian population.

Instead of sending warships and bomb-ketches to bombard Algiers, the English and French sent naval squadrons to show the flag, and "presents" and bribes to keep the favor of the dey and his ministers. We have lists of these "presents," some of them going to petty port officials, and most of them to the dey, his officers, and the more important reis. Curiously, the "presents" were rarely "enough"; the consular reports abound with stories of disappointment with the consul's bounty. One of the most striking stories comes from the early nineteenth century, when consul Broughton brought the dey a handsome musical snuff box with a clasp garnished with emeralds and brillants. The dey looked at the gift; then he asked the consul if his "king took him for a child to be pleased with the ting, ting, ting!" It had cost £1,500. The dey was equally unimpressed with the bale of fine English broadcloth that Broughton produced. It was of "poor quality." The consul returned the next day with a brace of pistols only to be asked: "Where are the guns that belong with them?" Broughton later remarked something about casting pearls before swine.

It is hard to know whether such surly, ungracious responses were mere playacting to secure more rings, watches, pins, fine cloth, et cetera, or simply boorishness common to uncultured men. The available evidence merely points to the problem of expectations and disappointments and the resultant headaches for the consuls. One French consul, exasperated and angry, wrote: "For the six days that I have been here one vexes me continually over the presents that I am obliged to give to this crowd of ingrates. Everyone wants some and they all talk about the quality of things given them by northern nations. If I listened to them it would cost 225,000 livres." As a matter of fact the costs mounted every decade perhaps in response to the falling profits from the corsairs' trade. An English consul who laid out gifts costing 50,000 talers points out that this was many times his own annual salary. The "presents" were the price of peace. When we see the consuls bribing for the favor of men ranging from the dey to a minor port officer we understand that the Algerians did not keep the peace solely because they wished to honor the treaties that existed between them and England and France. Perhaps these gifts are also evidence that the fear of naval reprisal was not as important as many believed: "presents" from the big naval powers and "presents" plus tribute from the smaller ones kept the corsairs on the leash and protected much of the commerce of the Mediterranean basin from their quasi-piracy. Portugal, Spain, the Spanish islands, and the petty Italian states furnished most of the "game" that eighteenth-century Algerian reis brought into port; only when the smaller northern states failed to come to an agreement about tribute did they furnish prize merchandise and slaves for sale in eighteenth-century Algiers.

XVI *The End of the Regency*

SEVERAL TIMES in the course of the eighteenth century French patience with Algerian interference in French commerce was almost exhausted, and the king's government seriously considered going to war to halt such acts. One of these times came in 1731: the Algerians captured a ship flying the French flag and made it a prize on the grounds that the captain and crew were all Genoese. A short time later, another reis captured fourteen French fishermen and sold them in the market at Algiers. The French consul's protests were of no avail. The king ordered Admiral René Duguay-Trouin with a squadron of four warships (224 cannons) to proceed to Algiers and demand that the treaty of peace be respected. The dey was Abdi Pasha, an old man, blind in one eye, suspicious of everyone. He had already escaped three attempts at assassination in his seven-year reign. When he finally did agree to discuss the problems, he brushed aside all the French complaints: the vessel and its crew were Genoese; so were the fishermen! But he did have a complaint of his own. He had assigned three hundred and fifty bales of wool to a French merchant, one M. Meschein, to be sold at Marseille, but Meschein had gone bankrupt, and the French court had confiscated the wool to satisfy his creditors. The wool belonged to the dey, and he was in high dudgeon over the tyranny of the French court. The French admiral suspected that the dey might be right about the wool and, also, that he had ordered the capture of Frenchmen to underline his complaint. Indeed, if there were no redress, further captures would undoubtedly occur. The admiral suggested negotiation.

In France it was admitted that there might be some grounds for the dey's complaint, but when the French consul, apparently through his own fault, also became embroiled with Abdi Pasha, the government decided upon a larger inquiry. M. LeMaire, whose experience in the Levant had given him considerable understanding of Moslem methods and characteristics, was appointed consul at Algiers with orders to report on probable and possible courses of action. LeMaire's letters written over the next twenty-odd years are some of the most valuable documents to give us insight into the government and problems of Algiers during this period. In marked contrast to his later ideas, in the early 1730s LeMaire was quite willing to consider armed conflict as the best means of forcing Algiers to live up to its obligations,[1] but, before the government at Versailles could decide upon such a course of action, the so-called War of the Polish Succession (1733–35) diverted French attention. It was Louis XV's father-in-law who lost the Polish throne but later secured one in Lorraine, a solution that in the future would bring that province into France. When the European problems relaxed, Tunis and Tripoli, rather than Algiers, became targets for French military action. Then Frederick II's "rape of Silesia" (1740) and the subsequent War of the Austrian Succession kept France and Europe embroiled with problems on the Continent until 1748.

It should surprise no one that after 1748 the French government again opened a discussion on the advantages of a war with Algiers. A whole list of complaints about the behavior of the Algerian reis as well as a chorus of pamphlets and letters reflecting "civilized" enlightened French opinion about the need for order in the world, urged some punitive action against the "barbarous piratical" states in North Africa, of which Algiers was by far the most important. Several pamphleteers pointed out that "civilized" Europe, if it wished, could easily rid the world of the plundering raiders from the Barbary Coast.

As the problem was considered at Versailles, however, it was not so simple. Nearly every memoirist started his discussion with the bombardments that Louis XIV had undertaken in the 1680s. Since that time Algiers had become better fortified, and the French navy no longer had the bomb ketches that had delivered the blows in that former time. On the other hand, the Algerian naval forces were weaker in 1750 than they had been earlier; their fleet consisted almost entirely of chebecks mounting less than thirty guns. These ships were faster and more maneuverable than the French warships, but unless two or three of them could close with a French frigate, they

1. At this period LeMaire suggested that the cost of maintaining eight to ten frigates of fifty-six to seventy guns would not be much more than the normal cost of maintaining the navy; at the same time, it would "exercise the sailors" and "bring dignity" to the king's service. He was obviously contemptuous of the Algerian naval power and underestimated the cost of maintaining a fleet in the North African coastal waters. (AAE Alg. XIII, fols. 109 and passim.)

had no chance of success, and any of the ships of the line could fight off à whole squadron of the Algerians. And yet these chebecks were dangerous to French commerce; they could be controlled only by convoys or by close blockade of the Algerian ports. This would be expensive and it would not absolutely assure the safety of French commerce. It was often observed that an important difference between 1682 and 1750 was the fact that Spain was now an ally and that therefore Spanish harbors would furnish the French forces with water, wood, food, and naval supplies. And yet there was considerable opposition to any joint Franco-Spanish action. The Spanish would demand the destruction of Algiers; this would offend the Ottoman sultan and endanger Franco-Ottoman cooperation. France did not require the obliteration of the corsair community, only its compliance with treaties. And even if the Spanish would be less rapacious toward Algiers, would they not, as the least price, demand a treaty of peace between Algiers and Spain? This of course was unfortunately contrary to French interests, for it would immediately introduce Spanish competition in the carrying trade and release Spanish merchandise from the threat of capture. LeMaire, who had suggested military action earlier, now suggested that an ambassador should be sent to Algiers to iron out all problems. He was writing at Versailles; obviously he saw himself as the ambassador.

While LeMaire and others considered French action, the "Albanian revolt" and the murder of the dey and his treasurer took place at Algiers. The new dey was a man known to have a violent temper, a man who liked to take over the role of executioner when he handed down a death sentence. Nonetheless LeMaire assumed that he could probably reach an agreement with him. His memorandum to this effect was dated in 1754; the coming crisis that produced the diplomatic revolution, and the Seven Years War gave him the opportunity to try to do so. He returned to Algiers, where, after a short turn in an Algerian prison resulting from a conflict with the dey, Franco-Algerian problems were settled by "presents" and a willingness to let bygones be bygones (1757).

French naval weakness in the Seven Years War resulted in many infractions of the Franco-Algerian Treaty of Peace and Friendship. When the war ended in 1763 the king's council ordered Admiral Suffren to prepare a plan for punishing Algiers. Suffren apparently took his task seriously; he even studied seventeenth-century naval experiences. Dutch Admiral Michiel de Ruyter proved to be one of his best sources. "I avow with pleasure," he wrote, "that one does not fear being fooled in following the advice of so great a man of war and of the sea."[2] The Admiral's proposals systematically covered the problems of controlling the Mediterranean in a manner that would force the Algerians to sue for peace. He would convoy shipping to the Levant and Cadiz, station chebecks and/or frigates to guard the southern coast of France, and cruise between Malta and the Azores. A flotilla of six warships stationed off North Africa would control the Algerian chebecks that might attempt to leave harbor. He assured the government that if there were three convoys each for the Levant and Cadiz "it will be impossible for the Algerians to do any damage" to French commerce. He showed his awareness of the Algerian potentials for war at sea by pointing out that the warships would need fewer soldiers, but the chebecks and frigates should have a large complement of marines to match the Algerians. Choiseul, Louis XV's great minister of foreign affairs, complimented the admiral on the fullness of his suggestions.

Suffren's memorandum was hardly dry before an incident at sea created a crisis. A French frigate, allegedly under the impression that it was dealing with a Saléan pirate, sank an Algerian chebeck; the whole crew was lost at sea. When the news reached Algiers the dey was furious; he threw the consul and his chancellor into prison, loaded with irons, confiscated all the French ships in the harbor, bastinadoed a French merchant on the pretext that he had fought with an Algerian corsair, and ordered the occupation of the French African Company's concession (the old Bastion of France) and the arrest of its inhabitants.

Admiral Suffren received orders to take two warships and a frigate to Algiers to see what could be done. His orders were explicit: he must "not enrage the dey who has the life of a French consul in his hands." Suffren anchored beyond the reach of the harbor guns and signaled that he had a package of letters for the dey. The Algerians must have understood that the admiral's orders were such that peace or war could result from the negotiations. M. de Fabry, who conducted the diplomatic exchanges for the admiral, has left us a superb account of the whole affair.

As usual, protocol and prestige presented the first hurdle for the discussions. The dey had insulted the kingdom of France by throwing the consul and his chancellor in prison; the mere fact that they had been subsequently released was a matter of minor importance. The

2. B.N., mss. franc. N.A. 9431, fols. 225f.

admiral ordered consul Vallière to have no intercourse with the dey; a French merchant in Algiers could act as an intermediary. When Suffren did manage to persuade the Algerians to allow Vallière to visit him on the flagship, the poor fellow suggested that he really should not return to the city. He liked the safety of the warship. Suffren decided, however, that he was at Algiers to negotiate, not to kidnap the consul. Finally it was a question of the honors and safety of M. de Fabry, who presumably would land and discuss terms. How many guns would salute him? Would he be safe from insults? Would the dey immediately return the compound to the French African Company and release its officers and men? These negotiations were slow. A winter storm in the last week of January 1784 forced the French warships to put to sea; when they returned on the 10th of the month the question of the salutes was settled. Consul Vallière left the flagship with three guns and six "Vive le roi!"; when he arrived at the mole he was saluted by five guns from the shore batteries. The dey then sent carcasses of beef, sheep, and chickens as well as bread and fresh vegetables to the fleet as a gift. Shortly afterward, de Fabry, properly saluted as the king's emissary, landed at the mole, bringing with him as a gift for the dey a Moslem slave whom he had rescued at Majorca.

The discussions lasted almost a week. Both sides paraded griefs and complaints; both accused the other of violations of the treaty. Finally on January 16th a codicile to the Franco-Algerian peace treaty was signed. It contained about the same terms that LeMaire had hoped to get in 1752. The important additions were simply the requirement that each signator would himself punish any seaman or other person who was subject to the signator's government, for any infractions of the treaty, and a clause preventing a Saléan pirate from selling at Algiers ships, cargoes, or crews that they might capture, plus requiring that the Saléan ships must leave Algiers within twenty-four hours after arrival. The Algerians were not particularly happy about the clause that announced that bygone offenses were bygone, and must be forgotten. In the next years there was a clamor in Algiers to end the treaty in 1789, when its time would run out. A hundred years was a long time, they argued, and many conditions had changed.

As 1789 approached, there were other reasons for reconsideration. The treaty with Spain, as we have seen, was concluded, but its terms were not implemented since the Spanish were still in Oran. However, when the treaty would come into effect, the corsairs would have trouble finding prizes that they could legitimately take unless the French treaty was ended. The French, on their side, argued that the treaty had been renewed in 1718, and so it would not really expire until 1818. Another crisis: a French warship sank an Algerian chebeck. The French government hastily insisted that it was a mistake, enlisted the support of the sultan of Turkey, and presented the dey with a handsome gift. At that moment the corsairs were about to depart for the Levant to join the Ottoman navy in the Black Sea in the war against Russia, so the conflict was smoothed over, with the French African Company paying a much larger annual payment for its concession on the coast. The crisis in France that emerged when the Estates General, summoned to solve interior problems, abruptly moved to give France a new constitution, made the problems created by Algiers minor and relatively unimportant. The Revolutionaries had more than events in North Africa to hold their attention.

By January 1793, when, after the execution of Louis XVI, the revolutionary French government had declared war on England as well as on most of continental Europe, high politics again impinged upon Algiers, for both the French and the English attempted to involve the dey in the war. The new dey, Hassan, a relative of the late dey, had been incompetent as treasurer, and he was still more so as dey. He became absolutely dependent upon two Jewish merchants, Naphtal Busnach and Joseph Baeri. They came to control the government of the regency. Like clever businessmen, they first advised that the dey steer a neutral course between France and England, but after 1794, when the news from Europe indicated that the French were the probable victors, they began to favor France. It should have been a great day for French policy, but the French consul at Algiers found himself caught up in a personal and family problem with the Committee of Public Safety. One of his relatives fled to Spain, and he soon had to leave his post. Events in Europe soon covered all other problems as the French moved from Convention to Directory after Robespierre and his friends were guillotined, and the new government's generals, including Napoleon Bonaparte, forced Prussia and Austria out of the war.

Then followed Napoleon's descent on Egypt. The sultan hurriedly urged the Algerians to join him in war against France, but the dey and his advisers read the lessons of the last few years differently: they had no intention of provoking Napoleon or the Directory. However, by 1802 Algiers was again caught in the net of Napoleonic politics. The petty Italian states had traditionally supplied the reis with prizes, but after Napoleon's campaign of 1800–1801 these states had become dependencies of Napoleon's growing sphere of power. He sent an emissary to Algiers to speak in a loud voice: if the regency did not mind its ways and submit to French will and stop molesting subjects of the first consul, Napoleon would do to Algiers what he had done to the Mameluke state of Egypt. The impression of French hegemony in Europe was not lessened when Admiral Nelson appeared before Algiers. He came to support a consul who had shown the bad judgment of inviting Moslem women to his home, but his orders gave him no authority to use force. He sailed away, leaving the impression that France was indeed all powerful, and England almost inconsequential.

Lack of prizes, lack of tribute money, difficulty in the collection of taxes endangered the dey's government. The arrogance of the dey's Jewish advisers did not help him much. In 1805 Busnach was murdered as he left the palace. Hassan quickly recognized the assassin's act to be for the good of the state, and to save himself he permitted the janissaries to sack the Jewish quarter. It did not save him. He, too, was murdered a few weeks later.

These murders were the beginning of a new era of disorder. The new dey, Ahmed, came to the throne, but the rioting continued; Ahmed's rival for power, the Agha, inspired indiscriminate looting and murder. At the end of a month Ahmed managed to arrest his rival, have him beheaded, and restore a measure of order to the community, but his problems would not go away. He was short of money to pay his soldiers, a situation fraught with danger to himself and the city of Algiers. The war in Europe was heating up: Austerlitz, Jena, Friedland, the division of the world between Napoleon and Czar Alexander. Ahmed tried to impose more tribute on the European powers that used the Mediterranean, but they had become part of the French Empire; Napoleon insisted that his domains needed no protection from Algiers. At Tilsit he and Czar Alexander had agreed that Napoleon could, when he was ready, take over Algiers and its beyliks as a colony or dependency of the French empire; he was not ready to act, but neither would he allow his dependent states to pay tribute to Algiers. When the money was not forthcoming, Ahmed's life was in hazard; he was murdered in November 1808.

The new dey, Ali er R'assel, was immediately faced with a demand that the treasury be opened and its contents given to the soldiers who had made him dey. He argued that the soldiers should only be paid their wages, that they could not violate the treasury. The next demand: the soldiers asked for the right to pillage the city of Aligers. This broke the solid front of the janissary corps. The married members and the coulougli were reluctant to see their relatives' houses invaded, with the sort of disorder that would inevitably follow. They began to form bands that were joined by some of the younger, more adventurous baldi. The unmarried janissaries organized against them. Neither dared to fight, but the organized life of the city came to a standstill. February 7, 1809, Ali er R'assel was murdered; the assassins elected one Hadj Ali to be his successor. Hadj Ali was a drug addict, a vicious man. He did manage to bring a little order into the life of Algiers, but he soon was at odds with the European community, especially with the French consul, who left his post and returned to France.

As we have noted, by the secret agreement with Alexander, Napoleon had Russian authorization for the conquest of Algiers. In 1808 he sent an engineer, M. Boutin, to Algiers to study the terrain and map out a project for the conquest. The problems that developed in Spain, however, forced a delay. After 1809 Spain became a serious problem for the Emperor; by 1811 Russia was on the verge of becoming one. The plans for a descent on Algiers were shelved in the archives; they were to be recovered, dusted off, and used in 1830.

The tumultuous events that followed Napoleon's decision to invade Russia overshadowed both the piratical depredations of Algerian corsairs and the little war between the United States and England. When the United States failed to send tribute in 1813, the dey and divan declared war on it, but there were no ships flying the U.S. flag in the Mediterranean, English convoys made English shipping in that sea safe, and the Algerians hesitated to capture ships belonging to the French empire. Ali Hadji tried to secure money by reopening the endemic conflict with Tunis, but even that failed to yield results. He was murdered March 22, 1815. His treasurer, Mohammed, became dey; he was murdered the first week in April 1815. Omer Agha became dey just in time to learn of the Treaty of Ghent ending the conflict between England and the United States. On June 17, 1815, Stephen Decatur fought a sea battle with the admiral of the Algerian fleet. As we have already noted, the Algerian commander was killed, his ships were captured, and the dey was forced to make peace with the United States that assured safe passage for American ships. A few weeks later, Lord Exmouth arrived at Algiers and imposed another treaty requiring freedom of passage for English, Sardinian, Sicilian, and Ionian ships. Without funds from these sources it was increasingly difficult to support the ever dwindling Algerian military forces.

There was more to come. Early in 1816 the English squadrons again appeared before Algiers. Lord Exmouth explained to the dey that the Congress of Vienna had decided upon the abolition of slavery and piracy; he demanded that the Algerians accept this decision and free its Christian slaves. The dey and the divan were both astonished and angry: how could the powers of Europe presume to interfere with an institution so firmly based in the customs and laws of their country, an institution approved by the Koran itself? The population, upon hearing this, were equally incensed. The English emissaries were jeered at and physically assaulted in the streets. The French consul warned that this would bring reprisals, but the dey refused to listen.

Reprisals came quickly. An Anglo-Dutch naval force totaling thirty-six warships arrived before Algiers. Lord Exmouth sent a boat ashore with a flag of truce and an ultimatum. While the Algerians were considering the latter, the Anglo-Dutch fleet moved quietly into a position allowing it to enfilade the mole and the harbor. The emissaries were returning to the flagship with a negative response to the ultimatum when the Algerians suddenly realized that the fleet was in a position to pour fire on their ships and fortifications. Someone ordered the guns on the mole to fire. There were three shots. They were answered by a murderous fire from the ships as the entire fleet blazed away, killing the Algerian cannoneers, smashing their guns, sinking or burning the ships in the harbor. It was a fatal blow for the Algerian navy as well as a terrible loss of life. The Turks and the Moorish auxiliaries fought bravely, but the blow had come unexpectedly—traitorously, the Algerians always believed. Indeed, the coup was possible only because the Algerians accepted the flag of truce as evidence of Anglo-Dutch good faith. The European consuls continuously reproached the Algerians of bad faith—perhaps Europeans could also be tarred with that brush.

When the cannonade finished, Omer quickly made peace on Anglo-Dutch terms. He did not know that the allied ships had used up practically all their powder and shot; they could not possibly have mounted another attack. The peace was dictated by Lord Exmouth: abolition of the institution of slavery, freedom for existing Christian slaves (some twelve hundred in all), and reparation of five hundred thousand francs. The Algerians could still make war on the lesser states and still could keep any captives as prisoners, but not as slaves. Even though the Algerian navy had suffered serious losses, within a year Sweden, Tuscany, and Denmark had signed treaties agreeing to pay tribute in return for the safety of their ships.

The Anglo-Dutch flotilla was hardly out of sight when the janissary militia revolted and pillaged the Jewish quarter of the city. Omer managed to quiet them down for a moment, but within the month he was strangled. Ali Khodja became dey, and with his arrival on the scene the regime that Kheir-ed-din Barbarossa had inaugurated by introducing Turkish janissaries into Algiers was about to come to an end.

The conflict between unmarried janissaries and their companions who were either married or the coulougli children of Turks, had dealt a blow to the morale and prestige of the corps. The fact that recruiting in the Levant had practically ended also eroded its viability. Ali Khodja was resolved to free himself from the tyranny of these soldiers. Hardly had he been installed in office, when he withdrew, with the public treasury, to the Casbah fortification guarded by two thousand Kabylie mercenaries. He then announced that any native Turks who might wish to withdraw to the Levant would be free to do so, but for those who elected to remain in Algiers, he would require strict obedience. Ali Khodja was a puritanical disciplinarian. He closed the taverns, expelled all women from the janissary barracks, and announced draconian disciplinary measures. A large section of the janissary immediately revolted, but the rebellion was quickly suppressed by an army of six thousand coulougli and Kabylie troops; the punishment was brutal. In the year 1818 Ali Khodja died of the pestilence, which was still endemic in Algiers. His successor, a weaker man and anxious to become secure in his position, granted amnesty to the janissary offenders and repealed some of the puritanical decrees; it was, however, too late for the janissary corps to recover its former position of power. When the French arrived in 1830 the janissary militia, less than two thousand five hundred men, was a minor factor in the resistance to the invasion.

The last decade of the independent existence of the Turkish regency of Algiers previewed the problems that the French were to encounter when they took over control of the territory. The beyliks were plagued with rebellions. Both Arab and Berber tribesmen, realizing the weakness of the dey's government and the decline of his military power, refused to pay taxes or to recognize the authority of their Turkish overlords. Beys who failed to restore order were either removed or strangled, but neither practice proved efficacious to the dey's treasury. Whatever taxes could be collected, the tribute paid by the lesser powers unable to protect their own ships, the payments from the European concessions at Calle and Oran, the occasional prize that could be sold for cash—all that hardly yielded enough money to pay the reduced military forces. It is not improbable that the regime would have collapsed of its own weakness even if the French had not decided to invade and conquer.

The anarchy inherent in such a regime made difficult the life of the European consuls. The Algerian authorities tried to keep just inside the limits that circumscribed the patience of the powers; in these last years the consulates of the Netherlands and Denmark were actually invaded and members of the staff (Berbers rather than Europeans) were taken away on charges of treason. The smaller states had no power to punish such behavior. The English, on the other hand, did bombard Algiers in 1824 when their consul was expelled from the city because of an altercation with the dey. A total of twenty-two warships fired on the city, but from a distance that made the bombardment of minimal damage. Finally, the English, like the other governments, gave in to the dey and appointed another man as consul; it was too expensive and unproductive to bombard the city. This convinced both the Algerians and the sultan of Turkey that Algiers was inviolable as long as the dey did not rouse all Europe against him. The assumption proved to be false; in 1830 a French expeditionary force landed at Algiers, conquered the city, and ended the life of the Turkish regency.

The problem that led finally to French military intervention had its origins in the era of the Directory (1796) when the two influential Jewish merchants, Baki and Busnach, supplied France with wheat, most of which belonged to the deylik rather than to the merchants. The Directory did not pay, but in 1801 Napoleon, as consul, recognized the debt and authorized payment. The money, however, was not forthcoming. Nothing was done to mollify the dey's irritation until after the restoration of the Bourbons; in 1818 a treaty was drawn up and signed, placing the debt at seven million livres, and two years later the chamber passed a bill authorizing the payment. At this point a group of French merchants brought suit for the collection of debts amounting to some five million livres that Baki and Busnach owed to them. The two merchants abruptly left Algiers in fear of their lives when the French consul explained to the dey that his money could not be recovered until the debts were settled and that he would receive only whatever was left after that settlement. This was incomprehensible to the dey. The money was his, not Baki's or Busnach's. How could a French court allow anyone to steal his money? When the French government refused to permit him to extradite the two merchants, he became convinced that he was being swindled.

The affair came to a head on April 30, 1827. It was an unfortunate coincidence that this was the end of Ramadan, a period when Moslem fanaticism reaches its peak. But even worse was the news that arrived: the Algerian fleet supporting the Ottoman navy in an effort to suppress the Greek rebellion was blockaded by a European naval expedition, and it had run out of supplies. It was even believed that the crews and marines were dying of hunger. What happened? The French consul chose this time to ask for the release of a ship flying a French flag but belonging to a subject of the Papal states! The dey was furious; he shouted his objections to French behavior, brought up all his complaints, and when the consul tried to reply, he struck him with a flywhisk and threatened to throw him in prison. French contempt for his regime, the injustice that he was suffering as a result of French court procedures, the European aid given the Greek rebels, and the final insult of a demand for the return of a "legitimate" prize had been too much for the dey. It also was too much for the French!

On June 11, 1827 a French squadron arrived at Algiers, embarked the French residents of the city and then proceeded to Calle to remove the Frenchmen connected with the concession there. After this was accomplished, the French instituted a naval blockade of Algiers.

The blockade went badly for both sides. The French did capture several Algerian corsair ships, but it was costly to maintain. Then came another "incident": two French ships were wrecked on the coast of Algeria. The crews, captured by the Berber tribesmen, were first treated as guests, then murdered, and their heads sold to the dey. This was fuel added to fire, an unfortunate situation that continued into July 1829, when the French sent an emissary to Algiers to attempt to end the conflict by negotiation. The dey, apparently believing that French willingness to negotiate was connected with serious political problems in France, refused to make concessions. There were serious problems in France where the Ultra party was gradually antagonizing the electorate, an electorate composed solely of wealthy and conservative families, but not as reactionary as the

Ultra party believed it to be. On October 8, 1829, Jules-Armand Polignac became prime minister; he was an arch-conservative/re-actionary who, like Charles X, had never learned anything new, nor forgotten anything old. He was resolved to stifle the crisis that was building up in the kingdom, if necessary by a coup d'état. Someone suggested that Algiers might distract French attention from the prob-lems created by the reactionary clerical legislation. At this point someone discovered the plans for a descent of Algiers drawn up by M. Boutin for Napoleon. They were complete, down to directions for the movement of troops overland for the final capture of the city. Here was a Napoleonic plan that could be implemented by the restored Bourbon ruler and make Frenchmen forget the glories of Napoleon. There were probably other reasons for the decision to make a descent on Algiers that was reached on January 31, 1830, but a most important one was the desire to make a diversion that would distract attention from the deplorable situation in France.

It was, however, still a question of the attitude of Europe. The Russia czar was enthusiastically in favor; the two German powers had no objection; the smaller states were in no position to make any. Only England and the Ottoman empire were opposed. The Turks tried to insist that Algiers was a part of their territory even though no one in Algiers paid any attention to the sultan's firmans. The sul-tan finally decided that his best policy would be to send an emissary to Algiers to urge the dey to come to terms; if that failed, perhaps it would not be a disaster since one attempt after another to assault Algiers had failed miserably—why not this one, too? The English were opposed; they did not want a French-controlled Algiers in the position to harass their Mediterranean commerce; they did not want a French revision of the status quo on the Mediterranean world. The English ambassador spoke loudly at Paris, but the French decided that the protests were largely made of paper and could be ignored. Thus there seemed to be no problems that would really stop the expedition being prepared in France's Mediterranean ports. The only thing to worry about would be the defenders; they had ample time to know that the French were planning a stroke against them.

Unlike the projects of Charles V's and O'Reilly's, the French plans for 1830 were well prepared. Boutin had been a careful or-ganizer, a good engineer, and he had made his plans after extended scrutiny of the terrain. By April 25 some six hundred vessels, of which three hundred were warships, were waiting to sail. The troops were put aboard on May 11–18 and on the 22d the entire armada left port. A storm forced them to put in at Palma for almost two weeks, but by June 12 the fleet was off the coast of Algiers, and on the 14th the first troops were put ashore. At this critical moment another storm threatened to treat the French much as a former one had mistreated Charles V, but the French were both luckier and more far-sighted; they had wrapped supplies and equipment in waterproof containers that could be thrown overboard and allowed to float to shore where they could be picked up by the troops that had already landed. Only a small part was treated this way, for the storm abated as quickly as it had come up, and the French had safe landing for men, horses, ambulances, cannons, fodder, food, powder, shot, and all manner of other war supplies. Algerian resistance to the landing was no more than token.

At this point the entire enterprise was endangered when the sultan, probably instructed by the English ambassador at Istanbul, sent a pasha to Algiers with orders for the dey to agree to any conditions of peace in return for an end of the invasion. If the dey should comply, the whole enterprise would be endangered. The French commander understood this. He managed to stop the ship carrying the pasha, and to send it away, along with the sultan's emissary, without allowing anyone to land or to make contact with the authorities in Algiers. The dey could not now assert that, yielding to the orders of his overlord, he was ready to make the French invasion unnecessary.

The invaders, however, did have to face troops and mounted horsemen from all parts of the Algerian regency. The three beys sent their best troops, and the tribesmen joined in a war against the Christian enemy, even more hated than the Turks, but these forces were largely undisciplined, poorly led, and quite unprepared to stand up against troops commanded by men many of whom had learned the art of war under Napoleon.

It would be unproductive to describe the progress of the invasion. Only at one point was there any danger of failure: on June 29 General Desprez believed a mirage that appeared before him and his staff to be evidence that Boutin's map was faulty. Several members of his staff urged him to reconsider, but he ordered a change of direction for his troops that could have spelled disaster for the whole mission. Fortunately for him the Algerians were not in any position to take advantage of his error before it had been corrected. In every other way the invasion moved with precision; on July 4 the last defenses of the city of Algiers were taken and the dey capitulated with the provision that he should be allowed to depart with his family and wealth under the protection of the French army. He wanted to escape with his life and possessions; someone else could decide what to do about peace.

The French army marched into Algiers watched by a surly crowd. The janissaries had locked themselves in their caserns, or, if married, had melted into the crowd of baldi. Obviously these erstwhile "lords" of Algiers were as much afraid of the populace of the city as they were of the French invaders. At the moment, with no government to deal with, the French hesitated and sought further orders from Paris. The victory came on July 4; July 26, 27, 28 witnessed a revolution in Paris. Polignac, his cabinet, and his king, Charles X, were forced to leave for England. The revolutionary government included the Marquis de Lafayette and Talleyrand, as well as Adolphe Thiers, a distinguished journalist-historian; François Guizot, a famous professor-historian; Casimir Périer, a rich banker, and others of like dignity—hardly men one would expect to find leading a rebellion that had erected barricades in the streets of Paris. These were the men, however, who had to decide what to do with Algiers. They were hardly willing to take the dictation of the English ambassador, who insisted that they should reestablish a native government and return to France, but they also had to face the opinion at home that had developed in Europe as a result of the revolutions in North and South America, namely that colonies were a burden as long as they could be of little use to the mother country, and rebellious as soon as they might become valuable. Nonetheless, the decision came down on the side of those who wanted to remain in Algiers and to establish a French regime in Algeria.

The decision was a fateful one. When the victorious French general secured the signature of the last dey of Algiers to a treaty that gave the French control and government over his city and land, there was very little that he really could convey to the French officers. The janissary army of occupation had already lost its power to rule. Indeed, in the whole territory, there were only about twenty-five hundred janissaries capable of bearing arms, and the Berber and Arab sheiks and emirs who ruled their tribesmen, as well as the townsfolk who were ready to assert authority over their communities, did not consider themselves bound in any agreement that the dey might make with the victors. In short, the conquering French army found itself in actual control over little more than the land on which it camped; its leaders were confronted with almost exactly the same problems that had bedeviled the last years of the Turkish regency. Both the countryside hinterland and the towns that had been in endemic rebellion for a decade or more were quite unwilling to accept the new rulers with any more grace than they had for the old ones.

If the French inherited the same problems, the impact of their rule was different from that of the Turks. No one should smile when Frenchmen write about their "civilizing mission" in Africa and elsewhere simply because sometimes French soldiers and bureaucrats applied methods and measures unsuited to this idealistic frame of reference. France did bring Western civilization to Algeria even though at times the process had a disrupting influence on ancient tribal customs and appeared to be little more than imposing French civilization on an unwilling people with bayonets and rifles. This Western civilization came in the form of modern economic order, more rational urbanization, extended education and public health services, and a greater respect for the rule of law, as well as the unplanned and unexpected preparation of personnel capable of directing and achieving a rebellion against French rule. No one who visits the former French colonies today will miss the fact that France had much to give to these peoples during the years that it ruled them. But all this was not planned in 1830, when the newly established July monarchy in France decided to replace the Turks as rulers of Algiers and its beyliks. It was destined to be the story of the next hundred and forty years of Algerian history.

Bibliography

Anyone writing a general history of the Turkish-corsair regency of Algiers will be greatly indebted to persons who lived there and wrote accounts of their experiences as well as to the officers of the European states who tried to keep their governments informed about conditions and problems. This study is no exception. The first four chapters rely heavily upon the historians, chroniclers, and geographers writing in the sixteenth century. Like every other student, I have found the work of Haëdo and Marmol invaluable; without them none of the books about the Maghrib in this period would have approached credibility. The seventeenth and eighteenth centuries saw the writing of more memoirs and travel books, but most important for the student are the letters and memoranda of the consuls, naval officers, and other officials who represented the European states at Algiers. Their letters are precious evidence with which to check the writings of travelers, slaves, merchants, priests, and others who have left us pictures and opinions about men and events in the area. It is unfortunate that there are not more documents written by Turks and Moors, either as officers or as travelers, that are available to those of us who have only European languages.

I have divided the materials that I have used into (1) letters and documents in manuscript and printed letters and documents produced at the time; (2) books and pamphlets and other materials written before 1830; and (3) scholarly and other works produced since 1830. I do not pretend that this bibliography is a complete statement of all the materials about the Turkish regency, nonetheless, it does provide a solid base for this study, and it should satisfy the needs of anyone wishing to look further into aspects of the history of the Turkish-corsair community of Algiers.

ABBREVIATIONS

AAE	Archives des Affaires Étrangères
AN	Archives nationales
A. de C. de A.	Archivo de Corona de Aragon
B.N.	Bibliothèque Nationale
B.M.	British Museum
R.A.	*Revue Africaine*

MANUSCRIPTS AND PRINTED PRIMARY SOURCE MATERIALS

MANUSCRIPTS

Public Record Office, London, 772-Sp. 71-1, 2, 3, 4. 772-IND. 13395-96.
Archives des Affaires Étrangères, Paris. France, M. et D., 792, 917, 297, 366. Algérie, M. et D., 12, 13.
Archives Nationales, Paris. K 1334.
Archivo de Corona de Aragon, Barcelona. Consejo de Aragon, Legajos, 555-62.
Bibliothèque Nationale, Paris. Ms. Franç. 16141, 16164, 167838, 15875, 15466, 16633, 10655, 19608, 5561, 19799, 23355.
British Museum, London. Newcastle Papers, Add 28093-32779; PS 8/10261.

PRINTED MATERIALS

Anderson, R. C., *The Journals of Sir Thomas Allen (1666-1678)*, Navy Records Society, 1940.
Barutell, Jan S. de, *Documentos sobre la armada de liga y batalla de Lepanto sacados del archivo de Simancas*, Madrid, 1842-43.
Bassett, René, *Documents musulmans sur le siège d'Alger en 1541*, Paris, 1890.
Berbrugger, A., "Les Casernes de janissaires à Alger," *Revue* (R.A.) vol. III, pp. 138-50.
———, "L'Expédition d'O'Reilly contre Alger en 1775," R.A. VIII, 172-87, 408-20; IX, 303-6; XI, 458-67.
———, "Mers el Kébir et Oran d'après Diego Saurez Montanes," R.A. IX, 251-67, 337-56, 410-29; vol. X, 43-50, 111-25.
Carrière, E., *Négotiations de la France dans le Levant au XVI siècle*, 4 vols., Paris, 1848-60.
Chappell, Edwin, *The Tangier Papers of Samuel Pepys*, Navy Records Society, 1935.
Clement, Pierre, *Lettres, instructions et mémoires de Colbert*, 7 vols., Paris, 1861-70.
Deny, J., "Charte des hospitaux chrétiens d'Alger en 1694," R.A. XVIII, 233-44.
Devoulx, Albert, "Le registre des prises maritimes," R.A. XV, 70-79, 149-60, 184-201, 285-99, 362-74, 447-57; XVI, 70-77, 146-56, 233-40, 292-303.
———, Les registres de la solde des janissaires conservés à la Bibliothèque Nationale d'Alger," R.A. LXI, 19-46, 212-60.
Dumont, Jean, *Corps universel diplomatique du droit des gens*, vol. III, Amsterdam, 1731.
Effendi, Ibrahim, *A Letter from the Government of Algiers to Admiral Russell*, London, 1695, Newberry case 6a, 160 no. 65.
Estado Mayor Central de Ejercito, Servicio Historico Militar, *Dos expeditiones Españolas Contra Argel 1541 y 1775*, Madrid, 1946.
Grammont, H. D. de, "Correspondance des consuls d'Alger (1690-1742)," R.A. XXXI, 164-212, 295-319, 341-49, 436-77; XXXII, 52-80, 117-60, 230-38, 308-19, 321-37; XXXIII, 122-76, 219-55. Also published as a book with the same title (Algiers, 1890).
———, "Documents Algériens," R.A. XXIX, 430-59; XXX, 399-402, 468-76; XXXI, 161-63.

————, "Lanfreducci et Othon Bossio, Colte et discours de barbarie," R.A., LXVI, 428–48.

———— (as trans.), *Relation des préparatifs fait pour surprendre Alger par Jeronimo Conestaggio*, Algiers, 1882.

————, "Relations entre la France and la Régence d'Alger au XVII siècle," R.A. XXIII, 5–32, 95–114, 134–60, 225–40, 295–330, 367–93, 409–48; XXVIII, 198–218, 273–300, 339–54, 448–63; XXIX, 161–71.

Instituto Historico de Marina, *La batalla naval del señor Juan de Austria segun un manuscrito anónimo contemporaneo*, Madrid, 1971.

Kaiser Karl V, *Correspondenz des Kaiser Karl V*, 3 vols., Leipzig, 1844–46.

Lanfreducci, François, *Côte et Discours de Barbarie* (preface, trans., Ch. Montchourt and Pierre Grandchamp), R.A. LXVI, pp. 429–548. Memorandum prepared for Grand Master of Knights of St. John, 1587.

Navarrete, F. N., Salva, M., and Baranda, P. S., *Coleccion de documentos inéditos para la Historia de España*, vols. I, III, XXXIX, XL, Madrid, 1846–62. These volumes are valuable for the Turco-Spanish war, 16th century.

Plantet, E., *Correspondance des Beys de Tunis avec la cour de France (1577–1830)*, 3 vols., Paris, 1893–1899.

————, *Correspondance des Deys d'Alger avec la cour de France*, 2 vols., Paris, 1889.

Powell, J. R., *The Letters of Robert Blake*, Navy Records Society, 1937.

Rouard de Card, E., *Traités de la France avec les pays de l'Afrique du nord: Algérie, Tunisie, Tripolitaine, et Moroc*, Paris, 1906.

Sue, M. J. E., *Correspondance de H. d'Escoubleau de Sourdis*, Paris, 1839.

Testa, I. de, *Receuil des traités de la Porte Ottoman avec les puissances étrangères*, Paris, 1864.

HISTORIANS AND CHRONICLERS: SIXTEENTH CENTURY

All writers dealing with the rise of the Turkish-corsair community in North Africa are dependent upon the work of Fra Diego Haëdo, a Benedictine monk who was prisoner at Algiers 1578–81. He was an inquisitive, intelligent, sensitive observer and questioner, and his works are fundamental to all subsequent western histories of Algiers. *Topographia e Historia General de Argel*, Valladoid, 1612; *Epitome de Los Reyes de Argel*, trans. by R. A. de Grammont, 188c–81 published as a book, Alger, 1881; and *Dialogos de la Captividad*, trans. by Molinervolle, Alger, 1897. The next significant history is equally important for the seventeenth century. Père Pierre Dan, superior in the convent of the St. Trinity and Redemption of Captives at Fontainebleau, was in Algiers part of the decade 1630–40. His *Histoire de Barbarie et ses Corsairs*, Paris, 1637, is a classic statement. Like Haëdo, Père Dan must be discounted for his Christian bias, but the book is a very valuable source. The next historian with significant material is Laugier de Tassy, *Histoire de Royaume d'Alger*, Amsterdam, 1725. Tassy was an officer in the French consulate at Algiers as well as naval commissioner for the Spanish king in the Netherlands. His account is marred because he could not resist telling the mythical account of Aroudj's infatuation with the wife of the ruler of Algiers whom he strangled. The "authentic letters" that he gives his readers are pure eighteenth-century French nonsense, but his accounts of his own times at Algiers are worth careful attention. Joseph Morgan, the English eighteenth-century historian of the Barbary, depended so much on Tassy's accounts that his work is little more than a translation of the Frenchman's history: Joseph A. Morgan, *A Compleat History of the Piratical States of Barbary*, London, 1750. The *Bibliothèque Nationale* has two manuscript drafts of a late eighteenth-century "history-commentary" by Abbé Raynal, *"Mémoire sur Alger,"* B. N. Mss. franc., 6429 fols. 102–61 (two drafts of the mémoire), is well informed for his time and well-written.

One of the most important books about the Maghrib written in the sixteenth century is the geography-chronicle of Luis del Marmol-Carvajal, *Description General de Affrica con todos los Sucessos de Guerra a Avido entre los Infideles y el Pueblo Christiano*, Granada, 1573, 3 vols. (There is a free French translation by Nicolas Samson, Paris, 1667.) Marmol was with Charles V in Tunis; he was a slave in Morocco, and he spent almost a decade traveling in the Maghrib. His descriptions of the land and its people are priceless. Three other Spanish chroniclers are also very useful. Alfonso de Santa Cruiz, *Cronica del Emperador Carlos V*, Edition de la Réal Academa de la Historia, Madrid, 1920–22, 3 vols.; Juan de Mariana, *A General History of Spain from the First Peopling of It by Tribal Til the Death of King Ferdinand*, trans. by Capt. John Stevens, London, 1699, and Prudencia de Sandoval, *Historia de la Vida y Hechos del Emperador Carlos V Maximo, Fortisimo, Rey Catholico de Espana y los Indias, y Tierra Firme del Mar*, first published Madrid, 1604. These three chroniclers were well informed about Spanish affairs of their day, and their accounts are well worth consideration. They bring a whiff of the contemporary into their history. An additional Spanish historian-chronicler deserving mention is the Jesuit scholar Pedro Abarca, *De Los Anales de Los Reyes de Aragon*, Salamanca, 1684. Another fundamental chronicle-geography was the work of the Christianized Arab scholar who wrote under the name Leo Africanus, *De Totius Africa Descriptions Libri*, Zurich, 1555 (French translation by Jean Temporal, Lyon, 1556). J. B. Gramaye's *Africae Illustratae Libri Decem*, etc. is little more than a rehash of Africanus and Marmol. The chroniclers and historians of the sixteenth and seventeenth centuries tell us the story of Aroudj and his brothers, but one of the most interesting and amusing accounts is by one Sinān Chaouch (whose name tells us that he was probably a messenger or emissary of the sultan), *Ghazewat Aroudj We Kheir-Ed-Din* (The pious exploits of Aroudj and Kheir-ed-din, founders of the Odgeac of Algiers). There are two translations: Sander Rang and Ferdinand Denis, *La Fondation de la Régence d'Alger*, 2 vols., Paris, 1837, B.N. LK8-141; and another by Venture de Paradis, the distinguished eighteenth-century scholar, probably written at the end of the eighteenth century. It is in manuscript, B. N. Mss. Franç. N.A. 892. The document was obviously produced by someone who either knew Kheir-ed-din very well and took down his stories, or someone well acquainted with such a person. The "pious" Kheir-ed-din could not have given a more sympathetic—and partly mythical—account of his exploits even if he had written it himself. There is one other Turkish account that should be consulted: Hoji Khalifeh, *History of the Maritime Wars of the Turks* (written c. 1645) trans. James Mitchell, London, 1831, B. N. J3-371. (Turkish title: A Gift to the Great Concerning the Naval Expeditions). This is a more straightforward account than the above, and it deals with the activities of the Ottoman navy in the Red and Black seas as well as in the Mediterranean.

The sixteenth-century French historian Seigneur de Brantôme attacked the problem of the sixteenth century by making biographical studies: he was obviously *au courant* with the information available at the French court as well as generally knowledgeable about Europe in his era. Pierre de Bourdelle, Sgr. de Brantôme, *Oeuvres Complètes*, Paris, 1864–82, 11 vols. Another French account was by Nicholas N. Dauphinois, *The Navigations, Peregrinations and Voyages of Nicholas N.D.* (trans. from the French in the *Collection of Voyages and Travels from the Library of the Earl of Oxford*, vol. I, pp. 701–707, MDCCXLV) His trip started 1551; he was chamberlain and geographer ordinary to Henri II, King of France.

The most widely read booklet about Charles V's African policy in the *Expeditio in Africam ad Algeriam*, Paris and Antwerp, 1542, Eng. trans., *A Lamentable and Piteous Treatise*, etc. reprinted in Harleian Miscellany, London, 1745; French trans., *L'Expédition et Voyage de l'Empereur Charles le Quint en Afrique Contre la Cité d'Arges*, Lyon, 1542. Sir Nicholas was a Knight of St. John. Sir Thomas Chaloner, also a Knight of St. John and also with Charles, wrote his mémoire in *De Republica Anglorum Instauranda*, Hakluyt, vol. II, pp. 99ff.

Fuentas, Diego de, *Conquesta de Africa donde se hallaran agora nuevamente recopiladas por Diego de Fuentas muchas y muy notables hazanas de particulares cavalleros*, Anvers, 1590. This little pamphlet presents "life histories" of many of our characters in this study.

Jones, Philip, *A true account of a worthy fight performed in the voyaga from Turkie by five ships from London against 11 gallies and two frigats of the king of Spaines at Pantalarea within the Straights.* Anno 1586, reproduced in Hakluyt, *Navagations, voyages, etc.*, vol. VII, pp. 229–38, Edinburgh, 1888. It was this "battle" that made the English welcome in Algiers at the end of the sixteenth century.

SEVENTEENTH- AND EIGHTEENTH-CENTURY TRAVELERS, GEOGRAPHERS

By the middle of the seventeenth century, western Europeans were rapidly developing a taste for travel literature, geographies, and compendiums of knowledge. As one would expect, the Maghrib contributed its part to this literature. Some of it is important source material for the historian. The following titles have been very useful in the preparation of this manuscript. I should note, however, that the memoranda prepared by English and French consuls that were in the Public Record Office, the Archives des Affaires Étrangères, and the Bibliothèque Nationale as well as the papers of Venture de Paradis also in the Salle des Manuscrits of the Bibliothèque Nationale (Ms. Franç. n.a. 3158, 3160, 9134–38, and Ms. Franç. 6429–30) were probably more useful than any of this travel and geography literature. Only Thomas Shaw proved to be as astute an observer as the men who were sent to Algiers to report on conditions for the information of ministers of the king.

The following were useful travel accounts or journals of visits to Algiers:

Anonymous, *État des Royaumes de Barbarie: Tripoli, Tunis, et Alger,* Rouen, 1703. Three letters presumably written by priests on a trip for redemption, with interesting comments on the society of each of the regencies.

Anonymous, *Several voyages to Barbary . . . with the hardships and sufferings and the redeeming of Christian slaves. With a journal of the siege and surrender of Oran,* 2d ed., London, 1736.

Britton, J., *Algiers Voyage, Journal or Briefe reportary of all occasions hapning in the fleet of ships sent out by the king, his most excellent Majestie . . . against the Pirates of Algiers . . . etc.,* London, 1671.

Broughton, Elizabeth, *Six Years Residence in Algiers,* London, 1838.

Brown, Dr. John. *Barbarossa, a Tragedy* (1832). An amusing theatrical piece performed at Philadelphia. It is based on the Zaphira story, but in this account Kheir-ed-din, rather than his brother Aroudj, is the murderer and would-be seducer. He is killed by Selim, son of Zaphira, at the end of the play.

Carcy, Mathew, *A short account of Algiers, containing a description of the climate . . . manners and customs . . . several wars . . . with powers of Europe from the usurpation of Barbarossa . . . to the present. With a concise view of the origin and rupture between Algiers and the United States,* Philadelphia, 1784, a little book with a title almost as long as the book itself to tell the people of the United States why they were having trouble in North Africa.

Croix, Abbé Nicolle de la, *Géographie Moderne,* 2 vols., Paris, 1769.

Dapper, Olfert, *L'Afrique,* Amsterdam, 1686. This book was translated into English with the same illustrations that were in the French edition.

D'Avity, Pierre, S.O.T.V.Y. gent. ord. de la c. de Roy, *Les Estates, Empires et princepautez du Monde,* Paris, 1615 (also printed in English the same year: see Newberry Ayer 137/a7/q615 and Case F 09.06.)

Dominici, Alfonso de'. *Trattato della miserie, che patiscono i fedeli christiani schiavi de' Barbari, e dell'indulgenze che sommi pontifici han concesse per lo riscatto di quelli,* Rome, 1647.

Dunton, John, *A true Journal of the Sallée fleet with the proceedings of the Voyage* (1636) Library of the Earl of Oxford, vol. II, pp. 492–98.

Fau, R. P. de la Mercy, "Description de ville d'Alger avec observation d'une éclipse du lune qui y arriva le 13 février 1729," R.A. CXXXIV, 250–56.

Faye, J. B. de la, *État des Régences de Barbarie Tripoli, Tunis et Alger,* The Hague, 1704.

Frejus, Roland, *Relation d'un voyage fait en Mauritanie par Roland Frejus de Marseille par ordre de S.M. en 1666,* Paris, 1670.

Grammont, H. D. de, and Piesse, L., "Un manuscrit du Père Dan, Les Illustres Captifs," R.A. XXVII, 11–35; 191–206; 355–79; XXVIII, 49–76.

Labat, J. B. ed., *Mémoires du Chevalier d'Arvieux,* 6 vols. Paris, 1736. These deal with seventeenth-century problems. D'Arvieux gives himself more credit than the evidence warrants.

Le Sieur Tollet, *Nouveau voyage fait du Levant en années 1731 et 1732, Alger, Tunis, Tripoli, etc.,* Paris, 1742.

Ogiley, John, *Accurate Descriptions of the Regions of Egypt, Barbary and Biledgered,* London, 1686.

Panati, Philoppo (trans. and with notes by Edward Blaquière), *Narrative of a Residence in Algiers,* London, 1818.

Rocqueville, Sieur de, *Relation du Royaume et du Gouvernement d'Alger,* Paris, 1686.

Shaw, Dr. Thomas, *Travels or Observations relating to several parts of Barbary and the Levant,* 2 vols., Edinburgh, 1808 (first publication in folio, London, 1738.)

Spragge, Sr. Edw., *A true and Perfect Relation of the Happy Success & Victory obtained against the Turks of Algiers at Bugia by his Majesties fleet in the Mediterranean under the command of Sr. Edw. Spragge, (May 1671),* London, 1671.

Tassy, Laugier de, *Traité de l'Esclavage des Chrétiens au Royaume d'Alger avec l'Estat présent de son gouvernement, de païs et de la manière dont les Esclaves Chrétiens son traitez et réchatez,* Amsterdam, 1731.

Tindall, Mat. Doctor of Laws, *An essay concerning the Laws of Nations and the Rights of Sovereigns,* London, 1694.

Venture de Paradis, "Alger au XVIII Siècle," R.A. XXXIX, 265–314; XC, 33–78, 250–77; CXI, 68–118. In manuscript, Bib. Nat. ms. franç. n.a., 892.

Villotte, S. J., P., *Voyages d'un missionaire de la Compagnie de Jésus, en Turquie, en Perse, en Armenie et en Barbarie,* Paris, 1730.

Vries, S. de, *Historie van Barbaryen en des zelf Zee-roovers,* 2 vols. Amsterdam, 1684.

ACCOUNTS OF SLAVERY AND REDEMPTION

There are a number of interesting books by men who were slaves in Algiers or other parts of the Maghrib, as well as accounts of "voyages of redemption." Dr. Ellen Friedman, in a study on Spanish captives in North Africa, that should soon be published, gives us the best list of these works by Spanish authors; the following works that I consulted were mostly available in the Newberry Library in Chicago.

Anonymous, *L'Esclave réligieux et ses avantures,* Paris chez Daniel Hartlmels, MDCXC.

D'Aranda, Emanuel, *The History of Algiers and Its Slavery* (trans. by John Davies), 1666.

Davis, William, *A True Relation of the Traveles and Most Miserable Captivity of William Davis,* Library of the Earl of Oxford, vol. I, 1745, pp. 475–88.

De la Motte, P., Comelin, Fran., and Bernard, Jos., *Voyage to Barbary for the Redemption of Captives,* Eng. trans., London, 1785.

Knight, Francis, *A Relation of Seven Years of Slavery under the Turks of Algiers Suffered by an English Captive Merchant,* London, 1640, and Library of Earl of Oxford, vol. II. (This account by Francis Knight is one of the more perceptive in this literature. He was a slave about the same time that Père Dan appeared in Algiers so the two authors either confront or—as more usual—confirm each other.)

Martin, Maria, *History of the Captivity and Sufferings of Mrs. Marie Martin who was Six Years a Slave in Algiers. Written by Herself,* Boston, Newberry Library case 4-5779.5.

Oakley, William, *Eben-Ezer or a Small Monument of Great Mercy Appearing in the Miraculous Deliverance of John Anthony, William Oakley, William Adams, John Jephs and John Carpenter,* London, 1675. (William Oakley writes of his book: "I wrote it and let a friend read it, but till I could prevail with a friend to teach it to speak a little better English, I could not be persuaded to let it walk abroad. . . . The stuff and matter is my own, the trimming and form another's." Thus he renders "Truth" to himself and "Justice" to his readers. Oakley was a slave from August 1, 1639 to June 30, 1644.)

Pellow, Thomas, *The History of the Long Captivity and Adventures of Thomas Pellow in South Barbary, 1720–1736,* ed. N. D. Newberry Library case Y 1565.

Phelps, Thomas, *A True Account of the Capitivity of Thomas Phelps,* London, 1685. Newberry Library, Bonapart collection, vol. 8.

Robinson, Henry, *Libertas or Reliefe to the English Captives in Algier,* London, 1642.

Underhill, Dr. Updyke, *The Algerian Captive or the Life and Adventures of Dr. Updyke Underhill, Six Years a Prisoner among the Algerians,* Hartford, 1816.

WRITERS AND SCHOLARS SINCE 1830

In the last century some eight to ten histories dealing with the Maghrib during the years of the Turkish occupation have been presented to learned or popular audiences in France, England, and Italy. One of the earliest, by Sir R. L. Playfair (*The Scourge of Christendom, Annals of British Relations with Algiers Prior to the French Conquest,* London, 1884) is in fact, an account of the activities, or part of the activities, of several English consuls in Algiers; the book is narrowly based on English materials and primarily concerned with English problems. The next book to be published (Grammont, H. D. de, *Histoire d'Alger sous la domination Turque,* Paris, 1887) is still a classic. Grammont taught himself to be an historian, and, in fact, he was a most important student of the Turkish regency both because of his histories and his publication of source materials. We no longer accept his interpretation of the driving forces in the regency, but we must admire his work. It should be pointed out, of course, that he was almost as narrowly focused on France as Playfair was on England. The next important study deals with all North Africa from antiquity to the French conquest: E. Mercier, *Histoire de L'Afrique Septentrionale depuis les temps plus reculés jusqu'à la conquête Française,* Paris, 1891, 3 vols. This book is a mine of facts not always digested, but valuable for checking details. Lane Poole's *The Barbary Corsairs* was published in 1890; it adds nothing to the story except that it is in English. Henri Garrot's *Histoire générale d'Algérie* (Paris, 1907) is a more general account intended for French audiences concerned with France's role in North Africa. World War I momentarily ended interest in Algiers, especially Algeria under the Turks, but in 1931, Ch. André Julien published his *Histoire de l'Afrique du Nord.* This is an excellent study covering Tunisia, Algeria, and Morocco from the Arab conquest to 1830. There was a new edition in 1966, and an English translation by John Petrie in 1970. Although Julien devotes only about sixty pages to the Turkish occupation, this book is well worth reading. The next study is by Sir Godfrey Fisher, *The Barbary Legend, War, Trade and Piracy in North Africa (1515–1830)*, Oxford, 1957; its author makes the quite correct assumption that European civilization of this period was crude, violent, unreliable in many ways, and then goes on to assume that the rulers and corsairs of the North African regencies were less guilty of any of these vices than Europeans. Every attempt to whitewash the men of Algiers that could be made is to be found in this book; it is absolutely astonishing to follow Fisher's efforts to show the North Africans as victims of European actions while they were always honorable men! Sir Godfrey has spent much time in research but has marred his book by a reverse prejudice. Pierre Hubac, *Les Barbaresques*, Paris, 1949, also tries to see the North Africans from their own point of view, but does not "whitewash" them. The best study of recent years is Salvatore Bono's *I Corsari Barbareschi*, Turin, 1964. It was published under the auspices of *Radiotelevisione Italiana*. The book is narrowly focused on the corsairs and their activity rather than the Turkish regency governments but, as such, is an excellent account. It also has a fine bibliography that emphasizes Italian sources usually not consulted by other writers—including the writer of this book. Peter Earl's *Corsairs of Malta and Barbary*, London, 1970, is more useful on the Knights of Saint John than on the Algerian corsairs. Earl has used the archives at Malta to bring us a better picture of the activity of the Christian corsairs. Another recent, more general, study, J. M. Abun-Nasr, *A History of the Maghrib*, London, 1971, presents an interesting pro-Arab approach to the problems.

For anyone who wishes to go beyond Julien or Mercier in the history of the Maghrib before the sixteenth century, he or she might consult E.-F. Gautier, *L'Islamisation de L'Afrique du Nord*, Paris, 1927, and G. Marçais, *Berberie Musulmane et L'Orient au moyen age*, Paris, 1946. Also see, Victor-L. Tapié, *France in the Age of Louis XIII and Richelieu*, New York, 1975, and Alberto Tenenti, *Piracy and the Decline of Venice, 1580–1615*, Berkeley and Los Angeles, 1967.

HISTORIES OF THE MAGHRIB AND ALGIERS

Boyer, Pierre, *La vie quotidienne à Alger à la veille de l'intervention française*, Paris, 1964.
Braudel, Fernand, *La Méditerranée et le monde Méditerranéen à l'Epoque de Philippe II*, enlarged 2d ed., 2 vols., Paris, 1966; New York, 1971. One of the most important historical studies, on any subject, of the mid-20th century.
———, "Les Espagnes et L'Afrique du Nord de 1492 à 1577." R.A. CXIX, 184–233, 351–410.
Conrotte, Manuel, *España y los países musulmanes durante el ministero de Floridablanca*, Madrid, 1909.
Friedman, Ellen, "Spain vs. Islam: Christian Captives in North Africa in the Early Modern Age." (This is a Ph.D. thesis, revised, that should soon be published. I had the privilege of reading it. It is extensively buttressed by work in Spanish archives and libraries. I have refrained from "pillaging"

this excellent study: Dr. Friedman's work should be presented under her own name.)

Guasch, Gil, *Ferdinando el catholico y los consulados catalanes en Africa.* Zaragoza, 1956.

Hubao, Pierre, *Les Barbaresques,* Paris, 1949.

Kahane, Henry, Kahane, Renée, and Tietze, Andreas, *La Lingua Franca in the Levant,* Urbana, Ill., 1958.

Masson, Paul, *Histoire des établissements et du commerce française dans l'Afrique barbaresque, 1560–1793,* Paris, 1903.

Mesnard, P., "Charles-Quint et les Barbaresques," *Bull. Hispanique,* LXI (1959), 215–35.

Monlau, Jean, *Les états barbaresques,* Paris, 1964.

Mulhagen, Marquis de, *Carlos y su Politica Mediterranea,* Madrid, 1962.

Nasr, J. M. Abun-, *A History of the Maghreb,* Cambridge, 1971.

Ontiveros y Herrea, Eduardo, *La Politica Nordafricana de Carlos I,* Madrid, 1950.

Prieto y Llovera, P., *Politica Aragonesa en Africa hasta la muerte de Ferdando el Catholico,* Madrid, 1856.

Sorgia, Giancarlo, *La Politica Nord-Africana di Carlo V,* Padua, 1963.

Tailliart, *L'Algérie dans la littérature française,* Paris, 1961.

Vilanova, J. M., *Una Politica defensiva Mediterrania in la Espagna del siglo XVI,* Zaragoza, 1956.

NAVAL HISTORIES

A number of naval histories deal with sixteenth-century war at sea. One of the most interesting writers on this subject is Admiral Jurien de la Gravière. He was a sailor with experience in the Mediterranean on ships powered by sails and a scholar quite willing to study and explore the evidence available to him. His books deserve to be read.

Jurien de la Gravière, *Les Chevaliers de Malte et la marine de Philippe II,* Paris, 1887.

———, *Les Corsairs Barbaresques et la marine de Soliman le Grand,* Paris, 1887.

———, *Doria et Barbarousse,* Paris, 1886.

———, *La Guerre de Chypre et la bataille de Lepante,* 2 vols., Paris, 1886.

The standard history for the Spanish navy is Duro, Cesareo Fernandez, *Armada Española desda La Union de Los Reinos de Castilla y Aragon,* vol. I, Madrid, 1895 (9 vols. in all, 1895–97).

The following two popular accounts are both readable and informative; Bradford knows the Mediterranean and he has used good source materials.

Bradford, Ernle, *The Great Siege,* New York, 1961.

———, *The Sultan's Admiral, a Life of Barbarossa,* London, 1968.

A recent little volume is interesting for its emphasis upon the construction of ships and placement of the guns (Guilmartin, John F., *Gunpowder and Galleys, Changing Technology and Mediterranean Warfare at Sea in the*

Sixteenth Century, London, 1974).

Armas, Antonio Rumeu de, *Piraterias y ataques navales contra las Islas Canarias,* 3 vols. in 5 parts, Madrid 1945-1950.

Bamford, Paul, *Fighting Ships and Prisons: the Mediterranean Galleys of France in the Age of Louis XIV,* St. Paul, Minn., 1973. (While this book does not deal with the Maghrib, it still is of great value for any study of naval problems in the Mediterranean in the seventeenth century.)

Christian, P., *Histoire des pirates et corsairs de l'Océan et de la Méditerranée depuis leur origine jusqu'à nos jours,* 4 vols., Paris, 1846-50.

Clowes, Wm. Laird, *The Royal Navy,* vols. II and III, London, 1898.

Corbett, J. S., *England in the Mediterranean, 1603-1713,* 2 vols., London, 1904.

Delarbre, J., *Tourville et la marine de son temps,* Paris, 1889.

Duro, Cesáreo Fernandez, *El gran Dukue de Osuna y su Marina, Jornados contra Turcos y Venecianos, 1602-1624,* Madrid, 1885.

Dyer, Florence E., *The Life of Admiral Sir John Narbrough,* London, 1931.

Field, James A., *America and the Mediterranean World, 1776-1882,* Princeton, 1969.

Garratt, G. T., *Gibraltar and the Mediterranean,* London, 1939.

Grammont, H. D. de, "Etudes Algériennes: la course," *Rev. Hist.* XXV, pp. 1-24. This is the best short account of the problems of the corsair reis. See also Chapter III in Bono, Salvadore, *I Corsari Barbareschi,* Turin, 1964.

Jal, A., *Abraham du'Quesne et la marine de son temps,* 2 vols., Paris, 1923.

Munido, Francesco-Felipe Olesa, *La Galera en la navegacion y el combate,* Tome I, *Eli bu qui suelto en el centario de la batalle de Lepanto,* Barcelona, 1971.

Roncière, Charles Bourel de la, *Histoire de la marine française,* Paris, 1932, 6 vols.

Rotalier, Ch. de, *Histoire d'Alger et de la piraterie des Turcs dans la Méditerranée,* 2 vols., Paris, 1841.

Routh, E. M. G., *Tangier, England's Lost Atlantic, 1661-1684,* London, 1912.

MALTA AND THE KNIGHTS OF ST. JOHN

Dockway, Lord Thomas (Grand prior of the Order in England), *A Briefe Relation of the Siege and Taking of the Citie of Rhodes by Sultan Soliman,* 1524.

Engel, Col. E., *L'ordre de Malte en Méditerranée (1530-1708),* Monaco, 1957.

Salvá, Col. Jaime, *Lo Orden de Malta y las acciones navales Españoles contra Turkos y Berberiscos en los siglos XVI y XVII,* Madrid, 1944.

ARTICLES IN LEARNED JOURNALS

Barbrugger, A., "Les consuls d'Alger pendant la conquête de 1830," R.A. IX, 57-60.

Bardoux, J. "Un vie d'un consul après de la Régence d'Alger," R.A. 65, 1924, 261-286.

Bourgues, Leon, "Sanson Napollon," *Rev. de Marseille et de Provence,* May-June 1886, May-June 1887.

Boyer, P. "Introduction à une histoire intérieure de la Régence d'Alger," R.A., 1966, pp. 297–316.

Braudel, F., "L'Economie de la Méditerranée au XVII Siècle," *Cahiers de Tunisie* IV, no. 14, pp. 175–97.

Cazenave, Jean, "Un Consul français en Alger au XVIIIᵉ siècle; Langoisseur la Vallée," R.A., 79, 1936, 101–122.

Capot-Rey, R., "La politique française et le Maghrib," R.A. CXXV, pp. 176–217.

Clarke, G. N., "The Barbary Corsairs in the Seventeenth Century," *Cambridge Historical Journal* XVIII, pp. 22–35.

Devoulx, A., "Assassinat du Pacha Mohammed Tekelerli," R.A. XV, pp. 81–89.

———, "La Marine de la Régence d'Alger," R.A. XIII, 384–420.

———, "Le Registre des Prises Maritimes," R.A. XV, pp. 73–77, XVI, 146–157, 234.

Emerit, Marcel, "Une Marine marchande barbaresque au XVIII siècle," *Cahiers de Tunisie* III, pp. 361–70.

Grandchamp, P., "La prétendue captivité de Saint Vincent de Paul à Tunis," *La France en Tunisie au XVII siècle 1651–1660* VI, pp. 1–20.

The following excellent articles by Andrew Hess are the result of work in the Turkish Archives at Istanbul as well as the sources usually consulted by Western scholars; Professor Hess has thrown much new light on Ottoman history:

Hess, Andrew, "The Battle of Lepanto and its Place in Mediterranean History," *Past and Present,* no. 57 (1972), pp. 53–73.

———, "The Evolution of the Ottoman Seaborne Empire in the Age of Oceanic Discoveries, 1453–1525."

———, "Firearm and the Decline of Ibn Khaldun's Military Elite," *Archivum Ottomanicum,* V (1974), *Amer. Hist. Rev.,* LXXV, 1892–1919.

———, "The Moriscos: An Ottoman Fifth Column in Sixteenth Century Spain," *Amer. Hist. Rev.* LXXIV, no. 1 (1968), 1–25.

———, "The Ottoman Conquest of Egypt (1517) and the Beginning of the Sixteenth Century World War," *Int. J. Middle East Studies* IV (1973), 55–76.

———, "A Rough Translation of Hyreddin Barbarossa's *Ghazavatname* for the history of the Moriscos as Taken from the Istanbul University MS," 2636 (Latin text by Ertugrul Düzdag)" Xerox manuscript.

Macabich, I., "Sobre la ofensiva franca-turca en la tercera guerra entre Carlos V y Francois I," *Hispania,* IX (1949), no XXXVII, pp. 640ff.

Mathiex, Jean, "Sur la marine marchand barbaresque au XVIII siècle," *Annalles* XIII, pp. 87–93.

Mesnard, P., "Charles Quint et Les Barbaresques," *Bull. Hispanique,* LXI (1959), pp. 215–35.

Pignon, Jean, "Osta Moratto Turco Genovese, Bey de Tunis, 1635–1640," *Cahiers de Tunisie* III, no. 11, pp. 331–62.

Rinn, L., "Le royaume d'Alger sous le dernier Dey," R.A. XXXXI, pp. 121–52, 331–50.

Robin, N., "L'Organisation militaire et administrative des Turks," R.A. XVII, pp. 132–40, 196–207.

Sevillano y Colom, Francisco, "Mallorca y la defensa de Bugia, (1515)," *Boletín de la Sociedad Arqueologica Luliana,* 1972, pp. 332–370.

Watbled, Ernest, "L'Établissement de la domination Turque en Algérie," R.A. XVII, pp. 287–99, 352–63.

———, "L'Expédition du duc de Beaufort contre Djidjelli (1664)," R.A. XVII, 215–31.

Index